Geography &
Ethnic
Pluralism

Geography & Ethnic Pluralism

Edited by
Colin Clarke
School of Geography, University of Oxford

David Ley
Department of Geography, University of British Columbia

and

Ceri Peach
School of Geography, University of Oxford

London
GEORGE ALLEN & UNWIN
Boston   Sydney

George Allen & Unwin (Publishers) Ltd,
40 Museum Street, London WC1A 1LU, UK

George Allen & Unwin (Publishers) Ltd,
Park Lane, Hemel Hempstead, Herts HP2 4TE, UK

Allen & Unwin Inc.,
9 Winchester Terrace, Winchester, Mass. 01890, USA

George Allen & Unwin Australia Pty Ltd,
8 Napier Street, North Sydney, NSW 2060, Australia

First published in 1984

British Library Cataloguing in Publication Data

  Geography and ethnic pluralism.
1. Pluralism (Social sciences)
I. Clarke, Colin, *19— –*   II. Ley, David
III. Peach, Ceri
305   HM276
ISBN 0-04-309107-5
ISBN 0-04-309108-3 Pbk

Library of Congress Cataloging in Publication Data
Main entry under title:
  Geography and ethnic pluralism.
Contributions by former students of Paul Paget,
presented to commemorate his interests and teaching.
Includes bibliographies and index.
1. Pluralism (Social sciences) 2. Ethnic relations.
3. Race relations. 4. Developing countries—Social
conditions. 5. Great Britain—Social conditions.
I. Clarke, Colin G. II. Ley, David. III. Peach, Ceri.
IV. Paget, Paul, 1918–
HM101.G296 1984   303.4'82   84–6319
ISBN 0-04-309107-5
ISBN 0-04-309108-3 (pbk.)

Set in 10 on 12 point Bembo by Alan Sutton Publishing Ltd, Gloucester,
and printed in Great Britain
by Butler & Tanner Ltd, Frome and London

To Paul Paget

Acknowledgements

The following organisations and individuals are thanked for permission to reproduce illustrative material:

Frontispiece reproduced by kind permission of the Steward of the Senior Common Room, Jesus College, Oxford; Figures 2.2–2.6 reproduced from *Kingston, Jamaica: urban development and social change, 1692–1962* (C. Clarke) by permission of the University of California Press, © 1965 by The Regents of the University of California; Figure 2.11 and Table 2.1 reproduced from *Social patterns in cities* (B. D. Clarke and M. B. Gleave, eds) Inst. Br. Geogs Special Publication, no. 5 by permission of the Institute of British Geographers; P. Kariya (3.1); Figures 4.1a–4.7 reproduced from *Outcast Cape Town* (J. Western) by permission of the University of Minnesota Press; Figure 5.1 adapted from *India's political economy, 1947–1977: the gradual revolution* map p. 2 (F. Frankel) by permission of Princeton University Press, © 1978 by Princeton University Press; Figure 11.1 reproduced from 'Space–time patterns of second wave Irish immigration into British towns' (Bronwen Walter), *Trans Inst. Br. Geogs* **5**, 298 by permission of the Institute of British Geographers.

The following are also thanked for permission to reproduce text material:

Cambridge University Press for permission to quote lines from *Colonial policy and practise* (J. S. Furnivall); Pantheon Books for permission to reproduce an excerpt from *The red and black* (E. Genovese), © 1971 by Eugene Genovese, reprinted by permission of Pantheon Books, a division of Random House, Inc.; Monthly Review Press for permission to reproduce an excerpt from *Labor migration under capitalism: the Puerto Rican experience* (History Task Force, Centro de Estudios Puertorriqueños), © 1979 by the Research Foundation of The City University of New York; Basil Blackwell for permission to reproduce an extract from *British black English*, © 1982 by David Sutcliffe.

Contents

List of tables

Frontispiece   Paul Paget. From a drawing by Juliet Pannett (1981) in Jesus College, Oxford.

Paul Paget: an appreciation

Some academics influence others by their writings; others have an impact through their teaching. Paul Paget belongs to the spoken tradition, and within that to the tutorial rather than the lecturing stream. In a system dominated by the exhortation to publish or perish, Paul's credit list was his pupils rather than his papers.

Paul taught across the breadth of geography, as is required by the Oxford tutorial system, but his main interest was in human geography and, within that, in social geography. It is for this reason that the present volume has been gathered from contributors who were previously taught or supervised by him and whose research has concentrated in this field. The contents represent the interests of a small subset within a larger and more widely distributed group of former students.

Paul's own publications were acute and brief,* but his pupils developed many of the ideas he had sketched in them. He was an inspiring tutor who, through an orientation to synthesis and comparative method, raised the 'big questions' which caught the imagination of potential researchers. In the synthetic view of man in place, drawing upon the earlier traditions of the Oxford and French schools of human geography, there was never any doubt among his students of their clear identity as geographers. Yet the success he achieved as a teacher reduced his potential as an author, for, the more his pupils developed his ideas, the less he felt able to publish them himself.

Paul Paget was born Ernest Paget on 10 November 1918. 'Paul' was a name given to him in his army days and which persisted. It was always a puzzle to those who could find only E. Paget on official lists. He was born in Pebworth, then in Gloucestershire, now in Worcestershire, the sixth and next-to-youngest child of a Vale of Evesham market gardener. His elder sisters took a major hand in his upbringing and called him 'Peter', in disregard of his baptised name.

He owed his scholastic career – so he claimed – to being a poor cutter of asparagus. Freed from this task because he made such a mess of the roots, he went to Chipping Campden Grammar School. The school shared with three neighbouring institutions a rotating, closed scholarship to Pembroke College, Oxford, which Chipping Campden usually filled with a science applicant. The candidate previous to Paul's attempt had failed to secure the award, but in the meantime the school had acquired a dynamic new geography master, R. P. Beckinsale, and it was decided that Paul, as the school's most promising candidate, should be given to Beckinsale, as the most promising teacher, to

* They are listed at the end of this appreciation.

vindicate the school's right to the scholarship. Thus Paul went to Pembroke and became a geographer.

In some universities geography grew out of geology. In Oxford, it developed out of history and, perhaps more specifically, out of the history of geographical exploration. Pembroke did not have a teacher in geography, but the College arranged for Paul to be tutored by J. N. L. Baker, a former historian, and a leading authority on the history of geography and geographical discovery. Paul was a prize pupil; he took a first in 1939 and a year later qualified as a school-teacher. Military service during the Second World War prevented him from entering directly on an academic career. After a spell as a subaltern with the Worcestershire Regiment, his geographical training and ability led him into intelligence work and he was posted to SHAEF before the Normandy landing. The interpretation of aerial photographs was to remain an enduring interest and he later taught the subject at Oxford. He was promoted Captain, saw active service in northern Europe, and after the war was stationed for a year in Jamaica. From this stemmed his sympathy for the Caribbean and its peoples.

The sixth child of a smallholder who had climbed into the cosmopolitan world of Oxford and become a staff officer, the man who had gained a first, but who was known by three different first names, was not entirely secure in the society into which events had carried him. He felt that circumstance, not his ability, was responsible. Lingering self-doubt remained with him when, on being demobilised, he returned to Oxford in 1946. He was appointed Departmental Lecturer in the School of Geography, and later, in 1951, a University Lecturer. In 1957, when Robert Steel resigned his Fellowship at Jesus College, to become John Rankin Professor at Liverpool University, Paul was elected to replace him and joined his former tutor, Baker, by this time Bursar of Jesus College. Paul was very much a College man, and moved into residence in the second quadrangle after his marriage broke down in the early 1960s. He held various College offices including Domestic Bursar, Tutor for Admissions, and Steward of Common Room; he retired in 1980 and was elected an Emeritus Fellow.

During his teaching career, Paul developed a number of key geographical principles which he introduced, in a typically modest way, into his tutorials in human geography. He was fond of asking his pupils to explore the relations between the quantitative and qualitative characteristics of population, and the formal and functional aspects of regions. His commitment to synthesis drew him for a while to the concept of the ecosystem and systems thinking as an elaboration of the regional method, while his recognition of the centrality of spatial relationships led to an early appreciation of core–periphery relations and such alluring essay titles as 'Ireland the outpost: discuss'! More seminal still was his emphasis on the perpetual disharmony between social and economic factors – a disharmony perhaps most explicit in colonial multi-ethnic polities where the society comprised an elite of white colonial masters and a subordinate stratum of indigenous or imported coloured labourers. Moreover, he invited his undergraduates to speculate about the significance for social relations of the spatial distribution of social groups. All these themes, but especially those relating to race, space, and society are echoed in this celebratory volume. It is a telling comment on the perspicuity of Paul Paget's view of geography and the world it studies that the synthetic, comparative method he championed, following the severe criticism it faced in the analytic fervour of the 1960s and 1970s, is today re-emerging as a form of highly respected scholarship.

Self-doubt and depression increasingly weighed on Paul, but his teaching remained an inspiration. The paradox is hard to explain, yet the impact he had on his pupils, as a gentle and broadminded man, and a thoughtful but self-effacing geographer, is the reason for this volume – a small token of appreciation for Paul Paget's encouragement of us to enter the field of social geography and, more especially, that of ethnic pluralism.

Publications

Paget, E. 1954. Settlements. In *The Oxford region*, A. F. Martin and R. W. Steel (eds), 158–64. Oxford: Oxford University Press.

Paget, E. 1956. Land use and settlement in Jamaica. In *Geographical essays on British tropical lands*, R. W. Steel and C. A. Fisher (eds), 181–223. London: George Philip.

Paget, E. 1960. Comments on the adjustment of settlements in marginal areas. *Geograf. Ann.* **42**, 324–6.

Paget, E. 1961. Value, valuation and the use of land in the West Indies. *Geog. J.* **127**, 493–8.

Introduction: Pluralism and human geography

DAVID LEY, CERI PEACH and COLIN CLARKE

Even today, a geographer confronting the title of this chapter might well expect a discussion of geography's own plural paradigms, the loss of intellectual integration in the subject, and the attendant dangers of eclecticism (Berry 1980). Such a response would invoke the sociology of knowledge rather than our intended subject, the sociology of place. Until recently there has been very little sensitivity within human geography to the social differentiation of places and, indeed, little appreciation of sociology or social theory. Thus a preliminary task of this introduction must be to review the concept of pluralism as it is used in this volume; secondly, we will consider in more detail the traditional neglect of social differentiation by geographers, and outline some contemporary theoretical perspectives on social segmentation, most of which have only recently come to the fore in human geography. The next section will provide a more direct introduction to the essays in the book. Finally, we will suggest some promising generic concepts emerging from these contributions for a comparative approach to the geography of plural societies, a field that has often consisted of perceptive but non-cumulative local studies. We will attempt, perhaps ambitiously, on the basis of the chapters that follow, to develop a set of geographic heuristics appropriate for the understanding of plural societies.

Geography and plural societies

Pluralism as a concept presents one of the more intractable problems to interdisciplinary dialogue in the social sciences, for it carries at least three separate meanings. In political science, the school of pluralism refers to the existence of a rotating set of dominant interest groups, where political alliances are issue oriented, and where numerous cross-cutting cleavages in society negate the likelihood that any single group will assume the status of a more or less abiding elite. The pluralist position emerged from a number of empirical United States' studies of community politics in the 1950s and 1960s. It has since lost popularity on a number of grounds, not least its use of a consensus model of society and its rationalisation of abstention by the majority from political action (Saunders 1979). However, in the context of more turbulent local politics in the past 15 years, the concept of political pluralism has recently regained favour in a somewhat revised form, as attention has been directed to the actions of key decision-makers in the allocation of resources, as these gatekeepers, usually in government, are swayed by the lobbying of diverse and shifting interest groups in their distribution of consumption items (Cawson 1978, Saunders 1979, Ley 1983).

A second tradition of pluralism is associated with developing areas, and was invariably encountered by students under Paul Paget's tutelage at Oxford. The theory of the plural society was a product of J. S. Furnivall's detailed accounts of the primarily colonial societies of South-East Asia during the interwar period (Furnivall 1939, 1956). As Furnivall's theory is discussed in the first three chapters in this book (see the essays by Demaine, Clarke and Ley) only its broad outline will be covered here. For Furnivall, pluralism implied a colonial and inherently unstable society, where a dominant but alien minority exercised control over an indigenous majority. Thus, within the plural society, there were usually overlapping cleavages of race, culture, class and authority. Ironically, therefore, pluralism in this sense is defined in a manner which is the reverse of its conventional meaning in political theory. For political scientists, pluralism implies dispersed power; in developing areas (following Furnivall), pluralism requires concentrated power, and as such it is a manifestation of elite theory.

The third meaning of pluralism is less specific and comes closer to its everyday usage. Here, social segmentation is regarded as weaker than in Furnivall's plural society, and differentiation is along fewer dimensions, commonly of a sociocultural type. This diluted form of pluralism is compatible with theories of assimilation where essentially residual areas of, for example, diet, religion, social networks or even language may remain, although socio-economic, ideological, or political integration of a group into mainstream society has already occurred. Ethnicity is often the key ingredient of what may be essentially a voluntary form of cultural differentiation; ethnic and perhaps life-style identities may be assumed or not, largely at will. M. G. Smith (1965) refers to such a situation as one of cultural heterogeneity, which he distinguishes carefully from cultural pluralism; so, too, White (1978) is unwilling to permit the concept of pluralism to be applied to symbolic communities defined by voluntary identities and social networks, while Gans (1979) sees such groups as transient, and subordinate to longer-term pressures to acculturation. While noting the strength of this argument, there remain important exceptions to it within the advanced societies. Ethnic identities may be more abiding and less superficial than is suggested (Jews providing perhaps the clearest example among Caucasian minorities), and racial identity continues to be a major social cleavage; moreover, as long as overseas migration exists, ethnic diversity will continue to be replenished and sustained. In addition (and this can only be touched on here), attitudinal and life-style diversity appears to be compounding in the advanced societies with the consolidation and politicisation of life-style groups (gays, feminists, fundamentalists, ecologists) especially in metropolitan areas. In everyday cultural and political life this less complete form of cultural pluralism appears far from trivial, if largely untheorised. It is weaker because it does not incorporate all of the overlapping variables of Furnivall's model, so that, for example, such sociocultural minorities do not usually assume political control and may not occupy distinctive economic niches as in the colonial state.

As a result, a number of theorists are qualifying the firm and somewhat inflexible definitions of a plural society offered by Furnivall and Smith (Smooha 1975). Pluralism is interpreted instead as a continuous rather than a discrete variable. At one end of the continuum lie the colonial tropical societies, with their pronounced patterns of social segmentation, while at the other are the more subtle cleavages of the advanced nations. It is this sense of pluralism as a continuum which underlies the essays in this volume.

Towards a sociology of place While pluralism is usually conceptualised in cultural terms, in part no doubt because of the role played by anthropologists in the development of the concept, cultural dimensions do not of course exhaust the potential segmentation of a society. In this section we will briefly review the ways in which human geographers have discussed social diversity in their analysis of man–environment relations.

Historically, geography as a discipline showed limited appreciation of social diversity. As long as its guiding paradigm emphasised the potency of the physical environment, there was a tendency to present human response in a socially uncritical form, where man was seen in a generic rather than a differentiated manner. Significantly, one of the primary forms of human diversity that was recognised was race, for racial characteristics could be assigned a derivative status as adjustments to environmental variations. Even the French school of human geography (following Vidal de la Blache, who ascribed a more favourable role to human creativity in the face of the physical environment) wrote of regional societies in an undifferentiated manner; a regional *genre de vie* was treated as monolithic and devoid of internal social diversity (Buttimer 1971). It was Max Sorre, a later member of the French school who, in extending its methodology from rural agrarian societies to the contemporary city, challenged an undue emphasis on social uniformity. In the city, he noted, the salient milieu of human activity is less often physical than it is interpersonal (Sorre 1957, Buttimer 1978). Thus it was in urban geography that a *rapprochement* between geography and sociology began, resolving the unfortunate schism between Vidal's followers and those of Durkheim (Berdoulay 1978), and with it emerged a more sophisticated perspective by geographers on social diversity.

During the 1950s, urban geographers began to replicate and, in some cases, extend the research tradition of human ecology, a branch of urban sociology concerned with man–milieu relationships in the city. Over the past 25 years, work in this field has become truly interdisciplinary, with a substantial cross fertilisation of research effort (Theodorson 1961, Schnore 1961, Berry & Kasarda 1977, Entrikin 1980, Peach 1975, 1980). Indeed, a distinction drawn by Robert Park, that 'human ecology . . . seeks to emphasize not so much geography as space' (Park 1967, 56), merely confirms how blurred disciplinary identities have become, for today many would define geography itself as the science of spatial relations. Human ecology has as a primary objective the study of the geographic distribution of social groups in the city, and spatial patterns of change through time. A series of research tools has been developed to measure the spatial impress of social differentiation, including segregation indices, social area analysis, and factorial ecology (Timms 1965, Herbert 1971).

Whereas the underlying dynamic of human ecology is one of economic separation through competitive interpersonal relations in the urban land market, empirical studies have often been concerned with racial- and ethnic- rather than class-based social areas (Morrill 1965, Rose 1972). A seminal early study examined patterns of ethnic and socio-economic segregation in Belfast as they had developed through time (Jones 1960). The attention given to segregation by race and ethnicity has tended to challenge the rather mechanis- tic view that ecological processes invariably follow the dictates of the urban land market, for clearly social groups are not assigned to housing according to a simple law of market power. Cultural biases and preferences also control segregation patterns. To some extent, residential patterns are volitional and freely chosen, to some extent they are culturally rather than economically prescribed, most notably in the discrimination against ethnic and racial minorities, leading in the most polarised cases to the existence of a dual housing market (Berry 1979).

While an emphasis upon spatial patterns has permitted considerable quan- titative precision and comparative studies of residential differentiation through time and across space, a purely cartographic analysis also has its limitations. In the colourful words of Emrys Jones: 'atlases of social data are rather like cases of butterflies – very pretty and telling us something, but the butterflies are dead' (Jones 1972). Moreover the animation of the map to reveal the social worlds which lie behind it is no simple matter for, as Olsson (1969, 1974) has cogently argued, there is a serious problem of geographic inference in moving from the statistical data of map distributions to underlying social processes. There is no unequivocal relationship between spatial pattern and antecedent and consequent social process.

The dual challenges to human ecology of economic determinism and a confining bias toward spatial pattern have led to some conceptual and methodological departures in the past decade which are attempting to reassem- ble the convergence that Park originally sought between the spatial pattern and the moral order of the city. Recognising the shortcomings of cartographic analysis for an understanding of the causes and consequences of spatial patterns, social geography has adopted more commitment to the examination of social interaction, of attitudes as well as patterns, and the use of such methodologies as social surveys, unobtrusive measures, and participant observation (Jackson & Smith 1981). Peach (1980), for example, has examined the structuring of social interaction in the case of intermarriage through ethnic segregation; Ley (1974) has considered the implications of almost total racial segregation for the development of ghetto-specific social worlds; while Boal has been conducting important ethnic research in Belfast for over a decade, tracing the mutual interrelations between space and society in the city's ongoing ethnic conflict. (Boal & Douglas 1982). This research orientation is represented in this volume by essays examining segregation and identity among West Indians in Britain (Peach), residence, encapsulation and marginality among British Asians (Robinson), and segregation, interaction, and assimilation among Irish immigrants to England (Walter). The conceptual and methodological shift from the human ecology of the 1950s and 1960s may intimate a shift also in the underpinning philosophy of science. The fundamentally positivist orientation of spatial analysis has given way consecutively to behavioural analysis through surveys, and more recently to such philosophies of meaning as phenomenology and pragmatism in the examination of such questions as the construction of place, identity, and social worlds (Ley 1977, Jackson 1981, Smith 1981).

The processes of culture building represent the completion of the transition from the objective realm of spatial patterns to the subjective realm of social worlds. But within such a transition there is the potential weakness that an internalisation of the argument will occur, precluding a full appreciation of inter-group relationships. The experience of place is a product not only of inter-subjective meanings but also of external relations. Each social group enters an arena where its life chances are a product of market power, status, and political authority. In an important conceptual paper, Harvey (1971) has suggested that much of urban politics consists of action by different interest groups to marshal political power behind their own claim on society's resources. In an ever more closely managed and planned society, political strength as well as market power provides access to desired ends. There is, in short, a politics as well as an economics of consumption (Pahl 1979, Ley & Mercer 1980). Political authority was a central ingredient of Furnivall's view of the plural society, and it provides a major theme of a number of essays in this volume, including an understanding of the landscape of apartheid (Western), imperial–indigenous relations on Easter Island (Porteous), and inter-group relations in the Caribbean (Clarke), India (Hawthorn), and Canada (Ley).

In addition to cultural and political divisions considered above, society is also segmented by gender (see Henshall's chapter) and social class. In colonial South-East Asia, class and caste provided overlapping cleavages, and this remains true for a number of the societies considered in the chapters which follow. Economic divisions were, of course, integral to the market-power basis to human ecology, and this emphasis has been revived in Marxist views of class, though in place of an emphasis on market exchange and gradations in the socio-economic order, Marxist analysis argues for a simple two-class model predicated upon the pure capitalist mode of production. There is not space here to discuss this position in any detail; for advanced societies it has been argued most fully in geography by Harvey's structural analysis (1973, 1978a, b). The weaknesses in this position include the problematic relations between the theoretical model of capitalism and actual societies, the tendencies toward philosophical idealism, and a reductionism which discounts cultural and political factors as having any significant effects before the 'logic of capital' (Duncan & Ley 1982). What is at issue is not, of course, the pervasiveness of economic inequality, but rather the imputed source of those divisions and assertions for its invariable theoretical primacy. Pluralists acknowledge the simultaneous existence of cultural, political, and social segmentation, but are not prepared to accept the invariable reduction of one form to another or the *a priori* primacy of any one factor. These are approached as historical contingencies rather than theoretical certainties (Smooha 1975).

A similar theoretical fracturing has occurred within the metropolis–hinterland or core–periphery model of development. This model has several compatible sources, including Furnivall's studies in South-East Asia, and the staple theory of economic development documented in Canada by Harold Innis. Within geography, A. A. L. Caesar's views on the economics of centre–periphery relations in Britain are relevant (Caesar 1964), as are the modernisation studies carried out by Berry, Gould and his students, and others (Gould 1970, see Brookfield 1975) and, perhaps at a different scale, Mackinder's concept of heartland and margins in world geopolitics (Gottman 1980). The modernisation perspective in particular has recently been criticised by geographers influenced by dependency theory where core–periphery relations are set in the context of political economy, and the exploitative relations are between a dominant core and a dependent periphery. While dependency theory is itself treated more sceptically today than five years ago (Harriss & Harriss 1979, Browett 1981, Ede 1982), the metropolis–hinterland model remains an often effective heuristic in analysing a range of social relations over space (see Jackson's essay). As elsewhere in the social sciences, it is only when a rich concept is applied in a more mechanical and deterministic manner that its weaknesses become apparent. This has appeared, for example, in some of the recent literature on internal colonialism. Hechter's (1975) celebrated study of the Celtic fringe in Britain suffers from this limitation, as he attempts unconvincingly to collapse the cultural resilience of Celtic nationalism to fundamentally economic lines of domination. It is clear from the data that Celtic resistance is multidimensional, implicating both cultural and economic factors, and that reductionism in either direction is unwarranted (Agnew

1981). So, too, a geographically unsubtle analysis of regional economic inequalities tends to exaggerate exploitative core–periphery relations, and minimise the realities of differential resource richness between regions. A failure to give due weight to the geographic variability of resources exists not only in Hechter's analysis but in other studies by non-geographers. In North America, for example, historic patterns of core–periphery relations (and associated charges of 'the development of underdevelopment') are being challenged – and may even be reversed – by the current exploitation of the massive resource base of the West, combined with the demise of the industrial heartland. There is far more variability to core–periphery relations than overly abstract theories might suggest.

The necessity for geographical sensitivity in appraising the sociology of place is perhaps an appropriate point to conclude this section. As geographers examine social differentiation in regional context with more care, they enter a genuinely interdisciplinary forum where they have much to give as well as much to receive from related social sciences.

The structure of the book

Pluralism represents the triumph of history and inertia over entropy. History and belief in a common descent are the electrical charges that bind members of an ethnic group together, while entropy is the force that moves the universe towards random mixing of its population. The core problem of pluralism for Furnivall and for Paget was that distinct ethnic groups coexist within the same political unit, but are not part of the same society; they might share the same nationality yet be ethnically distinct; they might be economically integrated while remaining socially separated. 'As individuals they mix, but only in the market place, in buying and selling. There is a plural society with different sections of society living side by side but separately within the same political unit.' (Furnivall 1948, 304.)

The scale of the political unit within which pluralism exists may vary considerably. The essays in this volume form a continuum of scale from the subcontinental (Hawthorn on India, Demaine on South-East Asia, and Ley on Canada) to the microscale (Porteous on Easter Island). They range from the specifically rural (Henshall on women farmers in the Caribbean) to the clearly urban (Western on the apartheid model, Peach on West Indians in London). Several of the essays deal with the linkage between the two (Peter Jackson on Puerto Rican migration, Robinson on South Asians in Britain and Bronwen Walter on the Irish migrants in Britain).

However, in presenting these essays, three main themes stand out: (1) a reappraisal of Furnivall's original concept; (2) an analysis of pluralism in different Third World settings; and (3) the pluralism of ex-colonial dependants absorbed within the metropolitan state.

Furnival revisited   It is appropriate that the first essay in this collection, by Demaine, re-examines the applicability of Furnivall's thesis in its original South-East Asian setting. Demaine reviews the argument that, given that colonialism was responsible for pluralism, independence should promote a more assimilated society. In fact, Demaine argues that more than colonialism was involved in the creation of pluralism. He distinguishes between cellular pluralistic societies and what may be termed 'side-by-side' pluralism. Cellular societies are the products of distinct or isolated areas, while 'side by side' pluralism is most common when ethnic minorities have arrived to fill a particular economic niche. The difference is that of between-area distinctiveness and within-area distinctiveness. Demaine shows that in the post-Independence period, the indigenous populations have pushed through legislative programmes and other forms of coercion to oust the ethnic immigrant groups from their niches. Indonesian pogroms, Vietnamese boat people, and Malaysian legislation have all secured this goal. Pluralism is alive and fighting in post-colonial South-East Asia.

Clarke's essay examines pluralism in the contrasted Caribbean societies of Jamaica and Trinidad. Jamaica exemplifies a classic case of Creole stratification which, in its origin, involved three ranked cultural segments, legally under-pinned by slavery and correlated with shades of colour: Trinidad's Creoles have had a similar social structure and history but account for only 60 per cent of the population, because the remainder comprises a large co-ordinate East Indian segment, the result of indentured immigration in the decades after slave emancipation.

Clarke compares these societies, using three interrelated models of pluralism set out by M. G. Smith – cultural, social and structural pluralism. At the beginning of the 19th century, the social structure of Jamaica and Trinidad consisted of a ranked order, from the base up, of slaves, freemen and citizens. Structural pluralism transformed cultural pluralism (based upon transmuted and syncretised European and African traits) into social pluralism in the public domain. Until after the Second World War, Jamaica and Trinidad were plural societies whose differentially incorporated non-white segments were dominated by white minorities. For almost 300 years in Jamaica and 150 years in Trinidad, structural, social and cultural pluralism were locked into a mutually self-sustaining system, which could be broken only by rebellion or by uniform incorporation on the basis of democracy. Only when Britain began a long process of constitutional decolonisation by introducing adult suffrage in the 1940s did the ballot box at last replace coercion by the military and the police as the final arbiter of the social order.

But in neither Jamaica nor Trinidad could universal incorporation abolish competition along racial and cultural lines. The three ranked segments in Jamaica and the two co-ordinate segments in Trinidad regrouped to struggle for political power at the elections. In Jamaica, the brown cultural category provided essential leadership skills for both major political parties, in each case seeking the electoral support of the black lower stratum. Political organisation in Trinidad transformed the two major cultural categories, East Indian and Creole, into mobilised corporate groups.

While Clarke's analysis is in terms of hierarchical and 'side-by-side' pluralism, Ley's contribution ranges from the cellular plurality of the discontented Provinces of Canada to the internal re-sorting of ethnic groups within cities. However, the thrust of the essay is at the national level. Ley's essay focuses on the difficulty of forging a common will from a cellular society which is simultaneously regionally plural (with substantial differences between provinces) and internally multicultural (with power and status problems within each province). The physical determinist explanations of such pluralism is contrasted with the Marxist determinist explanation. Ley argues that the patchiness of resources within the Laurentian Shield has led to the formation of separate nodes of development, like a set of beads strung out along the Canada–USA border. He shows the inverse relationship of the economic wellbeing surface, which rises from the east to the west of the country, and the social wellbeing surface, which is angled in the opposite direction. The confrontation of economic and social ends has its starkest expression in conflict between multinational oil exploitation and native people's land rights in the fragile environment of the North-West Territories. There are separatist tendencies in this cellular society in both east and west. However, although they pose a common threat to destroy the Federation, their political causations are different. In the west, in British Columbia and Alberta, the roots are in the business community. Newfoundland, with its hint of offshore oil riches, also falls into this category. In Quebec, on the other hand, the roots of separatism are cultural, and may run against the economic interests of the Province. In his examination of the core–periphery argument, Ley shows that Canada now presents a reversal of the traditional case, with power moving from the centre to the periphery. In his discussion of class versus ethnicity, ethnicity seems of more crucial political significance.

Pluralism in the Third World The four essays by Western, Hawthorn, Porteous and Henshall deal with different aspects of pluralism in the Third World. In Furnivall's description of a plural society, groups mixed economically but not socially. John Western's essay deals with South Africa, where total segregation is regarded by the Nationalist party as an ideal to be achieved rather than as a neutral statement of fact. Western's essay, a distillation from his powerful book (Western 1981), shows an extreme form of sociospatial engineering producing a city which will allow economic integration (Whites need the Black and Coloured workforce) while minimising social contact. The moral justification of apartheid, proposed by the Nationalist party, is that it both minimises social friction and allows for full, separate development of each group. Western hypothesises the shape and ethnic distribution that would result from 'egalitarian' segregation, and concludes that it bears little relationship to reality. Then he approaches the problem from a different perspective. Suppose that the aims were to dominate through segregation, rather than just to share space; suppose that Whites had first choice; suppose that they wanted to increase their physical distance from those from whom they felt most socially remote (and frightened); suppose they used those whom they feared least as a barrier. Applying such exploitative rules to the physical and historical base of Cape Town, Western produces a map that corresponds over 80 per cent with the real, racially exploitative city.

There are echoes of Ley's essay on the cellular plurality of Canada and of Demaine's comments on the non-homogeneity of ethnic minority groups in Hawthorn's essay on caste, class and regional politics in India. Hawthorn argues that what seem to be parallel strands of policy within a single political party are, in fact, internally contradictory. These policies raise expectations, sharpen inter-class and inter-caste antagonisms, and produce either political paralysis (as they did under Nehru) or political convulsion (as they did under Mrs Gandhi). India is a country on the continental scale, with enormous regional, linguistic, religious, economic and social differences. Nehru's Congress Party came to power at Independence in 1947 committed to socialist industrial development, rural equity and democracy. However, to achieve democratic power the party had to rely on the narrow top tier of the traditional class and caste hierarchical structures in rural areas (where the large majority of the population lived). These controllers of the rural vote bank were antagonistic to reform which would remove this power. Thus, to maintain power, Nehru's Congress had to forego the rural reform for which it was elected, and at the same time it reinforced the power of traditional classes and castes. Nehru's paralysis of power was eventually succeeded by his daughter's political convulsions. Mrs Gandhi found that by removing the ballot boxes from the villages and mixing them before the count, she could break the recriminatory control of the village vote bankers. She could appeal directly to the masses and destroy the political power of the traditional tier in the social class and caste hierarchy which held them down. What this upper class lost in political power it sought to restore by personal violence. Local communalism was the cost of national democratic success. But, having achieved political power, Mrs Gandhi's Congress lacked the economic power to deliver her promises. She was forced towards progressively more autocratic control. Hawthorn predicts that the internal conflicts between her aims of efficiency, equity and democracy must result in the subordination of two of these aims to the third, with explosive results.

Porteous's essay on Easter Island is at a totally different scale. Colonial penetration of the island between 1860 and 1877 reduced its native (Rapanui) population from 4000 to 110. However, the orientation of the essay is in an unusual direction. Porteous argues that, of the three groups which struggled to control the island, the Chilean government, the church and CEDIP (the 'exploitative' company which effectively controlled Easter Island for sheep-ranching purposes until the 1950s), the exploitative company was most responsive to the native peoples' needs. The church interpreted the traditional Polynesian diet of yams and sweet potatoes as meaning that the natives were deprived of Chilean staples. The natives' traditional lack of dress was portrayed as a denial of clothes. Traditional burials with feasts and singing were castigated as improper, and the company, which defended these traditional customs, was regarded as trying to ensure the perdition of the masses. The Chilean government indulged in a cycle of disputes with the company, peaking every 20 years or so, just before the negotiations to renew the lease to the company. The government used the island to distract attention from problems nearer home – a tactic not altogether unknown in some of Chile's neighbours. The government took effective control from the company only when it could see its own financial advantage. The company, it is true, was selective in the native customs which it encouraged but, as the Rapanui observe, the company did with one man what it now takes 500 to accomplish under the Chilean government.

Janet Henshall's essay attempts to broaden the horizons of what has been defined as 'plural'. The key elements of plurality generally recognised in the Caribbean are those of culture, colour and race. Clarke's essay in this volume has shown how, in Jamaica, where race is held constant, shade of skin colour significantly affected the social status. His essay also demonstrated that colour cleavage continued to stratify the Creole population of Trinidad, but that the deepest line of plurality lay between Afro-Caribbeans and the East Indians. Henshall offers a feminist–revisionist interpretation. By examining the role of women farmers in a predominantly Afro-Caribbean setting (Nevis) and in a predominantly East Indian setting (Trinidad), she argues that the role of women is more similar *across* the racial divide than it is to men's agriculture *within* the ethnic group.

Plurality and dependency in the metropolis   The final four essays in this volume deal with ethnic groups drawn from the spatially and economically dependent periphery into the metropolitan heartland. Jackson's essay deals with the centre–periphery relations of Puerto Ricans and the United States. Peach deals with the survival of island identity within the West Indian population in Britain, while Robinson applies a similar theme to South Asian identities in Britain. Finally, Walter examines the ethnic identity of the Irish, the largest individual ethnic group in Britain.

Jackson's essay divides into three main parts. In the first he contrasts the traditional push–pull type of analysis of Puerto Rican migration to the mainland with Marxist structuralist analysis. In the traditional analysis, population is seen as exerting pressure on resources, while in the Marxist analysis the modes of production are seen as creating crises for population. The marginal nature of the Puerto Rican economy is shown, and the integration of its population into a unitary US labour market, controlled by the pulse beat of the US economy, is demonstrated. In the second section, Jackson explores how economic dependency has led to change in Puerto Rican ethnic identity on the mainland. Puerto Rican concepts of race are multidimensional and take account of skin colour, hair type, nose and lip type and cast of features. American attitudes to race, on the other hand, are dichotomous – either you are white or you are not. Thus, enormous ranges of shadings and differentiations, which are recognised on the island, become collapsed into two categories in New York. Residentially, Puerto Ricans overlap from the black ghettos to the white population; the blacker Puerto Ricans are concentrated in the blacker part of the overlap, while the lighter skinned are on the outside. Rather than forming a binding group between black and white, Jackson argues that the Puerto Rican population is being fragmented. Blacker Puerto Ricans in turn seek to distance themselves from the American blacks – 'the darker your skin, the louder your Spanish!' The final section and conclusion are bleak. Dependency holds the population in thrall. The independence movement is the province of an increasingly violent intellectual fragment of the population.

Pluralism in Peach's essay rests not on the perpetuation of ethnic difference through a dominant power, but through voluntary continuity. In several of the essays, the heterogeneity of single ethnic groups has been discussed. Demaine hints at it in relation to Chinese ethnic minorities in South-East Asia; it forms a central point of Hawthorn's discussion of Indian politics. Peach argues, in his essay, that although West Indians in Britain are perceived as a single ethnic group (and may, in fact, become one), they remain differentiated by island of origin. He shows how the insular worlds of the Leeward and Windward islands may be traced within the overall distribution of West Indians in London, north of the river: Dominicans and St Lucians around Paddington, Montserratians around Finsbury Park. South of the river the population is Jamaican. However, he also produces some evidence of the convergence of different island Creoles to form a new Jamaican–English dialect. Peach's essay also echoes a point made by Porteous and Jackson about the transactional quality of ethnicity. Identity is not an absolute quality: it emerges in relation to interaction between individuals or groups. Porteous shows how the Rapanui appear naked, defenceless and exploited to the missionaries, but as adventurous, enterprising sheep stealers to the company. Jackson shows how white Puerto Ricans may become black in mainland America. Peach notes how the use of Creole varies according to circumstances and defines social and emotional relationships.

While Peach's essay concentrates on the within-group and voluntary aspects of Afro-Caribbean differentiation, Robinson's essay deals with the testing problem of separating the relative strengths of internal and external constraints on the segregation of Asian immigrants in Britain. By taking these contrasting groups, the South Asians and the East-African Asian population, he is able to show how different aims and aspirations in the face of similar external pressures by the white population nevertheless produce different social outcomes. Robinson's work demonstrates that the South Asian populations (from a variety of ethnic origins) have common aims of making money to improve their status at home in India, Pakistan or Bangladesh. Desire to save money, coupled with desire to maintain contact, through proximity, with relatives, friends, and community services such as the mosque, have led to spatial concentration and segregation. Yet within this concentration and segmentation is a further spatial sorting. The Punjabis and the Gujaratis are internally separated from one another, not only in the broad sectors of the town, but by workplace and by school. Even within the schools, sociometric analysis shows further inward-looking encapsulation. Paradoxically, the inward lookingness and orientation towards the myth of return not only separates South Asians from contact with native whites, but makes them unaware of hostility and discrimination in British society. East-African Asians, on the other hand, have no myth of return. They have nowhere to go. Their aspirations are largely entrepreneurial, middle class and directed towards making progress in Britain, Canada or the USA. They are more segregated from Pakistanis and from Bangladeshis than they are from whites. The proportion of East-African Asians with white friends is larger than for the South Asians. However, their upward and outward aspirations make them more aware of white hostility and discrimination, a finding which has parallels in David Ley's US ghetto sophisticates (Ley 1974).

While Robinson's essay concentrates on aspirations, the final essay in this collection, by Bronwen Walter, deals with the variable of time in assimilation. Walter shows that later waves of Irish migration to Britain have had different regional concentrations. Earlier movements this century (and in previous centuries) concentrated in Scotland and the North West, while the postwar movements have focused on the Midlands and South East. By drawing samples from Bolton in the North West and Luton in the South East, she is able to contrast the outcome of the assimilation process between an old-established and a recent centre of Irish immigration. Her evidence shows substantial, if not complete, structural assimilation in Bolton, while Luton illustrates considerable ethnic distinctiveness. In Bolton, outmarriage had occurred in the second and subsequent generations, and there was lapsing from Catholicism. Friendship patterns were dominated by English rather than Irish connections, and there was no support for the existence of an extended Irish community. There was a slight decline for the ethnic proportion with distance, while non-Irish friendships were maintained in all areas of the town. This indicated structural assimilation at both the neighbourhood and urban level for Bolton. For Luton, the picture was the opposite. There was a much higher proportion of first generation Irish, a high proportion of in-marriage and selection of Irish friends (although in contrast to the West Indian pattern of island identity, Irish maintenance of regional identities had collapsed down to a more general national identity). A majority of Luton friends were Irish, and the network operated at the town level rather than that of the neighbourhood.

The coldness of the English, reported in Luton, was mirrored in the local press which treated the Irish as if they were invisible, leaving social and religious functions unreported.

A framework for the study of pluralism

Social inequality   Social inequality involves a number of criteria – class, race, culture, ethnicity, caste and gender – several of which may operate simultaneously, often in harmony. Classes are bounded groups whose positions in the social hierarchy derive from past and present divisions of labour, associated with various modes of production. To distinctions of wealth are added those of prestige and power, and these three aspects are often correlated in the class hierarchy. A racial group is distinguished by virtue of its physical characteristics from which, in popular opinion, moral, intellectual and other attributes are believed to derive. Racism is the dogma that one group is condemned by nature to congenital inferiority and another to superiority.

Cultural categories display unique combinations of institutional features, for example, in family organisation and religion. Ethnic groups simultaneously have a clear sense of identity based upon a shared tradition, including a language, and a sense of racial or biological descent. Ethnicity unites elements of race and culture, but not all culture is ethnic – nor is all race ethnicity. If we follow Hutton's definition of a caste system as 'one whereby a society is divided up into a number of self-contained and completely segregated units, the mutual relations between which are ritually determined in a graded scale' (Hutton 1961, 50), it is obvious that it is a special case of ascriptive stratification, and that it is applicable only to populations in the Indian subcontinent and to Indian communities overseas.

Race and culture are discrete phenomena; however, they often share some of the characteristics of other stratification systems and may coincide with – and reinforce – other criteria of social inequality, such as class. The major distinction between race and class is that class is often relatively mutable, while race, in van den Berghe's words 'is an extreme case of status ascription making for rigid group membership' (1967, 24). Yet even racial and cultural groups have changed their status through conquest and colonisation, and as a result of the demographic and democratic shifts that have accompanied the ending of Western Imperialism. Moreover, individuals may percolate upwards through the racial and cultural hierarchy as a result of occupational mobility or politics, while acculturation and miscegenation may result in assimilation. Racial and cultural (including ethnic) identity may be achieved despite class division; less commonly, class consciousness may transcend cultural and racial boundaries.

Even more immutable than race is gender, and the status of women as a deprived category the world over deserves special attention. Together with men, they belong to all classes, all races, and all cultural groups in all societies, but their material situation *vis-à-vis* men ranges from a common exclusion from civil rights via the sex-specific disenfranchisement of women, to universal incorporation through adult suffrage. However, even in the latter case, women often remain 'invisible' in public life, and are socialised to accept inferior education and employment. But despite Henshall's argument that East Indian and black women farmers in the Caribbean are more similar to one another than to men in their own ethnic group (Ch. 7), which is not a disproval of the significance of cultural pluralism *per se*, the perennial theme of each chapter of this book is the salience of ethnic pluralism as *a* crucial aspect of social divisiveness the world over.

Pluralism: Smith versus Gordon   Two different sets of ideas about pluralism underpin the various chapters of this book, though both points of view agree in emphasising the importance of culture *vis-à-vis* class. M. G. Smith's model (Smith 1965, 1969) is directly descended from Furnivall's work (Furnivall 1939, 1948) and stresses the persistence of cultural distinctions in society. Institutionally defined segments may be ranked or occupy co-ordinate positions; they may themselves be subdivided by class. Cultural segments are frequently correlated with colour or racial distinctions, and some segments have their own unique social characteristics, such as caste. The political system that is most conducive to the establishment and maintenance of cultural pluralism is one of dominance, typically associated with colonialism. Dominance is the antithesis of democracy and both creates and implies dissensus. Dissensus is inherent in pluralism; and the system of dominance ensures that acculturation is limited and directed.

Gordon sets *his* ideas about pluralism in a more permissive class-based framework, which stresses assimilation; 'the goal of cultural pluralism, broadly speaking, envisages a society where ethnic groups would be encouraged to maintain their own communal social structure and identity, and preserve certain of the values and behavioural patterns which are not in conflict with broader values, patterns and legal norms common to the entire society' (Gordon 1978, 160). Gordon's scheme, in contradistinction to Smith's, is based on consensus and inevitable group acculturation once critical conditions have been met; the existence of democracy is implicit. Gordon identifies seven stages or sequential steps in the process of ethnic assimilation: cultural, structural, marital, identificational, attitude receptional, behavioural receptional and civic. According to this scheme, 'cultural assimilation, or acculturation, is likely to be the first of the types of assimilation to occur when a minority arrives on the scene'; but, as he adds, this process may take place 'when none of the other types of assimilation occurs simultaneously or later', and the completion of the stage of 'acculturation only' – the first step – may continue indefinitely, as his reference to the United States confirms (Gordon 1964, 77). However, once structural assimilation has taken place (that is, the inter-penetration of prime group membership), Gordon regards the remaining five stages of his system as inevitable.

Furnivall's ideas are reviewed by Demaine in a post-colonial context (Ch. 1); Clarke and Ley explicitly employ Smith's formulation of pluralism (Chs 2 & 3), and Smith's notions of cultural pluralities are implicit in the essays of Western (Ch. 4), Hawthorn (Ch. 5), Porteous (Ch. 6) and Henshall (Ch. 7). Gordon's model is used by Walter (Ch. 11) and also provides the context for Peach's chapter (Ch. 9). The tension between social and economic forces discussed by Jackson (Ch. 8), and the problems of encapsulation and marginality explored by Robinson (Ch. 10) straddle both models. Gordon's scheme of assimilation is applicable to the demise of cultural pluralism under conditions of democracy and voluntary acculturation; it can be used in some cases as an adjunct, in others as an alternative, to Smith's version of the plural model.

Pluralism and politics   Pluralism has often been construed as a peculiarly colonial phenomenon, but while colonies are quintessentially plural, conditions of pre- and post-colonial pluralism are widespread (see Chs 1–8). Moreover, many West European countries now have enclaves of recent immigrants from former colonial territories who have transformed class-based, metropolitan societies into culturally pluralistic ones by a process described as 'colonisation in reverse' (Chs 9–11).

Nevertheless, some of the most complex and oppressive types of cultural pluralism, such as those underpinned by slavery and indentured service, have resulted from colonialism; and it is worth underlining the importance of the relationship between the status of a society (as colony or self-governing state) and the power of its constituent cultural groups (Chs 1–3). Even after decolonisation, new states are frequently beset by two major problems; persistence of ties of economic and psychological dependency, which frustrate the creation of a sense of national purpose and perpetuate underdevelopment and emigration (Ch. 7); and lack of a national identity, the inheritance of pluralism sired by colonialism (Chs 1, 2, 3 & 5).

Laissez-faire attitudes on the part of new political elites have perpetuated the economic *status quo* in most Third World pluralistic societies. Politicians are generally coloured, but economic power often remains in the hands of traditional entrepreneurs or foreign enterprise. Despite having the vote, the underprivileged masses may have achieved little improvement in their socio-economic position, for political power is now typically vested in the hands of the colonial elite's former allies, who previously belonged to the middle stratum of Third World society.

South Africa and Malaysia represent polarised examples of government responses to the allocation of resources in post-colonial society. South African independence in 1910 was achieved before majority African rule was considered desirable by the British; since the late 1950s racial stratification has been codified by *apartheid*, and Africans, in practice, have largely been confined to resource-weak homelands, and have entered the towns only as temporary labour. In contrast, Malaysian independence has transferred political power from white into Malay hands, and legislation has been enacted to give Malays a stake in the economy proportional to their status as a majority. The Malay language is now compulsorily the medium of instruction in schools, a change which the economically powerful Chinese have condemned as inspired by sectarian motives and as hostile to themselves.

Whatever the government's motives, the introduction of democracy often exacerbates cultural distinctions in post-colonial societies. Competition to fill the political vacuum created by the demise or departure of the colonists, coupled to intense rivalry over access to scarce national resources, has created political parties out of cultural groups, excited inter-communal friction, and led to racial politics in Trinidad (Ch. 2), the Emergency and rural strife in India (Ch. 5) and constitutional crisis in Canada (Ch. 3). 'Decolonisation' of company enclaves may also perpetuate the very same problems as those experienced under managerial rule: neglect of social services, lack of sympathy for local customs and ecology, exploitation for the benefit of outsiders (Ch. 6).

Space and pluralism   Although we have argued that cultural pluralism (like class) inhibits the random mixing of populations, we have averred that it is not always possible to predict social forces from spatial patterns and *vice versa*. Geographers are aware that the interrelationship between society and space is essentially complex. But, despite scale-linkage problems, it should be possible to compare social situations at national, regional and local levels.

Generally speaking, Chapters 1–3 and 5–8 involve national-level analyses, while Chapters 4 and 9–11 are essentially urban (or local) enquiries; in fact, Chapter 2 contains national comparisons together with urban case studies. The burden of these urban essays is essentially in conformity with two of social geography's most important principles: that the social structure of the city cannot be understood in isolation from the forces which operate in the society where it is located; and that the spatial expression of these forces is most clearly explicit in residential structures. Hence, urban segregation is not only an expression of social propinquity and distance, but also an eloquent statement about social distance in the society as a whole.

At the intermediate or regional scale, the principal contribution is Chapter 3, which explores the intersection of regional, ethnic and core–periphery relationships in the pluralistic society of Canada. These various issues are mediated through the provincial system of the Confederation and are therefore swiftly transformed into national problems. In Trinidad, on the other hand, regional-ethnic disenchantment gives rise to political opposition but not to separatism. Regionalism and spatial segregation in countries of continental scale are infinitely more potent, politically, than in small islands.

Insularity deserves elaboration as a spatial theme. Chapters 1, 2 and 6 deal explicitly with island situations, though only in Chapter 6 is insularity examined substantively. In Easter Island insularity has ensured closure of the tiny Rapanui group and generated sufficient social power for the cohesive community to outwit apparently more powerful outsiders. Spatial separation and isolation involved in insularity lend a strength of purpose to the underprivileged that is often lacking in more accessible mainland communities.

Two types of tutelage are inherent in Furnivall's model; the subordination of the colonial society to the Mother Country, and the subservience of the coloured (indigenous or imported) elements in the labour force to white capital. A third theme involves the scaling down of international relationships of dependency to the regional level, as expressed in the link between the city and its hinterland. Prior to 1970, Montreal and Toronto were net extractors of Canadian regional surplus (Ch. 3); but the workings of peripheral capitalism are most clearly exemplified in Puerto Rico's dependent relationship with the United States (Ch. 8).

South Africa provides the most dramatic example of internal colonialism. The objective of *apartheid* is not separate-but-equal development; rather, the goal is domination of blacks by whites through spatial separation and differential access to resources. In this *herrenvolk* democracy, as in the Caribbean during slavery, only whites are full people enjoying all civil liberties. Blacks are inferior beings, confined to homelands or the periphery of cities. Yet despite their outcast status in society, they are essential to the workings of the white, capitalist system – as in Furnivall's scheme – because they provide a reservoir of cheap labour.

More subtle aspects of ethnicity are discussed in Chapters 9–11, which deal with urban life in Britain. These demonstrate the gradual assimilation of old and new Irish, compared to the high degree of ethnic and racial segregation generated by West Indian and Asian immigrants. Factions within these immigrant groups, notably islanders among the West Indians and East Africans and South Asians among the Oriental populations, are also intensely segregated spatially, and at very small scale, from their major non-white reference groups. Spatial segregation undoubtedly reinforces friendship, kinship and marriage-distance patterns among these various segments and between them and the white population.

Solutions to pluralism   Social justice demands the integration of cultural sections on the basis of a national system of civil rights. This is precisely the topic addressed by Smith (1969). He argues that pluralism has its most severe implications where culturally defined groups are excluded from the resources of the public domain, either because they lack equality before the law and are unable to vote, or because their possession of these rights is violated in practice (Ch. 2). Under these circumstances, cultural distinctions cease to be a personal matter and become criteria for group discrimination.

Black slavery in the Caribbean provided an example of cultural pluralism which was so legally and politically entrenched that the term 'structural pluralism' has been applied to it (Ch. 2). This system of grave inequality was abolished by the colonial powers in the 19th century, though invariably in the face of local elite opposition. However, Western's account of *apartheid* in South Africa provides a timely reminder that some societies still exist in which the mass of the population is categorised as of inherently lower status and, accordingly, is treated as less than full human beings.

It is also salutary to recall that the vast majority of colonial populations in the British Empire were non-citizens of their own societies as recently as 1945. One of the great revolutions of the postwar period has been the simultaneous, or near simultaneous, acquisition of independence and citizenship in former Third World colonies. Like most great social experiments, in the short term there have probably been as many failures as successes; yet one important principle has been reiterated and another established; that people should be able to make up their own minds about what they want for themselves and their country, and that self-determination ought not to be the prerogative of whites.

With the notable exception of South Africa, independence has meant majority rule; but because of cultural plurality, successor states have had to cope with pressing minority problems. The complexity of this issue is elaborated in Chapter 1, in which Demaine deals at length with the economically dominant but politically weak Chinese in South-East Asia. Citizenship has been offered to the Chinese in Thailand, Malaysia, the Philippines and Indonesia, but usually only the local-born have been eligible. Even where citizenship has been available, many have refused naturalisation because of their unwillingness to cast in their lot with their country of residence and their desire to maintain links with China.

The liberal solution of political and legal incorporation (while allowing culturally distinct populations to retain, lose or develop their institutional uniqueness) is, unfortunately, not the only one practised. Elimination, and expulsion, as well as dominance, are time-honoured methods of coping with pluralism. Genocide of the Chinese in Indonesia and Vietnam (Ch. 2) are events which confirm that the Nazi attempt to liquidate the Jews for racial and ethnic reasons was not a unique historical event.

If the origins of pluralism lie in immigration, emigration (both forced and free) has frequently been envisaged as 'a solution'. Mass movements of Indians from Burma and more recently of Chinese from Vietnam (the 'boat' people) have simplified the cultural complexity of the sending country (Ch. 1). The partition of the subcontinent of India along religious lines provides a classic case of forced migration stimulated by the extreme solution of secession; the very antithesis of *apartheid*, yet giving rise to a similar pattern of spatial segregation.

Fears of domination and discrimination may lead to revolution and partition; even an affluent democratic country like Canada is a victim of fissiparous tendencies (Ch. 3). This brings us up against a fundamental problem. Should pluralistic societies seek to resolve their problems by stressing the will of the majority at the expense of minorities (such as the Malays *vis-à-vis* the Chinese –

Ch. 1), or should nationhood be actively expressed through a more equal treatment and projection of all cultures (as, for instance, in the case of Canada's multi-cultural policy expressed within a bilingual framework)? Or should these issues be ignored in the hope that the problem will resolve itself if removed from the spotlight? (This is largely the solution adopted in the Commonwealth Caribbean, perhaps because no one people can be said to be more indigenous than the others.)

We may conclude, then, that pluralism has many guises. The problem is most crucial where legal and political exclusions commit whole sections of the population defined by race, culture or some other ascriptive factor, to a subordinate status. 'Solutions' range from integration to elimination or expulsion, from spatial dominance to partition. Ideally, in democratic society, legal and political incorporation is the essential first step, the *sine qua non* of democracy itself.

But we must not mistake the semblance for the reality. In Britain, race relations seem at first glance reasonably safe, set in the matrix of British institutions, especially if Irish integrationist experience can be taken as a model (Ch. 11). However, access to jobs and housing is not freely given to black and Asian immigrants. Without vigilance, *de facto* discrimination will produce a dual housing market and a systematically disadvantaged Asian and West Indian segment in British society; culturally determined, racially visible and differentially incorporated, very much as their forebears were in their countries of origin in colonial days (Chs 2 & 3). It is not by chance that disenchanted black youths in Britain (Ch. 9) are expressing their new and rebellious Afro identity through the very same cult, Ras Tafari, that developed in Caribbean colonial society in opposition to white imperialism, cultural domination and racism.

References

Agnew, J. A. 1981. Structural and dialectical theories of political regionalism. In *Political studies from spatial perspectives*, A. D. Burnett and P. J. Taylor (eds), 275–89. Chichester: J. Wiley.

Berdoulay, V. 1978. The Vidal-Durkheim debate. In *Humanistic geography*, D. F. Ley and M. S. Samuels (eds), 77–90. London: Croom Helm.

Berry, B. J. L. 1979. *The open housing question.* Cambridge, Mass.: Ballinger.

Berry, B. J. L. 1980. Creating future geographies. *Ann. Assoc. Am. Geogs* **70**, 449–58.

Berry, B. J. L. and J. Kasarda 1977. *Contemporary urban ecology.* New York: Macmillan.

Boal, F. W. and J. N. H. Douglas (eds) 1982. *Integration and division; geographical perspectives on the Northern Ireland problem.* London: Academic Press.

Brookfield, H. 1975. *Interdependent development.* London: Methuen.

Browett, J. 1981. Into the cul-de-sac of the dependency paradigm with A. G. Frank. *Aust. N.Z. J. Sociol.* **17**, 14–25.

Buttimer, A. 1971. *Society and milieu in the French geographic tradition.* Chicago: Rand McNally.

Buttimer, A. 1978. Charism and context; the challenge of La Geographie Humaine. In *Humanistic geography*, D. F. Ley and M. S. Samuels (eds), 58–76. London: Croom Helm.

Caesar, A. A. L. 1964. Planning and the geography of Great Britain. *Adv. Sci.* **21**, 230–40.

Cawson, A. 1977. Pluralism, corporatism, and the role of the state. *Government and Opposition* **13**, 178–98.

Duncan, J. S. and D. F. Ley 1982. Structural marxism and human geography; a critical assessment. *Ann. Assoc. Am. Geogs* **72**, 30–59.

Ede, K. B. 1982. Underdevelopment and regional inequality. *Area* **14**, 27–32.

Entrikin, J. N. 1980. Robert Park's human ecology and human geography. *Ann. Assoc. Am. Geogs.* **70**, 43–58.

Furnivall, J. S. 1939. *Netherlands India*. Cambridge: Cambridge University Press.

Furnivall, J. S. 1948, 1956. *Colonial policy and practice*. New York: New York University Press.

Gans, H. J. 1979. Symbolic ethnicity; the future of ethnic groups and cultures in America. *Ethnic Rac. Stud.* **2**, 1–20.

Gordon, M. M. 1964. *Assimilation in American Life*. New York: Oxford University Press.

Gordon, M. M. 1978. *Human nature class and ethnicity*. New York: Oxford University Press.

Gottmann, J. (ed.) 1980. *Center and periphery*. Beverly Hills, Calif.: Sage.

Gould, P. R. 1970. Tanzania, 1920–63; the spatial impress of the modernization process. *World Politics* **22**, 149–70.

Harriss, B. and J. Harriss 1980. Development studies. *Prog. Hum. Geog.* **4**, 577–88.

Harvey, D. W. 1971. Social processes, spatial form and the redistribution of real income in an urban system. In *Regional forecasting*, M. Chisholm (ed.), 267–300. London: Butterworth.

Harvey, D. W. 1973. *Social justice and the city*. London: Edward Arnold.

Harvey, D. W. 1978a. Labor, capital and class struggle around the built environment in advanced capitalist societies. In *Urbanization and conflict in market societies*, K. R. Cox (ed.), 9–37. Chicago: Maaroufa.

Harvey, D. W. 1978b. The urban process under capitalism; a framework for analysis. *Int. J. Urban Reg. Res.* **2**, 101–31.

Hechter, M. 1975. *Internal colonialism; the Celtic fringe in British national development, 1536–1966*. Berkeley: University of California Press.

Herbert, D. T. 1971. *Urban geography; a social perspective*. New York: Praeger.

Hutton, J. H. 1961. *Caste in India*. London: Oxford University Press.

Jackson, P. 1981. Phenomenology and social geography. *Area* **13**, 299–305.

Jackson, P. and S. J. Smith (eds) 1981. *Social interaction and ethnic segregation*. London: Academic Press.

Jones, E. 1960. *The social geography of Belfast*. Oxford: Oxford University Press.

Jones, E. 1972. The nature and scope of social geography. In *Social geography*, 11–23. Milton Keynes: The Open University.

Ley, D. F. 1974. *The black inner city as frontier outpost; images and behavior of a Philadelphia neighborhood*. Washington, DC: Assoc. Am. Geogs.

Ley, D. F. 1977. Social geography and the taken-for-granted world. *Trans Inst. Br. Geogs* NS **2**, 498–512.

Ley, D. F. 1983. *A social geography of the city*. New York: Harper and Row.

Ley, D. F. and J. Mercer 1980. Locational conflict and the politics of consumption. *Econ. Geogr* **56**, 89–109.

Morrill, R. 1965. The Negro ghetto; problems and alternatives. *Geogl Rev.* **55**, 339–61.

Olsson, G. 1969. Inference problems in locational analysis. In *Behavioral problems in geography*, K. R. Cox and R. G. Golledge (eds) 14–34. Evanston, Ill.: Northwestern University Studies in geography no. 17.

Olsson. G. 1974. The dialectics of spatial analysis. *Antipode* **6** (3), 16–21.

Pahl, R. 1979. Socio-political factors in resource allocation. In *Social problems and the city*, D. T. Herbert and D. M. Smith (eds), 33–46. Oxford: Oxford University Press.

Park, R. E. 1967. The urban community as a spatial pattern and a moral order. In *R.E. Park on social control and collective behaviour*, R. Turner (ed.), 55–68. Chicago: University of Chicago Press.

Peach, C. (ed.) 1975. *Urban social segregation*. London: Longman.

Peach, C. 1980. Ethnic segregation and intermarriage. *Ann. Assoc. Am. Geogs* **70**, 371–81.

Rose, H. M. 1972. The spatial development of black residential subsystems. *Econ. Geogr* **48**, 43–65.

Saunders, P. 1979. *Urban politics; a sociological interpretation*. London: Hutchinson.

Schnore, L. 1961. Geography as human ecology. *Econ. Geogr* **37**, 207–17.

Smith, M. G. 1965. *Stratification in Grenada*. Berkeley: University of California Press.

Smith, M. G. 1969. Some developments in the analytical framework of pluralism. In *Pluralism in Africa*, L. Kuper and M. G. Smith (eds), 415–58. Berkeley: University of California Press.

Smith, S. J. 1981. Humanistic method in contemporary social geography. *Area* **13**, 293–8.

Smooha, S. 1975. Pluralism and conflict; a theoretical exploration. *Plural Societies* **6**, (Autumn), 69–89.

Sorre, M. 1957. *Rencontres de la géographie et de la sociologie*. Paris: Rivière.

Theodorson, G. (ed.) 1961. *Studies in human ecology*. New York: Harper and Row.

Timms, D. 1965. Quantitative techniques in urban social geography. In *Frontiers in geographical teaching*, R. Chorley and P. Haggett (eds), 239–65. London: Methuen.

van den Berghe, P. L. 1967. *Race and racism: a comparative perspective*. New York: Wiley.

Western, J. 1981. *Outcast Cape Town*. Minneapolis: University of Minnesota Press and London: George Allen & Unwin and Cape Town: Human & Rousseau.

White, N. R. 1978. Ethnicity, culture and cultural pluralism. *Ethnic Rac. Stud.* **1**, 139–53.

Part A

REAPPRAISALS OF FURNIVALL

1 Furnivall reconsidered: plural societies in South-East Asia in the post-colonial era

HARVEY DEMAINE

Despite its widespread use in Western societies in recent years, it should not be forgotten that the term 'plural society' owes its origin to the development of certain distinctive characteristics in the social structure of the European colonies of the tropical world in the course of the late 19th and early 20th centuries. The term was coined by the British economist and administrator, J. S. Furnivall, on the basis of his experience in the civil service in Burma and of comparative studies of the whole South-East Asian region, notably in the Netherlands Indies (Fig. 1.1).

Furnivall makes extensive use of the term 'plural society' in a series of publications dating from the last years of the colonial era in South-East Asia (Furnivall 1939, 1942, 1945, 1948). Perhaps the most detailed argument occurs in his classic work *Colonial policy and practice*, in which he defines the plural society in terms of '. . . different sections of the community living side by side, but separately, within the same political unit . . . Each group holds by its own religion, its own culture and language, its own ideas and ways. As individuals they meet, but only in the market place, in buying and selling . . . Even in the economic sphere there is a division of labour along racial lines. Natives, Chinese, Indians and Europeans all have different functions, and within each major group, subsections have particular occupations' (Furnivall 1948, 304–5).

Furnivall believed that such a situation was distinctive of the then colonial tropical economy. He conceded that outside the Tropics, and indeed in the Tropics in the pre-colonial period, society might have plural features, but submitted that, in general, these mixed populations had 'at least a common tradition of . . . culture, and, despite a different racial origin, they meet on equal terms and their relations are not confined solely to the economic sphere' (Furnivall 1948, 305). Thus, such Western societies and traditional tropical societies in the pre-colonial period had a common social will which tended to control economic forces; by contrast, in the tropical colonies, no such common social will existed to set a bar to the immigration that created the plural society and which was left to the free-play of economic forces (Furnivall 1948).

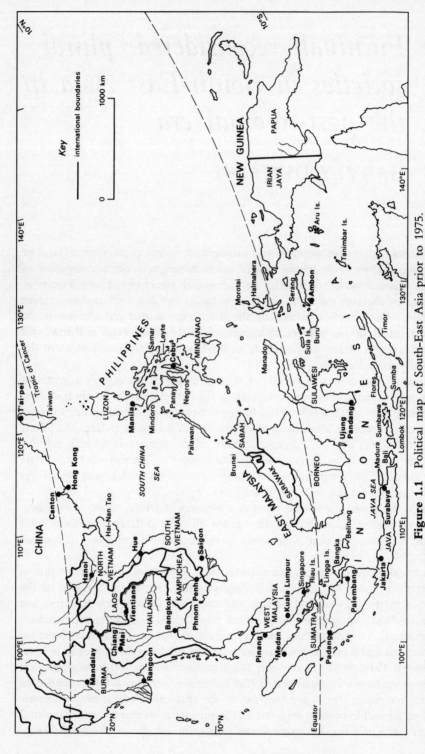

Figure 1.1 Political map of South-East Asia prior to 1975.

Note: Kampuchea was known as Cambodia before June 1982; Borneo is frequently referred to as Kalimantan (Borneo); Timor became the 27th province of Indonesia in July 1976. Since 1975 Vietnam has been reunified and Saigon renamed Ho Chi Minh City.

Furnivall's concept of the plural society has been widely criticised for its rather narrow basis, in particular the limitation of the term to the particular context of the modern colonial situation in tropical latitudes under the influence of European industrial expansion and *laissez-faire* capitalism (Smith 1969, 429). It has been argued that, contrary to Furnivall's assertion, plural societies did exist in pre-colonial societies in the Tropics (Kuper & Smith 1969) and even in pre-industrial European societies (Morris 1957, 125).

Such criticisms have considerable validity and even in the context of the tropical colonies that were the focus of Furnivall's studies, his emphasis must be open to doubt. It is an implicit assumption in Furnivall's argument that decolonisation should bring about a steady dissolution of the plurality of the former colonial society, an assumption that Smith (1969, 429) has also criticised in relation to the existence of pluralism in long independent ex-colonial territories such as South Africa, in particular, and in Latin America. On the other hand, Maurice Freedman, discussing the Chinese immigrant community which formed a major element in the 'plural society' of South-East Asia recognised by Furnivall, has argued that there has been a history of 'weathering down' of separate cultures in the region and that it can be expected in the longer perspective that cultural assimilation and the consequent erosion of plurality should occur with time in that context (Freedman 1965).

It is this issue of whether plural societies are maintained in the post-colonial context in tropical lands and of the changes that might occur in them that is the focus of the present chapter. In particular, it seeks to answer such questions in the context of the subject of Furnivall's original study, South-East Asia, almost two decades after Freedman's initial assessment of the situation in relation to the Chinese. A reassessment at the present time offers a longer view than that available to Freedman, and South-East Asia, in any case, provides a longer time perspective on pluralism and decolonisation, since most of the territories of the region have been independent for many more years than their African and Caribbean counterparts. South-East Asia is also interesting in that the newly independent states form a fascinating contrast with the one country that was not colonised politically by the European powers, Thailand. Despite its continuing independence, however, Thailand did receive the same influx of immigration by Chinese and to a lesser extent Indians as the rest of the region, but the maintenance of political power by the Thai elite allowed a much longer period for adjustment.

Elsewhere in the region independence, as in the case of most other ex-colonial territories, has brought to power the group who could claim to be the indigenous population of the respective territories. Such new governments, although they have rightly been concerned with economic progress, have also had a major task in the development of a sense of national unity in the territories they have inherited, territories which, in some cases, had never had any real functional unity in advance of the Western colonial presence and whose people also had common interests only in their desire to remove the domination of the colonial power.

In the case of the plural societies of South-East Asia, even this broad statement needs qualification. To some extent a common social will towards the continuation of colonial rule had been created by the colonial rulers within those elements of the plural society most closely associated with them: the Chinese and Indian immigrant groups largely imported to assist colonial economic development, and to a lesser extent the indigenous minority groups given special privileges under colonial rule. European withdrawal left such groups at best in an equivocal position, at worst in an untenable one, calling for changes in attitude or other action.

Of course, the need for adjustment has been common among all minorities in newly independent ex-colonial territories, but in South-East Asia this adjustment has been complicated by the fact that the region lies central to the countries of origin of both its main immigrant communities. The proximity of the subcontinental states of both India and China with their considerable cultural traditions inevitably provided competition for the loyalties of the immigrants and, indeed, allowed extensive return migration at all times. Such conflicts of loyalties were heightened in the period of decolonisation after World War II, which had also created in India a major independent subregional power which the bulk of the South-East Asian Indian community could regard as their homeland. On the other hand, India's strictly non-aligned political stance has posed few problems for the minorities in the countries of South-East Asia and elsewhere. By contrast, China, always politically independent, has become a much more important factor with the rise of communism and its eventual securing of power on the mainland after 1949. Whereas under the Nationalist governments, in power from 1911, there had been a state with which the Chinese in South-East Asia could identify and from which the community gained significant cultural leadership, with the Communist take-over there arose an obvious threat to the new states of the region in the form of a 'fifth column' operating on behalf of a power pledged to foster ideological world revolution. The reality of this threat was demonstrated at an early stage in the form of the Malayan Emergency and it has continued to have a profound impact upon the Chinese community in the region and upon attitudes towards it.

Such circumstances make a discussion of plural societies in South-East Asia in the post-colonial period extremely interesting, offering the possibility of widely varying changes in the societies described by Furnivall. In order to understand them fully, however, it will be necessary to examine briefly the situation that existed in the colonial period, to point out some features of the colonial plural society not highlighted by Furnivall. Fortunately, since Furnivall's publications, there has emerged a rich literature focused on the immigrant communities of South-East Asia, with major works on the region as a whole by Mahajani (1960) and Purcell (1965), as well as a series of texts on individual countries (Skinner 1957, 1958; Wickberg 1965; Purcell 1967; Sandhu 1969; Arasaratnam 1970; Chakravarti 1971). Naturally, any review such as this must draw heavily from the studies by these authors.

The development of the plural society in South-East Asia

The population of South-East Asia has long been characterised by its diversity. Successive elements of migration into the region created plural features in the traditional societies found there, as Furnivall (1948, 306) himself recognised. Lee has made the point that features of pluralism existed in the lack of fusion between hill peoples and plainsmen and the scattered alien traders within the territory. However, he argues that, prior to European contact, a 'plural society' did not exist 'in the sense of several groups struggling to occupy the same land or the same occupations', there being rather 'a cellular society of different cultural, linguistic, ethnic and economic communities living their separate lives in different parts of the country and stratified socially within themselves' (Lee 1980, 123).

With the entry of the European economic system into the region, particularly in the later period of its expansion when the trading companies which had blazed the trail were replaced by formal colonial administrations, further elements were added to this plurality. All too often it proved impossible to enlist the native population in the task of resource development which had become the main focus of European interest. It is true that where agricultural development comprised mainly the expansion of cultivation of traditional food crops, it was relatively easy to recruit native labour from the traditional heartlands of the respective territories, where increasing population pressures were leading to the spontaneous search for new frontiers of settlement (Adas 1974, Tanabe 1978), but even so there were constraints on development in the limited capital available to the native population, in the need for extensive water control works in the deltaic environments being colonised, and in the difficulty of organising the marketing of small amounts of surplus produce from a mass of small farms. Where the agricultural system was completely new, as with the plantations, indigenous labour was more difficult to recruit. Moreover, the organisational problems went further than the agricultural sector. Whereas it was sometimes possible to administer the newly acquired territories through the indigenous administrative system, as was the case with the Dutch in most of Java, often this traditional system had broken down in the shift to colonial rule and it went beyond the capabilities of relatively small numbers of Europeans to administer their new territories adequately and to control law and order.

It was into such occupational niches that the European colonial powers sought to introduce or to encourage the introduction of immigrants from outside the territories in question. In some cases this meant immigration from more advanced areas within the region, such as the import of Vietnamese into

Table 1.1 Growth of immigrant populations in South-East Asia, 1800–1960.

Year	Malaya Indians	Malaya Chinese	Singapore Indians	Singapore Chinese	Burma Indians	Burma Chinese	Indonesia Chinese	Thailand Chinese	Philippines Chinese	Indochina Chinese
1807									7 000	
1812	*Penang* 1 000	7 558								
1815										
1817	*Malacca* 2 986	1 006								
1821			132	1 159						
1828							*JM* 94 441		5 708	
1833	*SS* 12 749	15 153	2 324	8 517						
1850			6 284	27 988						
1851	*SS*									
1860		34 796					*JM* 149 000 *OI* 72 000	440 000		
1864							*JM* 175 000 *OI* 85 000			
1870								1.5 mill.		
1871	*SS* 11 501			54 572						
1872	21 888	50 043								
1876										
1879	*Perak*	20 373							30 797	
1880					150 000					
1881	*SS* 29 093	87 095	12 138	86 766	243 123					
1884		*Selangor* 28 236								
1886								1.5 mill.		
1889							*JM* 207 000 *OI* 137 000		93 567	*Cochin* 57 000

Year											
1891	SS 37 634 / FMS 20 435	105 149 / 164 753	16 035	121 908	420 830	37 000				JM 242 000 / OI 219 000	3 mill.
1900							120 000			JM 277 000 / OI 260 000	
1901	SS 39 050 / FMS 58 637	116 939 / 310 328	17 845	164 581	568 263						
1903											
1906	268 269	704 941	28 454	224 230	743 288	122 000					
1911								41 802			
1918						149 000				JM 384 000 / OI 425 000	
1920							293 000	43 802			
1921	439 000	856 000	32 687	321 575	887 077						
1930						194 000				JM 582 000 / OI 751 000	
1931	571 000	1.285 mill.	50 860	423 793	1.018 mill.						
1933								71 638			
1937							326 000		525 000 (China born)		
1939							918 000				
1941	531 000	1.885 mill.	68 978	729 473				117 487			
1947									2.315 mill. (ethnic)		
1955								100 971	181 626 (Nationals)		
1957	707 000	2.334 mill.	124 084	1.090 mill.							
1960									409 508 (Nationals) / 348 408 (China born)		

SS = Straits Settlements (Penang and Malacca). FMS = Federated Malay States (Perak, Selangor, Negri Sembilan, Pahang). JM = Java and Madura only.
OI = Outer Indonesia. Cochin = Cochin China.
Compiled from Purcell (1965), Sandhu (1969) and Chakravarti (1971). See these authors for details of original sources.

Cambodia and Laos or Javanese and Sundanese into Sumatra, but, on the whole, immigration meant the Chinese and, to a lesser extent, the Indians.

Chinese and Indian contact with South-East Asia has a long history, chiefly associated with the maritime trade route through the region linking the two great civilisations to the north and west (Wheatley 1961, Coedès 1964). However, although it has been argued otherwise (Majumdar 1963), settlement by Chinese and Indians in the region has been relatively recent, and mainly consisted of small trading communities living in colonies alongside important indigenous cities, much as did the early European traders (Mabbett 1977a, b). Such colonies were chiefly Chinese, and so successful were they that, as European control was consolidated, the Chinese were deliberately encouraged to reside in such entrepôts as Jakarta, Penang and Singapore.

Nevertheless, the numbers involved in such communities were small. Table 1.1 attempts to give estimates of the numbers of the immigrant communities in South-East Asia in the colonial period. Whatever their reliability, such statistics serve to show that even in the first half of the 19th century immigrant growth was relatively slow. In the Straits Settlements, not including Singapore, for example, the Chinese community was still under 50 000 in 1871, whereas that in Perak in 1879 is estimated at just over 20 000. In Indonesia, although Widjojo has amply demonstrated that Dutch statistics of the period should be used warily, growth of only 39 000 is recorded in the Chinese community in the whole archipelago over the period 1860–70 (Widjojo 1970, 11 ff.).

More dramatic increases were recorded in the last quarter of the 19th century and the early years of the 20th century. In several countries, the immigrant communities doubled in numbers within the space of one or two decades (see Table 1.1). Important as the actual numbers are, however, they mask very significant differences between the importance of the immigrant communities in the various territories in proportional terms. Thus by 1931, whereas the Chinese community of Malaya had risen to 33.9 per cent of the total population and in Singapore they had come to be the overwhelming majority with 76 per cent of the total, in Indonesia the much bigger Chinese community of 1 233 000 formed only 2 per cent of the total population of 60.7 million recorded in 1930. Similarly, although the Indian community in Malaya represented 15.1 per cent of the population of that state, the larger community in Burma reached its greatest recorded proportion of 6.9 per cent in 1931.

The new influx of immigrants in the last quarter of the 19th century and after was the movement that created the plural society as recognised by Furnivall, with its different ethnic groups – the indigenous populations, the immigrant Chinese and Indians, and the European elites – all apparently occupying their specific place within the society. It is important, however, to guard against oversimplification in this respect, since none of the communities and immigrant groups were in any way homogeneous. Both the so-called

'Chinese' and 'Indian' communities were diverse linguistically: the Chinese belonged to at least five major and several minor language groups (Purcell 1965, 6), and the Indians in Burma comprised four language groups, each over 100 000 strong (Chakravarti 1971, 191–2).

Perhaps of greater significance to the overall argument is the difference in occupation structure exhibited within the various communities. In Burma, one part of the Indian community consisted of agricultural colonists of the Arakan region, who had moved overland out of Bengal in search of an extension of the land frontier; there was also a substantial community of so-called 'Mountain Chinese' settled in the Shan States who had migrated from Yunnan. Burma with its overland migrants is perhaps atypical of the region, but nevertheless there were significant differences in the occupational structure of the more typical 'maritime' immigrant communities.

To a large extent such differences relate to the period of colonisation. The earliest immigrants were almost exclusively concerned with trade and commerce, forming something of a commercial middle class within the emerging plural societies. In Indonesia, for example, the Chinese were used by the Dutch from the 18th century as tax-farmers: they leased large areas of land, including whole villages, from the native rulers and were responsible for the delivery of the produce, labour and rent due from that territory to the Dutch ruling class (Purcell 1965, 407). Furnivall quotes Dutch sources indicating that the Chinese had the lease on approximately 14 per cent of the villages belonging to the East India Company and comments that 'they [the Chinese] had in fact become necessary to both Dutch and natives as middlemen' (Furnivall 1939, 46).

The same picture of a predominantly trading community was true of the Chinese elsewhere in the region at a later date. On the mainland, the traditional orientation towards China of most of the region's commerce enabled the merchants from that country to build up a monopoly position and, as rice sales expanded in the colonial period, it was the Chinese who dominated that trade at all levels in Siam and Indochina.

In Indochina there was little demand for Chinese in other enterprises and there they remained a relatively small trading community, but in Siam and most of the other colonies of the region, the expansion of exploitation of natural resources created a demand for labour that altered the whole structure of the immigrant communities. From the last quarter of the 19th century, particularly in Malaya, but also in Burma, Siam and Indonesia, the former trading communities became swamped with a massive influx of 'new' immigrants to work in the mines and plantations and as general labourers. Often these immigrants were from new source areas and created a degree of occupational specialisation between different Chinese linguistic groups. In Malaya, too, where Indian immigration became significant, there arose a similar division between the two groups, with the Chinese specialising in trade and mining, and the Indians working as estate labourers (Table 1.2).

Table 1.2 Racial composition of the gainfully employed population of Malaya*.

Industry	Chinese	1931 Indians (%)	Malays	Chinese	1957 Indians (%)	Malays
agriculture	27.0	17.0	55.0	26.9	13.6	58.5
(estates)	(23.1	73.5	2.8)	(28.2	52.8	18.6)
(market gardens)	(	NA	)	(70.4	1.3	28.3)
(*padi* cultivation)	(	NA	)	(4.1	0.1	95.8)
mining	76.5	13.5	8.5	68.8	11.5	17.2
(tin mining)	(82.4	11.1	4.9)	(67.7	15.0	15.6)
manufacturing	72.0	6.5	20.0	67.2	12.2	18.9
transport	55.0	22.5	20.5	50.1	18.5	27.5
commerce	78.3	11.5	8.5	70.1	15.6	12.1
services	46.0	25.0	24.5	42.7	15.3	33.0
others	70.0	10.5	12.0	60.0	18.0	20.0
all occupations	44.2	18.5	35.8	42.4	14.2	40.9

* The column for 'Other races' has been omitted and therefore the percentages do not total 100.
NA = not available.
Source: Sandhu (1969).

There are a number of surveys and censuses highlighting the relative specialisation of the various communities within the plural societies of South-East Asia in the 1930s. These emphasise the importance of the immigrant groups in trade, in primary processing and in some sectors of the mining industry; of the Europeans in the higher echelons of the administration and in large-scale industrial enterprises; and of the indigenous population in agriculture. Yet enough has been said in the preceding discussion to demonstrate that it would be wrong to view the 'plural society' that had been created in purely pyramidal terms. In particular, the distinction between the early trading group among the immigrant communities and the later labouring group has been stressed in a Marxist context by the Russian scholar Simoniya. His distinction in terms of the bourgeoisie and the working class is valuable in stressing that in the plural society that developed in the colonial period each of the segments contained its own separate class structure, so that members of the various segments were found in varying proportions at most levels of society (Simoniya 1961).

This point has been taken up by Skinner in his study of the Chinese in Thailand. Taking the 1947 census statistics, he points out that, whereas the ethnic Thai are predominant in the highest occupational status categories, in particular in government in the absence of a European ruling elite, in more general terms the percentages of each group in the various occupational categories are remarkably similar, especially in what he terms the low and mid–low status groups (Skinner 1957, 300 ff.). Of course, as Skinner (1957, 310) himself suggests, it may be argued that Thailand, lacking the European elite, does not constitute a valid example of Furnivall's plural society, but it does serve to support the evidence from elsewhere denying the simplistic view of class stratification merely along ethnic lines in such societies. Such a division in class terms may also help to explain the growing distrust with which the immigrant communities as a whole came to be viewed in the early decades of the 20th century, for latent competition between the ethnic groups was present at all levels of society other than among the ruling elite. This competitive situation became crucial in the steadily worsening economic situation of the 1920s and 1930s. As Adas points out with regard to Burma, while economic expansion was rapid enough to offer opportunities for all, there was little dispute between the communities; however, economic downturn and increasing competition for a smaller cake led to distrust and even fighting between them (Adas 1974, 166).

Increasing competition in the economic sphere in the 1920s and 1930s was heightened by changes in the social characteristics of the immigrant communities, arising from their greater numbers. Initially, the immigrant trading groups, given their relatively small numbers, had tended to become at least partially assimilated by the host population within which they lived. Many early traders took wives from among the native population and the offspring of such alliances steadily created such communities as the Baba Chinese of Malacca and the other Straits Settlements and the Peranakans of Indonesia. These and other similar groups had very distinct identities and life-styles, those mentioned combining an outward display of adoption of Malay cultural practices with a continued attachment to traditional Chinese education, but with a language (*Bahasa Melayu tionghoa*) that combined elements of Malay, Chinese, English and Dutch. Assimilation progressed even further in Thailand in the absence of the European elite. Here the immigrant Chinese had a ruling elite with which they could more easily identify in cultural and racial terms. It has been implied below that the Thai elite remained distinct, but some assimilation did take place even at the highest levels. Phraya Taksin, the general who reasserted Thailand's independence after the sacking of Ayuthia by the Burmese in 1767, was the son of a Chinese tax-farmer; the first king of the present Chakri dynasty was his son-in-law; and over time a substantial proportion of the elite may have acquired Chinese blood, though still regarding themselves as Thai.

Even in Thailand, however, the ability of the Chinese to become assimilated into the Thai culture was put under increasing pressure by the intensity of immigration in the 19th century. The sheer numbers made further assimilation difficult but, at the same time, changing attitudes among the immigrants themselves began to erect further barriers. As the various migration statistics clearly demonstrate, more than ever before the new migrants to South-East Asia saw themselves as short-term settlers, seeking only to earn funds to establish themselves and their families back in their homelands. The transient nature of these communities was reflected in their imbalanced sex ratios. According to Rangoon Port Health Authority figures, adult women regularly made up only 7–8 per cent of the arrivals from 1913 right through to 1938 (Chakravarti 1971, 189), and in the Philippines, the 1918 census enumerated women as comprising only 7 per cent of the Chinese community (Purcell 1965, 505).

Increasingly, however, the immigrants did stay on and the discrepancy between the sexes began to narrow. Where there was a long-established community, as in Java, even by 1920 and enumerating only those of Chinese nationality, there were 83 females per 100 males, whereas in the Outer Islands of the Indies, with their more recent experience of immigration, the figure was 37 (Central Office for Statistics in the Netherlands Indies 1925, 32). The ratios in Malaya climbed steadily; the Chinese community showed an increase from only 21.5 females per 100 males in 1911 to 48.6 in 1931 and to 81.5 in 1947, and the ratio of women to men in the Indian community rose from 32 to 51.4 and to 68.7 per 100 over the same period (Purcell 1965, 223; Chander 1972, 29). As the number and proportion of women increased, so any tendency towards assimilation through marriage with native women declined.

The increase in the numbers of immigrants from the latter part of the 19th century and their growing separation in demographic and, indeed, spatial terms, as a result of extreme immigrant concentrations in the large cities of the region, were accompanied by a further factor emphasising their separation, at least in the case of the Chinese. The rise of the Nationalist government in China gave the Chinese in South-East Asia for the first time a cause that aroused their loyalty and with which they could identify. The Nationalists, moreover, soon began to interest themselves in the affairs of the Chinese in the Nanyang, particularly in the issue of education for which none of the colonial powers in the region had shown much concern. Separate Chinese schools were sponsored in several countries, with little or nothing conceded to the separate cultural conditions of the communities in which the Overseas Chinese found themselves. These schools began to support the idea of a 'state within a state' in the territories of South-East Asia, and through this medium of instruction the Chinese became even less committed to the lands in which so many of them had become resident.

These developments in the sphere of education became an increasing issue in independent Siam in the period prior to World War II, with regulations insisting on a minimum Thai language content in the weekly curriculum being laid down as early as 1918 and being progressively hardened thereafter until many Chinese schools were closed after 1939. This Thai attitude was merely a reflection of the growing nationalism of the peoples of South-East Asia themselves, in part stimulated by the nationalism of the Chinese and naturally first seen in the country that had retained its independence. Such movements spread throughout the region among the educated elite in the course of the

1920s and 1930s and as they developed, so the position of the colonial elite and the immigrant communities became one of their prime and easier targets.

It was not only in relation to education that the pressures of the growing nationalism were felt. In the economic sphere, too, there were calls for restrictions on the role of the minorities. Here once again Thailand was to the fore with increased taxes on aliens and restrictions placed on the activities of Chinese vendors, but the Philippines, in connection with the application of American legislation, and Burma, after her separation from India in 1937, both also sought to reduce the economic power of their immigrant communities.

The introduction of these restrictive measures serves to indicate the growing tide of feeling among the indigenous population throughout the region towards the immigrant communities planted in their midst by economic developments in the colonial period. From being alien communities generally accepted and acceptable in the context of their role in assisting foreign trade up to the middle of the 19th century and even being regarded as *pauk paw*, or neighbours, in some parts of the region, the immigrants had become unassimilable by virtue of their increased numbers, their association with the colonial regimes which had become the targets of South-East Asian nationalisms, their growing separation through more balanced sex ratios and separate education systems and, in the case of the Chinese in particular, by their own growing nationalism which oriented them towards a greater interest in the politics of China and caused them to neglect the aspirations for independence of their adopted homelands. Already by the onset of World War II the plural societies of South-East Asia were subject to major stresses; in the postwar period of independence those stresses have continued, sometimes to breaking point.

Changing plural societies since independence

The Second World War can now be seen as a crucial turning point in the development of South-East Asia. The Japanese invasion of the region not only constituted a direct challenge to European supremacy by an Asian power, but also gave many nascent nationalist movements in the region their first experience of limited autonomy, albeit under strict Japanese control. After the Japanese defeat, the clock could not be put back. In quick succession the Philippines (1946) and Burma (1948) were awarded independence and Indonesia was at the same time wresting hers from a reluctant Netherlands. By 1954 the French had been defeated at Dien Bien Phu and the Geneva Conference had led to the creation of four independent states in Indochina, with Vietnam divided at the 17th parallel. In 1957 the problems of the 'Emergency' had evaporated to the extent that the Federation of Malaya could be formed, later to be joined by Singapore and the British Borneo territories in the Federation of Malaysia.

As suggested by Freedman, the achievement of independent status by the countries of South-East Asia between 1946 and 1963 offered the possibility of the steady erosion of the 'plural society' in the region. Of course, independence meant the rapid reduction of the former European elite group, but equally it opened the way for the immigrant communities to become assimilated with the culturally similar indigenous populations through the adoption of a common language, common national institutions and to some extent a common culture. As has been suggested, this process had already gone some way in the pre-war period in independent Thailand, at least among the elites of the two communities. Even here, however, it has been shown that economic competition and conflicting nationalisms had begun to institutionalise racial differences in the period prior to World War II, and it seems likely that assimilation was limited lower down the social scale. Indeed, throughout the region, protest and legislation had been aimed at immigrant groups, who had increasingly developed their own social and educational systems emphasising their separation and lack of commitment to their territory of residence. With independence, which brought political power to the indigenous populations of the respective territories, readjustment was thus required of all sections of the population. In particular, the immigrant communities could justifiably be asked to demonstrate their commitment to the new state if they wished to be accepted as equal partners in it. The indigenous groups could reasonably question such commitment, particularly in view of the fact that in both the Indian subcontinent and China circumstances had also changed in the immediate postwar period, the countries of the former gaining independence, the latter a new form of government under Mao Tse-tung. On the other hand, the immigrant communities could reasonably expect to be given the same rights as the indigenous people in return for their commitment to the new states.

Political events throughout the region in the immediate postwar period at once affected the social situation within the countries of South-East Asia by putting an immediate brake on immigration. Independence brought with it more stringent laws limiting entry (Amyot 1972, 63) and the rise of a strong, highly organised government structure in Communist China in any case led to a virtual cessation of migration from that source after 1949. The general halt to the process of immigration brought with it changes in the social structure of the immigrant communities. The number of aliens actually born outside the receiving country began to decline steadily and there was an equalisation of their sex ratios as they took on the demographic characteristics of a normal resident group. In Peninsular Malaysia, for example, by 1970 only 12.1 per cent of the Chinese population had been born outside the country and the Chinese sex ratio had risen to an almost normal 97.9 females per 100 males; the ratio for the Indian community had similarly risen from 68.7 per 100 in 1947 to 88.2 per 100 in 1970 (Chander 1972, 29; Malaysia 1976a). Moreover, the relative proportion of the immigrant communities in the total population tended to fall. In Malaysia, both the Chinese and the Indians began to lose ground to the host Malay community; the Chinese continued to grow in percentage terms to comprise 38.4 per cent of the population in 1947, but by

1970 that proportion had fallen to 35.4 per cent (Purcell 1965, 223; Chander 1972, 31).

Indeed, in some parts of the region the postwar period saw a reversal of the overall migration trends, as the immigrants questioned their futures in the independent states. In some cases the reversal was dramatic. In Burma, the Indian community, already drastically reduced in the course of the Second World War when the bulk of the community then numbered at 900 000 attempted to return to India overland on what Tinker (1975) has termed the 'forgotten long march', were further deterred by the civil war of the period 1948–52 and finally by the nationalisation measures of the Ne Win government after 1962. Chakravarti (1971, 186) has quoted Indian newspaper estimates of the Indian population in Burma at the end of the 1960s as a mere 250 000, a figure that as yet cannot be verified in the absence of detailed returns from the census of 1973.

The substantial reduction in the numbers of the Indian community in Burma has been paralleled elsewhere in the region in the case of the Chinese, sometimes in violent fashion. In Indonesia it is estimated that between 1953 and 1960 up to 100 000 Chinese may have returned to the newly created People's Republic of China, some attracted by the utopia which seemed to be offered by the new regime in Peking, but some equally discouraged by the increasingly nationalist measures being adopted by the new government. More significant, however, was the pogrom conducted against the Communist Party of Indonesia (PKI) in 1965, following that party's attempt to overthrow the army leadership. Although Chinese involvement in the coup and in the party was not exclusive, the PKI's association with Peking meant that the pogrom was largely directed at the minority community. Estimates of those killed in the disorder that followed range from 250 000 to half a million, a substantial proportion of them ethnic Chinese (Mackie 1976, 115).

Even more recently Vietnam has attempted to solve its minority problem with draconian measures. The deterioration of relations with China since 1975, in particular over the two countries' relative influence in Kampuchea, has led the Vietnamese to consider the substantial Chinese community in their midst as an internal threat to security. Of course, in the context of the spread of the Communist revolution to South Vietnam after 1975, the mainly business community of Saigon-Cholon constituted the major capitalist group which could only be viewed with suspicion as potential saboteurs of the socialist transformation of the economy. However, in the first instance, the Vietnamese leadership sought to enlist the co-operation of this group in the development of a mixed economy in the South, and it was only with the unwillingness of the Western world to provide financial aid on a larger scale and its increasing economic isolation that Vietnam adopted a more aggressively socialist policy towards the South in which the Chinese business community had little role. These policies undoubtedly encouraged the exodus of the Chinese by land and sea, and there can be little doubt that the Vietnamese at one level or another actively encouraged the departure of this potentially destabilising element. The actual numbers of refugees and the proportion of Chinese within them is a matter of some uncertainty, given the likelihood that many have perished at sea; estimates put the number of ethnic Chinese leaving North Vietnam for China in the course of 1978 as 160 000, including two-thirds of the registered Chinese population in the Haiphong area (*Far Eastn Econ. Rev.* 1979, 127), and the total number of boat people between May 1975 and mid-August 1979 was put at over 290 000 (Richardson 1979, 34), of whom perhaps 60–70 per cent were of Chinese origin (*Far Eastn Econ. Rev.* 1979, 127). The exodus, which has continued on a smaller scale since 1979, may have cut the Chinese population of Vietnam by over half a million, possibly reducing it by 50 per cent. It seems that the figure of 700 000 – 3 million Chinese still waiting to leave is a gross exaggeration of the total Chinese population (*Far Eastn Econ. Rev.* 1980, 111).

In Burma and Vietnam the departure of a major proportion of the alien minority group has reduced the problem of its assimilation and integration into the independent state to minor proportions; in both countries, it is rather the problem of indigenous ethnic groups which has taxed the authorities. Elsewhere in the region, including Indonesia, the immigrant communities have suffered no major numerical reduction. In these cases, independent governments have continued to follow policies seeking to alter the separate and advantaged (as they have seen it) position of the minority groups, while endeavouring to draw them into partnership with the host community in an attempt to consolidate the new political units in the region. The operation of these measures has, however, varied from country to country and, in some cases, they have tended to polarise positions between communities further and to maintain rather than reduce plurality. The policies followed may be considered under three headings: in relation to nationality and citizenship, economic opportunity and education. These will be discussed briefly below.

Nationality and citizenship   Foremost among the issues upon which the new states have tested the commitment of the immigrant communities has been the issue of nationality and citizenship. This has been particularly important in the case of the Chinese, given the claims of the Nationalist government in the pre-war period to speak for its overseas nationals and the continuing interest of the People's Republic in their situation. It could reasonably be argued that if the immigrant groups wish to continue to enjoy the same rights as the host community, then they should take up citizenship of their adoptive country; this in turn would speed up integration. However, in order for such groups to take up citizenship, this must clearly be facilitated by the laws of the new government and the willingness of the ruling group to receive them. Unfortunately, in South-East Asia in the period since independence the degree of willingness has varied significantly between countries and over time.

Paradoxically, perhaps, it is the Philippines with its relatively small immigrant community which has had some of the most restrictive laws. Here, Coppel (1972, 23) has suggested that citizenship is out of reach of all but the most wealthy of the Chinese community, so that as many as 200 000 Chinese do not have such rights. In Indonesia, too, the situation has become more restrictive over time. The earliest declarations of the republican government favoured equality and justice for all minorities in the hope of speeding up the assimilation process and the creation of a unified society out of the varied populations of the various islands. Prior to independence a curious situation had arisen, whereby Chinese born in the Netherlands Indies were Dutch subjects except when they travelled to China when they became Chinese citizens. This bizarre compromise was changed by the Indonesian government in 1949 by offering citizenship to all Chinese born in Indonesia, if they did not actively reject it within 2 years. Spurred by the rise of the new China and worried about ill treatment during the revolution, some 390 000 Chinese duly took that opportunity. This legislation did not include the foreign-born Chinese, but these were addressed in the dual nationality treaty signed with China in 1955, but coming into force in 1960. Under this treaty those of Chinese origin were required to reject *Chinese* nationality within a 2-year period, if they wished to become Indonesian citizens. Accompanied by a 1958 citizenship law stating that from this time only a child whose father was an Indonesian citizen would obtain citizenship by birth, the treaty closed the door to all alien Chinese from 1962 onwards (Willmott 1961, 42). In fact, since 1969 the dual nationality treaty has been inoperative, but the provisions of the act remain. Estimates vary, but probably between 40 and 65 per cent of those with dual nationality opted for Indonesian citizenship (Amyot 1972, 63; Coppel 1972, 22; Jenkins 1979a, 40). Added to the 390 000 Chinese nationals noted above, this process has left something between 1.1 and 1.5 million Chinese in Indonesia who have not taken up Indonesian citizenship (Mabbett & Mabbett 1972, 3), although recent government estimates are rather lower at 850 000 – 972 000 (Jenkins 1979a, 42).

The policies of Thailand and Malaysia have been rather more liberal. Until 1976 in Thailand anybody born on Thai soil of whatever nationality had the right to citizenship, although since then this has not applied to children of alien fathers. In Malaysia, too, the original proposals in the prelude to independence for varying restrictions on citizenship according to length of residence were slowly liberalised, so that by 1953 over half of the Chinese community had become citizens. Similar principles were adopted by the 1957 Federal Constitution and by the Federation of Malaysia in 1963. In general, the principle of *jus soli* now applies, except that at least one parent must be a citizen or permanent resident of Malaysia, and for those born elsewhere there are limited residential qualifications.

Therefore, in both these countries it may be taken that, given the virtual halting of immigration, a general process of assimilation of the minority groups in the population into citizenship will take place, with only the older generation who chose not to apply for citizenship on a residential basis remaining as aliens. Given equality of citizenship, such minorities might expect equal rights in other directions. In the Philippines and Indonesia, on the other hand, the restrictions placed upon the right to citizenship have led to a distinction being made between citizens and non-citizens, and the latter can scarcely be expected to have full commitment to their country of residence, unable as they are to compete on the same terms as its citizens. Such differences are particularly relevant when it comes to the consideration of economic questions, since the policy of restriction begun in the 1930s has continued into independence. However, as will become apparent, there is no perfect correlation between the economic opportunities offered to citizens and non-citizens; and in the Malaysian case, in particular, other considerations have overridden those of citizenship.

Economic nationalism and the plural society Attempts by independent governments to reduce what they have seen as economic domination by the immigrant communities have been common to all countries in South-East Asia. In general, these efforts have been made through further legislation aimed at reducing the control of the means of production by aliens. These enactments were framed to achieve a dilution of the economic interests of the ex-colonial powers, but as many of the immigrants, for one reason or another, have not been awarded citizenship in certain countries, this legislation has naturally applied to them, too. Indeed, certain legislation has been directed specifically at economic sectors dominated by the immigrant groups. Both the Philippines and Indonesia, for example, barred aliens from the retail trade, in the former case on an overall basis, in the latter merely from rural areas and small towns. In Indonesia, the Sukarno regime couched legislation in terms of the need to divert manpower and resources into technology and industry, but it was seen by the Chinese minority as sufficiently anti-Chinese to provoke a further departure to the mainland. Legislation in the Philippines has been even stricter. Most land and property titles must be held by Filipinos, and mineral prospecting, the operation of fishing vessels and the establishment of rural banks are among the enterprises that must be run by nationals or by corporations with more than 60 per cent of Filipino capital.

As Amyot (1972, 92) has suggested, legislation of this type can be beneficial in accelerating the process of assimilation by encouraging the immigrant groups to apply for citizenship, relatively easily secured in some countries and certainly available in Indonesia for all Chinese at one time or another. It has, moreover, encouraged an increasing movement towards partnership between non-national Chinese and local entrepreneurs, which has tended to flourish in Thailand and Indonesia, particularly under the Suharto regime.

Such a possibility has not been open under the other system by which governments have sought to reduce the domination of the immigrant groups: the process of state nationalisation. As has been seen above, this attempt in

Burma after 1962 and in Vietnam after 1977 has been a major factor in reducing the immigrant communities in those states. A variation on this theme of nationalisation which deserves closer attention, however, is that which has been adopted in Malaysia, where the government has set up state corporations designed to hold equity in trust for the Malay majority (*Bumiputras*) in an effort to increase the participation of that group in sectors of the economy in which they have been traditionally poorly represented. Agencies, such as the Majlis Amanah Rakyat (MARA), Perbadanan Nasional Berhad (PERNAS), the National Petroleum Corporation (PETRONAS) and the Bank Bumiputra, will then transfer shares to Malay individuals as their incomes and savings increase. This strategy is, in fact, just one part of that country's so-called 'New Economic Policy', which was adopted in 1971 following the race riots that occurred in Kuala Lumpur after the election of 1969. This New Economic Policy incorporates two related elements, the eradication of poverty and the restructuring of Malaysian society so that 'the identification of race with economic function and geographical location is reduced and eventually eliminated' (Malaysia 1976, 7). In esssence, the aim is to remove many of the elements of plurality from Malaysian society.

The restructuring of society involves three principal areas: employment by sector, employment by occupation and the ownership of share capital of limited companies, which was mentioned above. In the first area the objectives imply a rising Malay share in the secondary and tertiary sectors of the economy and a rising Chinese share in agricultural employment; thus it is intended that the share of Malays in secondary employment will increase from 31 per cent in 1970 to 52 per cent in 1990, whereas the Chinese share will fall from 60 to 38 per cent over the same period. In specific occupations the restructuring is also to be substantial, with gains for the Malays in all occupations except that of agricultural worker; a particularly rapid increase is planned for the category of administrative and managerial worker, with a rise from 22 per cent of the total in 1970 to 49 per cent in 1990. This restructuring is to be carried out in the context of rapid economic growth so that the changes are to be effected by controlling the ethnic division of new employment opportunities rather than by an absolute reduction in employment in any sector or occupation for any group. Thus almost 65 per cent of all jobs in the secondary sector should go to Malays, whereas over 60 per cent of agricultural employment should go to non-Malays (Young *et al.* 1980, 64). Similarly, it is at the expense of foreign-owned capital, which provided 63 per cent of the share capital of limited companies in 1970, that redistribution in this sector is aimed; the target is for this proportion to fall to 30 per cent by 1990, with the Malay stake increasing from 1 to 30 per cent – including the public trust agencies – and the non-Malay nationals' share increasing from 34 to 40 per cent.

To bring about this restructuring, the government has launched a wide variety of measures. Apart from the establishment of public agencies to buy share capital in trust, Malays have been given preference in public sector jobs, credit has been provided strictly for Malay enterprises, price preferences have been given for Malay suppliers and quotas set for public construction contracts. The Industrial Co-ordination Act of 1975, moreover, regulates employment and equity through a system of licences (Young *et al*. 1980, 75). Already such measures have had effect: Malay manufacturing employment had increased to 33 per cent of the total by 1975 and employment in administrative and managerial occupations to 32 per cent. Meanwhile, the Malay share in corporate equity had increased to 12.4 per cent by 1980, although the bulk of this continued to be held by public agencies rather than by Malay individuals (Peyman 1981, 43).

Education and changing pluralism   The call for greater participation in skilled employment among the Malays in Malaysia also has implications in the third area of policy to be discussed, education. To expect Malays to take up a greater proportion of the positions in business, managerial and technical fields has meant that general educational levels of the group have had to be improved. To this end, fundamental changes have taken place in the Malaysian educational system since independence, generally aimed at offering advantage to Malay students.

In post-independence Malaysia the government was initially faced with a whole range of schools catering for individual ethnic communities. It sought to rationalise this situation by the institution of a basic curriculum to be taught at primary level through two types of school: full national schools with instruction only in English and Malay, and national-type schools with instruction in Chinese and Tamil but with some training in English and Malay. This latter provision was to open the way for non-Malay students to enter education at the secondary level, where instruction was to be chiefly in English or Malay. The minority languages were not dismissed altogether with the option for one-third of the time in national-type (English language) schools to be taken up with Chinese language and culture; moreover, private Chinese schools which had numbered over 1000 in 1950 were not forcibly closed. Most of these were, however, pressurised by the demands of parents and finance to convert to national-type schools, and the Chinese and Indians tended to opt for the English-medium education which had served them well in the colonial period. Thus by 1966, when the intake into all primary education had increased 2.8 times, that into the English stream showed a rise of 4.8 times over the 1947 level (Rudner 1977, 85).

However, this trend was rapidly reversed in the following decade by a change of policy on the part of the Malaysian government, which sought to use education as the focus for asserting Malay norms in national identity. This involved the conversion of all English-medium schools and universities to Malay-medium in a gradual process scheduled for completion in 1983, thus removing the alternative for the immigrant minorities and forcing them to compete with Malays on the latter's terms. English-language enrolments at primary level had fallen to a mere 108 per cent of their 1947 levels by 1974 and have continued a downward trend since. Schools using Chinese- or Tamil-media were not immediately affected, but were essentially reduced to the status of a terminal primary system. Nevertheless, many parents switched to these schools with the idea of continuing fee-paying education abroad.

To some extent the policy followed by Malaysia since the late 1960s was a reflection of similar efforts made elsewhere in the region. Only in the Philippines has there been little effort to increase assimilation by integrating the Chinese schools into the national network. In Thailand, as has been noted above, the battle was largely fought in the pre-war period and in Indonesia there has been an increasing strictness towards Chinese schools. At first, given the general lack of educational development in the country, the Indonesian government recognised the need to maintain Chinese schools, but they received no subsidy from the government, and it was left to the competing pro-Peking and pro-Taipei factions among the Chinese community to finance themselves. After 1952, however, the government began to impose requirements that the Chinese schools should teach a certain amount of *Bahasa* Indonesia and these controls were steadily tightened. The year of revolts in the Outer Islands in 1957 brought a halt to the foundation of any new schools and saw restrictions on the use of textbooks; within a year the number of Chinese schools was halved and then halved again as the schools backed by Taiwan were closed down. Those associated with Peking suffered the same fate in the period after 1967, and although special schools aimed exclusively at alien Chinese were established under the national education programme in the years after 1969, these were limited in number and had been assimilated by 1974–75 (Suryadinata 1978, 153 ff.).

The plural society in South-East Asia: assimilation or maintenance?

In the context of these developments in national policies since independence, it is now possible to turn back to Freedman's thesis that in the longer term the immigrant minority communities of South-East Asia will be assimilated, as they have been throughout history. Of course, Freedman was talking exclusively of the Chinese, and in ethnocultural terms it may be argued that the Indian minority may be much more difficult to absorb within South-East Asian societies. Nevertheless, with the decimation of their numbers in Burma, the Indians now remain a relatively small community in proportional terms except in Malaysia and for most of the countries of the region the argument applied by Freedman to the Chinese does carry with it the implication of the steady erosion of the 'plural society' as it existed in the colonial period.

There is much to support Freedman's argument in the evidence we have assembled. The conditions that created the 'plural society' – open international frontiers in a largely *laissez-faire* economic system controlled by colonial powers – have disappeared. Freedman quotes the case of Thailand, the one country of the region not formally colonised, to demonstrate how a steady stream of Chinese immigrants from the 18th century onwards has been substantially absorbed, with existing Chinatowns merely 'the not yet assimilated portion of a much larger historical population of Chinese' (Freedman 1965, 34). He points out that where nationalism produced a confrontation in Thailand in the 1930s and in the early postwar period, repressive measures worked merely in the direction of pushing people to become Thai. The evidence from Skinner has supported this argument, and although his findings relate to the elite, Skinner concluded that this group was leading the whole community into greater accommodation with wider Thai society (Skinner 1958, 227 ff.). Moreover, there is evidence from other countries of assimilation between the host community and certain sections of the immigrant groups, leading to the creation of such communities as the Babas and the Peranakans.

On the other hand, it has also been noted that the separation between the host and immigrant was increased in the later period of immigration by the development of the immigrants as larger and more demographically stable communities, by their geographical concentration in and within cities, and by the institutionalisation of ethnic differences by legislation enacted towards the end of the colonial period and by independent governments. However well intentioned they have been, and in general they have followed the Thai format of seeking to push the immigrant communities into assimilation, these policies may have helped to maintain the very barriers against that assimilation.

With the departure of a large proportion of the immigrants from Burma and Vietnam, and in view of their relatively small numbers in the Philippines, it is to Indonesia and Malaysia that one must turn for a final assessment of the situation. Even in Indonesia, despite the relatively small proportion of the Chinese in the total population, it must be said that the assimilation forecast by Freedman still has a long way to go. Connor (1973, 20) has argued in another context that 'assimilation is not a one-directional process; if not completed it can be reversed', and Indonesian legislation has created the possibility of such a reversal. Thus, although the long established Peranakan community does seem to be tending towards 'Indonesianisation', having largely been awarded citizenship and having adopted Indonesian names in significant numbers, not all Chinese are Peranakans and not all non-Peranakans are Indonesian citizens. Thus, whereas the Peranakans have scarcely been affected by anti-alien legislation and since 1957 have been obliged to go through an Indonesian language education system, the non-citizen Chinese until relatively recently have been educated separately and severe obstacles have been placed in the way of their assimilation, particularly in the economic sphere. In recent years, especially following the anti-Chinese sentiments which surfaced during the anti-Japanese riots inspired by the visit of Prime Minister Tanaka in 1974, President Suharto has issued further policy directives which, at face value, suggest a new mood of discrimination against non-indigenous (non-*pribumi*) Indonesians, including debarring them from participation in new foreign joint ventures except in partnership with *pribumis*. This legislation thus affects even the Chinese who are Indonesian citizens, and if it were to be turned into effective policy, it would begin to create a group of 'second-class' Indonesian citizens, mainly Chinese.

Indications are, however, that such directives have been more rhetoric, designed to calm tensions, than reality and there is overwhelming evidence that the Suharto government, with its pragmatic, development-oriented policy, has rather sought partnership with the Chinese minority. In seeking to mobilise development capital from home as well as overseas sources, it has turned to the Chinese business community, both citizen and non-citizen. Where there have been restrictions on non-citizen participation, these have been circumvented by arrangements with *pribumi* licence-holders, often the ruling military elite themselves. This system, variously known as 'Ali Baba' or *cukongism*, promises to increase the degree of co-operation between the Indonesian and Chinese elites, but in the face of economic problems at other levels of society, the identification of the Suharto regime with the non-citizen Chinese in particular is serving to increase its unpopularity. Suspicion of the economic position of the Chinese amongst the Indonesian community continues, as is clear from the anti-Chinese riots of 1980 in the cities of Surakarta and Semarang, and recent suggestions of President Suharto's willingness to solve the citizenship question by a blanket grant to all Chinese may do little to solve the basic economic jealousies that exist.

Assimilation thus has some distance to go in Indonesia, but progress here seems more likely than in Malaysia in the short term. It appears that the efforts of the Malaysian government to equalise economic and social opportunity through the New Economic Policy of positive discrimination towards the Malays are meeting with problems. Although this policy stresses that the shift will only be made in the context of expanding opportunities for all groups or at the expense of the foreign investors, largely composed of British companies dating from the colonial period, to the immigrant groups, particularly the Chinese, it often seems like discrimination *against* them. This, and the attempt to build a national culture largely in Malay terms, is causing many of the immigrants to consider their positions in relation to that culture in the light of their own heritage. One writer has suggested that 'the pursuit of a Malaysian national culture will be meaningless and even counter-productive, unless that culture is itself a reflection of certain general and overall social ends, and is not in itself a sectarian product' (Clammer 1975, 17). For some at least of the immigrant community the policies do seem to be just such a sectarian product. Even the Baba Chinese, the early assimilationists among the Chinese community, have not found their position easy, and there has been some turning back towards Chinese learning and culture even in these circles (Clammer 1975, 11). In political terms it would appear that there is a continuing search by the Chinese community for a party to represent their interests, with a suspicion that their former representatives in the Malay Chinese Association (MCA) and Gerakan have allowed themselves to be drawn into a Malay-dominated government for individual economic advantage under similar terms to the Ali Baba system in Indonesia.

The situation in Malaysia does not suggest assimilation of the immigrant communities in the short term, and it must be doubted whether even here Freedman's 'longer view' will be sufficient. In Malaysia the sheer size of the immigrant community makes assimilation by a majority which is only slightly larger especially difficult; when some of that majority are immigrants of no greater vintage than some of the members of the minority communities, it is even more problematic. The colonial period institutionalised the differences between the communities in Malaysia; the New Economic Policy, although a bold and necessary attempt at social engineering, may only assist in further separation of the communities. Perhaps here, as in no other case in South-East Asia, the plurality created in the colonial period must be recognised and a national culture built upon it.

References

Adas, M. 1974. *The Burma delta. Economic development and social change on an Asian rice frontier*. Madison: Wisconsin University Press.

Amyot, J. 1972. *The Chinese and the national integration in South-East Asia*. Monograph no. 2. Bangkok: Institute of Asian Studies, Faculty of Political Science, Chulalongkorn University.

Arasaratnam, S. 1970. *Indians in Malaysia and Singapore*. Kuala Lumpur: Oxford University Press for the Institute of Race Relations.

Central Office for Statistics in the Netherlands Indies 1925. *Statistical abstract for the Netherlands Indies, year 1925*. Weltevreden.

Central Statistical Office, Indonesia 1975. *Population of Indonesia 1971*, series D. Djakarta.

Chakravarti, N. R. 1971. *The Indian minority in Burma*. Oxford: Oxford University Press for the Institute of Race Relations.

Chander, R. 1972. *1970 Population and Housing Census of Malaysia, community groups volume*. Kuala Lumpur: Jabatan Perangkaan Malaysia.

Clammer, J. R. 1975. Overseas Chinese assimilation and resinification: a Malaysian case study. *S.E. Asian J. Social Sci.* **3**, 9–24.

Coedès, G. 1964. *Les états Hindouisés d'Indochine et d'Indonesie*, 3rd edn. Paris: de Boccard.

Connor, W. 1973. The politics of ethno-nationalism. *J. Int. Affairs* **27**, 1–21.

Coppel, C. 1972. The position of the Chinese in the Philippines, Malaysia and Indonesia. In *The Chinese in Indonesia, the Philippines and Malaysia*, 16–30. London: Minority Rights Group.

Department of Statistics, Malaysia 1976a. *1970 Population and Housing Census of Malaysia*. Vol. 1: *Basic population tables*. Kuala Lumpur: Department of Statistics, Malaysia.

Far Eastn Econ. Rev. 1979. *Asia yearbook 1979*. Hong Kong.

Far Eastn Econ. Rev. 1980. *Asia yearbook 1980*. Hong Kong.

Freedman, M. 1965. The Chinese in Southeast Asia: a longer view. *Asian Rev.* **2**, 24–38.

Furnivall, J. S. 1939. *Netherlands Indies: a study of plural economy*. Cambridge: Cambridge University Press.

Furnivall, J. S. 1942. The political economy of the tropical Far East. *J. Roy. Centr. Asian Soc.* **29**, 195–210.

Furnivall, J. S. 1945. Some problems of tropical economy. In *Fabian colonial essays*, R. Hinden (ed.), 161–84. London: George Allen & Unwin.

Furnivall, J. S. 1948. *Colonial policy and practice. A comparative study of Burma and the Netherlands Indies*. Cambridge: Cambridge University Press.

Jenkins, D. 1979a. The Jakarta solution. *Far Eastn Econ. Rev.* 21 September, **105**(38), 38–40.

Jenkins, D. 1979b. The traders who came to stay. *Far Eastn Econ. Rev.* 21 September, **105**(38), 40–2.

Kuper, L. and M. G. Smith (eds) 1969. *Plural societies in Africa*. Los Angeles: University of California Press.

Lee, Y.-L. 1980. Race, language and national cohesion in Southeast Asia. *J. S.E. Asian Stud.* **11**, 122–35.

Mabbett, H. and P.-C. Mabbett 1972. The Chinese community in Indonesia. In *The Chinese in Indonesia, the Philippines and Malaysia*, 3–15. London: Minority Rights Group.

Mabbett, I. 1977a. The Indianization of Southeast Asia: some reflections on prehistoric sources. *J. S.E. Asian Stud.* **8**, 1–14.

Mabbett, I. 1977b. The Indianization of Southeast Asia: some reflections on historical sources. *J. S.E. Asian Stud.* **8**, 143–61.

Mackie, J. A. C. (ed.) 1976. *The Chinese in Indonesia*. Melbourne: Australian Institute of International Affairs.

Mahajani, U. 1960. *The role of the Indian minorities in Burma and Malaya*. Bombay: Vera.

Majumdar, R. C. 1963. *Ancient Indian colonisation of Southeast Asia*. Baroda: University of Baroda.

Malaysia 1976. *Third Malaysia Plan 1976–80*. Kuala Lumpur.

Morris, H. S. 1957. The plural society. *Man* **57**, 124–5.

Peyman, H. 1981. But how long will this non-stop sunshine last? *Far Eastn Econ. Rev.* 28 August, **113**(36), 43.

Purcell, V. 1965. *The Chinese in Southeast Asia*, 2nd edn. Oxford: Oxford University Press.

Purcell, V. 1967. *The Chinese in Malaya*. Kuala Lumpur: Oxford University Press.

Richardson, M. 1979. How many died? *Far Eastn Econ. Rev.* 26 October, **106**(43–4), 34.

Rudner, M. 1977. The economic, social and political dimensions of Malaysian education policy. In *Appetite for education in contemporary Asia*, K. Orr (ed.), 62–91. Monograph no. 10. Canberra: Development Studies Centre, Australian National University.

Sandhu, K. S. 1969. *Indians in Malaya*. Cambridge: Cambridge University Press.

Simoniya, N. A. 1961. *Overseas Chinese in Southeast Asia: a Russian study*. (Translation.) Annapolis: Joint Publications Research Service.

Skinner, G. W. 1957. *Chinese society in Thailand: an analytical history*. Ithaca: Cornell University Press.

Skinner, G. W. 1958. *Leadership and power in the Chinese community in Thailand*. Ithaca: Cornell University Press.

Smith, M. G. 1969. Some developments in the analytic framework of pluralism. In *Pluralism in Africa*, L. Kuper and M. G. Smith (eds), 415–58. Berkeley and Los Angeles: University of California Press.

Suryadinata, L. 1976a. Indonesian policies toward the Chinese minority under the New Order. *Asian Survey* **16**, 770–87.

Suryadinata, L. 1976b. Ethnicity and national integration: an Indonesian case. *Asia Q.* 1976, 209–34.

Suryadinata, L. 1978. *Pribumi Indonesians, the Chinese minority and China. A study of perceptions and policies.* Kuala Lumpur: Heinemann (Asia).

Tanabe, S. 1978. Land reclamation in the Chao Phraya Delta. In *Thailand: a rice growing society*, Y. Ishii (ed.). Honolulu: University of Hawaii Press.

Tinker, H. 1975. A forgotten long march: the Indian exodus from Burma 1942. *J. S.E. Asian Stud.* **6**, 1–15.

Wheatley, P. 1961. *The golden Khersonese.* Kuala Lumpur: University of Malaya Press.

Wickberg, E. 1965. *The Chinese in Philippine life 1850–1898.* Southeast Asian Studies no. 1. New Haven: Yale University.

Widjojo Nitisatro. 1970. *Population trends in Indonesia.* Ithaca: Cornell University Press.

Willmott, D. E. 1961. *The national status of the Chinese in Indonesia 1900–1958.* Ithaca: Cornell University Press.

Young, K., W. C. F. Bussink and P. Hassan 1980. *Malaysia: growth and equity in a multiracial society.* Baltimore: Johns Hopkins University Press.

2 Pluralism and plural societies: Caribbean perspectives

COLIN CLARKE

When I was an undergraduate 25 years ago, it was rare for geographers to incorporate social theory in their teaching, but Paul Paget made Furnivall's work on pluralism in South-East Asia a fruitful starting point for his Oxford tutorials on the social and spatial aspects of multiracial societies (Furnivall 1939, 1948). My own interest in pluralism, initiated by Paget, was reinforced when I started my doctoral research on Jamaica and became aware of M. G. Smith's (1960) anthropological restatement of Furnivall's model to provide a framework for analysing Caribbean societies.

By the time I began research, Vera Rubin had already edited a symposium volume entitled *Social and cultural pluralism in the Caribbean*, in which the leading pluralists and some of their critics set forth their interpretations of West Indian social structure (Rubin 1960). As these papers showed, the Caribbean is an excellent proving ground for Furnivall's ideas, since, although the region lacks indigenous cultures, the social, cultural and racial circumstances of the societies are comparable in complexity and inequality to those of South-East Asia. The Caribbean has had the longest experience of European tutelage of any Third World region; its economic development until the Second World War was dictated by the sugar plantation; its major cultural components were introduced through the importation of coloured labour managed by a white plantocracy under conditions of slavery and indenture.

In his contribution to Rubin's symposium, and in numerous other books and articles, Smith (1960, 1961, 1965a & b) argued that British West Indian society could not be explained by consensus nor by reference exclusively to colour–class distinctions – though throughout the islands there was a high correlation between phenotype and socio-economic status; rather, the social structure comprised a plurality of cultures imposed by colonialism, the sugar plantation and slavery. This plural model, derived from Third World research and not from hypotheses imported from developed countries, provided me with an anthropological insight into the historical and geographical development of Kingston, Jamaica, the study of which I prepared as a thesis under Paul Paget's supervision and later published as a book (Clarke 1975).

In this chapter I trace Smith's extension of his early work on social and cultural pluralism into legal and political spheres. I then examine the evolution of the interrelationship between these various modes of pluralism, using as a context the social history of Jamaica and Trinidad. These are the largest Commonwealth islands, and exemplify the two types of plural structure in the Commonwealth Caribbean. My intention is to demonstrate the usefulness of social theory to an understanding of the social and spatial differentiation of these two islands. But after my introduction to plural theory, the empirical sections on Jamaica and Trinidad aim to blend disciplinary perspectives, for, as Fleure remarked, 'geography, history and anthropology are a trilogy to be broken only with a severe loss of truth' (Fleure 1918).

Pluralism and plural societies

Cultural pluralism   The term pluralism, as it is used in the social sciences, has four principal sources of origin. The first, employed particularly by American political scientists, identifies pluralism with democracy. According to this viewpoint, the plural polity separates powers and builds in democratic checks and balances, while a multiplicity of autonomous organisations and interest groups – political, business and labour – compete freely with each other for political control.

The second strand in pluralist thought focuses specifically on ethnicity. As early as 1924, Horace Kallen, an American political scientist, drew attention to ethnic pluralism in the United States, stressed its association with family and ancestry and its involuntary nature, and advocated the legitimacy of ethnic differences. A similar point of view informs Milton Gordon's work, in which he identifies seven stages or sequential steps in the process of assimilation: cultural, structural, marital, identificational, attitude receptional, behaviour receptional and civic (Gordon 1964).

Kallen's political formulation focuses on consensus rather than conflict and Gordon's scheme emphasises rapid group acculturation, but J. S. Furnivall's conception of pluralism is rooted in dissensus and the persistence of cultural distinctions. Furthermore, Furnivall is concerned not with ethnicity and democracy but with cultural domination and colonialism. Describing conditions in Burma and Java, Furnivall noted:

'. . . the first thing that strikes the visitor is the medley of peoples – European, Chinese, Indian and native. It is in the strict sense a medley, for they mix but do not combine. Each group holds by its religion, its own culture and language, its own ideas and ways. As individuals they mix, but only in the market place in buying and selling. There is a plural society with different sections of the society living side by side but separately within the same political unit. Few recognise that in fact all members of all sections have material interests in common, but most see that on many points their material interests are opposed.' (Furnivall 1948, 304)

Furnivall's ideas have been refined and amplified by M. G. Smith and Pierre van den Berghe, who have, independently, produced similar classificatory models – the fourth source of ideas pertaining to pluralism. Both writers accept the state as a generally satisfactory definition of society, and they are in substantial agreement when van den Berghe argues,

'societies are pluralistic insofar as they are segmented into corporate groups that frequently, although not necessarily, have different cultures or subcultures and insofar as their social structure is compartmentalized into analogous, parallel, noncomplementary but distinguishable sets of institutions' (van den Berghe 1967, 34).

Institutional analysis is the cardinal feature of Smith's early work on pluralism. 'I hold', he writes, 'that the core of a culture is its institutional system. Each-institution involves set forms of activity, grouping, rules, ideas and values' (Smith 1965a, 79). Smith also argues that 'the institutions of a people's culture form the matrix of their social structure, simply because the institutional system defines and sanctions the persistent forms of social life' (Smith 1965a, 80).

What does Smith mean by institutions? The principal institutional systems that are involved in defining a population's culture and social relations are family, kinship, education, religion, property, economy and recreation. People who practise the same institutions – either the entire range or a selection of them – and for whom they have the same values and significance form a cultural section in the society. Smith clarifies his argument about cultural similarities and differences by citing the case of religion. He emphasises that 'variants of Christianity share common basic forms of organization, ritual and belief' (Smith 1965a, 84), whereas Christianity, Hinduism and Islam do not. He concludes that societies typified by minor features of differentiation, but which have common basic forms of organisation are culturally heterogeneous – the term homogeneous is reserved for small non-differentiated societies – and that societies that express institutional cleavage are culturally pluralistic.

Structural and social pluralism Subsequent to his work on cultural pluralism, Smith (1966, 1969, 1974) has developed the idea of structural pluralism. This occurs when population aggregates are differentially incorporated into society on a legal or political basis – for example, as slaves, freemen or citizens. Smith contrasts differential incorporation with uniform incorporation, when each individual adult has full voting rights and equality before the law; and equivalent incorporation, where a consociation is established and the separately incorporated sections have parity (Smith 1969, 435). Differentially incorporated sections are called corporate categories by Smith. They are assemblages of individuals discernible because of their caste-like identity (for example, slaves). Corporate categories that develop their own internal organisation become corporate groups, and in hierarchical societies are usually the super-ordinate elements (Smith 1966).

Smith identifies three variants of pluralism: cultural, structural and social (Smith 1969, 440). Cultural pluralism involves institutional differences which, of themselves, do not generate corporate social difference; provided they are restricted to the private domain through universal incorporation, they are of personal importance but do not have structural implications for society as a whole. As Smith observes, under universal incorporation, 'within limits set by law, differences of familial or religious practice are private options of equivalent status and indifference in the determination of individual civic rights' (Smith 1969, 435). Structural pluralism requires differential incorporation of the cultural sections; where it occurs, it creates social pluralism through the projection of institutional differentiation from the private into the public domain. Structural pluralism is either based upon or creates cultural pluralism through differential access of the sections to the society's resources. Smith concludes that 'uniform incorporation proscribes social pluralism, though it is equally consistent with cultural uniformities or cultural pluralism among its citizens' (Smith 1969, 440). Hence, structural pluralism always involves social and cultural pluralism, and social pluralism always involves cultural pluralism; but social pluralism may occur apart from structural pluralism when culturally distinct segments are or claim to be equal in rank and are linked in a consociation. This latter case does not occur in the Caribbean.

Where cultural variations do generate corporate social differences, Smith distinguishes between the social sections or segments formed in this way and social classes. In his view, classes are 'differentiated culturally with respect to non-institutional habits and value systems which may co-exist as alternatives on the basis of common values basic to the class continuum' (Smith 1965a, 53). In contrast, social segments possess their own value systems. They may be ranked hierarchically or may occupy parallel positions in the social order. Moreover, each section may be internally stratified by class.

The pros and cons of pluralism Proponents of cultural pluralism agree that circumstances to which the term is applied are extremely diverse. van den Berghe notes that 'societies range from maximally pluralistic, when the segments belong to unrelated cultural traditions, to minimally pluralistic, when only sub-cultural differences based on age, sex, class, "race" or caste, are present' (van den Berghe 1967, 134). However, some of these minimally pluralistic conditions would not qualify as pluralistic at all when measured against M. G. Smith's institutional yardstick, though one or two of them might form the basis for differential incorporation.

Critics of cultural pluralism claim that it emphasises institutional differences and neglects the importance of shared values (Rubin 1960). Others contend that it lays insufficient stress on distinctions of race and class (Wagley 1960). Another critic, referring to the problem of institutional analysis, has enquired 'at what point variations within an institutional sub-system become great enough to warrant our identification of two separate sub-systems?' (R. T. Smith 1961).

Notwithstanding these reservations, most of which can be answered only in the context of empirical research, it will be shown that cultural pluralism provides an extremely useful classificatory framework for examining complex societies. As a system of institutional analysis, it is open-ended and independent of race and colour – though race and colour can be fed in at a later stage; it facilitates the study of acculturation and places race in broad, historical and sociocultural contexts; it does not predicate a system of social stratification, yet it permits class concepts – either Marxist or bourgeois – and ideas about political domination to be deployed.

Relations between cultural sections are often symbiotic and maintained by patron–client links, but force or the threat of force is invariably a feature where a minority culture – or corporate group – is dominant. The plural model of differential incorporation demands – and supplies – an alternative interpretation to the one adopted by the consensual school of American sociology – whose ideas converge with those of the American school of pluralist political science (Parsons 1952), namely, that a common system of values is essential to stability in social systems and that without consensus societies cannot exist. van den Berghe (1967) applies the term plural society indiscriminately to pluralistic societies, and focuses on the tension between agreement and dissent in all culturally diverse situations, but M. G. Smith (1969), although conceiving pluralism more broadly, reserves the term 'plural society' for situations of minority-culture domination – the extreme case where structural, social and cultural pluralism coincide.

Marxism, identity and types of pluralism   Structural pluralism has something in common with Marxist perspectives on conflict, yet it avoids reducing the analytical framework to an economic dimension. Cultural pluralism emphasises the central importance of institutions, but these are broadly conceived and allow attention to be given to the currently fashionable, economic aspects of human behaviour, as well as to the racial and cultural variables that many Marxists would dismiss as 'false consciousness' – a capitalist device to divide the working class into mutually hostile bands. In this context, it is interesting to note that both pluralists and Marxists agree in interpreting racism as a means of justifying inequality – however it is conceived.

Eugene Genovese, the historian of American slavery, is one of the few scholars to discuss the attention Marxists should give to cultural *vis-à-vis* economic factors in social relationships.

'The confusion between Marxism and economic determinism arises from the Marxian definition of classes as groups, the members of which stand in a particular relation to the mode of production. This definition is essentially "economic" but only in the broadest sense. Broad or narrow, there is no reason for identifying the economic origins of a social class with the developing nature of that class which necessarily embraces the full range of human experience in its manifold political, social, economic and cultural manifestations. That the economic interests of a particular class will necessarily prove more important to its specific behaviour than, say, its religious values as an ahistoric and therefore an un-Marxian assumption. Since these values are conditioned only originally and broadly by the economy, and since they develop according to their own inner logic and in conflict with other such values, as well as according to social changes, an economic interpretation of religion can best serve as a first approximation and might even prove largely useless.' (Genovese 1971, 223)

The non-Marxist sociologist, Leo Kuper, views ethnicity as much more potent than class and observes, 'ethnic sections have an origin, as basis for existence, external to and preceding the societies in which they are incorporated'. He contrasts these with classes 'that emerge only in social interaction', and concludes that, in comparison with classes, ethnic sections are likely to have 'more enduring, comprehensive and unique histories, a greater affinity perhaps for sentimental elaboration of identity, and a larger capacity for reasserting exclusive loyalties, after long periods of increasing commitment to broader, more inclusive civic loyalties' (Kuper 1969, 461).

In addition to institutional aspects of pluralism, there are important aspects of culture associated with ethnicity and identity, based on shared features such as race, national background or language. Identity can rapidly be adapted and developed – as in the case of black identity in the USA or of the Ras Tafari cult in Jamaica. Both these protest movements had their origins in structurally pluralistic situations and each has attempted to transform corporate categories into corporate groups.

Excluding ethnic movements, pluralism has often been construed as a peculiarly colonial phenomenon. But, although colonies are quintessentially plural societies in the strict sense used by M. G. Smith, it is clear that there are widespread conditions of pre- and post-colonial pluralism. Moreover, many West European countries now have enclaves of recent immigrants from former colonial territories who have transformed class-based, metropolitan societies into culturally pluralistic ones by a process of 'colonisation in reverse'.

Pluralistic situations have many origins: conquest, forced labour, forced or free migration. However, I intend to focus on the historical evolution of two examples of pluralism that developed in the Caribbean under conditions of extreme differential incorporation. The first case, typified by Jamaica, involves ranked segments whose hierarchical relationship has been bolstered, historically, by racism; the second, exemplified by Trinidad, began with a social

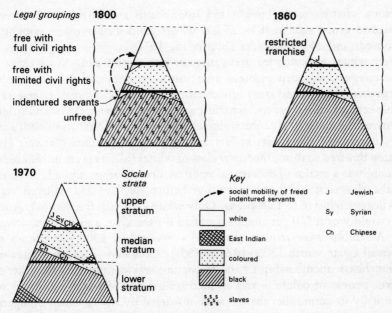

Figure 2.1 Race and status in Jamaica.

pyramid like Jamaica's, but has developed into a structure where two parallel segments of equal status compete for power.

Jamaica: a case of Creole pluralism

Captured by Britain from Spain in 1655, Jamaica rapidly developed as a sugar colony. Planters of British stock divided the island into estates and imported slaves from West Africa to provide the labour force. By the late 18th century cane fields covered the well drained coastal plains and embayments and penetrated the interior valleys. A plantation monoculture was established with sugar as king, and slave society was compartmentalised into almost 800 estates which were serviced by a dozen ports, most notable among which was Kingston, with a population of about 24 000 (Clarke 1975).

Citizens, freemen and slaves   From the beginning of the British colonial period, the major strata of Jamaican society were differentially incorporated as white freemen and black slaves; and, when miscegenation became more prevalent in the mid-18th century, an intermediate coloured element was formed through the manumission of the illegitimate offspring of the white elite (Fig. 2.1). These legal strata determined that whites alone were potentially full citizens: the brown emancipated population enjoyed only limited civil rights; slaves, whether blacks or illegitimate offspring of whites, were non-persons, chattels to be bought and sold. Status and power were inversely related to group size: in 1825, 25 000 whites controlled a colony with 40 000 coloureds and 340 000 blacks (Brathwaite 1971).

Free whites were divided occupationally into an elite and a lower class. The elite category included planters, merchants, attorneys, surveyors, lawyers, clergymen, doctors and army officers; the lower class comprised overseers and book-keepers, storekeepers, wharfingers, manufacturers, clerks and soldiers. Many of the early 19th century elite earned between £2000 and £4000 a year; they dominated the courts of law and officered the militia (Stewart 1823). Within this free stratum, the lower class of whites (like its peers in 18th century Britain) was a victim of differential political incorporation, though, in contrast to the slaves, it did have protection before the law and enjoyed certain privileges exclusive to Europeans. Only white Christian freemen who owned a freehold worth £10 per annum qualified for the vote, and representatives to the Assembly were required to have a freehold of £300 per annum or a personal estate worth £3000 (Renny 1807). Thus even if many whites were enfranchised, membership of the legislature was confined to the elite.

Free people of colour – and an increasing body of free blacks who were eventually to outnumber them – were restricted by law to urban occupations until the early 19th century, since it was feared they would incite plantation slaves to rebellion. Free coloured people were prevented from voting, testifying in criminal suits, holding political and administrative appointments, and, until 1816, from driving carts (Heuman 1981). Emulating the lower class of free whites, they gravitated into artisan work and retailing. In contrast, the small group of wealthy coloured people who had been educated abroad and had either inherited property and money from their white fathers or who had been successful in business on their own account, ranked economically, but not legally or socially, on par with the white elite.

The legal standing of the free people of colour was fully shared by the Jews. But whereas the free coloureds and free blacks were discriminated against because they were not white, the Jews, who were Portuguese Sephardim and ranked high in the colour spectrum of the society, were penalised for not being Christian. However, their disabilities were less onerous than those experienced by Jews in Britain at that time: they were permitted freedom of worship and were able to own property and undertake trade. The Jewish upper class in the 18th century was composed of merchants engaged in commerce with Spanish America, and the lower class supplied the slaves with salt fish, butter and cheap manufactured articles (Clarke 1975).

The relationship between masters and slaves, which provided the cornerstone of Jamaican society in its formative period, was legally defined in two documents, the *Code Noir* of 1696 and the *Consolidated Slave Laws* of 1792. These defined the obligations of masters to feed and clothe their slaves and to release them from work on Sundays; established limits to the mobility of slaves; and proscribed slave gatherings. But the protective clauses, which forbade such excesses as mutilation, were negated by the very existence of the master–slave relationship: for not only did whites frame the slave laws, but they also administered them in the courts. Furthermore, slaves were prevented from testifying against white persons, though they themselves could be convicted on the evidence of other slaves. Even the punishment meted out to masters and slaves who were found guilty of the same offence was grossly unequal: 'self-defence was a capital crime in a slave – and murder a fifteen pound penalty in the oppressor' (Southey 1827, 18).

Although Jamaica's slaves formed a homogeneous corporate category, they were internally differentiated by occupation, colour and place of birth. Plantation slaves were normally divided into three or four groups, each with a black driver. The great gang consisted of the strongest men and women, though the second gang tackled exactly the same work: digging cane holes, cutting cane, loading and unloading the carts *en route* for the sugar mill. Slaves who were weakly, elderly or pregnant made up the third gang, and the hog gang or grass gang comprised children who collected fodder for the stock and did light tasks such as weeding (Patterson 1967).

Drivers were not the only privileged slaves. Some worked in the sugar factories as boiler men and coopers. Brown slaves, both men and women, monopolised the least onerous tasks of domestic work. In the towns, slaves were engaged in port labour, in jobbing and retailing, especially on behalf of coloured owners, though here domestic work was undoubtedly the largest employer of female slaves. Further to these occupational and colour distinctions, to be Creole (West Indian born) or African involved different advantages and burdens. Africans performed the most onerous tasks and were denigrated by the more acculturated Creoles as 'salt water' Negroes (Clarke 1975).

Estate, colour and culture   It is tempting to describe Jamaica's major social strata during slavery as white, brown and black, but this is accurate only as a shorthand. By no means all whites were masters and all blacks enslaved. A small but growing number of blacks were free, either through manumission or self-purchase, and there was a small class of white immigrants, indentured under the deficiency laws to expand the arms-bearing population and to ensure that strategic trades did not fall into the hands of Negro artisans. After a minimum period of 4 years these indentured servants were released into the ranks of the lower class whites, unlike the slaves, who, whether black or coloured, usually lost their liberty for life (Williams 1944).

An unambiguous relationship between colour and status existed only in the upper stratum. A white skin – or acceptance as being white – was a prerequisite for full civil status; no compensatory attribute would normally qualify coloureds or blacks as 'full people', though under exceptional circumstances non-whites could be declared white by a special act of the Jamaica Assembly (Heuman 1981). The 'white bias' permeated all levels of society.

Possession of a white skin, aquiline nose, straight hair and thin lips became a badge of status, and gradations from the 'bad' features of the black to the 'good' features of the European, exemplified by mulattoes, quadroons, mustees and mustifinos (who were legally treated as white), formed stages on the road to whiteness and high rank. Moreover, the white bias carried cultural connotations: everything European was desirable; Africa was to be denigrated.

Jamaica's legal estates determined not only the status of the corporate categories but the cultures they practised. African traits were largely eroded under the system of slavery; the free people of colour (and the free blacks), while orientating themselves towards Europe, syncretised the behaviour of masters and slaves; and the whites practised a Creole version of 18th century British culture (Brathwaite 1971).

Males of the white elite took coloured mistresses, euphemistically called 'brown girls', and by preference those that were free. The lower class of whites was too poor to qualify for the attentions of coloured women, and their mistresses were usually black slaves. These unions were impermanent and never confirmed by matrimony. Coloured women, however, treated the keeper relationship as marriage, and preferred associations with whites to legal unions with brown men. Coloured men therefore resorted to black concubines – like lower class white men. Slaves – in quest of patronage – often tried to persuade young white immigrants to accept their daughters as mistresses (Clarke 1975).

Although mating between the strata followed a pattern that was structurally hypergamous, it was essential only for the lower class of whites and free people of colour. Among other groups alternative types of union with members of their own race were possible. White elite men married women of their own colour: like the Jews they practised both matrimony and concubinage. Unions between coloured people were rare, were usually legalised by marriage, and frequently involved the former mistresses of white men. Nuclear households were common among the slaves by the early 19th century, but involved serial polygamy: 'temporary connexions which they form without ceremony and dissolve without reluctance' (Edwards 1819, 98). Although concubinage was the norm, marriage was recorded among slaves in Kingston at the end of the slave period.

With few exceptions, whites were nominal members of the Anglican Church, yet masters made little or no attempt to baptise or educate their slaves. The Anglican Church also neglected the free people of colour, who were therefore ripe for proselytisation by the Wesleyans in the 1790s. By 1817, one-third of the Methodist congregation in Kingston was coloured (Clarke 1975). Among the slaves the most significant cultural group was the Coromantin from the Gold Coast, and their pantheism and ancestor cults were gradually adopted by the entire slave population. Even Creole slaves lived in fear of the spirits of the dead, and often engaged *obeah* men (practitioners of black magic) to manipulate malevolent *duppies* (ghosts). Christian baptism was looked upon by slaves as a protection against black magic. This presented a major obstacle to the success of the non-conformist missionaries at the end of the slave period and the problem was compounded by the frequency with which black bible leaders channelled slaves into unorthodox beliefs and established breakaway cults of an Afro-Christian type (Curtin 1955).

Education reflected and reinforced the pattern of culture developed by the various groups in Jamaica. Whites neglected local educational institutions, yet spent considerable sums on sending sons to English public schools and universities. Girls, however, were usually kept at home and adopted the speech and manners of their black nurses. In the second half of the 18th century, Wolmer's was the only secondary school in Kingston and the majority of its pupils were Jews or free people of colour. The slaves, by contrast, remained an illiterate, Creole-speaking group whose folk hero was Anansi, the spiderman and trickster of Ashanti legend; and their skills were manual and agricultural (Brathwaite 1971, Clarke 1975).

Fission and fusion   The 'white bias', which is really a euphemism for 'white racism', conditioned many of the Jamaican non-whites to accept the status quo, but the maintenance of the social order depended even more on the solidarity of the upper stratum and its ability to exploit divisions between and within the subordinate corporate categories. The whites feared that any alteration in the relationship between the three legally defined strata would threaten the stability of Jamaica's society (Smith 1965a). Thus advocates of slave emancipation were denounced, non-conformist clergymen were obstructed, and white and coloured liberals were ostracised or driven into exile. In the final analysis the cohesion of Jamaica's plural society depended on force or the threat of force. The political and legal supremacy of the whites was reinforced by the whip, by the British military detachment, and by the local militia, which was under white control but had substantial numbers of free, coloured, non-commissioned officers.

Slave opposition to servitude took many forms: malingering, magicoreligious activities, suicide, abortion and running away. Indeed, by 1750 two major maroon (runaway) communities had been established in the mountainous interior of Jamaica and had achieved treaties of recognition with the British government. Collective, as distinct from individual, opposition to slavery, was a peculiarly African phenomenon, especially during the 18th century. Twenty-nine rebellions took place in Jamaica over a period of 150 years, and the Coromantins were prominent in many of them. But tribal rivalry undermined slave organisation, and Creole slaves were uninvolved in insurrection until Daddy Sharp's rebellion, on the eve of emancipation, in 1831 (Higman 1976).

Social change   Notwithstanding adamant elite opposition to change, the legal framework of Jamaica's grossly inegalitarian Creole society was dismantled by the British government in the early 19th century. The free blacks, free people of colour and Jews were granted full civil rights in 1830, following a long campaign which had involved petition of the House of Commons (Heuman 1981); the slaves were emancipated in 1834 and their period of apprenticeship was ended in 1838 – exactly 30 years after the slave trade had been abolished in the British Empire. Since emancipation, no legal distinction has been made between Jamaicans on the basis of colour, though until recently the white bias remained important socially, psychologically and symbolically.

Creole structural pluralism, though mitigated by the civil rights movement of the 1820s and slave emancipation, persisted throughout the 19th century because of differential political incorporation. By the middle of the 19th century, Jamaica's export economy was sinking into decline, yet white plantocrats and merchants, Jews and elite browns – the beneficiaries of the old order – monopolised political power and attempted to retain the bankrupt estate system in the face of labour defection (Hall 1959, Eisner 1961). Emancipated blacks moved into the interior to form a reconstituted peasantry, but were at first of limited political significance because of the restrictive property and income qualifications of the franchise. In 1865, however, in the wake of the Morant Bay Rebellion, the Jamaica Assembly abdicated its constitutional rights in favour of Crown Colony Government, the main effect of which was to place control of the island's destiny in the hands of white expatriate officials – and white Creole planters and professionals. The rapid advance to power of the brown and black middle stratum was halted, and the potential voting strength of the burgeoning group of black peasant freeholders was neutralised (Heuman 1981).

Two other changes took place in the 19th century that had lasting effects on Jamaica's social structure. The period of Crown Colony government ushered in a period of intense infusion of Victorian values. Increasing emphasis was placed on sobriety, chastity, marriage and church-going, and this touched the lower stratum and provided a social veneer. However, to this day, low status Jamaicans suffer through their inability to live up to Victorian standards of morality, family organisation and religious behaviour (Clarke 1975).

The second change involved not so much an alteration within Creole culture as a supplement to it. The complexity of Jamaican society was increased by the arrival of East Indian indentured labourers between 1850 and 1917 for work on the sugar estates and banana plantations, and by the free immigration of Chinese and Syrians after 1890. Each group in its distinctive way has penetrated the Creole stratification and been acculturated to one of Jamaica's ranked plural cultures. According to Gordon's (1964) model of assimilation, each ethnic group has experienced acculturation in religious, educational and family spheres and enjoys civic assimilation, but on all other counts they remain ethnically and racially distinct. Syrians and Chinese have used trade, education and phenotype as entrées to high and medium status in urban areas; East Indians remain a rural enclave within the black peasantry and rural proletariat (Lowenthal 1972). Miscegenation on a large scale has affected all these immigrant groups, but they have retained their racial purity by shedding their mixed offspring into the ranks of the 'coloured' and 'black' strata.

Neither of these changes – cultural and racial – affected the pervasive pattern of differential incorporation. Even in the late 1930s under modified Crown Colony Government only 5 per cent of Jamaicans had the vote; politics remained an elite preserve and the reins of government were held in expatriate hands (Hughes 1955). The conjunction of a restricted franchise with economic depression created severe labour disturbances on Jamaica's estates and water-fronts out of which grew a political party, the People's National Party, and a trade union, the Bustamante Industrial Trade Union. Pressure was mounted for the vote and for independence from Britain. Universal adult suffrage was granted in 1944 and after a period of two-party democracy Jamaica became independent in 1962.

Social and cultural pluralism   Structural pluralism was formally abolished by adult suffrage in 1944, but Jamaica's cultural pluralism, together with most aspects of social pluralism, remained at independence (Smith 1961). Members of the upper stratum married before they mated, and household headship was invested in males. They were nominal members of the denominational churches, and the highest ranking ones usually Anglican. Secondary educa-tion, often acquired overseas, was a hallmark of this group. In the middle stratum, marriage and extramarital mating existed side by side, though illegitimacy was despised; fundamentalist Christian values were prevalent, and educational standards were generally good.

Illegitimacy was the norm among the lower stratum and household headship invested in males or females, depending on the composition of the domestic unit. Mating preceded both co-residence and marriage and half-siblingship was common, especially in urban areas. Common-law unions typified this stratum, yet social bonds tended to be matrifocal. Most low status Jamaicans were denominational Christians but large numbers belonged to American-based sects or to syncretic Afro-Christian cults. Access to secondary schooling was rare, absenteeism from school was commonplace and illiteracy was widespread.

Occupational and linguistic differences coincided with cultural segmenta-tion. Standard English with a Jamaican accent was spoken by the upper stratum who controlled business and the professions; members of the middle stratum spoke standard English and the Creole dialect, depending on which better suited the occasion, dominated the bureaucracy – until 1944 its upper levels were a white preserve – and filled subordinate, white-collar positions in the private business houses; the lower stratum spoke Creole only, and remained tied to manual, personal service and agricultural pursuits, most notably plantation labour and peasant farming (Smith 1961).

Using census data for 1960 the spatial interrelationship between major

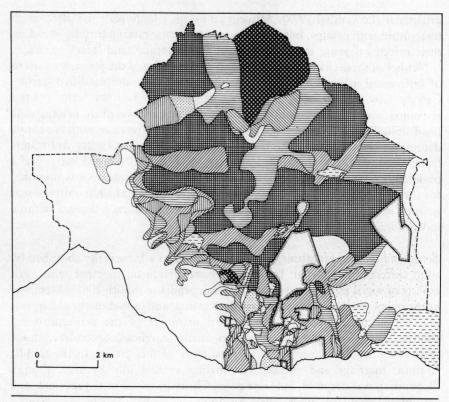

	Secondary school education	Common law union	Non-denominational Christian
Group I			
	>50%	<20%	<50%
	>50%	<20%	>50%
Group II			
	<50% >10%	<20%	<50%
	<50% >10%	<20%	>50%
	<50% >10%	>20%	<50%
	<50% >10%	>20%	>50%
Group III			
	<10%	<20%	<50%
	<10%	>20%	<50%
	<10%	<20%	>50%
	<10%	>20%	>50%

Figure 2.2   Kingston, 1961: social and cultural groupings (based on Clarke 1975, Fig. 76).

institutions can be explored for Kingston, Jamaica's capital city, which had a population of 376 000 on the eve of independence (Fig. 2.2). The lower stratum, characterised by common-law unions, Afro-Christian cults (non-denominational Christian) and poor educational standards, was concentrated in West Kingston and spatially segregated from areas of high cultural status, most of which were located in the central and northern suburbs. Persons of high status were typified by access to secondary (grammar school) education, low levels of non-denominational Christianity and a high incidence of marriage. Differentially acculturated to each, the median element occupied the middle ground, culturally, socially and geographically, between the upper and lower strata (Clarke 1975).

This evidence depicts an urban community split into three cultural segments which form an hierarchy. Moreover, the index of socio-economic status, compiled from occupational combinations in each enumeration district ranked from high (100) to low (300) (Fig. 2.3), corresponds closely with the pattern of institutional pluralism; and the distribution of whites (Europeans, Fig. 2.4), browns (Afro-Europeans, Fig. 2.5) and blacks (Africans, Fig. 2.6) coincides with the location of the upper, median and lower strata, respectively.

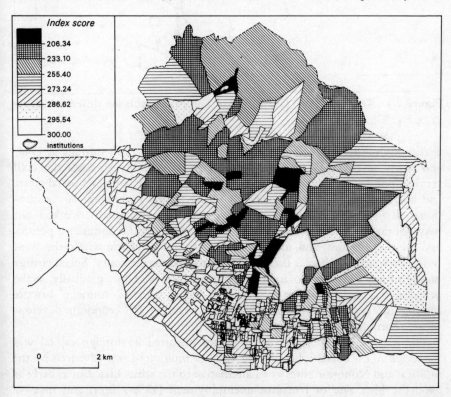

Index score

- 206.34
- 233.10
- 255.40
- 273.24
- 286.62
- 295.54
- 300.00

institutions

0   2 km

Figure 2.3   Kingston, 1960: socio-economic status (based on Clarke 1975, Fig. 54).

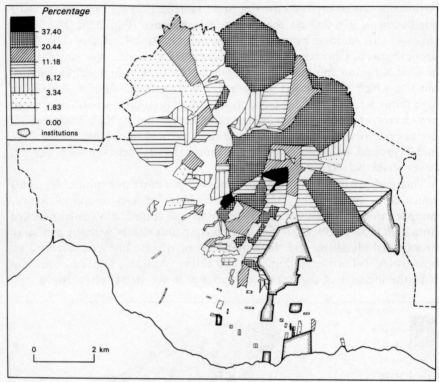

Figure 2.4 Kingston, 1960: distribution of European population (based on Clarke 1975, Fig. 77).

Although differential incorporation was replaced by adult suffrage in 1944, and many blacks subsequently achieved social mobility through the civil service, politics, trade and education, at independence Jamaica's social strata had not been culturally transformed. During the 18 year period of constitutional decolonisation (1944–62), an agreement was gradually worked out between the upper and median strata. The median stratum dominated politics and the trade unions, and advocated Jamaican independence within the West Indies Federation, whereas the upper stratum ran the economy. Social change was promised to the electorate, but it could be achieved only gradually, as the peripheral capitalist system – based on sugar, bananas, tourism, bauxite mining and tax-incentive manufacturing – matured and economic development occurred (Clarke 1974).

The pattern of export-led development nurtured by foreign capital was paralleled in the social sphere by the ideal of multiracialism, advanced by the political and economic elites as an alternative to the white bias. But as early as 1960 the high rate of Jamaican unemployment (13 per cent) and massive emigration to Britain were calling into question the capacity of capitalism to

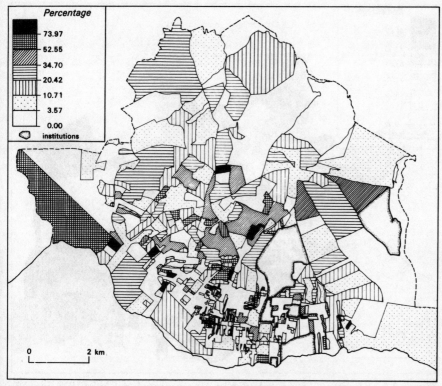

Figure 2.5 Kingston, 1960: distribution of Afro-Europeans (based on Clarke 1975, Fig. 80).

develop the Jamaican economy at sufficient speed and with adequate concern for social welfare; and the West Kingston slum was already a breeding ground for the anti-white, anti-imperialist and anti-capitalist cult of Ras Tafari (Nettleford 1970), whose impact on socialism in Jamaica was to be substantial during the Michael Manley period (1972–80).

Jamaica as a model This sketch shows how the three major elements in Jamaica's social structure were differentially incorporated during the 18th century and how the hierarchical distinction between slaves, freemen and citizens became a temporal sequence of change experienced by blacks (and browns) over a period of about a hundred years. In 1800 Jamaica was a plural society, in the strict sense of the term, with a dominant and all-powerful minority: structural pluralism transformed cultural pluralism – based upon transmuted and syncretised European and African traits – into social pluralism in the public domain. Severity of structural pluralism was reduced by slave emancipation, but uniform incorporation of the middle and lower strata – by the removal of the property-restrictive franchise – was delayed until as recently

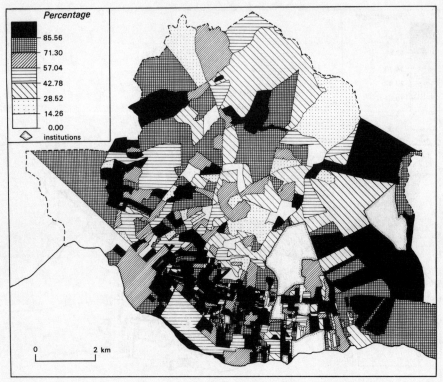

Figure 2.6 Kingston, 1960: distribution of Africans (based on Clarke 1975, Fig. 79).

as 1944. Jamaica entered independence in 1962 as a culturally pluralistic society but with a legacy of social pluralism. A major achievement of the Manley government of the 1970s was the partial removal of the stigma attached to folk culture, especially as far as illegitimate births were concerned.

Jamaica exemplifies a classic case of Creole pluralism, which in its origin involved ranked cultural segments, legally defined and correlated with colour. All other types of present-day Caribbean society can be related to it. The people of small homogeneous islands, for example, Barbuda and Anguilla, are culturally similar to Jamaican peasent communities. Haiti and the Windward Islands resemble Jamaica, but their whites have gone and they have brown elites instead. Cuba in 1850 was like Jamaica in 1800, but massive white immigration in the early 20th century swamped the Creole stratification and reduced the non-whites to enclaves in a class-based hierarchy.

Other examples of late immigration disrupting the Creole stratification are provided by Trinidad and Guyana. Between 1845 and 1917 tens of thousands of Indian indentured labourers were brought in to work on the nascent sugar estates. In Trinidad they account for 40 per cent of the population; in Guyana they are the majority. Yet in both territories they form a segment that is in many ways external to the Creole stratification and adds a more complex plural dimension to it.

East Indians in Creole Trinidad

Trinidad was a Spanish colony until captured by Britain in 1797. Neglected throughout most of the Spanish period, Trinidad began to develop as a slave plantation society only after the Cedula of 1783 permitted the immigration of Catholics from the French Antilles with skills in plantation management and sugar manufacturing. Despite considerable investment by British planters after Trinidad was formally annexed in 1815, this trilingual society remained markedly underpopulated and underdeveloped. In 1834, at emancipation, it had barely one-fifteenth of Jamaica's slave total and the sugar industry was still in its infancy (Wood 1968).

As in Jamaica, white masters occupied the apex of the social pyramid, black slaves the base; free coloureds, descendants of white masters and slave women, acquired an intermediate position between the two extremes. But interracial contact was less constrained than in other British West Indian colonies. After centuries of Spanish neglect, plantation slavery was only just becoming established (Newson 1976). English-speaking whites were outnumbered by Spanish colonists and French émigrés, and the free coloureds – French, English or Spanish in speech – were more numerous than all the whites put together (Wood 1968).

After emancipation a plentiful supply of cheap labour was essential to maintain the profitability of the plantation system and to enable it to expand into the substantial tracts of virgin, fertile territory on the edge of the Gulf of Paria. However, the slave trade in the British Empire had been abolished in 1808, and indentured immigrants from India alone could meet the labour needs of the plantocracy. The first immigrant ship arrived in 1845, and by 1917, when the Indian government terminated the traffic, 143 900 Indians had arrived in Trinidad, of whom 33 000 had exercised their right to a return passage.

Although blacks left the estates to squat in the vast tracts of Crown Land or to settle in the capital, Port of Spain, which already had more than a quarter of the island's entire population, the Indian immigrants gradually placed the plantations on a sound footing. By 1866, sugar output reached 40 000 tons, three times the level attained in the 1830s. Greater racial and cultural complexity accompanied these economic advances (Wood 1968). The Indian element in Trinidad's population increased from 27 400 in 1871 to 70 200 in 1891, and its contribution to the island total over the same period expanded from 22 to 32 per cent (Fig. 2.7).

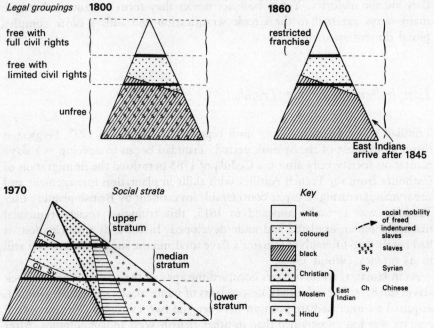

Figure 2.7   Race and status in Trinidad.

Provenance and settlement of the Indians   Most of Trinidad's indentured
Indians came from the North-West Provinces and Oudh, Bihar and Bengal,
and passed through Calcutta; only a small proportion were shipped from
South India via Madras. Outstanding source areas for the emigrants were the
450 mile section of the Ganges Plain from Delhi to Benares and the region
between Benares and the Himalayas (La Guerre 1974). Less than 15 per cent of
the emigrants were Muslims. Among the Hindus (85 per cent), a wide range
of castes was represented: agricultural castes, low castes and outcastes made up
two-thirds of the migrants, but high ranking Brahmins and Kshattriyas
accounted for 10 per cent (Weller 1968, Wood 1968).

At first, Creole society viewed the Indians as transients who would leave the
island once their contracts expired. In 1853, however, the Colonial government decided that although indenture would remain a 5 year term, Indians
would have to live in the island for a further 5 years before they were eligible
for their free return passage. Thereafter, demographic factors ensured the
permanence of the Indian community. By 1871, more than one in seven of the
Indians had been born in Trinidad, and by the early 1900s the local born
outnumbered Indian immigrants; for these Trinidadians India would never be
home. During the second half of the 19th century, as the Indians changed from
sojourners to settlers, from coolies, as they were derisively called, into East
Indians, they formed large, racially homogeneous enclaves in the sugar belt

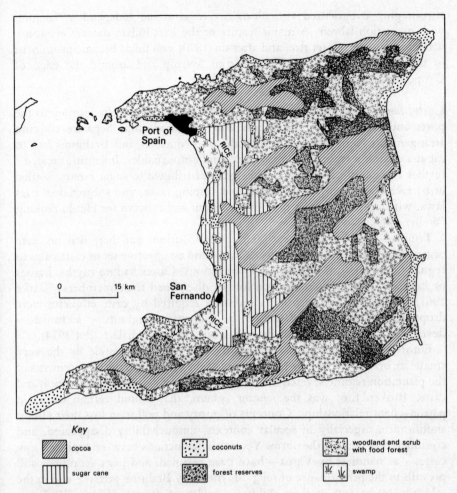

Figure 2.8 Trinidad: land use.

south of Port of Spain and in the canefields of the Naparimas around the second town of San Fernando (Fig. 2.8) (Ramesar 1976, Brereton 1979).

A key factor in the development of the East Indian settlement pattern was the Crown Colony's decision in 1869 to release land for small scale farming. Many Indians commuted their return passage for land: by 1916 they had 90 000 acres (39 200 ha) under cultivation, two-thirds of it in cocoa, by then the island's main crop, and East Indian cane farmers outnumbered their black counterparts by four to three (Wood 1968).

At first, East Indian settlement beyond the perimeter of the plantations was dispersed, but after 1870 government-planned villages were set up around Chaguanas and south of San Fernando (Wood 1968). Garden plots were laid out in acreages too small for subsistence and were sited next to sugar land, thus

encouraging experienced agriculturalists to combine independent farming
with plantation labour. A major feature of the East Indian peasant economy
was the growing of wet rice, and after the 1870s *padi* fields became prominent
in the cultural landscape of the Caroni Swamp and around the edge of
Oropouche Lagoon.

Caste, family and religion   Dissolution of caste began on the journey to the
ports and continued in the depots and on board ship. Separate cooking
arrangements were provided for Hindus and Muslims, but Brahmins had to
eat at a common table with lower castes and untouchables. Indenture created a
further erosion of caste: East Indians were distributed to sugar estates, settled
in barracks, allocated to cultivating and reaping tasks, and subjected to pass
laws, which restricted their mobility, without any concern for Hindu ranking
(Weller 1968, Wood 1968).

Trinidad-born Indians knew their caste affiliation, but there was no caste
organisation, no caste council – *panchayat* – and no effective set of caste rules to
regulate interpersonal relations and obligations. Castes had no myths, heroes
or heritage of their own, and no longer disciplined their members (Clarke
1967). Niceties of grammatical expression required by caste etiquette were
dropped, and the descendants of the Calcutta emigrants – *kalkatiyas* –
developed a simplified Hindi derived from Bhojpuri dialect (Jha 1974).

Enforcement of strict caste endogamy was made impossible by the very
small size of, and sex imbalance in, many of the castes, and the requirements of
the plantation regime severed the link between occupational specialisation and
caste. Broken too, was the *jajmani* system, that bound certain castes in
patron–client relationships. Concepts of purity and pollution lost their Hindu
significance, especially in secular contexts; untouchability disappeared, and
commensality became the norm. Yet status distinctions between high and low
castes – as manifest by Varna – have been retained, and caste sentiment still
prevails in the performance of religious rites – by Brahmin priests – and in the
selection by parents of their children's brides or grooms (Clarke 1967).

Nineteenth century Indian immigrants were neither families nor uprooted
communities, but individuals picked to fill the recruiting agent's quota.
Agents had the utmost difficulty in obtaining women – which the quota often
required – and the immigrants' sex ratio fluctuated from year to year.
Trinidad's East Indian males outnumbered females by three to two in 1891,
and the ratio approached parity only in 1946. Despite the imbalanced sex ratio
among East Indians, racial endogamy was maintained. Sexual relations – even
illicit ones – between East Indian men and black women were rare, and as late
as 1946 mixed East Indian–Creole offspring numbered only 8400 in the census,
or just over 4 per cent of the East Indian total.

The North Indian, patrifocal nuclear family was preserved in 19th century
Trinidad. As in India, East Indian brides were expected to be virgin and
women who were separated or widowed were not allowed to remarry by

Hindu rites. Ironically, despite retention of simplified customary marriage rituals, most Trinidad-born East Indians were illegitimate by Creole standards. Traditional Hindu marriages 'under the bamboo' were not legally recognised until 1946 – a few years after official sanction was given to Muslim unions, and a century after the first Indians had arrived in Trinidad. As a result, as late as 1946, almost two-thirds of East Indian women aged over 15 were classified in the census as common-law wives.

The tenacity of the Indian family was paralleled by the retention of Indian religious activities (Niehoff & Niehoff 1960, Klass 1961). Within 15 years of the beginning of indentured settlement in Trinidad, Hindu temples had been built on the estates and *saddhus* (holy men) were tramping the roads. Goat sacrifice in propitiation of Kali Mai was carried out by the lower castes in the second half of the 19th century (Morton 1916), though most Hindus have now abandoned animal sacrifice and accept Brahminical orthodoxy.

Immigrant Brahmins and their local-born pupils re-established a priesthood, officiating at marriages and performing domestic *pujas* (ceremonial offerings) for their clients. But the cast-exclusive nature of the priesthood, the use of a dead language (Sanskrit), and the Brahmins' inability or unwillingness to educate the lower castes have left Hinduism largely traditional and ritualistic.

Urdu-speaking Muslims were everywhere a minority in the East Indian population, yet they achieved a high degree of organisation, explicable, perhaps, by their regular meeting for worship in the mosque. Muslims were less tolerant of Christianity than the Hindus; they avoided the proselytising activity of the missions and isolated themselves from Creole society.

East Indians of all backgrounds acquired new traits as well as experiencing cultural loss. Some of the most outstanding changes were brought about by the Christian missions – Catholic in the north and Presbyterian in the south. Services were in Hindi and Sunday schools gave basic instruction to East Indian children. As a result of conversion, the Hindu proportion of the East Indian population dropped from 80 to 65 per cent between 1901 and 1946. In contrast, the Muslim proportion grew steadily yet continuously, but by 1946, when Muslims accounted for 17 per cent of East Indians, even they were outnumbered by the combined total of southern Presbyterians and northern Catholics (19 per cent).

Canadian Presbyterians devoted themselves to improving East Indian education, and opened many schools in the 1870s with the financial backing of the government and the estates. By 1896 there were more than 56 Canadian Mission Indian Schools, as they were popularly known, and a handful of East Indian converts had been trained to teach in them (Morton 1916). Hindu and Muslim boys attended the Presbyterian schools into their teens, and larger numbers were converted – especially those wanting further education and white collar jobs, particularly in teaching.

By the end of the Second World War, three-fifths of the East Indian elite – Christian, Hindu and Muslim – were Presbyterian-trained (Kirpalani *et al.* no

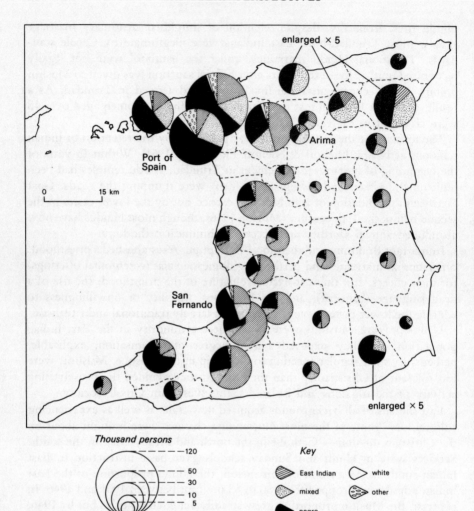

Figure 2.9 Trinidad, 1960: race and colour.

date). But this education was for boys; most East Indian girls were kept at home until they married. Despite the widespread provision of primary schools, illiteracy, especially among Hindus, remained the distinguishing feature of the East Indians; according to the 1946 census, 37 per cent of the men and 66 per cent of the women were illiterate in English.

Society and space   At the end of the colonial period the principal feature of Trinidad's social structure remained the dichotomy between Creole and East Indian (Fig. 2.7). The term Creole, as used locally, excluded the East Indian population together with the small Syrian, Portuguese, Chinese and Carib minorities. Creoles were white, brown or black, and, as in Jamaica, phenotype corresponded closely with socio-economic status. Out of a total population of 1 million in 1960, Creoles accounted for over 60 per cent; the breakdown by colour groups was: whites 2 per cent, browns 16 per cent and blacks 43 per cent. East Indians made up 37 per cent of the island's total, but they were still segmented into their major religious groups: Hindus (23 per cent of Trinidad's total population), Muslims (6 per cent) and Christians (8 per cent).

Leaving aside the neighbouring island of Tobago, which is a political dependency with almost all its population black, Trinidad divided into five racial–cultural zones. The western sugar belt and its subsidiary rice-growing areas, lying between Port of Spain and San Fernando, together with the Naparimas and the sparsely populated south-west peninsula, were predominantly East Indian (Fig. 2.9). Port of Spain and its associated conurbation stretching along the Eastern Main Road towards Arima contained more than 250 000 inhabitants, over 90 per cent of whom were Creole. San Fernando, with 40 000 population, was the only other town of note. Almost three-quarters of its inhabitants were Creole, but East Indians formed a sizeable minority – the largest proportion that East Indians achieved in any Trinidad town. The north and east of Trinidad were rural, sparsely populated and largely black, except for Nariva where there was a pocket of East Indians. By far the most racially heterogeneous locality was the central uplands, where mixed communities of blacks and East Indians subsisted by small-scale cultivation supplemented with cocoa farming. The outstanding feature of the spatial pattern was the dichotomy between town-dwelling Creoles and rural Hindus and Muslims. Whites, coloureds, blacks and Chinese were only weakly segregated from one another at the national level, and the three East Indian groups were closely aligned (Fig. 2.10). Christian East Indians were more urbanised than Hindus and Muslims, resided in close proximity to Creoles of mixed ancestry, but segregated themselves from Negroes.

Two correlates of racial segregation merit further discussion: occupational specialisation and endogamy. Professional occupations, a preserve of the white elite and coloureds in the 19th century, had been entered by educated blacks and East Indians, notably urban Christians: at the other social extreme, small farming involved blacks and East Indians. Otherwise, occupations and race were polarised: white-collar jobs were Creole dominated, whereas urban marginality was strongly associated with low-status blacks; agricultural labouring in the sugar industry devolved on Hindus and Muslims; oilfield workers were predominantly Creole. Sometimes occupational specialisation was very precise, particularly among town dwellers. East Indians were prominent in retailing, road haulage, and petrol station and cinema ownership. Brown and black Creoles dominated the civil service and police force, and these enclaves were seen by East Indians as the means whereby the Creole government-party extended its control over the society (Williams 1969).

Polarised in space yet occupying approximately co-ordinate socio-economic positions, the Creole and East Indian segments were notably endogamous: a

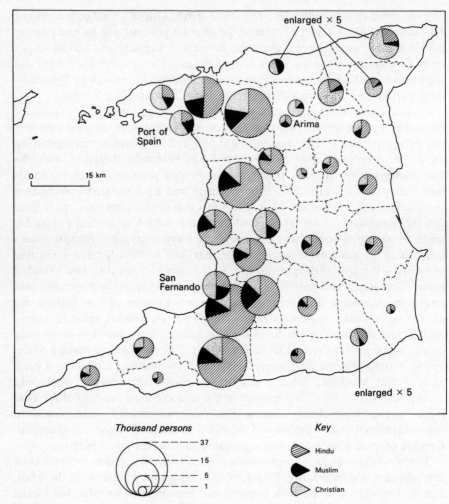

Figure 2.10   Trinidad, 1960: religious groupings among the East Indian population.

reflection of institutional incompatibilities and racial antipathy. Among the
black lower class, female household headship was common; mating, as in
Jamaica, was usually initiated by visiting; and the majority of births were
illegitimate. As women grew older, visiting tended to be replaced by
concubinage and by the time they were in their 40s most had been legally
married – as had most whites by their mid-20s. East Indians, unlike blacks,
stressed early marriage and male household headship. Moreover, East Indian
parents arranged their daughters' and sons' marriages. Parental control of the
choice of marriage partner, together with the practice of settlement exogamy
among Hindus, negated the potential for East Indian outmarriage provided by

residential mixing in small urban communities such as San Fernando (Clarke 1971).

Social and cultural pluralism in San Fernando   By focusing on another urban situation at the end of the colonial period, it is possible to explore some of the complexities of cultural pluralism in Trinidad. The town selected is San Fernando, which had 40 000 inhabitants in 1960. The white population, which is of marginal interest here and is spatially discontinuous in distribution, has been omitted from the analysis. Eighteen racial and cultural characteristics have been intercorrelated (Table 2.1) and the first and second highest coefficients in each column have been grouped using linkage analysis (Fig. 2.11) (Clarke 1973).

The linkage diagram depicts two groups: one focuses on the inevitably negative correlation between blacks (Negroes) and East Indians; the other is structured by the bond between secondary education and males in non-manual occupations, and by the strong inverse relationship that each of these variables has with less than standard 6 education. Moreover, the two major groups are loosely linked by various aspects of family structure. Common-law unions were associated with low occupational status and poor education. Many lower-class Hindus and Muslims (as well as blacks), whose original marriages had foundered, resorted to consensual cohabitation. Female household headship was essentially a black cultural phenomenon and associated with visiting relationships rather than with marital or common-law unions.

These two major statistical groups involve 17 of the 18 variables used in the analysis. Taking the highest and second highest coefficient for each variable, five nodes may be identified. In rank order of the number of correlation bonds, these nodes are East Indian and non-manual occupations; Negroes; less than standard 6 education; secondary schooling (Fig. 2.11).

Duplication of institutions characterised East Indians and Negroes. Thirteen of the 16 cases where the Negroes and East Indians are correlated with other variables involve a change of sign as one moves from one group to another (Table 2.1). Comparison of the correlations for the mixed and Negro populations also supports the cultural pluralism hypothesis for Creoles. Eight of the 16 cases where the mixed and Negro populations are correlated with other variables record a change of sign; these eight cases refer to the Chinese, orthodox Christians, other Christians, Presbyterians, females in common-law unions, secondary schooling, less than standard 6 education, and males in non-manual occupations.

This statistical analysis shows that both Creole and East Indian elements in San Fernando were divided into cultural segments. The Creole segments were ranked as in Jamaica, but among East Indians, hierarchical and parallel positions were noted, with Presbyterians recording a superior occupational status to Hindus and Muslims, and one comparable to the Creole mixed group. In some cases the minor cultural segments were distinguished by two

Table 2.1 Matrix of Spearman rank correlation coefficients for racial and cultural characteristics for the population of San Fernando

Variables	Negro	East Indian	Chinese	Mixed	Denominational Christian	Other Christian	Presbyterian	Hindu	Muslim	Female, head	Female, common law	Female, visiting	Female, married	Secondary school	Less than standard 6	Standard 6 or 7	No education	Males in non-manual occupations
Negro	1.0	*-0.67*	-0.41	-0.25	**0.62**	0.41	*-0.47*	-0.46	-0.38	0.40	0.28	*0.56*	-0.34	-0.52	0.30	**0.58**	-0.35	-0.61
East Indian	**-0.67**	1.0	-0.25	-0.09	-0.37	-0.16	**0.58**	**0.79**	**0.50**	-0.26	0.05	-0.40	0.20	0.06	0.17	-0.51	*0.65*	0.16
Chinese	-0.41	-0.25	1.0	0.41	-0.29	-0.19	0.24	-0.02	0.23	0.13	-0.15	-0.25	-0.10	0.43	-0.27	-0.17	-0.26	0.58
mixed	-0.25	-0.09	0.41	1.0	-0.25	-0.15	0.15	-0.35	-0.04	0.26	-0.13	0.11	-0.29	0.42	-0.48	0.23	-0.33	0.53
denominational Christian	*0.62*	-0.37	-0.29	-0.25	1.0	-0.38	0.05	-0.39	*-0.43*	0.35	0.19	**0.57**	-0.17	-0.33	0.27	0.45	-0.12	-0.41
other Christian	0.41	-0.16	-0.19	-0.15	-0.38	1.0	-0.06	-0.16	-0.09	0.10	0.32	0.22	-0.19	-0.48	0.25	0.46	-0.06	-0.43
Presbyterian	-0.47	0.58	0.24	0.15	0.05	-0.06	1.0	0.26	0.09	-0.05	-0.13	-0.08	0.31	0.19	-0.06	-0.13	0.31	0.30
Hindu	-0.46	**0.79**	-0.02	-0.35	-0.39	-0.16	0.26	1.0	0.34	-0.43	-0.01	-0.49	0.29	-0.10	0.15	*-0.54*	**0.67**	-0.04
Muslim	-0.38	0.50	0.23	-0.04	-0.43	-0.09	0.09	0.34	1.0	0.02	-0.01	-0.36	0.05	-0.02	0.06	-0.21	0.26	-0.14
female, head	0.40	-0.26	0.13	0.26	0.35	0.10	-0.05	-0.43	0.02	1.0	-0.01	0.46	**-0.65**	-0.02	0.03	0.34	0.26	-0.09
female, common law	0.28	0.05	-0.15	-0.13	0.19	0.32	-0.13	-0.01	-0.01	-0.01	1.0	0.23	*-0.36*	-0.44	0.71	0.06	0.37	-0.56
female, visiting	0.56	-0.40	-0.25	0.11	0.57	0.22	-0.08	-0.49	-0.36	*0.46*	0.23	1.0	-0.29	-0.32	0.24	0.44	-0.10	-0.40
female, married	-0.34	0.20	-0.10	-0.29	-0.17	-0.19	0.31	0.29	0.05	**-0.65**	-0.36	-0.29	1.0	0.14	-0.20	-0.12	0.14	0.24
secondary school	-0.52	0.06	*0.43*	0.42	-0.33	**-0.48**	0.19	-0.10	-0.02	-0.02	-0.44	-0.32	0.14	1.0	*-0.74*	-0.39	-0.33	**0.88**
less than standard 6	0.30	0.17	-0.27	*-0.48*	0.27	0.25	-0.06	0.15	0.06	0.03	**0.71**	0.24	-0.20	*-0.74*	1.0	0.13	0.49	*-0.75*
standard 6 or 7	0.58	-0.51	-0.17	0.23	0.45	*0.46*	-0.13	-0.54	-0.21	0.34	0.06	0.44	-0.12	-0.39	0.13	1.0	-0.40	-0.28
no education	-0.35	0.65	-0.26	-0.33	-0.12	-0.06	0.31	*0.67*	0.26	0.26	0.37	-0.10	0.14	-0.33	0.49	-0.40	1.0	-0.29
males in non-manual occupations	-0.61	0.16	**0.58**	**0.53**	-0.41	-0.43	0.30	-0.04	-0.14	-0.09	*-0.56*	-0.40	0.24	**0.88**	**-0.75**	-0.28	-0.29	1.0

Highest coefficient in each column shown in **bold** type; second highest coefficient in each column shown in *italic* type.
Source: 1960 census enumeration district data.

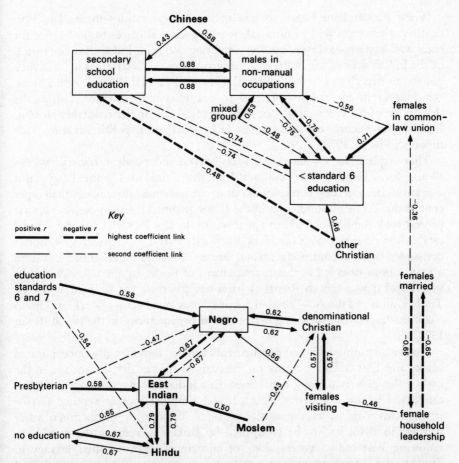

Figure 2.11 San Fernando: linkage of highest and second highest correlations for each racial or cultural characteristic, based upon enumeration district data from the 1960 census.

or three institutions alone; in others the entire range of institutional differences was involved, and the institutional practices themselves were quite distinct if not mutually incompatible.

Pluralism and politics A similar but more entrenched pattern of plurality obtained at the national scale, where East Indians and blacks are separated spatially and socially as a result of economic location – and mutual antipathy. During the second half of the 19th century East Indians and blacks internalised white racist stereotypes of one another. East Indians abused blacks as 'niggers' and black denigrated Indians as 'coolies'. 'Like monkeys pleading for evolution, each claiming to be whiter than the other', even today, in Naipaul's perceptive phrase, 'Indians and Negroes appeal to the unacknowledged white audience to see how much they despise one another' (Naipaul 1962, 80).

When East Indians began to join national organisations in the late 19th century, they eschewed multiracial, working-class alliances in preference for their own racially exclusive bodies. So strong was East Indian fear of erosion of the Indian way of life under pressure from Creole society that in 1922 they countered British and Creole proposals for constitutional advance with a plea – which was refused – for proportional or communal representation. During the depression of the 1930s, however, several radical East Indians, notably Hosein, Roodal and Rienzi, began to forge links with black politicians and trade unionists (Ryan 1972).

They aspired to a multiracial, socialist and independent society, whose ideals, for a while, were embodied in the Trinidad Labour Party. But working-class electoral success was out of the question, since fewer than 6 per cent of the Trinidad population in the 1930s qualified for the vote; so popular protest took the form of labour agitation. In the late 1930s Rienzi and Roodal established close ties with the black-led Butler Party. In October 1936 Butler demanded better accommodation and wages for oil and sugar workers. Within a year, labour riots led to the imprisonment of Butler by the white establishment, and it was left to Rienzi, a barrister, to create the Oilfield Workers' Trade Union and the All-Trinidad Sugar Estates' and Factory Workers' Union – still the largest and most important labour organisations in the island (Ryan 1972).

Notwithstanding this rapprochement among differentially incorporated blacks and East Indians, voting on the basis of the restricted franchise in the early 1940s polarised along racial lines: East Indian areas returned East Indian candidates to the Legislative Council, and a similar pattern typified Creole strongholds. And, when the legislature, on the eve of the introduction of adult suffrage in 1946, had to be compelled by Britain to remove the restriction requiring East Indian voters alone of all groups to prove their literacy in English, the scene was set for a new and even more pernicious bout of racial politics, this time hallowed by 'one man, one vote' and the multi-party democratic system.

Since 1956 Trinidad's blacks and browns have supported the People's National Movement (PNM) (Oxaal 1968), and the party, under mulatto leadership, has won six consecutive elections. During the decade 1956–66 – in the middle of which Trinidad followed Jamaica out of the West Indies Federation and into a separate independence – parliamentary opposition devolved first upon the People's Democratic Party, which was created and headed by the executive of the orthodox Hindu association, the Sanathan Dharma Maha Sabha, and, after 1958, upon the Democratic Labour Party (DLP) (Malik 1971). The DLP was originally a coalition of opposition groups, but its leadership was largely Brahmin and its voting strength depended upon Hindus and, after 1960, Hindus, Muslims and Christians (Fig. 2.12). This political bifurcation of the electorate was convenient to Creole and East Indian political leaders. They transformed Trinidad's major cultural

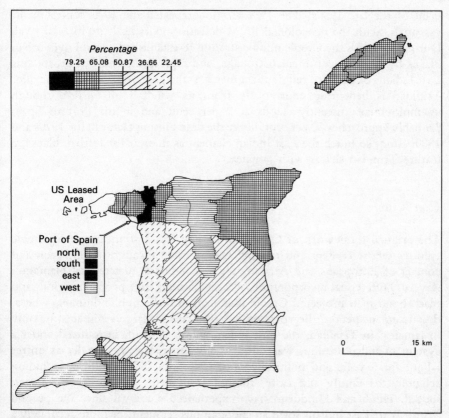

Figure 2.12 Trinidad and Tobago general election, 1961: PNM candidates, percentage of the total vote.

categories into corporate groups; whipped up racial antagonism at election periods – yet stressed multiracialism at other times; and encouraged their followers to respond to their opponents' ethnic revival by seeking and sustaining their own cultural roots.

Confrontation between Creole and East Indian became less intense during the 1970s, though mulatto hegemony was maintained. Black power disturbances and an abortive mutiny in the defence force in 1970 split the Creole segment along lines of internal cleavage and disturbed, for a time, the PNM's control of Port of Spain's marginalised blacks (Oxaal 1971). East Indians, fearful of the black power outburst and frustrated by alleged Creole gerrymandering and fixing of voting machines during the 1960s, refused to take part in the 1971 election, and all Trinidad's seats returned PNM candidates. Another major political change took place in 1976, with the electoral demise of the DLP and the emergence of the United Labour Front (ULF), based upon a voting alliance of black oilfield workers and East Indian sugar labourers – an echo of the late 1930s. The 1981 election repeated the 1976 contest in its essentials, with the neocolonial PNM defeating its radical, multiracial rival. During the 1970s the Creole middle stratum re-established control over urban blacks by using government patronage, and represented itself to prosperous East Indians of all three religious segments as the guarantor of the status quo. Trinidad is benefiting enormously from its windfall oil wealth, though unemployment currently stands at 9 per cent, and in the Port of Spain probably approaches 20 per cent; hence the destabilising factor in the 1970s and 1980s is not so much the East Indian element as marginalised urban blacks, a feature Trinidad shares with Jamaica.

Conclusion

The original framework of Caribbean society was a stratification of Creole cultures whose content and ranking were created through immigration and contact of Europeans and Africans under conditions dictated by plantation slavery. Differential incorporation of white citizens, free people of colour and black bondsmen projected Creole pluralism into the public domain, where, despite emancipation, the vote and independence, it largely remains, notably in Jamaica. In Trinidad, the East Indian ethnic element, introduced under a system of indentureship, was differentially incorporated – legally as unfree labour for 5 years and politically until 1946. But Indian culture, including religion, the family and caste, though simplified, remains largely intact: indeed, Hindi and Hinduism have experienced a revival since the Second World War. East Indians form an endogamous segment, or more accurately a series of religiously defined segments external to the Creole stratification, with Christians closer to Creole behaviour and values than Hindus and Muslims. In Jamaica, ranked Creole pluralism does not produce obvious spatial segregation – except in Kingston. In Trinidad, however, co-ordinate Creole–East Indian pluralism is expressed spatially as an island-wide phenomenon, and is underpinned by urban–rural distinctions; but within-town segregation, on a racial and cultural basis, is low, largely because the major segments are occupationally stratified and Creoles and East Indians have approximately equal access to housing markets.

M. G. Smith's three types of pluralism have been explored here in the context of social aspects of British West Indian history. Until after the Second World War Jamaica and Trinidad were plural societies whose differentially incorporated non-white segments were dominated by whites. For almost 300 years in Jamaica and 150 years in Trinidad, structural, social and cultural pluralism were locked into a mutually self-sustaining system which could be broken only by rebellion or by uniform incorporation on the basis of democracy. Only when Britain began a long process of constitutional decolonisation by introducing adult suffrage in the mid-1940s did the ballot box, at last, replace coercion by the military and the police as the final arbiter of the social order.

But neither in Jamaica nor Trinidad could universal incorporation abolish social pluralism overnight. The three ranked segments in Jamaica and the two major co-ordinate segments in Trinidad regrouped to compete for political power at the elections. In Jamaica, the brown cultural category provided essential leadership skills for both political parties – the People's National Party and the Jamaica Labour Party – in each case seeking the majority support of the black lower stratum. Political organisation in Trinidad transformed the two main cultural categories – East Indian and Creole – into corporate groups. The major electoral polarisation was between East Indian and black; but Trinidad politics of the 1960s also involved a struggle between brown Creoles and Brahminical Hindus for control of the society.

Plural societies based upon differential incorporation are inherently unstable. The Jamaican riots of 1938 were an echo of Morant Bay in 1865, which was itself preceded by numerous slave outbreaks; and disenfranchised blacks and East Indians collaborated in the 1937 disturbances in Trinidad. In all these instances the white oligarchy called on British troops to pacify the colony. Since uniform incorporation was introduced, rebellion has had other causes and targets. Jamaican black power protest in 1968 and similar violent events in Trinidad in 1970 exposed the disaffection of the urban poor whose marginality in both instances had been created by Creole governments; in each case either the local defence force or the police retained control. Since 1975, the pursuit of radical, multiracial policies for the benefit of manual workers has been based upon East Indian–black co-operation in Trinidad; unlike the labour protest of 1937, the multiracial movement has taken place within the democratic framework of elections. Its target is no longer a white elite, but the brown, conservative ruling class.

The three models of pluralism set out by M. G. Smith cover the range of circumstances from domination to democracy, cultural retention to acculturation. Furthermore, the three plural modes are related. Differential incorporation creates the specific circumstances of cultural pluralism, projects them into the public domain, and prevents full acculturation. Acculturation and assimilation are possible only under conditions of uniform incorporation, and may not occur fully even then if individuals prefer to retain their cultural distinctiveness.

Uniform incorporation is indispensable if social pluralism is to be removed from the public to the private domain. However, in modern democracy cultural pluralism (or acculturation) will only be achieved where governments are determined that cultural and racial factors will not be manipulated for political ends. These circumstances are likely to be rare, especially in recently independent, successor states to colonial plural societies whose experience of equality and liberty has been brief. As the histories of Trinidad and Jamaica show, the path leading from social to cultural pluralism is likely to be a long one: under imperialism it took more than a century to transform slaves into citizens.

Acknowledgements

I am indebted to David Lowenthal and M. G. Smith for their careful criticism of an earlier draft of this chapter.

References

Brathwaite, E. 1971. *Creole society in Jamaica, 1770–1820.* Oxford: Clarendon Press.

Brereton, B. 1979. *Race relations in colonial Trinidad 1870–1900.* London, Cambridge and New York: Cambridge University Press.

Clarke, C. 1967. Caste among Hindus in a town in Trinidad: San Fernando. In *Caste in overseas Indian communities,* B. M. Schwartz (ed.), 165–99. San Francisco: Chandler.

Clarke, C. G. 1971. Residential segregation and intermarriage in San Fernando, Trinidad. *Geog. Rev.* **61**, 198–218.

Clarke, C. G. 1973. Pluralism and stratification in San Fernando, Trinidad. In *Social patterns in cities,* B. D. Clark and M. B. Gleave (eds), 53–70. Special publication, no. 5. London: Institute of British Geographers.

Clarke, C. G. 1974. *Jamaica in maps.* London: University of London Press.

Clarke, C. G. 1975. *Kingston, Jamaica: urban development and social change.* Berkeley, Los Angeles and London: University of California Press.

Curtin, P. D. 1955. *Two Jamaicas: the role of ideas in a tropical colony 1830–1865.* Cambridge: Harvard University Press.

Edwards, B. 1819. *The history, civil and commercial, of the British Colonies in the West Indies,* 5th edn, Vol. 2, London: Whittaker, Reid, Nunn.

Eisner, G. 1961. *Jamaica, 1830–1930.* Manchester: Manchester University Press.

Fleure, H. J. 1918. *The trilogy of humanities in education.* Aberystwyth: University of Wales Press.

Furnivall, J. S. 1939. *Netherlands India: a study of plural economy.* Cambridge: Cambridge University Press.

Furnivall, J. S. 1948. *Colonial policy and practice: a comparative study of Burma and Netherlands India.* London: Cambridge University Press.

Genovese, E. D. 1971. *In red and black.* London: Penguin.

Gordon, M. 1964. *Assimilation in American life.* New York: Oxford University Press.

Hall, D. 1959. *Free Jamaica 1838–1865.* New Haven: Yale University Press.

Heuman, G. 1981. *Between black and white.* Oxford: Clio Press.

Higman, B. W. 1976. *Slave population and economy in Jamaica 1807–1834.* London and New York: Cambridge University Press.

Hughes, C. A. 1955. Adult suffrage in Jamaica 1944–55. *Parliament. Aff.* **8**, 344–52.

Jha, J. C. 1974. The Indian heritage in Trinidad. In *Calcutta to Caroni: the East Indians of Trinidad,* J. La Guerre (ed.), 1–24. London: Longman.

Kallen, H. M. 1924. *Culture and democracy in the United States.* New York: Boni and Liveright.

Kirpalani, M. J. *et al.* No date. *Indian centenary review.* Port of Spain: Guardian Commercial Printery.

Klass, M. 1961. *East Indians in Trinidad.* New York and London: Columbia University Press.

Kuper, L. 1969. Ethnic and racial pluralism: some aspects of polarization and depluralization. In *Pluralism in Africa*, L. Kuper and M. G. Smith (eds), 459–87. Berkeley, Los Angeles and London: University of California Press.

La Guerre, J. 1974. *Calcutta to Caroni: the East Indians of Trinidad*. London: Longman.

Lowenthal, D. 1972. *West Indian societies*. London: Oxford University Press.

Malik, Y. K. 1971. *East Indians in Trinidad: a study in minority politics*. London, New York and Toronto: Oxford University Press for the Institute of Race Relations.

Morton, S. E. 1916. *John Morton of Trinidad*. Toronto: Westminster.

Naipaul, V. S. 1962. *The middle passage*. London: André Deutsch.

Nettleford, R. 1970. *Mirror mirror: identity, race and protest in Jamaica*. Kingston: William Collins & Sangster.

Newson, L. 1976. *Aboriginal and Spanish Colonial Trinidad*. New York and London: Academic Press.

Niehoff, A. and J. Niehoff 1960. *East Indians in the West Indies*. Publications in anthropology, no. 6. Milwaukee: Milwaukee Public Museum.

Oxaal, I. 1968. *Black intellectuals come to power*. Massachusetts: Schenkman.

Oxaal, I. 1971. *Race and revolutionary consciousness*. Cambridge, Massachusetts and London: Schenkman.

Parsons, T. 1952. *The social system*. London: Tavistock.

Patterson, H. O. 1967. *The sociology of slavery*. London: MacGibbon & Kee.

Ramesar, M. D. 1976. Patterns of regional settlement and economic activity by immigrant groups in Trinidad: 1851–1890. *Social Econ. Stud.* **25**, 187–215.

Renny, R. 1807. *An history of Jamaica with observations on the climate*. London: Cawthorn.

Rubin, V. (ed.) 1960. *Social and cultural pluralism in the Caribbean. Ann. N. Y. Acad. Sci.* **83**. New York: New York Academy of Sciences.

Ryan, S. 1972. *Race and nationalism in Trinidad and Tobago*. Toronto: University of Toronto Press.

Smith, M. G. 1960. Social and cultural pluralism. In *Social and cultural pluralism in the Caribbean*, V. Rubin (ed.). *Ann. N. Y. Acad. Sci.* **83**, 763–77. New York: New York Academy of Sciences.

Smith, M. G. 1961. The plural framework of Jamaican society. *Br. J. Sociol.* **12**, 249–62.

Smith, M. G. 1965a. *The plural society in the British West Indies*. Berkeley, Los Angeles and London: University of California Press.

Smith, M. G. 1965b. *Stratification in Grenada*. Berkeley and Los Angeles: University of California Press.

Smith, M. G. 1966. A structural approach to comparative politics. In *Varieties of political theory*, D. Easton (ed.), 113–28. Englewood Cliffs, NJ: Prentice-Hall.

Smith, M. G. 1969. Some developments in the analytic framework of pluralism. In *Pluralism in Africa*, L. Kuper and M. G. Smith (eds), 415–58. Berkeley, Los Angeles and London: University of California Press.

Smith, M. G. 1974. *Corporations and society*. London: Duckworth.

Smith, R. T. 1961. Review of *Social and cultural pluralism in the Caribbean*, V. Rubin (ed.). New York: New York Academy of Sciences, **83**. In *American Anthropologist* **63**, 155.

Southey, T. 1827. *A chronological history of the West Indies*, Vol. 3. London: Longman, Rees, Orme, Brown & Green.

Stewart, J. 1823. *A view of the past and present state of Jamaica*. Edinburgh: Oliver & Boyd.

van den Burghe, P. 1967. *Race and racism: a comparative perspective*. New York, London and Sydney: Wiley.

Wagley, C. 1960. Discussion of M. G. Smith's paper, Social and cultural pluralism. In

Social and cultural pluralism in the Caribbean, V. Rubin (ed.). New York: *Annals of the New York Academy of Sciences* **83**, 777–80.

Weller, J. A. 1968. *The East Indian indenture in Trinidad*. Caribbean Monograph Series, no. 4. Rio Piedras: Institute of Caribbean Studies.

Williams, E. 1944. *Capitalism and slavery*. Chapel Hill: University of North Carolina Press.

Williams, E. 1969. *Inward hunger: the education of a Prime Minister*. London: André Deutsch.

Wood, D. 1968. *Trinidad in transition*. London: Oxford University Press.

3 Pluralism and the Canadian state

DAVID LEY

As I begin this chapter, Canadians are awaiting the imminent pronouncement of their Supreme Court upon due process for major changes in the Canadian constitution. If the constitution represents the essence of a state's institutional integrity, a proclamation of its social order, political unity and common ideals, then perhaps it is symptomatic that Canada has no indigenous constitution. Its founding charter, the British North America Act, remains (in September 1981) in London. Indeed, the federal government's attempt to repatriate the constitution and add an amending formula and a charter of rights is opposed by the governments of eight of the ten Canadian provinces, and presently awaits the deliberation of the highest court in the land. The persistent inter-governmental bickering and, indeed, the constitutional decision of the Supreme Court are acknowledged by many Canadians with a supreme disinterest, but none the less the differences behind the constitutional debate are substantial and have real effects on everyday life. Moreover, the dispute is one manifestation of a fractious national life, a plurality of interests articulated, mobilised and politicised.

Provincialism is not the only face of regionalism in Canada. In Quebec, a francophone government committed to separatism is in power and, having been rebuffed once in a provincial referendum for an ambiguous programme of 'sovereignty association', is now planning a new initiative to carry its 40 per cent minority vote to a majority next time. In the western Canadian provinces, several regional separatist movements have been spawned over the past 2 years, and in Newfoundland, a reluctant late arrival to confederation, the promise of offshore oil and gas has led to increasingly assertive declarations of provincial rights. But if regionalism is the dominant fact of Canadian disunity, a thesis we will consider in more detail below, it is by no means the only one. There is, for example, the social, economic and political question of the native people, which affects national corporate planning principally in the shape of an unresolved land claim, which recent government estimates suggest may cost more than $4 billion (Canadian) to settle over the next 15 years. Corporatism itself has both a public and a private complexion, and in recent years there has been marked acrimony in their mutual relations. Aside from normal complaints of over-regulation and over-taxation, foreign corporations (principally from the United States) are incensed at what they take to be the restrictive nationalist orientation of the federal government's foreign investment review agency, and its national energy policy, designed to Canadianise the energy sector through favourable tax breaks to Canadian corporations (including the public corporation, Petro Canada) and to nationalise, through purchase, a substantial proportion of foreign corporate activity in the energy field. This policy has angered conservative legislators in Washington and caused Canadian–American relations to reach their lowest level in many years.

Aside from the constitutional debate, there is populist support for at least some of these governmental initiatives. For example, in response to an impasse with the federal government over domestic oil prices, the oil-rich province of Alberta reduced its energy output to the rest of Canada. This policy had popular approval with many Albertans, and car bumper stickers began to appear in the province, inviting their fellow countrymen in central Canada to freeze in the dark. More generally, the politicisation of special interests has led to marked activism among citizens and organised groups. Recent conflicts have included a march on Parliament by home owners protesting against high mortgage rates (in excess of 20 per cent at the time), which was dispersed by the police; continuous discord between employees and management (in British Columbia, with the worst provincial strike record, the leader of the labour movement announced a war on employers); a demonstration against police harassment by homosexuals in Toronto; energetic attempts (now successful) by women's groups to dislodge the federal minister who was their Cabinet spokesman; ongoing confrontation between ecological groups and resource-based industry; and feuds between life-style liberals and neoconservatives for control of the elected boards of hospitals and schools, in order to advance their own view of ethics and morality. This is the social order of an advanced industrial nation such as Canada: segmented, pluralistic, contentious. It is little wonder that consensus models of society are no longer in vogue among social scientists, though it should be added that to date protest and conflict have been largely confined to legal forms of expression.

In this chapter I will examine three areas of sociocultural pluralism particularly noteworthy in Canadian national life in recent years: the native question, regionalism, and the status of a bicultural society. Other more squarely economic questions such as labour–management relations and conflict over local consumption issues will not be addressed directly. How does one conceptualise such pluralism? Is it complex and multidimensional, a confusion of cross-cutting cleavages, or as some would suggest, is it the manifold outworking of a single and simpler logic? Indeed, is the notion of pluralism itself an ideological subterfuge for some more deeply patterned system of domination?

The plural society in perspective

In its origins, the concept of the plural society was indeed predicated upon a fairly simple view of culture contact followed by a pattern of economic, social and political domination. The theory of the plural society emerged from J. S. Furnivall's detailed and comprehensive studies of the British and Dutch empires in tropical Asia. If we accept, on the basis of the copious evidence marshalled by Furnivall, the existence of plural societies in Burma and the Netherlands Indies during the phase of European colonialism in the form that Furnivall described them, several questions remain to be answered for contemporary study. First, does the theory still hold true following independence in those nations which provided Furnivall with his case studies? (see Ch. 1). If so, then it is not the colonial experience alone which provides sufficient conditions for the construction of a plural society; Furnivall himself noted during the interwar period the existence of pluralism in non-colonial tropical nations such as Thailand. Secondly, was pluralism a trait elsewhere in the colonial Tropics? From his fieldwork in the British West Indies, M. G. Smith (1965a & b) confidently extended the pluralism thesis to the British colonies in the Caribbean (see Ch. 2), as well as identifying plural societies elsewhere, for example, in pre-colonial Africa. Thirdly, to what extent may the existence of a plural society be identified outside the Tropics? This is the question to which this chapter is directed. Though a former outpost of the British and French empires in North America, Canada has for more than a century been a self-governing nation state, and is now one of the advanced nations of the Western world. Yet at the same time, like Australia and South Africa, another British dominion and former dominion. Canada's history has been characterised by internal strife and strong sectional interests, following social, ethnic and regional divisions (Hodgins *et al.* 1978). To what extent are the insights of Furnivall's theory of the plural society, assembled in a markedly different geographical context, relevant for an understanding of the divisions within the modern Canadian state?

But first the theory of the plural society needs to be more closely specified. The most fundamental feature of a plural society, according to Furnivall, is the absence of a common social will among the medley of peoples who 'mix but do not combine' (Furnivall 1956, 304). As a result there is no moderating social control upon raw economic forces: 'In the plural society the highest common factor is the economic factor, and the only test that all apply in common is the test of cheapness' (Furnivall 1956, 310). Consequently, 'In a plural society . . . the community tends to be organized for production rather than for social life' (Furnivall 1939, 459). The state has no social and cultural cohesion; it exists as a loose collection of self-interested individuals separated into well-recognised ethnocultural groups who are divided occupationally as well as culturally. Social order is sustained by a privileged minority, often (though not necessarily) the civil servants, the military and the businessmen of the colonial power.

In British Burma, Furnivall found the ideal type of a plural society, where industry, commerce and the cities were controlled by a British elite, Chinese traders and Indian labourers, whereas the Burmese themselves were largely members of a rural and pre-industrial society.

The spatial impress of a plural society has been demarcated by geographers in the Tropics. Research by Gould and his students (Gould 1970, Riddell 1970), tracing the diffusion of what they ambivalently call a modernisation surface in former colonial states, is the geographic representation of Furnivall's model. Beginning with a coastal mercantile outpost, often later to become the capital city of an independent nation, the development process and European penetration pass into the interior, emanating outwards from secondary colonial urban cores (Taafe et al. 1963). Although the invocation of central place theory in the diffusion process introduces a more subtle spatial argument, there are points of contact here with core–periphery models of development (Brookfield 1975), including, as we shall see later, the seminal views of Harold Innis on the economic history of Canada and the emergence of a strong set of regional identities.

Furnivall tended to emphasise the economy, the administration and the social organisation of the plural society. It was left to later writers, including Anthony King (1976) in his penetrating examination of the colonial city in British India, to fill out the cultural components of pluralism, as manifested in institutional forms, the symbolism of everyday life, and the built environment. It is also cultural pluralism which Smith (1965a & b) isolates in his extension of Furnivall's model to the British West Indies. In particular, Smith sees the distinctive feature of the plural society to be a diversity of institutional forms. The range of institutions varies somewhat in separate parts of Smith's discussion, but generally the list includes marriage, the family, religion, property, education, economic institutions, language and folklore; excluded are law and government (Smith 1965a, 14–15). Shared institutions imply a common social will and cultural homogeneity; however, divergent institutions suggest 'differences of social structure, ideational systems, and forms of social action' and hence cultural pluralism (Smith 1965a, 80). A second feature of the plural society drawn out of Furnivall's text is economic and political control by a sectional minority; when dominance is exercised by a minority then a true plural society is found, but when domination rests with a majority, there may be cultural heterogeneity, but not a plural society (Smith 1965b, 5). Indeed, Smith (1965a, 88) goes so far as to suggest that 'the distinctive feature' of plural societies 'is their domination by a cultural minority'.

Furnivall's thesis has not gone unquestioned, for in many respects it challenged the prevalent social theory of the interwar and immediate postwar period. Anglo-American structural functionalism held to an essentially consensus view of society, which set it against the view of the plural society emphasising strife and dissonance, the absence of a common social will. However, by the 1980s, intellectual fashion has shifted, and it is now

Parsonian structural functionalism which is treated more sceptically, whereas conflict theory is widely regarded as providing a more accurate portrayal of national and international social and political relations. Such an intellectual climate is likely to be more receptive to the conflict model of the plural society.

It is important, however, to distinguish between the thesis of the plural society as we have discussed it, and the concept of pluralism in political theory. In the latter case, pluralism refers to a theory of society that sees political control as shifting between a variety of elites and interest groups (Hewitt 1974, Saunders 1979). Thus there is no invariant association of interests in persistent political groupings; as issues shift, so do alliances and the activism and influence of different individuals. This picture is one markedly different from the societies Furnivall studied. Within the dominant European group there were admittedly marked differences from time to time between traders and missionaries, and there were additional national differences in the ideology of colonial rule between the British and the Dutch. None the less, the abiding analysis offered by Furnivall and Smith points to a ruling elite who exercised political, cultural and economic control over a majority of the population in the interests of the minority. Thus a sharp distinction must be drawn between the plural society and theories of political pluralism. The confusion is heightened by a problem of nomenclature, for in political theory attention is directed toward the locus of power, and a thesis suggesting that control is exercised by an elite is termed elite theory, which has conventionally been set in *opposition* to a pluralist theory of diffuse power. Thus a society with a dominant elite (the opposite to pluralism in political theory) would form the arrangement that Furnivall called a plural society!

Pluralism as a political theory has been developed particularly in the study of Western democracies. Furnivall's view of the European states was of a homogeneous society with a clearly defined, if not always recognised, common will. 'In the homogeneous society of western states', he wrote, 'the basic problem of applied political science is how best to ascertain and give effect to the common social will; in the plural society of the tropics the basic problem is to create a common social will' (Furnivall 1956, 488). This observation of the Dutch East Indies during the colonial era remained unchanged following independence, for in the mid-1960s Geertz noted that in Indonesia 'the whole political process is mired in a slough of ideological symbols, each attempting and so far each failing to unjumble the Republic's catalogue, to name its cause, and to give point and purpose to its polity' (Geertz 1973, 221). But if the absence of a national will continued to exist in post-colonial Indonesia, what of the advanced societies, and the picture Furnivall drew of the uniform social values of European nations, notably of England with its 'strongly homogeneous society' (Furnivall 1956, 454)? And what of the British dominions overseas?

Table 3.1   Canadian economic indicators by province (ranks).

Province (territory)	% population growth			Indicator Av. weekly wage	Lowest unemployment rate
	1966–71	71–76	76–81*	1976	1976
Newfoundland	6	6	4	5	9
Prince Edward Island	9	8	5	10	NA
Nova Scotia	7	9	8	9	7
New Brunswick	9	7	3	8	8
Quebec	8	10	9	4	6
Ontario	5	5	6	3	4
Manitoba	11	10	10	7	3
Saskatchewan	12	12	7	6	2
Alberta	4	3	1	2	1
British Columbia	3	3	2	1	5
Yukon Territory	1	2 ⎱ 11		NA	NA
North-West Territories	2	1 ⎰		NA	NA

* Preliminary estimate.
NA = not available.

Canada: economic development and social wellbeing

Canada consists of 10 provinces, extending from Newfoundland in the east to British Columbia in the west, and two sparsely peopled northern territories. There are marked regional variations within the Canadian nation along a range of historical, cultural, economic, social and political dimensions. But these dimensions are not positively correlated, so that the construction of composite provincial quality of life indices is not a simple task. Interestingly, Furnivall specified just such an asymmetry between economic development and social wellbeing in the plural society, a proposition which Paul Paget held as perhaps the most general principle in his teaching of regional and social geography: invariably, 'the rates of social progress are neither geared harmoniously to, nor synchronised with the rates of economic progress' (Paget 1960). In the plural society Furnivall noted how the desire for economic gain was liberated from the social control of custom, how economic forces were exempt from the direction of social will: 'in supply as in demand, in production as in consumption, the abnormal activity of economic forces, free of social restrictions, is an essential character of a plural society' (Furnivall 1956, 312).

If we examine the pattern of economic and social indicators at the provincial scale within Canada, we find just such an asymmetry between economic development and various measures of social cohesion (Tables 3.1 & 3.2).

Table 3.2 Canadian social indicators by province (ranks).

Province (territory)	Indicator % grooms not married in province of birth 1971	% no religion 1971	Divorce rate 1975	Abortion rate 1976	Criminal code rate 1976
Newfoundland	12	12	11	10	10
Prince Edward Island	9	11	12	12	12
Nova Scotia	7	8	7	5	8
New Brunswick	7	9	10	11	11
Quebec	11	10	3	8	9
Ontario	5	4	4	3	5
Manitoba	6	5	6	6	7
Saskatchewan	9	6	9	9	5
Alberta	4	3	1	4	4
British Columbia	3	1	2	2	3
Yukon Territory	1	2	5	1	2
North-West Territories	2	7	8	6	1

Economic indicators show a general increase from the economically depressed Atlantic provinces to the strong resource-based economies of the west (Table 3.1). But the social gradient is reversed, with spatial immobility and the retention of traditional values prevalent toward the Atlantic seaboard, whereas the western provinces and northern territories have the least favourable levels of social wellbeing (Table 3.2). Here rapid social and spatial mobility, the economic lure of the resource frontier, has severely eroded traditional customs and values. The negative correlation between social and economic indicators is remarkably consistent: in the mid-1970s Alberta, British Columbia, the territories and Ontario had the five highest economic scores and the five lowest social scores; the Atlantic region included the three provinces with the poorest economic performance but also three of the four with the highest performance on the social indicators.

The interplay between tradition and modernity reaches its most extreme form in the Canadian North. Particularly in the North-West Territories, with its native majority, one finds the essence of a plural society, in the juxtaposition between the mines and oil rigs of multinational corporations and the land-based native life-style of hunting and fishing. It is a conflict of economic demand versus social demand, of gain versus custom. In contrast to the stable rhythmic cycles of the native life-style is the lurching of the boom–bust cycle of northern development, where opportunistic investment is followed by opportunistic disinvestment (note the demographic boom–bust pattern in the territories during the 1970s in Table 3.1). In the conflict between homeland and frontier is captured that same tension between conservation and exploitation which Furnivall documented in the plural societies of colonial South-East Asia.

Canadian pluralism: tradition and modernity

Both Furnivall and Smith make brief illustrative allusion to Canada. In *Netherlands India* Furnivall notes that the plural society is not confined to the Tropics but may also be found in South Africa, the United States, or Quebec with its separation of race, language and religion, and even in western Canada with the coexistence of ethnic segregation by residence and occupation (Furnivall 1939, 446). This is a weak (if current) definition of a plural society, seeming to require merely variation according to one or two sociocultural variables. In a later volume, Furnivall's criteria were more demanding, and the examples of Canada, Australia, South Africa and the United States were introduced as representative of 'a society with plural features, but not a plural society' (Furnivall 1956, 305). Smith adopts an equally rigorous demarcation of nation states, recognising a three-fold classification of homogeneous, heterogeneous and plural societies. Although acknowledging the diversity of modern Western societies, Smith is unwilling to call them pluralistic, for he does not see a difference in basic cultural forms, but rather what he calls a cultural heterogeneity of secondary, essentially voluntary, elements. In his view, neither life-style nor class qualify as expressions of pluralism, for they do not require any shift of cultural institutions (Smith 1965a, 82). The most that Smith will allow, in the case of black society in the United States, is a localised pluralism in the American South where indeed a measure of institutional distinctiveness separates the races (cf. Ley 1974). But, he adds, the existence of local plural communities need not imply a national plural society. As for Canada, Smith is in accord with Furnivall that the absence of a small but dominant cultural elite identifies in Canada cultural heterogeneity but not a plural society. If we attempt to isolate the key ingredients of the discussion by Furnivall and Smith, we may define a plural society as having an ideological component (the absence of a common social will), an institutional component (divergent cultural forms), an economic component (differing forms of resource exploitation) and a political component (authority relations in which a minority is dominant).

Within Canada the clearest demarcation of a plural community in this classical sense lies in the juxtaposition between native and European values and institutions, and historically, a case could be made that in this regard the early phases of European colonisation did, indeed, create a plural society. The land treaties struck with native leaders introduced in the early years of settlement the full pluralist quartet of conflicting ideologies, divergent cultural institutions, separate economic objectives, and rule by an alien minority. Though there are dangers in oversimplifying the fate of native people in the various British dominions (Fisher 1980), none the less in each instance (save South Africa) they were rapidly outnumbered by European settlers. It is, of course, the fact of European settlement in the temperate latitudes of the dominions which introduces a decisive break in the society and history of the temperate as opposed to the tropical lands of the former British Empire (Price 1950). Indeed, it is the exception which proves the rule, for the numerical weakness of the white race in South Africa has been the dominant element of that nation's recent geopolitical history, and justifies its designation as a contemporary plural society in the strict sense (Western 1981, and in this volume).

But the political relationship between Canadians and their native people has none the less been equally asymmetrical, even if the tyranny has usually been that of a majority rather than a minority, and has arguably moved from a phase of direct oppression, through the period of paternalism to the present publicly articulated consultative relationship between the federal Department of Indian Affairs and Northern Development and the native peoples (Kariya forthcoming). Indians count for less than 2 per cent of the national population and remain the wards of the federal government. This term is used advisedly, for to be an Indian is to have a specified legal status. The definition of an Indian, his rights and benefits, and his claim to individual land ownership are all powers of the Indian Act; even in death an Indian's will has no legal force until endorsed by the Minister of Indian Affairs or a court of law. Thus the native people do not even experience an identical legal or governmental regime as do other Canadians.

The management of native affairs has, moreover, followed the same core–periphery or metropolis–hinterland pattern as Furnivall identified in colonial South-East Asia, with the centres of political and economic control located in the major cities of the Canadian South. Within this framework 'metropolis continuously dominates and exploits hinterland whether in regional, national, class, or ethnic terms' (Davis 1971). Gould's 'modernisation surface' shows, as in the Tropics, a hierarchical gradation with local hegemony being exercised in intermediate administrative centres such as Yellowknife which, as 'Ottawa North', have control over their local hinterlands while being subordinate to authority from major southern centres (Usher 1970, Ostergaard 1976).

This pattern is found among Indian reserves in British Columbia, where the map of the prevalence of a traditional life-style shows a distinctive regional variation (Fig. 3.1). This map was produced from a painstaking compilation of 41 indicators for 123 Indian reserves in the province; factor scores are mapped for the first component of a principal components analysis of the data matrix (Kariya 1975). Although some of the data may be suspect, the regional trend is clear and reveals a pattern consistent with a typical 'modernisation surface'. Traditional life-styles survive in districts remote from the heavily populated

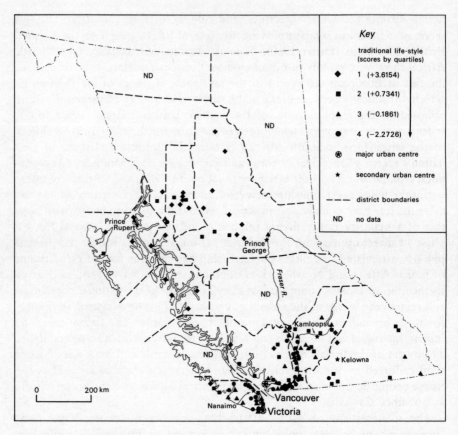

Figure 3.1 The geography of tradition and modernity among British Columbia Indian bands, 1969 (source: Kariya 1975).

south-west corner of the province; less traditional reserves are clustered not only in the south-west around Vancouver and Victoria, but also along the Fraser River, the major transport artery from the coast to the interior. Local effects are discernible around some of the smaller urban centres, notably Nanaimo and to a lesser extent Prince George and Prince Rupert. Each of these secondary centres represents an intermediate administrative division with a district office of the Department of Indian Affairs.

The history of external control and exploitation has, in the 1970s, led to a reaction by Canadian natives, revealing a dynamism in core–periphery relations we shall note again later. Sporadic opposition has occurred in the South, most notably in British Columbia where a wave of political mobilisation occurred among Indian bands in 1975, leading to the occupation of a number of regional offices of the Department of Indian Affairs, the throwing up of barricades on several reserves, and briefly and rather flamboyantly (for the eager media), the brandishing of firearms. In the Canadian North, native opposition has been more sustained and more ambitious, and has moved into a phase of institutional innovation (Loree 1976). Younger and better educated native leaders transcended local band interests and formed the Indian Brotherhood of the North-West Territories, an organisation that was not contained within existing white-dominated institutions and which made substantial political, economic and cultural claims for the native peoples. For the first time, the metropolis–hinterland model of exploitation was challenged, as an effective power base was assembled to speak for native interests. This process has continued as land claims and arguments for separate political institutions have coalesced in a self-government movement of the Inuit Tapirisat, urging a new political entity covering two-thirds of the North-West Territories controlled by the native people themselves (Morrisset 1981). Recently, notice was served of an application by native leaders to the United Nations to secure a separate status for a native homeland in the Canadian North.

The mobilisation of native interests was evident in the federal government's Mackenzie Valley Pipeline Inquiry, the Berger Commission (Berger 1977). The inquiry, set up to consider the impact of a proposed natural gas pipeline, rapidly expanded into an assessment of economic development in the North as it influenced native and environmental conditions. The report's title, *Northern frontier, northern homeland*, unambiguously juxtaposed the competing interests of core and periphery, and arrived at the historic judgement that construction of the pipeline should be delayed for 10 years to permit the settlement of land claims, native preparation and adjustment for northern development, and further investigation of ecologically fragile environments.

In making his judgement, Justice Berger was acknowledging that there was no common social will in the North: the economic prerogatives of frontier are in conflict with the social imperatives of homeland. So too, 'the more the industrial frontier displaces the homeland in the North, the greater the incidence of social pathology will be' (Berger 1977, Vol. 1, xxii). Nor is there a common set of cultural institutions in the North, and it was a recommendation of the inquiry that this dualism be sustained. 'The transfer of the control of the education of native children [to natives], with all that it implies in the way of institutions, finance, legislation, and language rights, must be part of the reordering of relationships between the native peoples and the federal government that is inherent in the settlement of native claims' (Berger 1977, Vol. 1, 184). In this manner the northern hinterland is seeking equality rather than subordination in its relations with the southern core. The federal government's acceptance of the main recommendations of the Berger Commission, and apparently conciliatory negotiations underway with native groups, suggest the possibility of a new order in which there will be pluralism without domination; in Berger's words, 'a new partnership of interests'.

Canadian pluralism: regionalism

But the abiding tension in Canada in the 1980s is not the native question, important though this is, but the country's fissiparous regionalism. Despite a 40 per cent minority vote in the May 1980 provincial referendum, some form of secession remains a real possibility in Quebec. In Newfoundland, which only entered federation in 1949 with a 52 per cent plurality, the prospect of offshore petroleum wealth after generations of economic depression has inspired a vigorous provincialism. At the prospect of Quebec's secession, a group of businessmen in the Atlantic provinces have begun canvassing for formal union with the United States. This view is shared by at least one elected member of the Saskatchewan legislature, while in the West generally there are also several brands of secessionist movements which during 1980 were able to attract over 2000 supporters to their rallies. No wonder, then, at the lament of Canadian intellectuals that 'The forces that glorified the progress towards a centralized nation–state with an all-encompassing nationalism appear to be in retreat. Regionalism focuses upon the parts rather than the whole: it emphasizes the pluralistic character of Canadian culture and the limited nature of the Canadian identity' (Westfall 1980). No wonder, either, that the identity crisis of the Canadian intellectual has become the abiding political crisis of the nation, not only because of rampant regionalism, but also, and closely linked with it, because of provincialism, the unrelenting impasse in federal–provincial relations which has soured Canadian national life over the past decade.

In Canadian geography and history the role of the physical environment in the nation's evolution has often been explored (Careless 1954, Merrill 1968); for his volume on Canada, Griffith Taylor used the subtitle *A study of cool continental environments and their effect on British and French settlement* (Taylor 1957). A focus upon the role of the physical environment was transmitted by Taylor to his student Andrew Clark who has, in turn, been a major influence upon the current generation of Canadian historical and regional geographers (Warkentin 1978). In a recent paper, Cole Harris (one of Clark's students) has argued for the significance of the Canadian Shield, a vast inhospitable environment, in severing the continuity of Canadian colonisation so that 'settlement proceeded in patches', and over the course of time a vigorous regionalism was founded which later assumed political expression within provincial boundaries (Harris 1979, 1981). A geographic basis to regionalism offers a plausible thesis, for today the Canadian ecumene is still reminiscent of a string of beads threaded along the American border, with 89 per cent of the land area devoid of permanent settlement. At the same time the nation is the second largest in the world, with a maximum east–west extent of over 5000 km at the broadest point.

In part, such a geographic interpretation overlaps with a dominant stream of historical writing that has stressed the role of the wilderness and frontier life on the forging of the Canadian identity. But it connects also with a second tradition of historical scholarship, which emphasises not only formal regions based upon environmental homogeneity, but also functional regions predicated upon the spatial organisation of territories by man, taking advantage of natural lines of transportation (Careless 1954, McCann 1982). In the penetration of the Canadian interior, the dominant geographical fact then becomes the navigable waterways which allowed movement along the St Lawrence River, through the Great Lakes, and into the lake and river systems of the Prairies and western Cordilleras. Through this natural routeway developed the commercial exploitation of the interior and a trade system orchestrated from the major eastern cities exporting staple products to Europe. There is a clear affinity between this mercantile viewpoint and the spatial model of the evolution of transportation systems in the colonial Tropics (Taafe *et al.* 1963).

In Canada this thesis was elaborated by the economic historian Harold Innis in his seminal work on the fur trade (Innis 1930). Innis introduced a profound reorientation of perspective, for rather than following the dominant American paradigm and considering the effects of the frontier upon the national character, the reverse relationship was stressed. The frontier was dependent rather than independent, a product of trade and eastern decision-making, a periphery relative to a dominant core, a hinterland to centralised metropolitan initiatives. In this relationship Innis stressed the commercial links between metropolis and hinterland in the organisation of staple exports, though he probably pressed the role of economic factors too far, as in his claim that 'Canada emerged as a political entity with boundaries largely determined by the fur trade' (cited by Eccles 1979). In a reassessment of *The fur trade in Canada*, Eccles has raised severe criticisms of Innis' scholarship, and in particular of what he sees as an economic determinism that overlooked military and political factors in the expansion of European interests in Canada. But what survives an otherwise comprehensive assault is the metropolis–hinterland model, for the posing of imperial geopolitical strategy rather than entrepreneurial enthusiasm as a major motive of European penetration simply refers the fate of the hinterland back beyond the Montreal merchants to the imperial courts of London and Paris.

The metropolis–hinterland association has proven a fruitful heuristic concept in an understanding of Canadian regionalism, and recently it has been revived, if in a less subtle form, by sociologists who have tied it to the development–underdevelopment model of A. G. Frank, arguing that regionalism is a facade for class relations forced by the imperatives of capitalist accumulation (Clement 1978, Cuneo 1978, Matthews 1980, 1981). 'Regionalism', writes Clement, 'is but one expression of more deeply rooted inequalities and social problems in Canada.' Neither geography nor history is implicated in this situation: 'it is not the product of some natural phenomenon like geography or resources or even historical accident'. Regionalism is quite simply a product of the development of underdevelopment, of a concentration of corporate and government control in central Canada and the sustained emiseration of the national hinterland. Interpretation of Canadian regional inequality therefore rests with dependency theory, which rewrites regionalism in class terms about the capitalist mode of production.

The spatial concentration of corporate control in central Canada has long been recognised – between them, Toronto and Montreal contain about 75 per cent of corporate head offices – and in *The Canadian Establishment*, Newman (1975) has persuasively argued for the existence of a national ruling class in Toronto and Montreal: 'the 1000 men who run Canada'. It is an elite with its own subculture of private clubs and private schools, where pedigree and the correct training are the elements of an aristocracy exercising social closure to outsiders (Porter 1965). Newman's portrait of a powerful and self-sustaining elite is compatible with dependency arguments (though, like Porter, he does not require them), and also with Furnivall's own thesis of the plural society which anticipated the latter development–underdevelopment schema.

This revival of the Innis hinterland–metropolis model is flawed by excessive claims. The suppression of geography is untenable, and parts company with Innis' sensitivity to the importance of variation in the physical environment. For it is not only the niggardliness of the Canadian environment which has prompted national disunity (as the frontier theorists have written), but so too has its wealth. However, Clement (1978) argues that 'foreign investment in manufacturing, because it has been so Ontario-centred, and in petroleum, because it has been so Alberta-centred, have added to the problems of regionalism in Canada'. The message is that foreign corporate capitalism has been the culprit in producing uneven development. But this is a geographically simplistic statement: there is investment in Alberta because there is petroleum in Alberta! Uneven development in large measure follows uneven resource distribution. In the case of southern Ontario the issue is less simple, though obviously there are spatial advantages of access to the Canadian market and, for American industrialists, proximity to their own manufacturing belt. The abolition of geography and the suppression of regional resource variation give altogether too much freedom to the unconstrained power of capital to create landscapes (Duncan & Ley 1982). The unqualified indictment against the corporations falters at another point. Inequality is measured in terms of per capita incomes, and in 1971 these were highest and growing fastest in Ontario and British Columbia (Cuneo 1978). But, Cuneo notes, these were also the provinces with the most powerful corporate presence, from which one might conclude that far from being prejudicial to the standard of living, the presence of corporations was beneficial.

There is a second major objection to the current overstatement of the metropolis–hinterland relationship. Ironically for a dialectical argument (Davis 1971), it is neglectful of historic change. Indeed, income data over a 40 year period (1925–65) show that little change occurred in the relative standing of the Canadian core and periphery (Merrill 1968). To this extent it could be argued that federal transfer payments have proven ineffective in bringing about greater equalisation, though this overlooks the possibility that without a national regional policy the income gap might even have broadened; suggestive here is the fact that by the mid-1970s federal transfer payments accounted for between a third and a half of net provincial income in each of the Atlantic provinces. But there is a more substantial issue. It is evident that the 1970s have proven a threshold in the relative fortunes of the Canadian regions. In Canada, as in the United States, rapid economic development of the West is redefining the economic power of core and periphery. For example, if we re-examine provincial income data supplied by Matthews (1980) in an application of dependency theory, we see that up to 1971 Ontario held its appointed position at the top of the income ladder. But by 1975 it had fallen to fourth position behind the three western provinces of British Columbia, Alberta and Saskatchewan, while substantial increases had also occurred in the Atlantic provinces. Matthews does not note the theoretical significance of this reversal for his model, but it is a trend which is confirmed by other indicators (see also Table 3.1). The most recent demographic estimates suggest that from 1971 to 1980 Ontario suffered a net *loss* of 65 000 inter-provincial migrants in contrast to a gain of 150 000 between 1966 and 1971 (Bourne 1978, 1981; Simmons 1979). Quebec, the other province of central Canada, performed even more poorly, losing over 200 000 net inter-provincial migrants through the 1970s. In contrast the western periphery of British Columbia and Alberta gained 340 000 migrants from other provinces, while even the eastern periphery of the Atlantic provinces registered a demographic reversal in the 1970s, benefiting from a net inflow of over 30 000 migrants from other provinces after sustained losses over several decades.

The demographic fortunes of core and periphery have been transformed. So rapid and decisive has this shift been, that in the second edition of *The Canadian Establishment*, Newman virtually doubled the entries of members of the elite noting that 'The most dramatic change within the Canadian power structure was the shift westward of the centre of gravity of Canadian corporate decision-making which followed the 1973 OPEC price hikes and the 1976 election of the Parti Québecois' (Newman 1975, 2nd edn, ix–x). The seemingly impregnable ranks of the Canadian Establishment, which Clement (1978) so uncompromisingly located in Ontario, have in 5 years been dispersed by economic development in the West and cultural nationalism in Quebec.

The distinctive character of regional movements also gives the lie to any schema that treats core–periphery relations in too mechanical a fashion (Williams 1980a, Agnew 1981). There is a marked divergence between western and Quebec separation which matches in large part the difference between Scottish and Welsh nationalism. Western separatism is primarily an economic response to regional prosperity and the perception of exploitation from the centre; its leaders are businessmen, its followers fiscal conservatives. Its arguments are those of discriminatory tariffs, inequitable transfer payments, federal encroachment upon provincial resources, and the suppression of western manufacturing by central Canadian interests, in short, 'the exploitation economy which draws income and wealth from western provinces to central Canada' (Blackman 1977). One political exercise by Alberta economists placed 'the opportunity cost of confederation' in foregone and lost economic activity at $800 for each Albertan by 1981, and concluded that 'Canada makes little economic sense' (Blackman 1977). In contrast, for Quebec and the Atlantic provinces, such an argument makes eminent sense, for they are major beneficiaries of federal transfer payments. It was the promise of such benefits that drew Newfoundland into confederation in 1949, and which has sustained the Quebec economy through the 1970s; from 1971 to 1974 the province received over $2 billion (Canadian) in equalisation payments alone, almost half the total disbursement of the federal exchequer.

A mechanical core–periphery model is particularly vulnerable in the case of Quebec regionalism (Canadian Review of Studies of Nationalism 1978). First, Quebec is geographically part of the core region. Secondly, it is a major recipient of federal transfer payments, so that the most convoluted logic would be necessary to prove economic exploitation. Thirdly, it has direct political links to the federal government (unlike Alberta and British Columbia) via its blanket support for the federal Liberal party, which in turn has come as close to forming a monopoly government in the Canadian parliament as a democratic system could theoretically permit. Yet Quebec intellectuals, including the current Premier, have been fond of citing internal colonialism as a rationale for political action (Thomson 1980). Their reference group, of course, is less the nation than the province; their objective one of *maîtres chez nous*. Conflict in Quebec is primarily that of the historic competition of regional elites, the ambition of francophones, especially the new middle class of professionals and intellectuals, to wrest provincial control from a dwindling anglophone minority (McRoberts 1979). The goal is not for control to pass to native Quebeckers, but for it to be assumed by French-speaking native Quebeckers. The secession movement is thus profoundly cultural and closely associated with Quebec's new middle class (Williams 1980b); it intersects with the federal government only in as much as the province's linguistic aspirations are at odds with the Canadian constitution.

Regionalism is, then, the fundamental cleavage contributing to Canadian pluralism, and attempts to cast it primarily in terms of class have achieved only modest success. Moreover, empirical studies of the nation's political cultures have shown regionalism to be a significant and independent factor in a comparison of class versus regional effects. One recent attempt to establish 'a theoretical tradition which identifies regionalism as functionally related to patterns of class formation in Canada' was not convincing (Ornstein *et al.* 1980). Using a large national sample, the relative strengths of region and socio-economic status were compared as predictors of political orientation. Region was the more effective predictor in the domains of federal party affiliation and political participation, whereas socio-economic status was somewhat more effective in predicting attitudes to political issues such as immigration and welfare. Recognising that socio-economic status is not a Marxian category, the authors sought to operationalise a Marxian concept of class from occupational data. But this more rigid definition of class was even less successful in comparison with regionalism in accounting for the variety of Canadian political cultures.

Canadian pluralism: multiculturalism

In a review of recent developments in the theory of the plural society, Smooha (1975) has noted how the more demanding framework of Furnivall and Smith has been relaxed, as the central concepts have become more flexible and elastic. Within Canada, the dominant interpretation of pluralism today is cultural pluralism (Driedger 1978, Anderson & Frideres 1981), a far less exacting

Table 3.3 Major source nations of Canadian immigrants (ranked).

1951	1968	1979
Britain	Britain	Vietnam
Germany	USA	Britain
Italy	Italy	USA
Netherlands	Germany	Hong Kong
Poland	Hong Kong	India
France	France	Laos
USA	Austria	Philippines
Belgium	Greece	Portugal
Yugoslavia	Portugal	Jamaica
Denmark	Yugoslavia	China

Source: Innes (1980).

concept than Furnivall's discussion of the overlapping cleavages of class, status and power or Smith's definition of institutional diversity. Canadian cultural pluralism has been anchored around bilingualism, a historic fact confirmed and guaranteed in the British North America Act of 1867. A bilingual, bicultural state fitted a population that in 1881 identified itself as 90 per cent English or French. This arrangement has been sustained up to the 1970s, and its further development was the mandate given to the Royal Commission on Bilingualism and Biculturalism which issued its report in 1970. Indeed, assimilation into the cultures of the two dominant groups has been the major objective of immigration policy this century (Palmer 1975).

However, substantial demographic shifts, particularly in the postwar period, have complicated the bicultural model. Whereas Europeans accounted for 88 per cent of Canadian immigrants between 1950 and 1955, by 1974–78 the figure had fallen to 37 per cent; by the latter period Asian immigrants accounted for 26 per cent of all arrivals, and Latin America and the Caribbean furnished another 18 per cent. In 1979, admittedly an unusual year with the extensive Vietnamese refugee programme, the Asian component had risen to 45 per cent of all immigrants. This transition is clearly evident from rankings of the leading source countries of immigrants (Table 3.3). In 1951 six of the leading nations were in north-west Europe, but by 1968 the southern European regional grouping was more conspicuous. Finally, in 1979 seven of the leading 10 were Third World states, and six of these were Asian. Canadian bicultural policy has been strained by these developments, so that under protest from other ethnic groups, the 1970 Royal Commission added a fourth volume on non-English, non-French minorities, and in 1971 the government of Canada announced a multicultural policy within a bilingual context. By 1973–74 the federal multicultural programme had a budget of $10 million with further initiatives taken by a number of the provinces, though not by Quebec, which has consistently seen multiculturalism as a threat to francophone bilingual and bicultural claims.

Thus within Canada the North American ethnic revival of the 1970s is supported by explicit federal policy. How significant is this new ethnicity and the cultural pluralism associated with it? In his seminal volume on social stratification in Canada, Porter (1965) saw ethnicity as largely reducible to socio-economic status. In the United States, Gans (1979) has dismissed the new ethnicity as largely symbolic and in large measure an affectation, and in Canada, Brotz (1980) similarly sees multiculturalism as 'a choice of pizzas, wonton soup, and Kosher style pastrami sandwiches'. Both writers regard multiculturalism as secondary to more fundamental cleavages in society, and by implication the cultural pluralism derived from it is trivial before the higher shared aspiration to a middle class way of life.

But there is some evidence that such a view is an oversimplification, that ethnicity influences more significant realms of life and that it exercises an effect independent of socio-economic status in such areas as spatial segregation and occupational type. Whereas ethnic segregation in agricultural communities, particularly in the prairies, has been sustained over several generations (Anderson 1977, Schlichtmann 1977), 70 per cent of immigrants who landed in the 1970s settled in the ten major cities, so that it is within the metropolitan areas that recent ethnic segregation is most marked. Ethnic concentrations are in part a product of market power and housing availability but they also reflect patterns of choice (Richmond 1972). There is clear evidence that residential concentration is chosen by recent immigrants to take advantage of ethnic institutions, the extended family and other forms of community support. Similarly, and consistent with assimilation theory, later household choices may make the ethnic neighbourhood less important; in particular, access to better housing outside the inner city will lead to the decline of ethnic segregation invariably revealed by census data up to the 1960s (Balakrishnan 1976).

But there are important exceptions to this trend. In Montreal, Toronto and Winnipeg substantial regrouping of Jewish communities has occurred in high status suburbs. Indeed, Winnipeg offers some instructive examples of the differential voluntary segregation of various minority groups (Matwijiw 1979). A comparison of ethnic districts for six minorities over a 20 year period showed dispersal of the German and Scandinavian populations, the shrinking of compact Ukrainian and Polish areas, but the survival of distinctive neighbourhoods for the Jewish and French communities (Driedger & Church 1974). These varying spatial patterns were not related to social class or population size, but were clearly linked to the existence of ethnic cultural forms, particularly religious and educational institutions. Differential cultural identity offered the most consistent set of relationships to account for ethnic residential segregation (Driedger 1977). These results corroborated earlier research on minority segregation in Toronto which had also concluded that ethnic identity, defined in a multidimensional way, gave a more satisfactory interpretation of spatial patterns than social class (Darroch & Marston 1971). A similar conclusion has been reached by several recent empirical studies of ethnic segregation in the United States (Bleda 1979, Uyecki 1980), so that in a review essay Agocs (1979) was able to make at least the modest judgement that from the North American evidence 'it is clear that ethnic patterns of population distribution are not fully explained by differences in social class position'.

The close relationship which Porter (1965) and others have pressed between social class and ethnicity would similarly lead to the expectation that occupational status is closely constrained by ethnic status. Although simple correlations invariably reveal a relationship between the two, more discriminating analysis controlling other variables leads to a substantial reduction in the association, and reveals a steady decrease in the relationship between census periods. Reviewing a number of studies, Darroch (1979) concludes that ethnic affiliation as an independent factor 'has only a slight effect on occupational achievement and income in Canada'. However, ethnic job segregation, modest and decreasing through the 1960s except for a few minorities (Darroch 1979), has assumed new significance more recently, at least in Toronto with its high levels of immigration in the 1970s (Reitz et al. 1981). The extent to which ethnic occupational segregation is a result of cultural as opposed to socio-economic factors is unclear; however, there is reason to believe that the existence of ethnic social networks and gatekeepers makes an important independent contribution to job segregation (Anderson 1974).

Thus ethnic segregation exists both by residence and by occupation, but has no invariable relationship with socio-economic status. To this extent, the view that ethnic patterns may be collapsed to social class patterns remains unproven, and we are led to conclude that cultural pluralism introduces distinctive, if perhaps secondary, lines of cleavage in Canadian society not only in folklore and ethnic custom but also in more significant realms of life.

Conclusion

Our discussion of the native question, regionalism and multiculturalism by no means exhausts the range of Canadian segmentation. If less conspicuous than in Europe, and, as we have seen, secondary to regionalism in matters of political identification, social class or at least socio-economic status is an obvious determinant of attitudes and life chances, and is associated with its own form of domination and conflict in the workplace. In recent years there has also been marked conflict in the realm of consumption, with the mobilisation of social movements espousing opposing values in the case of urban development (Ley 1980, Ley & Mercer 1980), and in life-style and ethics, which have politicised such issues as abortion, homosexuality, the status of women and the teaching of evolution versus creation in the schools. Indeed, in some respects these life-style cleavages are perhaps more significant than ethnic variations, for disagreement over the status of the family, sexuality, religion and recreation manifests the diversity of basic cultural institutions which for Smith (1965a) is a primary expression of a plural society.

Finally, to address Furnivall's most fundamental question, is there within the present Canadian state a common social will? It is worth noting that in 1965 Pierre Trudeau, Canada's Prime Minister during the past turbulent decade of Canadian unity, similarly identified the role of a shared social will as fundamental to the survival of the nation: 'it becomes apparent that more than language and culture, more than history and geography, even more than force or power, the foundation of the nation is will' (cited in Williams 1980b). Although political declarations by Trudeau and others that the nation is strong are pure hyperbole, yet the overall balance of evidence would suggest there is a common will, at least for a majority of the population. National surveys have shown majority support for the integrity of the Canadian nation, even in regions of pronounced discontent (Kornberg et al. 1980). And, as I conclude this chapter, a constitutional consensus between the federal government and the provinces has been reached, at the eleventh hour, though at the cost of alienating Quebec, and initially, the native peoples, and other special interest groups.

But if it exists, the idea of Canadian unity takes a singularly unheroic form, aligned more with the comfort of a high standard of living than with historical and cultural ideals (perhaps this is why it is a source of such anxiety for Canadian intellectuals). To this extent, multiculturalism (and the cultural pluralism upon which it rests) may contribute more to national unity than to disunity, for in its celebration of ethnic diversity it contributes to the consumption options of the Canadian middle class. But there are more troubling cleavages, in Quebec, in the North, in the new life-styles in the major cities, and perhaps, in an era of deindustrialisation and recession in the Western world, in the future frustration of the consumptive appetite that has provided perhaps the major legitimation of the Canadian state. If this last eventuality comes to pass, and present indications are not encouraging, then the private fears of many Canadians may be realised with the discovery that their nation is more a convenience than a conviction. Then the string of beads comprising the Canadian ecumene may break apart, showing that all the while the country was 'a crowd not a community', 'a business partnership, not a family concern' (Furnivall 1956, 307–8).

References

Agnew, J. A. 1981. Structural and dialectical theories of political regionalism. In *Political studies from spatial perspectives*, A. D. Burnett and P. J. Taylor (eds), 275–89. Chichester: Wiley.

Agocs, C. 1979. Ethnic groups in the ecology of North American cities. *Can. Ethnic Stud.* **11**, 1–18.

Anderson, A. B. 1977. Ethnic identity in Saskatchewan bloc settlements. In *The settlement of the west*, H. Palmer (ed.), Ch. 10. Calgary: University of Calgary.

Anderson, A. B. and J. S. Frideres 1981. *Ethnicity in Canada*. Toronto: Butterworths.

Anderson, G. 1974. *Networks of contact: the Portuguese in Toronto*. Waterloo: Wilfred Laurier University Press.

Balakrishnan, T. R. 1976. Ethnic residential segregation in the metropolitan areas of Canada. *Can. J. Sociol* **1**, 481–98.

Berger, T. R. 1977. *Northern frontier, northern homeland*. Report of the Mackenzie Valley Pipeline Inquiry. Ottawa: Minister of Supply and Services, Canada.

Blackman, W. J. 1977. A western Canadian perspective on the economics of confederation. *Can. Public Policy* **3**, 414–30.

Bleda, S. 1979. Socio-economic, demographic, and cultural bases of ethnic residential segregation. *Ethnicity* **6**, 147–67.

Bourne, L. S. 1978. Emergent realities of urbanization in Canada. Research paper 96. Centre for Urban and Community Studies, University of Toronto.

Bourne, L. S. 1981. Unpublished. Living with uncertainty: the changing spatial components of urban growth and housing demand in Canada. Department of Geography, University of Toronto.

Brookfield, H. 1975. *Interdependent development*. London: Methuen.

Brotz, H. 1980. Multiculturalism in Canada: a muddle. *Can. Public Policy* **6**, 41–6.

Canadian Review of Studies of Nationalism 1978. Special issue on Quebec nationalism: **5**(2).

Careless, J. M. S. 1954. Frontierism, metropolitanism, and Canadian history. *Can. Hist. Rev.* **35**, 1–21.

Clement, W. 1978. A political economy of regionalism in Canada. In *Modernization and the Canadian state*, D. Glenday et al. (eds), 89–110. Toronto: Macmillan.

Cuneo, C. 1978. A class perspective on regionalism. In *Modernization and the Canadian state*, D. Glenday et al. (eds), 132–56. Toronto: Macmillan.

Darroch, A. G. 1979. Another look at ethnicity, stratification and social mobility in Canada. *Can. J. Sociol.* **4**, 1–25.

Darroch, A. G. and W. Marston 1971. The social class basis of ethnic residential segregation: the Canadian case. *Am. J. Sociol.* **77**, 491–510.

Davis, A. 1971. Canadian society and history as hinterland versus metropolis. In *Canadian society: pluralism, change and conflict*, R. Ossenberg (ed.), 6–32. Scarborough, Ont.: Prentice-Hall.

Driedger, L. 1977. Toward a perspective on Canadian pluralism: ethnic identity in Winnipeg. *Can. J. Sociol.* **2**, 77–95.

Driedger, L. (ed.), 1978. *The Canadian ethnic mosaic*. Toronto: McClelland & Stewart.

Driedger, L. and G. Church 1974. Residential segregation and institutional completeness: a comparison of ethnic minorities. *Can. Rev. Soc. Anthrop.* **11**, 30–52.

Duncan, J. S. and D. F. Ley 1982. Structural Marxism and human geography: a critical assessment. *Ann. Assoc. Am. Geogs* **72**, 30–59.

Eccles, W. J. 1979. A belated review of Harold Adams Innis, *The fur trade in Canada*. *Can. Hist. Rev.* **60**, 419–41.

Fisher, R. 1980. The impact of European settlement on the indigenous peoples of Australia, New Zealand and British Columbia. *Can. Ethnic Stud.* **12**, 1–14.

Furnivall, J. S. 1939. *Netherlands India*. Cambridge: Cambridge University Press.

Furnivall, J. S. 1956. *Colonial policy and practice*. New York: New York University Press.

Gans, H. 1979. Symbolic ethnicity: the future of ethnic groups and cultures in America. *Ethnic Racial Stud.* **2**, 1–20.

Geertz, C. 1973. *The interpretation of cultures*. New York: Basic Books.

Gould, P. R. 1970. Tanzania, 1920–63: the spatial impress of the modernization process. *Wld Politics* **22**, 149–70.

Harris, R. C. 1979. Within the fantastic frontier: a geographer's thoughts on Canadian unity. *Can. Geographer* **23**, 197–200.

Harris, R. C. 1981. The emotional structure of Canadian regionalism. *Walter L. Gordon Lect. Ser.* **5**, 9–30.

Hewitt, C. 1974. Elites and the distribution of power in British society. In *Elites and power in British society*, P. Stanworth and A. Giddens (eds), 45–64. London: Cambridge University Press.

Hodgins, B. *et al.* (eds) 1978. *Federalism in Canada and Australia: the early years*. Waterloo: Wilfred Laurier University Press.

Innes, F. 1980 (unpublished). *Some possible implications of recent Canadian immigration experience*. Department of Geography, University of Windsor.

Innis, H. A. 1930. *The fur trade in Canada*. New Haven: Yale University Press.

Kariya, P. 1975 (unpublished). *The spatial dimensions of level of living for Indian bands in British Columbia in 1969*. BA thesis. Department of Geography, University of British Columbia.

Kariya, P. (forthcoming). *Keepers and kept: British Columbia Indians and the Department of Indian Affairs*. PhD thesis. Department of Geography, Clark University.

King, A. D. 1976. *Colonial urban development: culture, social power and environment*. London: Routledge & Kegan Paul.

Kornberg, A. *et al.* 1980. Public support for community and regime in the regions of contemporary Canada. *Am. Rev. Can. Stud.* **10**, 75–93.

Ley, D. F. 1974. *The black inner city as frontier outpost: images and behavior of a Philadelphia neighborhood*. Monograph Series 7. Washington, DC: Association of American Geographers.

Ley, D. F. 1980. Liberal ideology and the postindustrial city. *Ann. Assoc. Am. Geogs* **70**, 238–58.

Ley, D. F. and J. Mercer 1980. Locational conflict and the politics of consumption. *Econ. Geog.* **56**, 89–109.

Loree, D. J. 1976. Some factors related to Indian organizational development in the Northwest Territories of Canada. *Plural Socs* **7**, 3–16.

Matthews, R. 1980. The significance and explanation of regional divisions in Canada:

toward a Canadian sociology. *J. Can. Stud.* **15**, 43–61.

Matthews, R. 1981. Two alternative explanations of the problem of regional dependency in Canada. *Can. Public Policy* **7**, 268–83.

Matwijiw, P. 1979. Ethnicity and urban residence: Winnipeg, 1941–71. *Can. Geogr.* **23**, 45–61.

McCann, L. D. (ed.) 1982. *Heartland and hinterland: a geography of Canada*. Scarborough, Ont.: Prentice-Hall.

McRoberts, K. 1979. Internal colonialism: the case of Quebec. *Ethnic Racial Stud.* **2**, 293–318.

Merrill, G. 1968. Regionalism and nationalism. In *Canada: a geographical interpretation*, J. Warkentin (ed.), 556–68. Toronto: Methuen.

Morisset, J. 1981. The aboriginal nationhood, the northern challenge and the construction of Canadian unity. *Queen's Q.* **88**, 237–49.

Newman, P. 1975. *The Canadian Establishment*. Toronto: McClelland & Stewart (2nd edn 1979).

Ornstein, M., H. Stevenson and A. Williams 1980. Region, class and political culture in Canada. *Can. J. Polit. Sci.* **13**, 227–71.

Ostergaard, P. 1976 (unpublished). *Quality of life in a northern town: a social geography of Yellowknife NWT*. MA thesis. Department of Geography, University of British Columbia.

Paget, E. 1960. Comments on the adjustment of settlements in marginal areas. *Geograf. Ann.* **42**, 324–6.

Palmer, H. (ed.) 1975. *Immigration and the rise of multiculturalism*. Toronto: Copp Clark.

Porter, J. 1965. *The vertical mosaic*. Toronto: University of Toronto Press.

Price, A. G. 1950. *White settlers and native peoples*. Melbourne: Georgian House.

Reitz, J. *et al.* 1981. Ethnic inequality and segregation in jobs. Research paper 123. Centre for Urban and Community Studies, University of Toronto.

Richmond, A 1972. *Ethnic residential segregation in metropolitan Toronto*. Institute of Behavioural Research, York University.

Riddell, J. B. 1970. *The spatial dynamics of modernization in Sierra Leone*. Evanston: Northwestern University Press.

Saunders, P. 1979. *Urban politics: a sociological interpretation*. London: Hutchinson.

Schlichtmann, H. 1977. Ethnic themes in geographical research on western Canada. *Can. Ethnic Stud.* **9**, 9–41.

Simmons, J. W. 1979. Migration and the Canadian urban system. Part III. Comparing 1966–71 and 1971–76. Research paper 112. Centre for Urban and Community Studies, University of Toronto.

Smith, M. G. 1965a. *The plural society in the British West Indies*. Berkeley: University of California Press.

Smith, M. G. 1965b. *Stratification in Grenada*. Berkeley: University of California Press.

Smooha, S. 1975. Pluralism and conflict: a theoretical exploration. *Plural Socs* **6**, 69–89.

Taafe, E., R. Morrill and P. Gould 1963. Transport expansion in underdeveloped countries: a comparative analysis. *Geogr. Rev.* **53**, 503–29.

Taylor, G. 1957. *Canada: a study of cool continental environments and their effect on British and French settlement*. London: Methuen.

Thomson, D. C. 1980. Canadian ethnic pluralism in context. *Plural Socs* **11**, 55–75.

Usher, P. G. 1970. (unpublished). *The Bankslanders: ecology and economy of a frontier trapping community*. PhD thesis. Department of Geography, University of British Columbia.

Uyecki, E. 1980. Ethnic and race segregation, Cleveland, 1910–70. *Ethnicity* **7**, 390–403.

Warkentin, J. 1978. Epilogue. In *European settlement and development in North America*, J. R. Gibson (ed.), 208–20. Toronto: University of Toronto Press.

Western, J. C. 1981. *Outcast Cape Town*. Minneapolis: University of Minnesota Press.
Westfall, W. 1980. On the concept of region in Canadian history and literature. *J. Can. Stud.* **15**, 3–15.
Williams, C. H. 1980a. Ethnic separatism in Western Europe. *Tijdschr. Econ. Soc. Geograf.* **71**, 142–58.
Williams, C. H. 1980b. The desire of nations: Québecois ethnic separatism in comparative perspective. *Cahiers Géogr. Québec* **24**, 47–68.

Part B

ASPECTS OF PLURALISM IN THE THIRD WORLD

4 Social engineering through spatial manipulation: apartheid in South African cities

JOHN WESTERN

'You go to bed, you dream about it – and I am not exaggerating at all. I stayed just beyond the railway line, and the railway line in South Africa is very often and most always an indication of the whole thing there, because you know a railway line, or a river, or something like that, is a line of demarcation between Whites on the one hand and Coloureds on the other hand in a very physical sense. In any case, for me it was the railway line, and I see this thing over there all the time.'

(Adam Small, a 'Coloured'[1] South African poet, interviewed at the California Institute of Technology, Pasadena, in 1971)

The Republic of South Africa provides striking illustrations of the inextricable link between space and society. The imposition of the policy of apartheid – strict racial segregation by law – is not simply some byproduct of supposedly racist White South African attitudes held towards those of their fellow citizens who are not White. Rather, it is a deliberate and not unsubtle attempt to maintain and enhance White social control through the manipulation of space. For a diminishing White ruling minority – falling now to one in six of the total population – spatial control is only one of the many means employed to perpetuate hegemony. Evidently, among the other methods employed are the maintenance of a strong, almost totally White army; an internal security apparatus whose secret police enjoy the broadest powers; the governmental direction of education, radio and TV; and the ever-increasing role of central government in the economy, manipulated to provide paths for White advancement while carefully channelling 'non-white' employment opportunities to maintain dependency. All these methods have received much attention from scholars, whereas *spatial* means of control seem until recently to have received relatively little.

Spatial control, however, is clearly central to government planning. Consider that in a country of 28 million people, up to 4 million Black Africans have been uprooted from where they were living and set down somewhere else. Such 'resettlement' has been imposed in order to conform to the 'Grand Apartheid' partitions of the Homelands or Bantustans policy. Furthermore, over 600 000 Coloured and Indian people (their combined population being 3¼ million) have been shifted within the cities from one part to another, under the auspices of the Group Areas Act. In Cape Town alone, a metropolis of approximately 1 150 000 persons, perhaps 200 000 have been removed from their homes under the Act. The aim of this removal is to maximise White economic and strategic security by achieving both racial homogeneity of residential areas and the required disposition of such areas relative to each other. The general resultant pattern is one of White occupation of central areas and of those geographical sectors with important facilities, with non-whites distanced at the city's periphery. The number of persons removed clearly indicates that an enormous effort has been made by the government to put its spatial plans into practice. We may therefore assume that spatial planning is absolutely fundamental to the continuing dominion of the apartheid system in South Africa. This being so, I shall attempt to construct a descriptive model of geographical apartheid, and to apply it to Cape Town – which only 30 years ago was the least racially segregated city in southern Africa.

The ideology of residential planning

In sociospatial planning in the Republic of South Africa the starting point is the polar opposite from what in the United Kingdom or in the United States is almost unconsciously professed to be the basic desirable goal. Although this goal is not achieved, public figures in these last two societies continually stress the conventional wisdom that somehow a 'mix' of social strata in a given area is societally wholesome: whether of socio-economic classes in the British new towns (Heraud 1968) or of races in the USA; whether the voice be that of a white United States senator[2] or of the Black Americans' National Urban Coalition.[3] The publicly expressed aims of the National Party in South Africa, which came to power on a pro-apartheid electoral platform in 1948, are the very opposite: that a 'mix' is undesirable, and that racially homogeneous neighbourhoods are for *everyone's* good, White[4] and non-white. Accordingly, in the South African Parliament in 1977 Senator P. Z. T. van Vuuren claimed:

'We make no apologies for the Group Areas Act and for its application. And if 600 000 Indians and Coloureds are affected by the implementation of that Act, we do not apologise for that either. I think the world must simply accept it. The Nationalist Party came to power in 1948 and said it would implement residential segregation in South Africa . . . And we shall implement that policy. We put that Act on the Statute Book and as a result we have in South Africa, out of the chaos which prevailed when we came to power, created order and established decent, separate residential areas for our people.'

A central justification for this viewpoint, that segregation is in the interests of all, is enshrined in the 'friction theory': the belief that any contact between the races inevitably produces conflict. Thus, Dr T. E. Dönges, Minister of the Interior, introducing the Group Areas Bill to Parliament on 14 June 1950, stated:

'Now this, as I say, is designed to eliminate friction between the races in the Union[5] because we believe, and believe strongly, that points of contact – all unnecessary points of contact – between the races must be avoided. If you reduce the number of points of contact to the minimum, you reduce the possibility of friction . . . The result of putting people of different races together is to cause racial trouble.'

This assertion is very simplistic, and induces Kuper *et al.* (1958), in their important study of Durban, to devote some time to evaluating its truth or otherwise. Basically, they correctly observe that the *conditions* under which contact occurs – that is, either equality or asymmetry of social relations – are what influence any potentiality for interracial friction. Yet the 'theory' may have some measure of sense to it, as may be illustrated by referring to certain propositions by Robert Sommer (1969) in *Personal space*. Sommer was tentatively exploring the notion that methods used by animals and birds to maintain their hegemony might have a measure of applicability to human society. If two individuals or groups are of differing status, then superordination–subordination may be maintained either by the superordinates arrogating to themselves spaces from which subordinates are excluded ('territoriality'), or, if territory is to be shared by superordinates and subordinates, then the latter must continually show deference to the former in a patterned ritual of etiquette ('dominance'). Thus

'[animal studies] show that both territoriality and dominance behavior are ways of maintaining a social order, and when one system cannot function, the other takes over . . . Group territories keep individual groups apart and thereby preserve the integrity of the troop, whereas dominance is the basis for intragroup relationships . . . Group territoriality is expressed in national and local boundaries, a segregation into defined areas that reduces conflict.' (Sommer 1969, 12, 14 & 15)

Now compare Sommer's formulation with Dr Dönges speaking for the Group Areas Bill in Parliament on 31 May 1950:

'Hon. members will realise what it must mean to those groups, always to have to adopt an inferior attitude, an attitude of inferiority towards the Europeans, to stand back for the Europeans, where they live alongside the Europeans, but if we place them in separate residential areas, they will be able to give expression to their full cultural and soul life, and that is why we say that separate residential areas must be established.'

The first half of this extended sentence is a precise delineation of 'dominance', whereas the second half is about 'territoriality'. Dr Dönges would doubtless assert that here both non-Whites and Whites are being offered the advantages, through the good offices of the government, of non-threatening, snug communal living, secure from 'friction', with law and order firmly and justly established. The negative overtones of the word 'apartheid' are thus misleading, unfortunate and, indeed, undeserved. Therefore, the phrase 'separate development' should be used, to indicate – just as with the homelands policy – that Whites and non-whites get fair shares of the urban pie in a separate but equal dispensation: according to Dr Dönges, 'The [segregative and property] restrictions imposed on one group are also imposed on the other group. Each group surrenders certain of its rights for the common good of all groups.'

Therefore, if we were to imagine what an 'ideally' segregated apartheid city would look like, we could simply plan four quadrants of a circle for each of the four major racial groups, and ascertain which group got allocated which quadrant by a roll of the dice. Or we would work out how large each group's sector of the circular city should be, in direct ratio to that group's proportion of the total population of the city: i.e. if Black Africans made up five-sixths of the city's population, then the Black African sector would account for $(360 \times 5)/6$ degrees or 300 degrees of the circle. But if we did either of these things we would not end up with anything that approached the present realities of Group Areas cities in South Africa.

However, we might choose to view government utterances about 'self-determination in their own areas' for all racial groups as being, at least partially, smoke-screening verbiage. We might choose to view Dr Dönges' words above on non-whites 'giving expression to their full cultural and soul life' as, at least partially, a politician's hyperbolical hypocrisy. And if we did so, and constructed an imaginary, ideal apartheid city upon the supposition that segregation is not the aim but that *domination* through segregation is, then our resultant city ends up being suspiciously like the Group Areas reality. In the planning of this city, every time that there is a decision as to who shall be put where, the Whites get first choice. Every time there is any advantage to be extracted from the nature of the terrain, as from the disposition of a gully for a barrier or heights for domination, then that physiographic advantage goes to the Whites. If we now do this, we shall find that what starts off seeming to be a rather chilling or even perverse conceptual exercise in spatial planning eventually becomes a tellingly close approach to Cape Town's segregated reality today.

The Group Areas city in theory

Basically, there is a common economy in South African cities, and it is thus in the workplace that members of all racial groups mix. Industrial areas, therefore, are in a residential sense 'common ground' – for nobody of any racial group lives there – although clearly they constitute *White* space in that Black African, Coloured and, noteworthily, Indian businessmen are not permitted equal access, being prohibited from establishing concerns in these areas. Racial interaction proceeds here, but on White terms. (In fact, the situation concerning industrial zones is a little more complicated than sketched here, and is also an area of some apparently important changes at present, a point I shall address in closing this chapter.)

In contrast to industrial zones, *residential* areas can be systematically and unambiguously segregated. Such segregation is, we have seen, publicly espoused by the government as a mechanism for the management of conflict, i.e. for the minimisation of 'friction'. This being so, a city arranged in concentric zones, with industry and commerce in large measure at its centre, makes a poor candidate for the basis of an ideal apartheid city. Its annular form means that persons of different races will continually be crossing each other's spaces commuting to and from downtown work . . . giving rise to 'friction'. Incidents of this nature occurred in the USA in the early 1960s, when tension sometimes reached such levels that rioting could be sparked off by an incident such as a Black child in the inner city being struck by a White commuter's car. A second, better candidate for the apartheid city is the sectorial plan. W. J. Davies (1971) notes that this was appreciated, for example, by the Group Areas planners in Port Elizabeth: the sectorial plan minimises criss-crossing of zones occupied by other racial groups. Most effective of all is the establishment of totally separate, single race 'ethno-cities' (Western 1981), whereby improved mass-transit facilities – such as electrified, high-density, commuter railway networks – permit economic interaction among a system of widely separated Black, White and Brown cities, between a multiracial labour force and its various workplaces. However, this chapter will not discuss this third, inter-urban segregative alternative, but rather the second: planned *intra-urban* racial segregation on a sectorial basis. Such planning is the business of the Group Areas Act.

First in the field with such a race-space plan was Durban. In this city, not at all Afrikaner Nationalist in political leanings but rather a stronghold of British colonial sentiment, segregation plans were being conceived *prior* to the introduction of the Group Areas Act. Already in 1922 a city ordinance providing for Whites-only residential areas had been enacted. Many Indians, most of whom were originally imported from the British Indian Empire after 1860 as 'coolie' labour for the Natal sugar plantations, had before long carved out a successful niche for themselves as shopkeepers and traders. Some of them accumulated enough capital to buy into erstwhile White residential zones in

Durban and in other Natal towns: 'penetration', as Whites termed it. The 1922 ordinance was followed by two Union government commissions into 'penetration' (in 1940–41 and in 1943), then by the 'Pegging Act' of 1943 (the Trading and Occupation of Land (Transvaal and Natal) Restriction Act, which 'pegged' the status quo with regard to interracial property transfers), and by the 'Ghetto Act' (the Asiatic Land Tenure and Indian Representation Act) in 1946. The Group Areas Act having become law in 1950, the members of Durban City Council's Technical [city-planning] Sub-Committee co-operated fully with the central government and presented their first report in November 1951. In it they offered seven principles or rules, cool and logical derivatives of the British-rooted town-planning of the time, whereby a segregated pattern might be achieved.

The first principle was that a residential race zone should have boundaries 'which should as far as possible constitute barriers of a kind preventing or discouraging contact between races in neighbouring residential zones'; that a race zone should have direct access, by the means of transport deemed 'most suitable for the group concerned', to working areas and to any non-racial amenities 'so that its residents do not have to traverse the residential areas of another race'; that it be large enough to develop into an area of full or partial self-government, and to provide appropriate land not only for all present or anticipated economic and social classes in the race group concerned, but also for group institutions, suburban shopping and recreation. Secondly, different race zones should not be juxtaposed: 'accordingly large areas offering scope for urban expansion not too remote from the group's places of employment are to be preferred' – note the advantages of a sectorial plan.

Thirdly, in order to give the maximum length of common boundary between working areas and residential zones, and thus reduce transport costs and difficulties, industry should be dispersed in ribbon formation. Fourthly, in planning the future Group Areas city, the present racial pattern of land ownership and occupation was 'not a material consideration', although, fifthly, 'settled racially homogeneous communities should not be disturbed except in so far as it is necessary to give effect to the postulates set out above'. Sixthly, 'different race groups may have differing needs in respect of building and site development', and so 'topographical suitability' for such varying needs must be considered. Finally, 'the central business area and the existing or potential industrial areas should not, in the initial stages, be earmarked for the exclusive use of any [one] race'.

These seven principles are now to be employed to deduce an ideal apartheid city. This assumes that the Durban principles were applied to Group Areas planning in all South African cities. Whether this is so or not cannot be definitely known. Although public hearings are held on Group Areas zoning in the locality concerned, the final deliberations are made in the administrative headquarters in Pretoria and then *ex cathedra* proclamations are issued. Nevertheless, W. J. Davies, in his painstaking study of the designing of Port

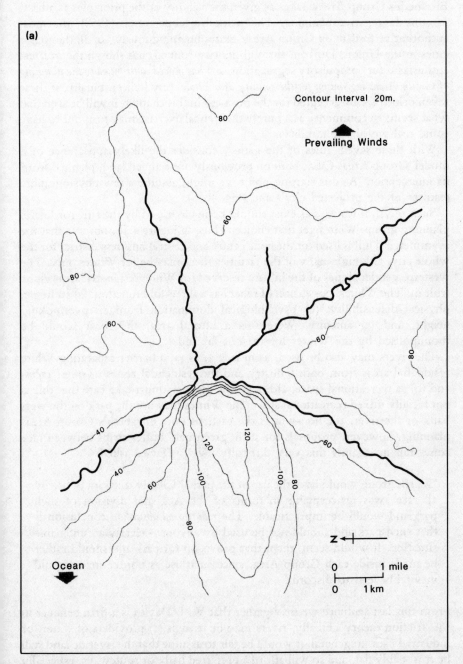

Figure 4.1 (a) Pristine site for an ideal apartheid city.

Elizabeth's Group Areas, takes as given the validity of the principles as a basis for this segregative planning. The work by Kuper *et al.* (1958), the most authoritative to date on Group Areas, states unambiguously: 'of all the major cities in the Union, Durban, through its city council, has shown the greatest enthusiasm for compulsory segregation, *and has indeed contributed to the planning of Group Areas legislation for the country as a whole*' (my italics). Finally, if these seven principles are accepted for the moment in this chapter, it will be seen that what seems to commence as a purely theoretical exercise may turn out to have some real-world applicability.

With these seven 'rules of the game', consider the likely appearance of a model 'Group Areas City', built on previously unoccupied land, planned from its interception. As our starting point we might assume a few physiographic features of the projected city's site (Fig. 4.1a).

Such physical features as exist should be made use of by the superordinate, planning group: Whites get first choice. Thus, in Figure 4.1b, observe that the asymmetrical hill is used for the civic centre and central business district for the whole city, although many of the facilities there may be for Whites only. The western, gentler slopes of the hill are reserved for White residential areas alone (rule 6). The Whites' possession of relief has a three-fold function: (a) strategic: physical defensibility; (b) psychological domination from an overlooking height; and (c) amenity. Were this a littoral area, the coast would be monopolised by the Whites for reasons (a) and (c).

The rivers may also be used, as in rule 1, as (a) a barrier separating White residential areas from both industry and the residential zones of other races; and (b) as recreational space, although the planners must take care that this is not racially mixed recreational space: the Whites may use the park on the west bank of the river, the non-whites the east. In Port Elizabeth's Group Areas planning, however, proposals for such 'green belt' buffer strips between race zones ran up against this very difficulty. W. J. Davies asked:

'Which group would have the use of the parks? Clearly freedom of use by all races was unacceptable in terms of the Act, and division of such parkland would be impracticable. The *reductio ad absurdum* conclusion is that such parkland should not be used by anyone – clearly an untenable situation. It would seem, then, that provision for parkland should rather be made inside each Group Area, since such use as border strips would inevitably lead to discord.'

From this last sentence we may gather that W. J. Davies is a firm believer in the 'friction theory'. Finally, rivers may be used as (c) providers of water for industrial uses. In general, it would be fair to assume that the riverine land will be reasonably flat, and so will afford a preferred path for routeways, especially railways, thereby increasing the likelihood of riparian industrial establishment.

Industry is located in accordance with rules 1 and 3. It separates Whites from

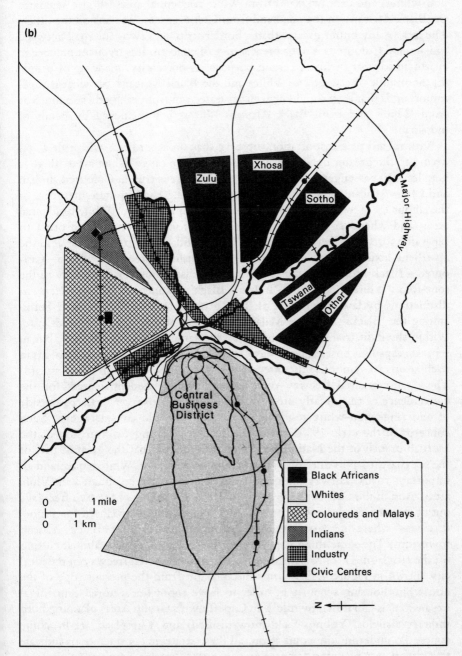

Figure 4.1 (b) An ideal apartheid city.

non-whites, and is down wind from White residential areas.[6] It also separates the Black Africans on the one hand from Coloureds and Indians on the other. The lack of any buffer greater than a border strip[7] or a two-lane road between Indians and Coloureds is not a great source of concern. It is frequent practice in apartheid to treat them for certain purposes as one entity, made up of people 'in the middle', between the Whites and the Black Africans. So what is most important is that they should be well separated not from each other so much as from Whites and from Black Africans – as is here achieved by bands of industry.

With regard to transportation, observe that, in accordance with rule 1, (a) owing to the greater dependence upon the private car in White areas, there is here less rail passenger provision; (b) the converse is true in Coloured, Indian and Black African areas. The rail routes, as in rule 1, carry these members of the labour force to their places of work without passing near White residential areas; and whenever possible, rails and roads form buffer strips in order to separate more effectively the different 'racial' and 'ethnic' zones. (*Racial* in the apartheid lexicon refers to the legally established three-fold 'White'–'Coloured'–'Black' (formerly 'Bantu' or 'native') distinction, or frequently to the four-fold 'White'–'Coloured'–'Indian'–'Black' distinction. *Ethnic* refers to distinctions by law *within* each of these groups, such as Shangaan or Sotho among the 'Blacks', or Cape Malays or Griquas among the 'Coloureds'.) (c) Within the industrial zones all travel by the same roads and railways, but in separate capsules, buses and railway carriages being racially segregated. This in itself seems to symbolise the integrative limits of the common economy. (d) The circumferential freeway runs through White residential areas for the convenience of this greatly motorised population. However, it keeps outside of and rings non-white residential areas for strategic considerations. Such concerns in the early 1950s prompted the Race Zoning Commission of the Durban branch of the National Party to recommend that the greatest part of the sea coast, to a distance of 3 miles inland, should be in White hands, and all important roads, railway lines and water pipes should be situated in White areas. And in the October 1976 unrest in Cape Town one of the two freeways out of the city, Settler's Way, was stoned, and the highway closed for a time; this was where it passed wholly through Coloured or Black African townships. The same thing happened in the June 1980 unrest, almost cutting off the city from D. F. Malan airport. The circumferential freeway in the ideal city shown in Figure 4.1b is some distance out from the present edge of the non-white housing schemes in order to leave room for sectorial centrifugal expansion, as laid down by rule 2. In Cape Town's Group Areas planning both military airfields, Youngs Field (now disused) and Ysterplaat, are in White zones. To underline the point again, all these strategic considerations indicate that this is not planning for segregation *per se*, but for domination through segregation.

Concerning residential areas, the basis in Figure 4.1b has been the proportions of the various groups in the total Republic population. This assumes the present system of 'racial' and 'ethnic' categorisation, by which Whites are not subdivided 'ethnically' by law, whereas non-whites are. To assume such a system here is *not* to accept its validity as an analysis of the society's structure. Rather it is the legislated existential reality with which we are obliged to deal if designing according to apartheid's canons. By it we find that approximately 16.5 per cent of the population are White, 9.5 per cent Coloured, 3 per cent Indian, 18.8 per cent Zulu, 18.5 per cent Xhosa, 14.0 per cent Sotho, 8 per cent Tswana and approximately 10 per cent other Black Africans. As Malays account for only 0.6 per cent of the total population of the Republic, there is no 'Cape Malay' Group Area; instead they are subsumed under 'Coloureds'. These percentages do not imply – having allowed for the sectors of industry, commerce, transportation and open space – that it is in these proportions that the remaining angles of sectorial spread are assigned. For Whites are expected to live in more comfort at lower densities than non-whites.

Whites also have, as do a few well-off members of other racial groups, the one non-white domestic servant per household allowed by law to live on the premises in (structurally separate, by law) servants' quarters. This immediately imparts a basic unreality to the desired watertight residential segregation aimed for by Group Areas legislation. Clearly, however, the desirability of total segregation is outweighed by the unwillingness of Whites to forego the non-white domestic servants required by the South African Way of Life. 'White by night' may be strategically desirable for the 'White' towns, but it is not practical politics for the National Party to pursue it. Especially because it is appreciated that it is frequently *more* than one non-white person who is regularly sleeping in the servants' quarters overnight, *Die Vaderland* (21 November 1968) regrets that:

> 'People who call aloud for a solution of the race question continue to keep a small army of non-Whites in their homes or on their farms . . . It simply does not enter their heads to investigate who is sleeping on their property. Early in the morning it is not only Lyttleton that looks like a "black ant-heap". Let every Johannesburger, for example, take the trouble to stroll through the streets of his suburb between five and six in the morning. He will then see how potential thieves, thugs, robbers and so forth are exuded in their dozens from the backyards.'

Whites, then, living at lower densities, and with domestic servants on the premises, have an extraproportionately large space assigned to them in the ideal plan, as in rule 6. In Figure 4.1b the Whites and the Black Africans are allocated approximately equal areas, whereas their respective proportions of the total population are 16.5 and 71 per cent. Confirmation comes from present residential densities for the Johannesburg metropolitan area, planners proceeding from a rule of thumb ratio (persons per unit area) of 1 : 3 : 3 : 4 for Whites, Coloureds, Indians and Black Africans, respectively.

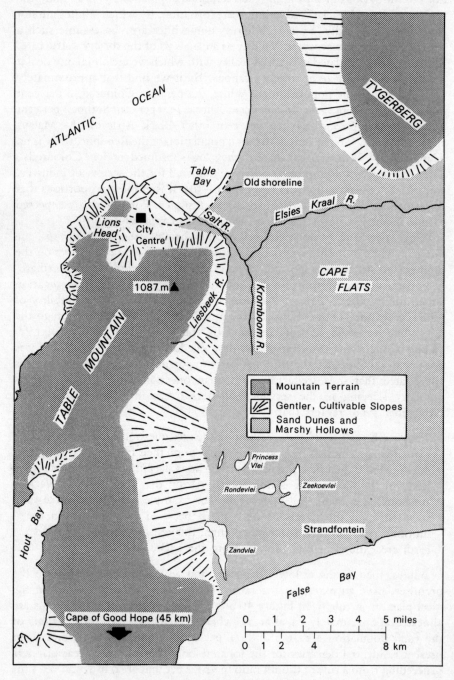

Figure 4.2 Generalised site of Greater Cape Town.

The design of each residential area for each group as defined accords with rule 1's requirements for size and compactness, supporting a local civic centre, small-scale suburban shopping, and recreation amenities. These are tangible provisions of 'separate development'. They are, however, separate but unequal. Suburban shopping centres in the non-white townships are not permitted on such a scale that they would offer too much competition to downtown store interests. Also of relevance here is that, outside of the homelands, Black African urban zones – 'townships' or 'locations' – were until 1978 officially deemed 'temporary' settlements, their inhabitants merely sojourners in 'White South Africa'. Thus, the argument ran, there was no need to provide commercial or social facilities here. So the 'primate' civic centre and central business district, attached to the White Group Area, dominates the whole city from its hilltop site: the focus of the metropolis is White.

The White zone having first choice for placement, the positions of the residential zones for all the other groups vis-à-vis the White zone accord to their various statuses as viewed by the Whites, who have total planning power. As Popenoe (1973) says:

'The extent to which a minority group of a particular ethnic status is segregated physically from other groups depends, in part, on its "social distance" from the majority group.[8] The broad principle here is that social distance is reflected in physical distance.'

W. J. Davies (1971) reports that in the Group Areas planning of Port Elizabeth: 'The Chinese were placed in closest proximity to the Whites because of the higher standard of living that this group had achieved in Port Elizabeth.' The Chinese also represented less than 2 per cent of the total population of Port Elizabeth at that time, and thus offered, as well as little threat to adjacent White status, little numerical strategic threat. It is this last, as well as the great social distance, that has led to the spatial distancing of Black Africans from Whites. And it is this interplay of relative numbers, relative White fears and relative statuses that in this model apartheid city places the Coloureds' residential areas closest to the Whites, then the Indians', with the Black Africans' townships furthest out.

Group Areas of Cape Town in theory

If such is the model apartheid city conjured up by hypothesis alone, how close an approach could actually be made to this city of White dominion in the case of Cape Town? Let us assume as 'given' as few characteristics of the city as possible. First, the physical site of the city is unalterable in all but a few rather minor respects: the 'made ground' of the docks and city centre foreshore where what was Roggebaai (*baai* = bay) has been infilled (Fig. 4.2). Secondly, the basic function of the city remains the same: a port and industrial centre with one of South Africa's main communications arteries running slightly north of east from the city towards the passes through the coastal mountains and, eventually, to the economic core of the country on the Witwatersrand. Thirdly, the general proportions of the various 'racial' and 'ethnic' population groups shall remain representative of the particular mix that Cape Town has possessed. That is to say, the proportions of these groups in the *total* South African population do not apply in this case. At which juncture, however, should one choose 'the norm' for Capetonian population proportions? Clearly, the proportions are not set but continuously changing. During this century there has been, as in other South African cities, a decline in the White proportion – which fuelled White demands for the perceived security of Group Areas. But as it is unavoidable that *some* date be chosen as a baseline for this plan, let it be 1948, when the Nationalists acceded to power and the Group Areas conception became a certainty. At that time the approximate proportions of the Cape Town population groups were 44 per cent White, 44 per cent Coloured, 11 per cent Black African and 1 per cent Indian. Fourthly, the pre-existing social geography and racial ecology of Cape Town in 1948 or thereabouts (Fig. 4.3) will, in accordance with rule 4, not in any way deter the planners or cause them to deviate from their projected ideal spatial arrangements. People, whoever they are, may be moved about as draughts on a board, with impunity. However, fifthly, because of the symbolic value of the 'Mother City' of South Africa beneath the tremendous towering backdrop of the face of Table Mountain, no attempt shall be made to change the location of the city centre, but rather it shall be cherished in its familiar site.[9] The planners of this ideal apartheid city are White South Africans, and to them the Mother City's central precincts, where van Riebeeck first set foot in 1652, partake of elements of 'sacred space'. Here are located so many of the historical and public institutions of White South Africa, all set beneath 'our national temple, our holy of holies', as Jan Smuts called Table Mountain shortly before his death in 1950. These precincts are central to the myth of origin and sense of nationhood of the Afrikaners, and so must remain *in situ*.

Based on these five characteristics, the resultant pattern would, it is suggested, be that of Figure 4.4. White settlement must command the higher ground and also most of the coast, for the purposes of defence, domination and amenity. Thus the Whites settle on the flanks of Table Mountain, be it on the western, Atlantic coast south from Green Point, or east from Oranjezicht to Observatory and thence south to Muizenberg (the Southern Suburbs). The eastern boundary of these White suburbs is fixed to the north by the Kromboom River. Southwards from its source, where there are no utilisable physical barriers, a strip of industry is placed, the barrier emphasised by a major arterial highway.

Further south still, we come to the lakes or *vleis*, large water-filled hollows among the Cape Flats sand dunes (see Fig. 4.2). What White use can be made

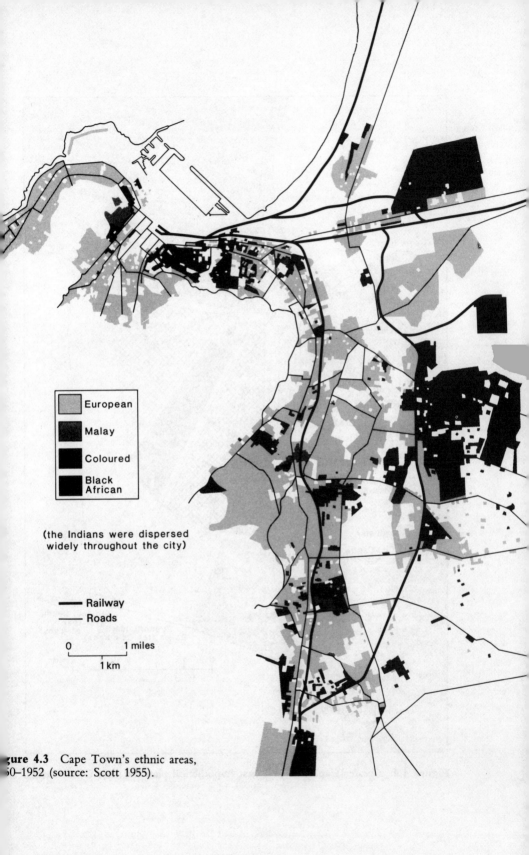

European

Malay

Coloured

Black
African

(the Indians were dispersed
widely throughout the city)

Railway
Roads

0   1 miles
1 km

gure 4.3 Cape Town's ethnic areas,
50–1952 (source: Scott 1955).

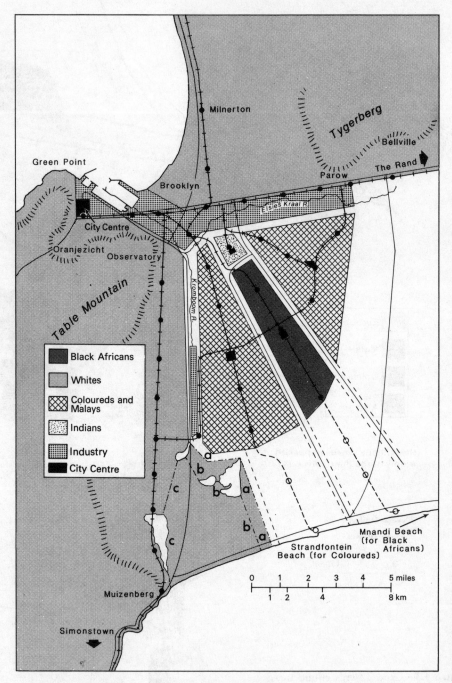

Figure 4.4 Greater Cape Town: a first hypothetical plan for ideal Group Areas.

of Princess Vlei, Rondevlei and Zeekoevlei? There are three options: (a) to monopolise, (b) to share (with Coloureds) or (c) to forego. Let us assume the Whites take option (a). This is to extend out from the flanks of the southern peninsula mountains on to the Cape Flats in order to make use of the amenity value of the *vleis*. There being no topographical barriers in this case, buffer strips will have to be created between White and Coloured, and White and 'future Coloured' areas (for observe the provision for centrifugal expansion of Coloured and Black African sectors eventually towards their False Bay beaches, Strandfontein and Mnandi, respectively). Or Whites may take option (b), which combines the amenity and barrier functions of the *vleis*. However, from the apartheid viewpoint there can be no option (b), for it would mean that if Whites were on the south and west banks and Coloureds on the north and east banks, then both groups would be *sharing* the *vleis*. We may anticipate the planners' reaction to this eventuality: referring to Port Elizabeth's parks and museums, W. J. Davies (1971) opines, 'the inevitable swamping of such amenities by non-Whites that would result must be seen in the light of current race relations attitudes and would inevitably result in friction'. We have already met such a conclusion with regard to green belt proposals in Port Elizabeth. If the Whites take option (c), they remain on the slopes of the mountain, west of the north–south freeway, and use Zandvlei as an extra buffer towards Muizenberg to the south. But then they forego the amenity value of Rondevlei and Zeekoevlei. As option (b) is no option, the choice lies between (a) and (c). Since once again, we assume that as with live-in domestics the Whites want segregation but not at a price that denies them amenities, we may posit that the Whites will choose option (a) and take the *vleis*; as their fear of the Coloureds is not so great, Whites will be prepared to live on the flat and not only on the higher land. This is in fact what has largely happened. White yachting and water ski-ing, and White waterfront homes proliferate on Zeekoevlei – separated from the Coloured Group Area of Grassy Park by the 100 yards or more of unbuilt-upon no man's land proclaimed to be an official 'border strip' on 8 November 1965.

The flanks of the other area of higher ground, the Tygerberg, are also reserved for Whites, south to the Northern Suburbs of Parow and Bellville. Furthermore, the coast north from the port and its associated area of industry, from Brooklyn to Milnerton, are also for Whites. This being so, it would immediately seem desirable that a link be made from the coast there, eastward to Parow, to create a continuous tract of White settlement; the gap is of under 10 km. It should be noted that William J. Davies (1971) accepts the creation of such continuity as a *sine qua non* in Group Areas planning in an analogous position, that of a Port Elizabeth–Despatch–Uitenhage 'White corridor' – although the gap in this latter case is at least twice as great as that from Brooklyn to Parow. If such a continuous White residential zone is created, linking Brooklyn, Parow and Bellville, it can with facility be separated from non-white areas to the south by an industrial strip along the primary communications artery. A final point is that, although residential use there is extremely implausible, the *whole* of commanding Table Mountain is zoned as a White Group Area.

The Whites, then, always get the advantageous sites, the first choice. The likelihood of this occurring had been predicted by the liberal politician Dr Edgar Brookes when he attacked the Group Areas Bill in Parliament in June 1950.

'He [the Minister] wants to divide it [the land] and to have the first pick too. We know what we are talking about on these benches . . . and we know what every honest member of this House will admit – hon. members who have been on the Native Affairs Commission in this House will admit – that what you get for a Native location in an urban area is a bit of land which nobody else wants. Just what is left. They know that. They know that that is so all over the country. Do you suppose, Mr. President, that if there is any allocation of land between Europeans and Coloured in the Cape Peninsula, that the Coloured people would get Newlands or Kenilworth? [High-status southern suburbs of Cape Town with at that time some Coloured enclaves or "pockets"] . . . The Hon. Minister knows they will not . . . This is the nature of this Bill: compulsory segregation administered by one race. And I do not trust the Hon. Minister to hold the scales equally between the races; I do not trust him in the least, to do so.'

Brookes' mistrust was to be wholly vindicated.

Returning to the model, the Whites claim, expectedly, an extraproportional amount of the space available, for their lower-density residential purposes. Both they and the Coloureds are numerous enough to be divided into two sections without doing violence to rule 1. Congruent with social distance, the Black Africans are placed as far away from the Whites as possible, beyond industry, and then further concealed by flanking Coloured zones, whose position is also congruent with social distance. There is no residential segregation *within* the Black African group because the proportion of those whose ascribed ethnic affiliation is other than Xhosa has always been minimal in Cape Town, currently amounting to only 4 per cent.

Rail and arterial road provision fulfills its anticipated buffer-strip functions, and moves non-white workers in segregated fashion to their jobs and to their beaches, with minimal crossing of each others' allotted zones. The main 'national road' freeway to Johannesburg runs at the northern edge of the major industrial strip, thereby being retained in White territory. The circumferential freeway, for similar strategic reasons, is also a good distance out from the present edge of the non-white townships, allowing for their anticipated sectorial expansion. It may be noted that the Whites, the most affluent, are therefore those who make the greatest demand for freeway provision, which

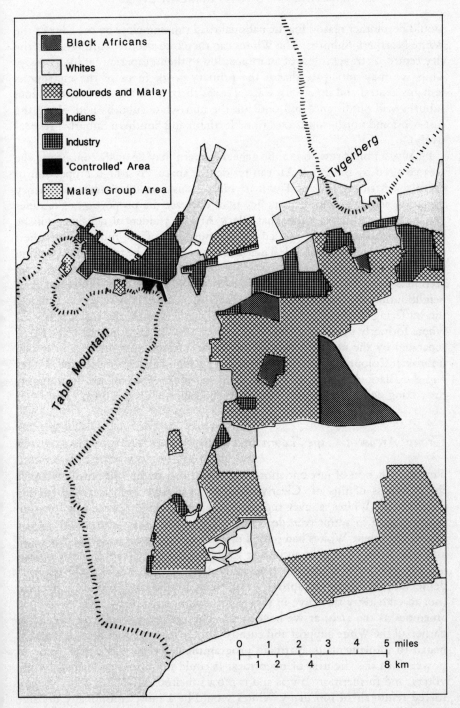

Figure 4.5 Greater Cape Town: actual Group Areas, 1979.

Legend:
- Black Africans
- Whites
- Coloureds and Malay
- Indians
- Industry
- "Controlled" Area
- Malay Group Area

Table Mountain

Tygerberg

0 1 2 3 4 5 miles
1 2 4 8 km

would be another reason for the national road running close by the edge of the White Northern Suburbs. The Whites can therefore also live furthest from the city centre, as travel is less of an imposition to them, especially if by freeway. Thus we may anticipate that if the primary work focus of the metropolis remains central and inner-city Cape Town, then, as in Figure 4.4, the White suburbs will outdistance and outflank the non-white suburbs both along the east–west and north–south axes (the Northern and Southern Suburbs, respectively).

Finally, a minor revision to the general pattern may be made concerning the area covered by the Black African residential space. As a high proportion of the Black Africans in Cape Town are male Transkeian migrants in dormitory barracks, and as government policy is to decrease the proportion of families yet further, we may assume that Black African residential densities will be higher than heretofore supposed for the purposes of the model. Thus their space requirement is lessened. Their zone may thereby be trimmed, by taking away its northernmost portion as delineated in Figure 4.4. The northernmost section is that which was city-centrewards, that most close to White residential neighbourhoods. So to remove it enhances, concomitant with social distance, the buffering of the Whites from the Black Africans by the Coloureds. For where formerly there were two Coloured residential tracts on the Cape Flats, separated by the northern part of the Black African zone, there is now one unbroken Coloured tract, thereby forming a solid barrier between the Whites and the Black Africans. The resultant disposition approximates in thought-provoking degree to the post-Group-Areas reality of Cape Town, Figure 4.5.

Group Areas of Cape Town in practice

The introduction of just one more real-world constraint will greatly enhance the goodness of this fit. Clearly, Group Areas have been imposed for the benefit of the Whites, as even the government-appointed Theron Commission was prepared to admit (van der Horst 1976). Now, there were tracts of the Cape Flats where Whites had settled prior to Group Areas – such as Pinelands and Lansdowne – where, according to the model, they 'should not be' (Fig. 4.6). However, it is just not practical politics in South Africa's 'Herrenvolk democracy' to attempt to uproot White voters for the sake of some model plan (nor to take away their live-in non-white domestics, nor their access to such amenities as the vleis, as we have seen). The present government needed to garner all the White support and enthusiasm for its cause that it could when it began to implement its apartheid programme, especially as it had come to power with the slightest of majorities. It could not afford to alienate White voters, and furthermore it was and is most solicitous of White solidarity, and forced removals of too many Whites would be a most emotionally divisive issue. Whites are much more difficult, then, to move about to fit the plan than

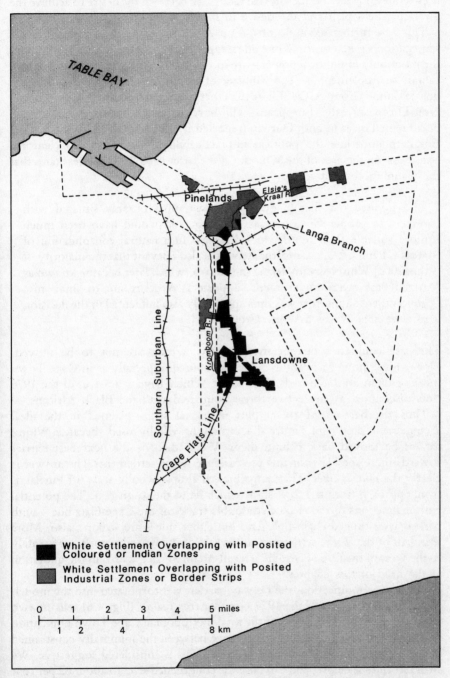

TABLE BAY

Pinelands

Elsie's Kraal R.

Langa Branch

Southern Suburban Line

Kromboom R.

Lansdowne

Cape Flats Line

White Settlement Overlapping with Posited
Coloured or Indian Zones

White Settlement Overlapping with Posited
Industrial Zones or Border Strips

0   1   2   3   4   5 miles
   1   2   4   8 km

Figure 4.6 White settlement on the Cape Flats before the Group Areas Act.

non-whites. In fact, a trade-off will take place between the desire to achieve the ideal apartheid plan and the desire to move as few Whites as possible.

This is a further example of Group Areas imposing segregation not for segregation's sake but for White advantage. If the costs to Whites – who hold the monopoly of political power – are too high, then the ideal segregative plan cannot be implemented. The Minister of the Interior may have said in the debate on the Group Areas Bill in 1950 that 'we must find living-room for the Non-Europeans, the Europeans will have to make sacrifices'. But well documented cases in both Durban (reported by Kuper *et al.* 1958) and in Port Elizabeth underline the political impracticability of attempting to enforce 'sacrifices' on the part of the Whites. Of the latter city, W. J. Davies states that the planning committee

'. . . pointed out that [a given] area was unfavourably situated with respect to proper Group Areas planning, and would have been much more suitable for Coloured development in a natural consolidation of areas C1 and C2 . . . Unfortunately, it is also relevant that the majority of the [2000] Whites already living in the area, which later became known as Algoa Park, were government supporters. A desire not to antagonise government supporters was thus apparently also influential in the decision to zone area W3 as a White Group Area.'

The case could not be put more baldly: Whites are not to be moved. Non-whites, however, can be moved as desired, especially as in Cape Town most of them are Coloureds, whom the Whites have at least until the 1976 riots discounted as any active threat compared with the Black Africans.

Thus the barriers of rivers plus industrial strips planned in the ideal arrangement shown in Figure 4.4 cannot be wholly used, because Whites cannot be moved back behind them. What, then, is the next best barrier towards the Cape Flats for this pre-existing White settlement? The answer is clearly the *railway lines*. The Langa branch almost wholly seals off Pinelands from approach from the townships which lie to the south-east. The potential barrier functions of the electrified double tracks of the Cape Flats line – with barbed-wire-topped chain-link fence on either side – are striking also. More than half of the White settlement to the east of the Kromboom River is safely to the west of the Cape Flats line – recall Adam Small's words in the quotation at the head of this chapter.

If this one modification, the railway barrier, is incorporated into the model, then a comparison with the 1979 Group Areas reality (Fig. 4.5) tells us two things. First, there is in terms of the total metropolitan Cape Town population an approximately 75 per cent congruence between the minimally constrained deductive model and actual Group Areas. This is considered suggestive. We shall return to it below, and can raise the congruence level to about 82 per cent with a little further scrutiny. Secondly, a map of 'residuals' is produced by this

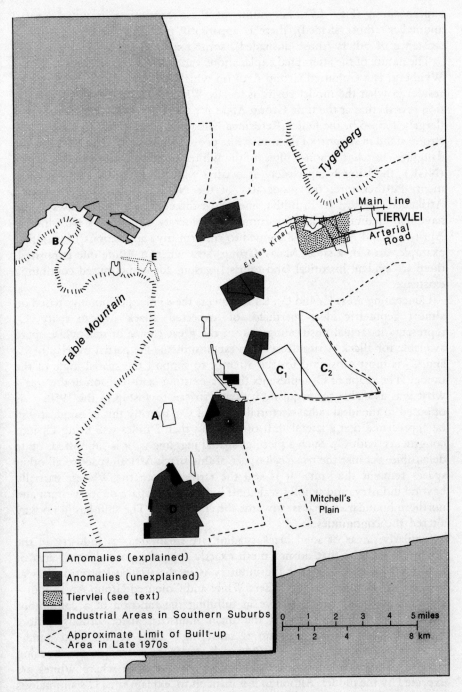

Figure 4.7 Spatial anomalies. See text for key to letters.

superposition (Fig. 4.7). For some of these continuing, residual 'spatial anomalies' (those shaded), there is apparently no logic; for the continuing existence of others (those unshaded), some explanation can be offered.

The nature of the attempted explanations varies. For example, area A, lower Wynberg, is a Coloured Group Area (in which Malays also are permitted to reside) in what the model posits as ideally White residential space. Investigation reveals that at the time Group Areas for Cape Town were being debated (largely 1953–57), the Dutch Reformed Mission Church (NGSK) took a very strong stand in support of the non-white people of this zone. The NGSK is the daughter church, for non-whites, of the Whites-only Dutch Reformed Church (NGK), the latter being closely associated with the National Party government. Furthermore, the moderator of the NGSK was a much respected Afrikaner, the Rev. D. P. Botha, one whose forcefully expressed views would have had credibility with government bureaucrats. (Interviews with him in April 1975 and August 1978 seemed to confirm my suppositions.) In another example, area B, a small Malay Group Area where a White one is posited, there are evident historical (and tourist) reasons for its permitted continuing existence.

Concerning areas C_1 and C_2, C_1 represents the *a priori* positioning, based on almost geometric ideal apartheid, of 'expected' Black African space; C_2 represents its actual positioning. Given the great choice of non-white space available for Black African township establishment, the partial overlap of C_1 and C_2 is most satisfying for the attempt to support the spatial logic of the model. The shape of C_2 represents the pre-existing land-division in the area – what was available for acquisition as an African township in the 1950s – as opposed to the ideal radial–sectorial shape of C_1. Bearing this in mind, it will be appreciated that a lateral shift of only less than 2 miles will bring C_1 into congruence with C_2. Such a piece of spatial juggling is, it is submitted, quite defensible, because the *relational* aspect of this Black African space to all other spaces remains the same. It is still the farthest from the Whites, partially beyond industry, and wholly sealed off by Coloured space on its western and northern boundaries (that is, towards the city centre). The shift has in no way altered the contiguities.

Similarly, areas of solid black shading are small areas of industry in the Southern Suburbs that do not mesh exactly with the posited small area of industry of Figure 4.4. Yet the industry is in the *relational* position it was predicted to occupy – at loci where White and Coloured Group Areas abut – although it is not very effective in fulfilling the function of a continuous border. The same is true of the main industrial strip: although more fragmented, its general position is satisfyingly close to what the model anticipated. Or finally, take area D, which covers the enormous new housing tracts of Retreat-Steenberg, a Coloured Group Area but where Whites are expected by the model. Although it is difficult to 'explain' area D's anomalous position, it is worth noting that although 'anomalous' in terms of the geometry of the ideal plan, in *relational* terms area D is less anomalous, especially as it can be seen to be lying on the Cape Flats side of that effective racial barrier again, the railway.

There is not space in this chapter to consider each of the other residual areas one by one,[10] but in summary, the areas shaded in on Figure 4.7 are those where it is felt no adequate explanation can be offered for their existence on what ideally should be the territory of a different racial group. The areas stippled are those where no adequate explanation is known for the existence of a residential area on what ideally should be an industrial zone. (This is viewed as being a spatial conflict of much less severity than that where two racial residential zones are confounded.) Much of area E is merely 'controlled' under the provisions of the Group Areas Act, which means it has no particular racial status at present – so it cannot be evaluated. For the other areas, some surmised partial 'explanations' can be advanced. What we are left with, in terms of the shaded and stippled areas, is a pattern demonstrating that well under 5 per cent of the Whites of Greater Cape Town are where they ideally should not be, about 20 per cent of the Coloureds,[11] 100 per cent of the Indians (who make up only 1 per cent or so of the metropolitan population) and perhaps 30 per cent of the Black Africans. This works out to about 18 per cent of the total population of Cape Town not being where it should be according to a highly ideal geometrical plan, subsequently tinkered with but not in any fundamental way modified.

Implications and conclusion

Is this approximately 82 per cent congruence suggestive? Is the reasoning process above circular (using a model constructed *ex post facto*) and invalid; or does it, as the author would claim, have some heuristic validity? If one is prepared for the moment to go along with the latter, it will be appreciated that there are two possible ways of accounting for the 82 per cent congruence. The first is that the figure is so high because the main lineaments of Cape Town prior to apartheid were already cast in a race–class mould, not so different from apartheid aims anyway; all the present government has done is to clean up most race–space anomalies. The second way is to view the government as strong willed, implacable and unwavering in its determination to achieve its decided goals since it came to power in 1948. The present social landscape of Cape Town, then, is due more to this Nationalist government than to what it received as a legacy from a British Imperial *laissez-faire* past.

This second interpretation is doubtless that which the government and its supporters would favour; and, especially, how the government would like its non-white subjects to view it: as omnipotent. The government cannot be deterred or deflected; it has its plans laid out and it does not change its mind; it does not bow to the pressure of the mass of public opinion (non-white); and any questioning of it that oversteps that mark which the government has already decided upon will be met undeviatingly and utterly predictably with force – the government holding nearly all the instruments for imposing its will, and not being hesitant to use them. If the minds of the non-white subjects can be convinced that the above is the case; and further, if as in Cape Town the mass of the non-white subjects are of the Coloured group who are a 'privileged' minority among the South African non-white population anyway and therefore equivocal about the value to them of radical societal change; *then* some indication is provided as to why so little overt physical resistance has occurred, at least until August and September 1976, to the forced removals of so many Cape Town citizens from their homes.

To compare Figure 4.5 (present Group Areas) with Figure 4.3 (P. Scott's (1955) 'ethnic areas' of 1950–52) is indeed to be struck by the simplification of the social geographic pattern, and to be drawn to the second interpretation above. However, the government is *not* omnipotent and is constrained to act pragmatically, certainly with regard to pre-existing White settlement and certainly with regard to the economy. It cannot change the functions (nor the history, nor the site) of Cape Town overnight, nor can it tear down the accreted fabric of the city everywhere and begin anew. In this sense the bulldozing during the 1970s of District Six – a largely dilapidated inner-city area of mainly Coloured occupancy, which had great symbolism for Coloureds' self-pride and sense of identity – is the exception.

Perhaps one could combine these two evaluations, and find a middle position. That is, the first interpretation above, that apartheid in Cape Town is merely an extrapolation of the socio-economic-cum-racial segregation that had gone before, I believe misses a real shift to more draconian spatial control: 200 000 people, after all, have been removed. T. J. D. Fair (1969), having observed the redrawing of Cape Town's space by Group Areas, considered the resultant pattern to be one of 'fragmented nuclei'. This is a somewhat unilluminating conclusion. I suspect, rather, that there is a good deal of underlying coherence to the pattern, for the reasons that have inhered in the spatial modelling above: Group Areas is a design for dominion – hence the second interpretation is valid. Yet, to view thus the present Group Areas of Cape Town as the perfect outworking of a total, implacable blueprint for segregation is also a partial view. The existence of 'anomalous areas' indicates this, as does the very nature of the 'explanations' offered for certain of these areas, such as in area A. It seems that some of the present Group Areas details were arrived at in a rather *ad hoc* manner, being partially susceptible to the efforts of pressure groups while the precise disposition of Group Areas for Cape Town was under deliberation. So one is left, perhaps inevitably, confronting the fact that even in the striking case of urban spatial manipulation that apartheid South Africa presents, both reality and explanation prove somewhat ambiguous and ill defined.

This apartheid modelling is, of course, time specific, being most applicable to the quarter century after 1950. Changes are occurring in the Republic that demonstrate that the government's separate development policy is to some degree malleable in the means that it employs, although its ends – continuing White political and economic domination – must remain unchanged. Thus certain apartheid planning details employed in this essay's model have begun to fall away. For example, on Zeekoevlei (see p. 129) there is now a pleasure boat slipway used by non-whites on the eastern shore of the lake. Buses (but not trains) were desegregated in Cape Town in 1979, and in Port Elizabeth and Uitenhage at the end of 1980. So were *some* of Cape Town's beaches, although this seems a very ill defined matter at the moment. Most noteworthily, after 4 years of gradually unfolding legislation and of modifications in Group Areas bureaucratic practice, it seemed by 1981 that non-white – especially Indian – traders were being allowed equal access to industrial–commercial areas. Yet at the same time, in certain places around the country, Indians were *still* being removed from their established residences and business premises. But in summary, despite these latter-day 'loosenings' of apartheid, it may be asserted that South Africa incontrovertibly provides one of the starkest examples of the conscious manipulation of space by a minority in order to sustain social relations of dominance in a plural society.

Notes

1 In South Africa the term refers to those persons officially deemed to be of mixed racial ancestry.
2 Senator William Proxmire referred to 'healthy, diverse communities with a mix of race, age, and income', in hearings before the Commission on Banking, Housing and Urban Affairs, in Washington, DC, on 7 July 1977.
3 See *Displacement: city neighborhoods in transition*, 2 and 25, July 1978. Washington, DC: National Urban Coalition.
4 Except for 'ethnic' differentiation among Whites, for which there is no provision in the Group Areas Act. See p. 122 for explanation of the terms 'racial' and 'ethnic' in the apartheid context.
5 The Union of South Africa became the present Republic of South Africa in 1961.
6 Another consideration of this kind might be to ensure that White residential areas are upwind of Coloured and Black African townships. For if these latter do not have domestic electricity, they will be using wood or coal for home heating and cooking, causing noxious air pollution. This strikes one very forcibly over Johannesburg, for example, where Soweto and Alexandra townships, only in part electrified, emit enormous amounts of acrid smoke.
7 Where there are no topographical features that may be used to inhibit contact between the races at the border of their respective zones, a 'border strip' – a veritable no man's land upon which no homes may be built – is frequently inserted by Group Areas planners (see p. 129).
8 It must be appreciated that in the sense of this quotation, the Whites in South Africa are the 'majority group'. They have a majority of power although they are in a numerical minority.
9 The sobriquet 'Mother City' was of course given by Whites, referring to where Whites first came to South Africa. Cape Town is equally the 'Mother City' for the Coloured people. The Black Africans, who have been historically somewhat 'strangers' in the Western Cape, can hardly be expected to feel it is *their* mother city, and I would surmise that Indians would have such an affective tie to Durban rather than to Cape Town. As a result of being the term continually employed by the dominant group, however, it seems that 'Mother City' is accepted general usage for Cape Town: note that a local Black African soccer team in Langa location, Cape Town, has (voluntarily) called itself 'Mother City' (Wilson & Mafeje 1963, Plate 10).

10   Such a detailed consideration is provided in Western 1981, pp. 110–20.
11   This figure, and that for Black Africans, excludes the Cape Flats shantytown squatters, now
     partially rehoused, for whom information is incomplete. They are living in Group Areas
     zoned for Coloureds, Indians, Whites, border strips, industrial use, and on unproclaimed
     land; they also occupy Black African space (not strictly the Group Areas' domain) (see Ellis *et
     al.* 1977).

References

Davies, W. J. 1971. *Patterns of non-white population distribution in Port Elizabeth with
    special reference to the application of the Group Areas Act*. University of Port Elizabeth,
    Series B, Special Publication no. 1. Port Elizabeth: Institute for Planning Research.
Ellis, G., D. Hendrie, A. Kooy and J. Maree 1977. *The squatter problem in the Western
    Cape: some causes and remedies*. Johannesburg: South African Institute of Race
    Relations.
Fair, T. J. D. 1969. Southern Africa: bonds and barriers in a multi-racial region. In *A
    geography of Africa*, R. M. Prothero (ed.), 325–79. London: Routledge & Kegan Paul.
Heraud, B. J. 1968. Social class and the new towns. *Urban Stud.* **5**, 33–58.
Kuper, L., H. Watts and R. J. Davies 1958. *Durban: a study in racial ecology*. London:
    Jonathan Cape.
Popenoe, D. 1973. Urban residential differentiation: an overview of patterns, trends,
    and problems. *Social Enq.* 43, 3–4 and 35–6.
Scott, P. 1955. Cape Town, a multi-racial city. *Geogr. J.* **121**, 149–57.
Sommer, R. 1969. *Personal space*. Englewood Cliffs, NJ: Prentice-Hall.
van der Horst, S. T. (ed.) 1976. *The Theron Commission report: a summary*. Johannes-
    burg: South African Institute of Race Relations.
Western, J. C. 1981. *Outcast Cape Town*. Minneapolis: University of Minnesota Press;
    London and Sydney: George Allen & Unwin; Cape Town, Johannesburg and
    Pretoria: Human & Rousseau.
Wilson, M. and A. Mafeje 1963. *Langa: a study of social groups in an African township*.
    Cape Town: Oxford University Press.

5 *Some political causes of caste and class hostility in India*

GEOFFREY HAWTHORN

India is large. It has a population of nearly 700 million, second only to that of the People's Republic of China, and twice what it itself had in 1947. It is economically diverse. 'At one jolly go', as Ashok Metra, an Indian economist, put it in 1969, and it is still true, 'one can traverse the entire spectrum of pastoral life, feudalism, mercantilist behaviour, unbridled capitalism, and blotches of socialist earnestness' (quoted in Hiro 1976, 3). It is culturally heterogeneous. It has 14 or 15 major languages, a multitude of local castes, several religions, and extremes of wealth and poverty and of simplicity and sophistication that are not perhaps exceeded anywhere else in the world. It defies generalisation.

Yet it is thought of as one country, and more importantly, governed and administered as one. *De jure*, and in an admittedly more complicated and qualified sense *de facto*, too, there is a single Indian state. There is thus some cause to believe that one can say something reasonably true and general and even unvacuous about Indian politics. And if that politics is in large part mediated by a single state, while deriving from and purporting to serve an almost unimaginably vast, various and by no means wholly civil society, then one might ask: what is the connection there between state and society? More precisely, with a particular interest in the extraordinary variety of the society, in its plurality of distinct and yet cross-cutting groups, one might quite reasonably ask: how has the connection between state and society itself affected that?

The origins of differentiation

The variety that the Congress Party inherited at independence in 1947 was the result of a long history of imperial domination. In the first place, invasion and occupation in the subcontinent have always resulted in a dominant stratum coming to extract a high proportion of the agricultural surplus: to begin with locally, by organising tribal and probably swidden cultivators into a bonded labour force in villages; then regionally, by organising the collection of 'tribute' from local landlords; and finally, with the British, nationally, by organising a more ordered and legally defined collection of revenue. But the differentiation was not only economic. It was also cultural. In the earliest historical phases, it involved the superimposition of different and originally alien forms of life upon the native ones and in time upon each other. During the Moghul empire, at its height in the 16th century, a widespread and, for a time, effective political hegemony was created in the name of an alien faith, although this hegemony, which left a simmering resentment to central rule, was never extended to the south. And then, with the British empire, yet another alien culture was superimposed upon the local Hinduisms and Buddhisms and the residual Islam. This is the only truly national culture that the subcontinent has ever had, although it has, of course, only ever been the culture of a small, if always crucial, elite.

The resultant mosaic, the geographical variety across the country and the economic and cultural differentiation at the most local level within it, has also, in the way that it has come about, had its political effects. It has done much, although in the nature of the case it is not easy to say how much, to reinforce the Hindu, or more exactly the Brahminical, view that the control of human and material resources, the realm of *artha*, is quite separate from that of the definition and pursuit of a virtuously integral form of life, the realm of *dharma*. That is to say, it has done much to produce a conception of politics as something quite separate from the pursuit of the moral life; accordingly, to produce a conception of politics quite at variance with that which we in one form or another inherit from Jews and Christians and Greeks in the West and which others inherit from Islam in the Middle East; in effect, to produce a conception and also a practice of politics which in their sophistication, in what we might be tempted to regard as their cynicism and opportunism, can be said to exceed even the most machiavellian of manipulations elsewhere (see Basham 1963, Tambiah 1976, 19–31). It has produced a sharp distinction between politics as practical action and politics as the pursuit of virtue. In an occupied society, for both occupiers and occupied, such a distinction serves many ends. Even in what is now an independent society, a society that is at least nominally committed to a more moral politics, it leaves more than mere traces.

For at least 100 years before independence, however, India was administered by the British. But this confused the politics of the country, as it added, not least through this confusion, to the more long-standing heterogeneities. To begin with, the British were themselves rather confused about what they were doing. Always interested in extracting wealth from the country, they disagreed among themselves about how to govern such extraction. On the one hand, what have been called the Utilitarians were convinced that the necessary conditions of economic, social and even political progress consisted in a free market in land and the establishment of an independent and responsible landlord class. Thus, in the name of utilitarianism in general and of Ricardian economics in particular, they sought to replace more traditional, non-market allocations of land by more modern, market principles, to establish titles of ownership and to settle a large degree of responsibility upon large landlords. Traditionalists, on the other hand, were both more sceptical of the general tenets of what may broadly be described as the utilitarian view (in English terms they tended to be Tories rather than Whigs) and more sceptical of the possibility of engineering an 18th century British social structure in India itself. Accordingly, they were less inclined to tamper with local arrangements, and more inclined to regard the proper purpose of British rule as being to exercise a benevolent paternalism.

However, because of what English historians still refer to as 'the Mutiny' in 1857, because of a growing hostility to British rule after 1918, because of other difficulties in administering the country after 1918, and especially after 1929, and because the Englishmen on the ground in India, the local administrators and military men, were temperamentally Tory, the Traditionalists, even if only by default, won the day. Having given a large degree of economic discretion to the landlords, to the large *zamindars* in the drier areas of the north and east, and to the smaller *ryots* in the wetter areas of the west and south, and having done much to reinforce lines of caste by establishing clear but distinct legal rights for the members of the different castes (for this in Madras, see the exceptionally illuminating article by Washbrook 1981), the British then largely retired, leaving the Indians themselves to accept the consequences. But the Indians came increasingly not to accept these consequences. Not only did they come increasingly to reject the idea of British rule; they also became more divided among themselves. For one consequence of British rule was to divide the more powerful in the countryside, those whose power lay in land, from the less powerful but better educated in the towns, those whose status, without real power, came from their professional service. The first, the landlords, did not greatly object to the British. At least, they did not widely voice any objections they may have had. The second, however, did. It was they who largely created and directed the Congress Party and so formed and then fuelled the movement for political independence.

After a second punishing war, of course, the British finally decided to leave the country and concede that independence. They conceded it to Congress, to this almost exclusively urban, middle-class party, but to a party that had by 1947 itself come to be divided, in at least three ways: among conservatives, like Sardar Patel, committed to economic and political development in an ortho-dox liberal–capitalist manner; radicals, like Jawaharlal Nehru, committed to economic and political development in a more directively socialist fashion; and those of a different, more indigenously Indian but also radical disposition, like Mahatma Gandhi and Jayaprakash Naryan, committed to an economic and political development that in their view should avoid both industrialisation and *étatisme* and rely instead upon a virtue that they somewhat optimistically held to lie in a moralistic and egalitarian culture, an inversion of the dominant strain, in the country's villagers. All three groups, however, were committed to a democratic state and, in that, to universal suffrage. It was this particular commitment, together with what in this respect were for Nehru the fortuitous deaths of Gandhi, in 1948, and Patel, at the end of 1950, which set the pattern of politics for the next 25 years. This was a pattern in which Nehru and Congress proceeded to create the conditions for their own paralysis. And this commitment to democracy and its consequences have in turn very clearly affected the lines of caste and class and community, of cleavage and coalition, which Congress inherited from the actions and inactions of its predecessors.

The dilemma of democracy 1947–66

In essence, Nehru's dilemma was simple. On the one hand, he was committed to economic development. In his view, a view affected and informed by what he had heard and read of English Fabians and Soviet planners before the Second World War, such development should consist in a commitment not merely to economic growth but also to greater equity, to secularism and so to social reform. Institutionally, therefore, development required some degree of directive planning and, through this, some reduction in the long-standing economic and social differentiations, most especially in agriculture, and some restraint upon the vested interests that these differentiations defined and expressed. On the other hand, Nehru, together with the entire Congress, was committed to universal suffrage and to a constitution, established in 1950, that clearly guaranteed a series of fundamental rights, including rights to property, even as it also urged positive discrimination in favour of the least privileged sections of the society. In a country more than three-quarters of whose population were rural, and so more or less directly involved in agriculture, the commitment to universal suffrage meant seeking the support of those outside the towns, those who, up to the time of independence, had played a much less important part in the party. But to do this, Nehru and those committed to his view of development had thereby to concede the interests of precisely that section which had to be challenged and even perhaps overridden, if that kind of development was to succeed.

The dilemma could have been resolved, of course, if this view of development had been the dominant one in Congress, and if the appeal to the voters in the countryside, the majority of whom were either small and marginal cultivators, often on share cropping tenancies, or labourers, could have been direct. But neither of these conditions obtained. Even after Patel's death, which removed the most powerful advocate for development within the existing structure, Nehru was neither strong in his own party nor, by virtue of this lack of strength, able effectively to challenge more conservative interests outside it. In the First Five-Year Plan, it is true, the Planning Commission did

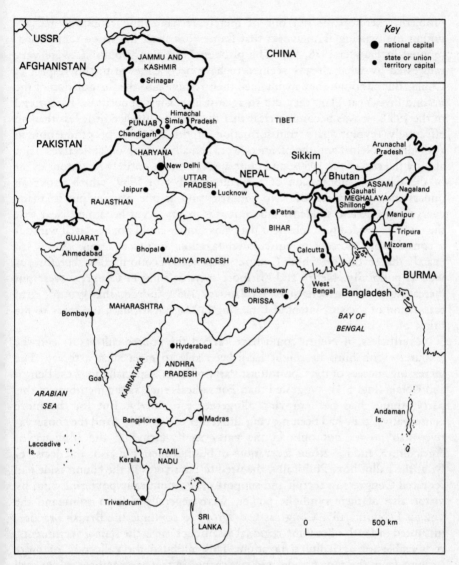

Figure 5.1 India's state boundaries in 1978.

advance a rather radical view. 'Corresponding to each stage of development', it argued, 'there tends to grow a certain economic and social stratification which is conducive to the conservation of gains from the use of known techniques. Such stratification has a part to play in social progress. But beyond a point, it hampers innovation and change, and its very strength becomes a source of weakness. For development to proceed further, a re-adaptation of social institutions and social relationships thus becomes necessary . . . The problem, therefore, is not one of merely rechannelling economic activity within the existing framework; that framework itself has to be remodelled' (quoted in Frankel 1978, 95). The planners, and Nehru himself, were very impressed by what already seemed to have been achieved in this respect in China. But although they maintained their resolve into the formulation of the Second Five-Year Plan, they did so against increasing opposition. By the end of the 1950s, it was becoming clear that this resolve implied little less than an effectively revolutionary transformation of the relations of production in agriculture. Nehru and the planners were actually talking of 'collectives'. But also by the end of the 1950s, and quite apart from the entirely fortuitous event of the Chinese suppression of a revolt in Tibet in 1959, which broke an understanding between the two countries and as one planner put it, made everything Chinese suddenly taboo, it was in any event becoming clear that the revenue needed to implement the plans simply could not be raised without a considerable increase in agricultural taxation; in the taxation, that is, of exactly that section on whom Congress depended. Economically, therefore, as well as politically, Nehru and his more socialist allies in Congress were put increasingly on the defensive. By January 1959, indeed, this group's firm reassertion of socialist intent at a meeting in Nagpur brought the party to the brink of division.

Nevertheless, if Nehru could have carried the poorer cultivators and the labourers with him, he might have been able to meet such a threat. The increasing success of the Communist Party of India, especially in West Bengal and Kerala (Fig. 5.1), suggested that. For radicals such as the members of this party, things had been moving altogether too slowly. But for the more conservative, they had been moving altogether too quickly. And the conservatives had power not only in the party itself, including the Ministry of Agriculture, and in various federations of businessmen, but also, and decisively, at the ballot box. Politically, the need to raise votes in the countryside had required Congress to recruit and support the economically powerful who, by virtue also of their symbolic power, were generally able to command the voters. Economically, Congress had agreed to continue the British practice, instituted in 1919, of making regional assemblies, now the state governments, responsible for agricultural taxation. This inhibited the collection of more revenue from the countryside, and any change in that arrangement might well have taken the new state governments, now packed with the landed interest, out of the party altogether. Congress would have been decimated and the country would have polarised into parties of the right and left. Changing the practice and raising the revenue might have been a risk worth taking, but it would only have been a risk worth conceiving if the left could then have won. Yet precisely by virtue of the powerful farmers' control of their local 'vote banks', this would have been unlikely. In any event, no one seems to have recommended the risk. Nehru's Congress was paralysed. The dilemma seemed irresolvable.

It was not, of course, quite so stark as this. Nevertheless, the complications all worked against Nehru and his allies rather than for them. Internally, there were fears for the constitution, resistance from the powerful industrial and financial community, growing hostility (with ancient roots) to control from what came to be called the 'Hindi heartland' across the north of the country, and an increasingly evident government incapacity administratively to effect institutional reforms. Externally, there were the deteriorating relations with China, and an increasing pressure from the United States, a source of money and of aid in kind to make up deficiencies in food grain, to modify and even to abandon what from Washington appeared to be an alarming drift towards communism. By the time of Nehru's death in 1964, his ambitions were in ruins. He and those who supported his vision of development had, simply, failed. The conclusions from the left and the right seemed to be correct. Either India had to modify its commitment to democracy and thereby allow a consequently more powerful Union government to press for real reform; or it had to retain its commitment to democracy, including its commitment to the guarantees of the wholly liberal constitution, and thereby allow only that development which was possible within the existing framework. The question for Nehru's daughter, therefore, as she came to power in January 1966, was whether the country should commit itself clearly to one or other of these options or attempt instead to continue to compromise between them, as Nehru himself had tried to do for 17 years.

From democracy to dictatorship 1966–75

The failure of that compromise would lead one to expect that political actions and inactions between 1947 and 1964 did little to change the extraordinary social heterogeneity in the country itself. In general, this is correct. Such change as there has been – sharpening of social definition and of expressed interest – has come since 1966, and especially since the periods of Emergency Rule between 1975 and 1977 and of the Janata administration between 1977 and 1980. What happened before 1964 was that the increasing power of the state governments, the consequence of Congress's determination to establish an impregnable base in the countryside, through government patronage, increased the power of the local patrons, and so increased the dependence of their own clients. This was itself reinforced by what are generally agreed to be the increasing economic inequalities of the agricultural development that was occurring, the 'green revolution' in the wheat-growing areas of the north and west, where, for ecological reasons, capital-intensive development was most feasible. Also, up to 1964, the increasing power of the state governments allowed more and more expression of regional hostilities to central rule. In so far as there were changes in the years before Mrs Gandhi assumed office, therefore, they were changes that served merely to clarify and only slightly to sharpen existing differences (for a fuller account of this period and references see Hawthorn 1982).

There was irony in the party's election of Mrs Gandhi: irony both in its causes and in its consequences. By the time that Lal Bahadur Shastri died at the end of his short period of office as Prime Minister between 1964 and 1966, the Congress machine in Delhi was effectively controlled by what came to be called 'the Syndicate': five state party leaders who had acquired their power in the preceding years. They naturally wished to maintain that power, and for this, Mrs Gandhi seemed to them to be ideal. She carried the prestige of her father, and so seemed likely to be able to bring popular support, but she had been a quiet member of the cabinet, only fourth in rank and apparently unambitious. She inherited a rapidly deteriorating economic situation, made worse by bad harvests in the mid-1960s and a devaluation against the dollar, forced upon her by the United States as a condition of further economic support; and she faced increasing anger from various but at this point still largely urban groups, who felt themselves to be suffering materially. For these economic reasons, and because of the continuing pressure from the increasingly powerful state politicians, she abandoned any lingering ideal of directive planning from the centre. In striking contrast to the First, the report of the Fourth Five-Year Plan recommended that the states be 'free to formulate their own plans on the basis of their own appreciation of the local problems, priorities, potentials, and past experience'. In this, it echoed the report of the Administrative Reforms Committee in 1968 that the states should be given 'full initiative and freedom of action' (quoted in Frankel 1978, 313 & 311).

Meanwhile, Mrs Gandhi's first general election in 1967 had been a debacle for Congress. The party lost the votes of the poor and disadvantaged in both town and country, failed to pick up more than one in four of the new voters, and was decimated where it was at its apparently most invulnerable. Three cabinet ministers, three chief ministers in the states, and, most surprising of all, three members of the Syndicate itself, lost their seats. The party was reduced in majority to 25 from over 100 in the Lok Sabba in Delhi, and lost control of Kerala, Madras, Orissa, West Bengal, Rajasthan, Punjab and even, at the heart of the 'heartland', Uttar Pradesh. For the first time since independence, opposition parties on the right and on the left managed to arrange effective coalitions to defeat it. But the victors were very varied: communists in Kerala and West Bengal; princes in Madhya Pradesh, Rajasthan, Gujarat and Bihar; militantly right-wing Hindi communalists in Uttar Pradesh; and militantly anti-Hindi communalists in the south, especially in Tamil-speaking Madras. Congress was beleaguered on all sides. The inability of previous administrations to do anything very substantial about reducing inequalities, the growing sense of economic constraint, and a dismay at a perceived loss of independence to the United States all served to explode what in retrospect seemed very clearly to have been the ticking bomb of Indian differentiations; and after the elections, with the appearance, for example, of private armies in Tamil Nadu (as Madras was significantly renamed) and of a revolutionary programme of agrarian reform in Kerala, promoted by the now ruling Communist Party of India (Marxist), of guerilla activity in the poorest areas of West Bengal and of a new Communist Party of India (Marxist–Leninist) to direct it, of strikes and demonstrations all over the country, including considerable violence and destruction of property, to which faction-ridden state governments responded by sending in the police, many asked whether the country might not blow apart altogether. It was India's most severe political crisis since Partition, and was certainly the most serious challenge that Congress itself had faced. At the heart of it was Mrs Gandhi.

The irony of the Syndicate's choice of what had seemed to be this weak but electorally attractive woman in 1966, therefore, was that in the conditions she inherited, she appeared to the electorate itself to be so weak, and so unattractive, that she seemed set to destroy the ground on which the Syndicate itself and all that it represented stood. And so there was irony in the consequences of that choice. For it was already clear in 1967, and quite evident by the time of the mid-term elections in 1969, in which Congress lost control of every single state, that the ability of the rich and their own patrons in the state governments to control the votes of the poor was almost everywhere diminishing. In Uttar Pradesh, for example, where politics had hitherto been in the hands of Brahmins and Thakurs and was not so deeply affected by linguistic and other cultural antagonisms, the new Bharatiya Kranti Dal (BKD; Indian Revolutionary party) had successfully appealed over the heads of these high-caste members of the economically and politically dominant rural class to lower-caste members of the Backward Classes. For the first time, poorer groups were speaking for themselves.

Moreover, the poor were increasing in number, both relatively and, because of steady population growth, absolutely too. In every single Indian state, there had been an increase in the 1960s in the proportion and number of agricultural labourers, such that by 1971 they came to constitute 26 per cent of all workers in the contry as a whole; similarly, there had been an increase in the same period in the number and the proportion of what the National Sample Survey classifies as 'marginal' cultivators, from 39 to 51 per cent. It was accordingly becoming clear that there were votes in appealing once again to 'socialism'. It was certainly becoming clear to Mrs Gandhi. She accordingly decided not to pursue the compromise that her father had sought and not to let the increasingly centrifugal forces have their way in an unfettered democracy. She decided to adjust that democracy in order to restore power to Congress and the centre.

Mrs Gandhi's first move was in the party itself. She gave her support to a socialist faction and in 1969 eventually divided the party into two: Congress (O), the old conservatives, and Congress (R), the radicals. Her second step was against the constitution, and although it was not entirely successful, it made it plain, as one of her cabinet later said after a judicial defeat, that executive power over the judiciary 'was the only way out for us'. Her third move, however, was to break what had been perhaps the single most crucial fetter on the articulation of the interests of the poor through the ballot box. She insisted upon the mixing of the ballot boxes themselves before the count, so that individual villages could no longer be identified. This protected the poor, as they had not been protected before, from retaliation from their patrons. Finally, she resorted to a shrill and sustained populism; declared *garibi hatao*, 'abolish poverty'; learnt the lesson of the communists, the communalists and the BKD, and herself set out to appeal over the heads of the established economic and political classes to the poor themselves.

It was a stunningly successful strategy. Congress (R) won a landslide victory in the 1971 election. It acquired a two-thirds majority in the Lok Sabha, sufficient to effect any constitutional change, and in the three state elections that were held at the same time, showed that the old vertical hold, the old pattern of patronage and electoral control, desperately maintained, in so far as it could be, by Congress (O), had largely broken. Nevertheless, if the election consolidated Mrs Gandhi's own position in the party, and if it appeared to give her and her allies an almost unqualified mandate for radical change through parliamentary means, it also, like all populist victories, created a very considerable hostage to fortune. Congress (R) now had actually to deliver what it had promised. Unfortunately, it could not do so. Expectations had been raised as never before, but the conditions for meeting them were not there. There had been no improvement in the organisational capacity of Congress or of the national, regional and local administrations. Indeed, the only really effective organisational capacity that there had been, in those very vertical ties which had hitherto prevented the smaller cultivators and the landless labourers, the Backward Classes and the Scheduled Castes, from expressing their view, had in many places begun to disappear or just crumbled altogether. Also, the planners, once again committed to that institutional reform which had been talked about in the First Five-Year Plan but abandoned by the time of the Fourth, were faced with the simple fact that quite apart from organisational incapacity they simply did not have the necessary revenue. Indeed, the state governments had actually reduced agricultural taxation after the 1967 elections, at the height of their power, the extreme point of the centre's weakness, so that by 1971, although agricultural income accounted for 45 per cent of GNP, agricultural taxation accounted for only 1 per cent of all tax revenue. Meanwhile, the World Bank and the International Monetary Fund were renewing their pressure for a less socialist path.

Mrs Gandhi was therefore in a new dilemma. Her father had been paralysed by the commitment to socialist change on the one hand and the political need to support the larger farmers on the other. She, by contrast, on the one hand acted to try to increase the power of the executive, mandated to do so, as she believed, by her electoral support, while on the other, threatened by increasing opposition from the business and professional communities, short of revenue and without an organisational infrastructure in the country itself, used that power to move towards what came for the first time, in a country that had hitherto been compared by some with China, by others with more liberal models, to be described as a Brazilian strategy. All the while, she spoke of 'socialism', incautiously revealing to a journalist, however, that she did so only 'because that was what went down well with the masses' (quoted by Nayar 1971, 78). It could not last, and it did not. Eventually, threatened by a technical objection to her own parliamentary election, and more seriously, by a rapidly growing opposition movement in urban Bihar amongst students and the pinched *petit bourgeoisie*, led by the old Gandhian socialist Jayaprakash Naryan, she revealed the full logic of her inadvertently Brazilian moves and declared, in June 1975, a State of Emergency.

Renewed differentiation and greater disorder 1975–81

The Emergency, she said in the September of 1975, was a response to 'growing indiscipline' and 'every section fighting for itself' (quoted by Rudolph & Rudolph 1978, 385–6). Liberally inclined political commentators had seen this coming. Drawing upon the argument that the introduction of universal or at least widespread suffrage in a varied, heterogeneous, plural, and hitherto colonial country tends to encourage the articulation of 'primordial' sentiments; making the more obvious inference that the introduction of suffrage encourages an articulation of interests first among the more powerful sections of a society and only then among the less; and lighting upon the obvious fact that India was a society stratified into castes, they predicted that what one has called 'the politics of arousal', of the middle against the top, would be followed by 'the politics of displacement', of the top by the middle, and eventually by a 'second displacement', of the middle by the bottom (for an appraisal of this literature up until 1978 see Hawthorn 1982; this particular formulation is from Narain 1979).

Marxists, although they had, of course, described it rather differently, had seen this coming too. But liberals tend to underestimate the power of material interests and their coalescence into classes; and Marxists tend to underestimate the power of social discrimination in India and the extent to which such discrimination, by caste and by other criteria of culture and status, can sharpen the lines of class. Certainly, the Backward Classes, the lower castes, in the countryside then tended and still tend to be the small and marginal cultivators; the Scheduled Castes and the Scheduled Tribes, where they are not still tribal, the labourers. What Mrs Gandhi triggered between 1967 and 1975 was a discontent of both caste and class.

Already in 1965, Béteille had predicted that members of the Backward Classes 'would make increasing use of political action to bargain for a better position in society' (see Béteille 1969, 134 & 142). It was a prediction confirmed in the election in 1977. In the eight main northern states, where politics had been in the control of the rich and high caste, Congress was reduced from 192 seats out of 280 to 5 out of 290. In the west and south, however, where politics had also been in the control of the same groups, it swept the board (Weiner 1978). In both areas, with the partial exception of Maharastra, where some of the old Congress machine survived (Schlesinger 1977, Manor 1978; for an account of this machine see Carter 1974), the 'vote banks' collapsed. The powerful groups had lost their power. Congress had been strong in the north, and had lost there. Congress (O) had already been destroyed and Congress (R) had suffered from the fierceness of the sterilisation programme and other frighteningly high handed moves during the Emergency. Non-Congress parties had been powerful in the west and south, and lost there. The Emergency had not had such dire personal consequences in these states, there had been a more visibly energetic attempt at some agrarian reform, and the non-Hindi speakers were alarmed by the aggressive communalism of the Jan Sangh faction in the Janata coalition.

At first sight, it may look as though the overall victory for Janata in the 1977 election indicated a preference for liberty over bread (Rudolph & Rudolph 1978, 394). At second sight, however, it looks as though what had caused the defeat of Congress in 1977 had also caused its victory in 1971 and its earlier reduced majority in 1967. Poorer classes and lower castes all over the country were repeatedly expressing their hostility to the richer and higher. By 1977 they were once again showing that they had come to see what Kadidal Manjappa, a former Congress Revenue Minister in Mysore and the grandson of a low-caste Vokkaliga labourer, had described in his autobiographical novel, *The martyr of Panjaravalli*, in 1966: the politics in the countryside had for too long been the preserve of avaricious rural magnates who held up the implementation of legislation intended to bring greater equality and justice to rural areas. Whatever they had said, successive governments had done very little to redress this state of affairs. The poor and low caste had rejected what Charan Singh, leader of the electorally successful Bharatiya Lok Dal (BLD; successor to the BKD) in Uttar Pradesh, was to describe as the 'urban bias' of Congress policies, the 'marriage of wheat and whisky' so convenient to the larger farmers and the industrialists (Singh 1979; he took the phrase from Lipton 1977; for the more extended view of the relations between agriculture and industry see Sau 1977).

Nevertheless, if the votes for the Janata in the north in 1977 and for Congress in the west and south were simply the votes of the poor and disprivileged (and in the north the personally harassed, too) against the rich, this was but a temporary phenomenon. That became clear in the 1980 election in which Congress (Congress (I) now replacing Congress (R)) swept back to power, and especially so in the 'Hindi heartland' (Gould 1980). Gould argues that this election revealed 'a return to more primordial regional and ethnic roots' (Gould 1980, 607). Others claim that already by 1978 the third of the three predicted phases had come: those at the bottom had at last displaced those in the middle (Narain 1979, 172–3). Each is only partly true; neither is entirely correct. Gould's own figures, and those of others too (e.g. Wallace 1980), reveal that the reconstituted BLD, now simply the Lok Dal, appealed to the Backward Classes, to those in the middle, and that Congress appealed to those both above and below them, to the elites on the one hand and to the Scheduled Castes or untouchables on the other; to those, that is, who either resented the increased power of the Backward Classes or simply feared it.

The breakdown of the 'vote banks' had not only destroyed much of the political power of the old elites: in the small and marginal cultivators of the Backward Classes, it had released a force in which resentment led to an increasing number of increasingly vicious attacks on those beneath. In 1976, there were 169 recorded instances of communal violence in the country as a whole, in which 39 people were killed and 794 injured. In 1978, there were 230 incidents, 110 deaths and 1853 injuries. By 1980, there were 421 incidents, 372 deaths and 2691 injuries (*Econ. Polit. Wkly* **16**, 1981, 833). Not all of these were attacks on Harijans or untouchables. Some were attacks on Muslims, some were attacks on other groups, and some, although it is not clear how many, reflected the rather distinct set of disturbances in the north-east. By 1980 it seemed clear, *pace* Gould, that a more distinctly class politics was now emerging across the country, and *pace* Narain, that those at the bottom, if by that is meant the Scheduled Castes and Scheduled Tribes, were far from having successfully and securely managed to articulate and promote their interests.

Nevertheless, it is important to see that it is not merely *class* politics that is involved here. In 1980 and 1981, the smallholders increased their strictly economic protests at rising inflation and consequently falling real incomes, exacerbated by the government's inability to deliver inputs. But at the same time, they increased their attacks on Scheduled Castes. There were increasing reports in 1980 of such attacks and of the use of the police in making them. In Gujarat, the state, ironically, in which Mahatma Gandhi had made his most successful appeals for peace and co-operation among castes, what has actually been described as 'caste war' broke out in 1981. It began, it is true, in the town, and not the country, in the anger of medical students at the quota for members of the Scheduled Castes, but it spread and as it did so was joined even by members of the state legislative assembly. In the towns, the ambitious but frustrated resented positive discrimination in favour of Harijans. In the countryside, at least in the north of Gujarat, the Patels, rich by virtue of their cultivation of cash crops, were coming to resent their loss of power in Mrs Gandhi's Congress (I), and appeared to be taking this resentment out on others, on Harijans and on Kshatriyas, Adivaris and Muslims, too.

As the planners in Delhi had once again reverted to a less radical intent, hoping only that the benefits from such development as there was would 'trickle down' to the poor, these poor, still deprived of any effective voice at the centre, were increasingly becoming the target of hostility from those who, although more prosperous, were increasingly agitated by the effects of inflation and by the loss of power and status it had brought. Even in West Bengal, where the state government made an attempt to register share croppers in its Operation Barga, up to half of the eligible *bargadars* were reported not to have registered because they feared retaliation from their landlords. The state government itself was hampered by a judicial decision that it could not rightfully act with tenants' associations, and it remained silent on other matters – the implementation of legislation limiting the size of agricultural properties, the raising of taxes on income and the enforcement of a minimum wage for agricultural workers (on Gujarat, see Bose 1981), Yagnik 1981; on changes in southern Gujarat over a longer period see Breman 1974; on Operation Barga in West Bengal see Dutt 1981, Khasnabis 1981, Rudra 1981).

Conclusions and consequences

One can argue that if an increase in income and some greater equity in its distribution are the central ends of economic development, then the one can for a time proceed without the other. Groups whose income does not initially increase may nevertheless for a time be content in their expectation that others' prosperity will eventually come to them. But if after some time it does not, they may well become restive. It is, of course, a conditional matter. In homogeneous societies, where there are few lines of culture or status to reinforce any lines of class, the initial expectations may be higher, the period of expectation may be longer, and if and when the expectations are not met, the reaction may be fiercer. In heterogeneous societies, like India, where the many lines of culture and status do reinforce the lines of class, the initial expectations may be lower, the period of expectation shorter, and if and when the expectations are not met, the reaction less fierce (Hirschman 1973).

There is also, though, a mixed condition. This is that of a heterogeneous society in which the government has at least nominally committed itself to softening the lines of culture and status and to redressing the inequities of class; but in which it has not in fact been able to do so. This can be the worst of all possible worlds. The experiences will be the experiences of a heterogeneous society; the expectations will be the expectations of a homogeneous one. The outcome can be, and in parts of the Third World, most especially in Latin America but also in Nigeria, for instance, and in Pakistan, has been, one of increasing internal hostility solved only by the state rounding on the discontents and directly or indirectly repressing them. This is the mixed condition to which India seems to have been moving. Inequities there of class and a public rhetoric of equality have together exacerbated perceptions of differences in culture and status. The governments, and especially Mrs Gandhi's governments since 1967, have spoken of equality but have acted otherwise and connived at the similar actions of others. At the same time, these governments have done much to undermine the only organisation capable of delivering any redress. Mrs Gandhi has forcibly re-expressed the combination of old cynicism and new moralism so characteristic of politics in India since 1947.

One can only guess at the political consequences of this for the future. India may even be approaching the point at which it learns the terrible lesson that a poor and heterogeneous society committed to efficiency and equity and also to some degree of expressive satisfaction for its constituent groups will find it more rather than less difficult to achieve these aims by means of parliamentary democracy with universal suffrage. What is already clear, however, is that the consequences of governmental action and inaction in India have been to exacerbate the multiple heterogeneity with which the country came to independence.

References

Basham, A. L. 1963. Some fundamental political ideas of ancient India. In *Politics and society in India*, C. H. Philips (ed.), 11–23. London: George Allen & Unwin.

Béteille, A. 1969. *Castes: old and new*. Bombay: Asia Publishing.

Bose, P. K. 1981. Social mobility and caste violence: a study of the Gujarat riots. *Econ. Polit. Wkly* **16**, 713–16.

Breman, J. 1974. *Patronage and exploitation: changing agrarian relations in south Gujarat*. Berkeley and Los Angeles: University of California Press.

Carter, A. 1974. *Elite politics in rural India: political stratification in western Maharastra*. Cambridge: Cambridge University Press.

Dutt, K. 1981. Operation Barga: gains and constraints. *Econ. Polit. Wkly* Review of Agriculture June, A58–A60.

Frankel, F. 1978. *India's political economy 1947–1977: the gradual revolution*. Princeton: Princeton University Press.

Gould, H. 1980. The second coming: the 1980 elections in India's Hindi belt. *Asian Survey* **20**, 595–616.

Hawthorn, G. P. 1982. Caste and politics in India since 1947. In *Caste ideology and interaction*, D. McGilvrary (ed.), 204–20. Cambridge: Cambridge University Press.

Hiro, D. 1976. *Inside India today*. London: Routledge & Kegan Paul.

Hirschman, A. O. 1973. The changing tolerance for income inequality in the course of economic development. *Q. J. Econ.* **87**, 544–65. Also in 1981, *Essays in trespassing: economics to politics and beyond*, 39–58. Cambridge: Cambridge University Press.

Khasnabis, R. 1981. Operation Barga: limits to social democratic reformism. *Econ. Polit. Wkly* Review of Agriculture June, A43–A48.

Lipton, M. 1977. *Why poor people stay poor*. London: Temple Smith.

Manor, J. 1978. Where Congress survived: five states in the Indian general election of 1977. *Asian Survey* **18**, 785–803.

Narain, I. 1979. India 1978: politics of non-issues. *Asian Survey* **19**, 165–77.

Nayar, K. 1971. *India: the critical years*. Delhi: Vikas.

Rudolph, L. I. and S. H. Rudolph 1978. To the brink and back: representation and the State in India. *Asian Survey* **18**, 379–400.

Rudra, A. 1981. One step forward, two steps backward. *Econ. Polit. Wkly* Review of Agriculture June, A60–A68.

Sau, R. 1977. Indian political economy 1967–1977: marriage of wheat and whisky. *Econ. Polit. Wkly* **12**, 615–18.

Schlesinger, L. I. 1977. The Emergency in an Indian village. *Asian Survey* **17**, 627–47.

Singh, C. 1979. The social origin of leadership. *Sunday* 18 November, 16–21.

Tambiah, S. J. 1976. *World conqueror and world renouncer: a study of Buddhism and polity in Thailand against a historical background.* Cambridge: Cambridge University Press.

Wallace, P. 1980. Plebiscitary politics in Punjab and Haryana. *Asian Survey* **20**, 617–33.

Washbrook, D. A. 1981. Law, state and agrarian society in colonial India. *Mod. Asian Stud.* **15**, 649–721.

Weiner, M. 1978. *India at the polls: the parliamentary elections of 1977.* Washington: American Enterprise Institute.

Yagnik, A. 1981. Second phase in caste war. *Econ. Polit. Wkly* **16**, 977–8.

6 *Easter Island: pluralism and power*

J. DOUGLAS PORTEOUS

'Did you ever expect a corporation to have a conscience,
when it has no soul to be damned, and no body to be kicked?'
(Edward, First Baron Thurlow)

In the neocolonial Third World, multinational corporations and host governments are major power groups competing for resource control. Public opinion
and the felt needs of minority groups are often much weaker forces. In a series
of papers I have explored the tangled relationships apparent in American-
owned copper-mining towns in Chile (Porteous 1972, 1974, 1978a). These
were characterised until 1970 by shifting allegiances among alien administrators, government officials, Chilean workers and local native Indians.

This experience, coupled with extensive literature search, enables two
general propositions to be put forward:

(a) Multinational corporations operating in the Third World are likely to
generate plural cultures, often expressed in the form of a company town
or estate (Porteous 1973). The resultant paternalist–dependency relationships are unlikely to be harmonious.
(b) Aboriginal populations frequently become powerless minority groups.
Their plight may be used as ammunition in the struggle for spatial control
between an apparently paternalist host nation and an apparently exploitative multinational corporation.

This chapter explores these propositions in terms of the group interrela-
tionships which characterised the company estate that emerged on Easter
Island in the late 19th century. It is a contribution to the modern history of
Easter Island, a subject until now wholly neglected in favour of prehistory and
archaeology (Porteous 1981).

The chief Easter Island protagonists from the late 19th to the mid-20th
century were the Chilean government, a multinational firm whose Easter
Island operation involved sheep ranching, a vociferous Chilean public opinion,
and the Rapanui, the original inhabitants of the island. These were not
undifferentiated groups. Unlike many studies of pluralism, which deal with

'imperialists', 'natives' and the like as monolithic entities with relatively simple relationships, I hope to demonstrate both the complexity of motives within each group and the complexity of relationships between the groups. The role of the church, for example, is often neglected in development studies, but was a major force behind public opinion and government action in the history of Easter Island (Mamak & McCall 1978).

Such a subtle portrayal demands a narrative rich in historiographic detail. I have therefore chosen to concentrate largely upon the period of 'company colonialism' on Easter Island, from 1888 to 1953. Within this period, the chief emphasis is given to the major power crisis which occurred during and after the First World War.

Background

Easter Island experienced its first major external impact in the 1860s when the efforts of Peruvian slavers, augmented by the work of French missionaries and a Franco-Scots sheep ranching group based in Tahiti, reduced the population from approximately 4000 to a mere 110 by 1877. To facilitate sheep rearing on the island the Rapanui remnant was confined to the 'reservation' village of Hangaroa.

Chile annexed the island in 1888, but a colonisation scheme led by Policarpo Toro proved a dismal failure. The sheep rearing operation was continued first by E. Merlet and Company, and then by the Compañía Explotadora de la Isla de Pascua (appropriately, the Easter Island Exploitation Company, henceforward CEDIP). The latter company was a subsidiary of the Scots-Chilean merchant multinational, Williamson–Balfour, and was based in Valparaiso with Merlet as manager. CEDIP purchased the bulk of the island from the Tahiti-based sheepmasters and, after the colonisation failure, leased the small government-owned area around Hangaroa.

Having begun, with Toro, the policy of leasing the government-owned property on Easter Island, successive Chilean governments found themselves involved in a recurrent drama. As the term of a lease contract approached, government interest in the island would rise, frequently stimulated by intense press campaigns and the resulting surges of public opinion. After a prolonged and often vicious altercation among government, company, press and public, a new contract would be promulgated and the company would be left to rule the whole island with little interference until the contract again ran out and the cycle was repeated.

The first cycle, or Toro colonisation period, ended with the disgrace of Toro and the assumption of control by Merlet in 1895–7. The succeeding cycles, based on 20-year contracts, peaked towards the end of World War I, again in the mid-1930s, and yet again in the early 1950s. During most of this period a single company was the effective sovereign of Easter Island. The struggle for control of the island was thus a three-way contest among the government, the *de jure* sovereign, fuelled by volatile public opinion; the company, the *de facto* controller; and the Rapanui, rulers *ab origine*. Although the contest for control continued throughout the period, this chapter concentrates upon the conflict that emerged during World War I, for this was the most severe of the several struggles and illustrates most clearly the interactions of the groups.

The company state is challenged

During the first decade of the 20th century the government and public of Chile paid scant attention to Easter Island. From 1890 Chile was intermittently represented on the island by an official known as the *subdelegado marítimo*, and as a further counterweight to the authority of the company manager, it was announced in 1902 that a native chief of the island should be elected. A minor press campaign mounted by the newspaper *El Chileno* in 1904 was waged on the grounds that Tahitian immigrants had taken over certain native lands, that Merlet was using forced labour to work the island, and that the living conditions of the natives were, in general, very poor. A naval expedition of 1904 dispelled these fears by establishing the absence of forced labour and the presence of only three Tahitians. In general, it appeared that all was well with Easter Island and the administration of Merlet and Company and the natives of the island lived in complete harmony. Throughout much of this period, however, the post of *subdelegado marítimo* was held by the CEDIP manager, who thus represented both company and government and consequently wielded absolute power on the island. It is quite conceivable, therefore, that the naval expedition was reporting the obviously favourable opinion of this island-based officer.

But, from about 1910, government interest was engendered by the outcries of influential citizens. At this time Easter Island was, in effect, merely a Chilean colony, having not yet been incorporated into a department or province. Citizens of Valparaiso, claiming that the island had communication links, 'albeit irregular', with their city, petitioned the central government to include the island in the Valparaiso *intendencia*. Moreover, since the turn of the century, groups of influential citizens in both Santiago and Valparaiso had become concerned with the conditions of life of the Easter Islanders, who were universally declared to be bowed beneath the yoke of the company.

Chilean authorities were also made aware of their colonial responsibilities by the actions of the islanders themselves. Throughout the period of alien domination, indigenous rebellions have periodically taken place. The murder of the last Rapanui king in 1899, possibly by Merlet, and Merlet's firing of Rapanui crops, provoked anti-company demonstrations in 1900. Twentieth century uprisings captured headlines in Chilean newspapers and even abroad, severely agitating both alien residents and mainland officialdom.

The Routledge archaeological expedition found itself embroiled in a major revolt during 1914, an outcome of the further abuse of power by Merlet. At this time Percy Edmunds, the harassed CEDIP resident manager, was the sole representative of both company and government. Antagonism towards CEDIP had been growing for some years, especially because of Merlet's desire to use the Rapanui as cheap or unpaid labour on the sheep ranch. In June 1914 Angata, an old woman, was led by a dream sent by God to declare that Merlet had died, that the island belonged to the Polynesians, and that a symbolic feast of company beef and mutton should be celebrated without delay. The year 1914 was the apogee of empire, and Mrs Routledge (1919) rather scornfully compared the rising to 'a Gilbertian opera'. The Rapanui claims, however, as presented to Edmunds, were no more unreasonable than the rash of expropriations of alien enterprise that has swept the Third World since independence. In this premature expropriation attempt the Rapanui declared, 'We desire to take all the animals in the camp . . . for you know that all the animals and farm . . . belong to us . . . There is another business . . . who gave the animals to Merlet also who gave the earth to Merlet because it is a big robbery. They took this possession of ours, and they give nothing for the earth, money or anything else . . .' (Routledge 1919, 142). As the white party totalled only seven persons, nothing could be done to prevent the islanders from slaughtering and eating cattle and sheep, from breaking into the wool warehouse, and from ranging over the whole island, previously out of bounds to them. In view of their former strong links with French-controlled Tahiti, it is perhaps significant that the rebels flew a home-made tricolour.

The siege of the ranch house was relieved only by the arrival of a Chilean warship, the *General Baquedano*, whose captain, though restoring order at once, was clearly unsympathetic towards CEDIP and the British Scientific Expedition. He was unable to guarantee the safety of the latter, and considered the Rapanui had 'behaved very well not to murder Mr. Edmunds'. With the ensuing death of Angata and the exile of several young islanders to Chile, the rebellion came to an end.

Easter Island's 'native question' soon became an issue on the mainland, however. A persistent campaign for the liberation of the island swept through Chile in 1915–17. Opposition to the company was overtly based on CEDIP's treatment of the Rapanui. Motives of profit and prestige were apparent, however, in government opposition to the company's claim to own most of the island and in the assertion that, under new management, the island could be of much greater economic value to Chile.

The company's treatment of the indigenes

In early 1916 the anti-company campaign found a leader in Rafael Edwards, Bishop of Dodona and Vicar Military of Chile. Military chaplains had been sent out to Easter Island on several of the Navy's annual visits. During their short stays on the island they performed baptisms and marriages which may have been awaiting official blessings for a year or more.

Bishop Edwards was shocked at the reports brought back by his chaplains. The Rapanui were apparently living in appalling conditions, bereft of outside help. In June 1916, therefore, the bishop left Valparaiso on the *General Baquedano* for an extended investigation of social conditions on Easter Island.

During his absence, a growing concern about the forgotten inhabitants of the remote Chilean colony began to manifest itself in occasional newspaper articles of a speculative nature. It was known, for example, that leprosy was endemic on the island, and the demand of the *subdelegado* that a walled leprosarium should be built was met with enthusiasm by a society that regarded the disease with horror (*La Unión* 16 March 1916). On his return, the bishop revealed that the lepers had been relegated to two huts outside Hangaroa where, lacking clothes, beds, cooking utensils, food and medicines, they lived in an 'unbreathable atmosphere which provokes nausea'* (*La Unión* 22 July 1916). The bishop continued, 'men and women, young and old, the lepers appear to be walking corpses, brutally mutilated . . . it is a spectacle whose horror sets the nerves on edge, paralyzes the heart, and excites simultaneous feelings of pity and indignation within the breast' (*La Unión* 18 November 1916).

Only a dozen or so lepers existed in 1916. But the plight of the 250 other islanders also drew attention; as early as 1914 a newspaper article had asserted that the indigenes were totally naked and suffering from hunger and thirst. So poor were their conditions of life that they were said to have petitioned the Chilean government to allow them to migrate *en masse* to Tahiti.

> 'Poor Islanders! Except for the Bishop of Dodona, who has concerned himself with them? Who has taken one second from the busy affairs of his daily life to consider the state of material and moral abandonment in which they live, whose fruits are nakedness, hunger, ignorance, and impiety? Who has raised his voice to implore pity for these unfortunate fellow countrymen? No one!' (*La Unión* 12 May 1916)

After the return of the bishop, these assertions were to be larded with abundant factual information.

To Bishop Edwards, Easter Island appeared a rich and potentially productive land. The condition of the native inhabitants was therefore all the more starkly exhibited. His reports depict a broken race, almost entirely naked, eating only what the earth spontaneously produced, idle, shiftless and unwilling to work. This description was fully in accord with contemporary

---

* All quotations (except those from Edmunds and Green) are from the Spanish and French and are the author's translations.

opinion of the Polynesians who, having ceased to be 'noble savages', had not yet absorbed the Euramerican work ethic. There was clearly a gross lack of fit between Easter Island actualities and the bishop's ideals.

Responsibility for the plight of the islanders was laid squarely at the door of CEDIP (Bienvenido de Estella 1920). Little thought seems to have been given to the almost total failure of successive Chilean governments to control company activities and ameliorate the living conditions of their island citizens. As is common in company–state situations, the entrepreneur, even when not guilty, becomes the most convenient whipping boy when problems emerge.

In 1914 CEDIP had been accused of depriving the Rapanui of their land, of giving almost all of the scarce sweet water supply to the stock, and of driving the inhabitants from the coasts into the mountainous interior where the land was less fertile. Company permission was apparently required to leave Hangaroa, and should a hungry indigene be found stealing a sheep for his starving children, he was deported to mainland Chile on the next boat, there to die from the dual operation of unaccustomed climate and homesickness. There was some substance to these charges, although the frequency of deportation was much exaggerated. Moreover, the relocation of the Rapanui in fertile Hangaroa gives the lie to claims that the indigenes had been driven into the interior.

Bishop Edwards added to these charges, stating that hunger among the Rapanui was in part due to company intransigence and the introduction of new wants. The former reliance on the abundant indigenous products had been reduced to 'a few bananas, some sweet potatoes, other roots . . . raw or badly-cooked fish . . . a little sugar cane' (La Unión 18 November 1916). The growing preference was for imported foodstuffs, available only at the company store, where prices could be set at whim. In one instance, the bishop speaks of a sack of flour costing 100 pesos (the equivalent of one month's rent of the leased government lands). Consequently, among the Rapanui 'bread and flour are unknown; there is no maize, no potatoes, no rice, no coffee, no tea, no maté . . . nothing' (La Unión 18 November 1916).

Bishop Edwards clearly had no training in Polynesian ethnology. He clearly expected the Rapanui to be tea-drinking Chileans. Indeed, his scornful description of their actual diet closely conforms to the traditional Rapanui diet. To this rather culture-bound view Bishop Edwards added that although the island abounded in sheep, meat was rarely available to the inhabitants. When meat was given to Rapanui workers during the shearing season, they were forbidden to take it home for their families. All agricultural progress was hindered by the existence of only a single plough.

Working conditions were also said to be poor, and the CEDIP was accused of instituting a regime of forced labour. This had resulted in neglect of indigenous agriculture during those periods when the Rapanui were required to shear sheep, load and unload vessels, and other non-regular occupations. Where cash wages were given, they immediately returned to CEDIP via the company store. A letter was referred to in which Merlet had apparently asked the captain of the *General Baquedano* to sanction forced labour. If the Rapanui proved unwilling to work, the company resorted to a lock-out, during which no work was offered, no goods were sold and no native products were bought. This resulted in severe distress among the indigenes. In sum, Edwards suggested, the native inhabitants had become slaves of the company, which operated the island in a feudal manner reminiscent of the traditional *encomiendas* of the Spanish–American Empire (*La Unión* 17 December 1916).

The immediate practical response to these reported outrages was a major drive to collect a wide variety of useful goods, from ploughs to needles, which could be sent to relieve the wants of the islanders. Of prime importance was the collection of clothes. European clothing had been worn on Easter Island since the days of the late 18th century explorers, from whom garments were stolen in quantity. This requirement providentially coincided with mainland demands that the islanders be clothed, savage laxity in dress being perceived as sinful.

Private charity produced a considerable array of goods, although it is not clear whether the 20 ploughs and sundry sewing machines requested by the bishop were forthcoming. As an added attraction to those who wished to relieve the sufferings of 'the poor indigenes of Easter Island . . . completely abandoned . . . without material or spiritual aid', all who contributed were guaranteed indulgences by the Church for 100 days. In December 1916 a charity committee began work in Valparaiso, a city chosen not simply for its tenuous shipping links with the island, but because it was 'the city from which the light of evangelism and civilization was carried to Easter Island' (*La Unión* 1 December 1916).

The company response

CEDIP did not remain quiescent under this hail of accusation. In a business-like fashion Henry Williamson attempted to rebut the bishop's accusations point by point, although his letters to the press were hopelessly outnumbered by those of the company's detractors. In dealing with the question of Rapanui treatment, Williamson incisively observed that the issue depended wholly upon one's perceptions of and attitudes towards indigenous conditions of life. Any solution depended 'upon the prism through which one looks':

'An evangelical missionary may consider that the company has been inhumane because it has not converted the indigenes from idolaters into catholics, from ne'er-do-wells into workers, from communists into respecters of private property, from immoral ways to chastity, from dirty to clean, from herbivores to carnivores. But a simple mortal might judge that the company, which is neither the government nor the church, has done quite enough in procuring houses for the natives, in inducing them to formalize their marriages, in preventing them from fighting and killing each other, in clothing the nearly naked females, in giving them land which they can cultivate if they so desire, and offering them ploughs and oxen, in providing them a daily wage when they feel like working, and respecting their desires when they do not . . .' (*La Unión* 20 November 1916)

Though it is now impossible to judge the truth of the matter, Williamson's company had clearly done a great deal more for the Rapanui than had the Chilean government or the Catholic church.

The literary output of Bishop Edwards and his chaplains during the period 1918–21 reveals a crusading spirit, amounting at times almost to zealotry. Father Bienvenido de Estella (1919), in particular, made claims about the work of the church which were refuted by Vives Solar (1920), a Chilean official who had lived several years on Easter Island. One detects a paternalism as great as Williamson's in Bienvenido de Estella's (1919) choice of titles, such as 'Six months among the Easter Island *kanakas*'.

An altercation that took place between Bienvenido de Estella and a CEDIP official reveals the polarity of attitudes between church and company (Bien-venido de Estella 1920). In the second decade of the 20th century, Rapanui funerals still involved a great deal of feasting, singing and dancing. Regarding this as barbarous, the two priests instructed the islanders to behave in a more civilised manner. Company officials remonstrated, suggesting that the islanders should be permitted to retain their traditional ways. The reaction of the missionaries was to heap abuse upon the 'egotistical, monopolistic entre-preneurs' who refused to recognise the duty of all Westerners to bring the light of civilised morality to those still living in heathen fastnesses. On the other hand, one might question the company's altruism in that the selective support of native customs has been used by almost all colonialists as a means of entrenching their ultimate control.

It is axiomatic in any discussion of company towns or estates that the company is castigated for its treatment of its workers. Taking the middle ground between the protestations of CEDIP and the accusations of Bishop Edwards, one might well commend the company for its restrained interfer-ence with indigenous life-styles and question the bishop's concern with imposing his rigid standards of behaviour upon the entire population of a cultural group with a social ethos diametrically opposed to that espoused by this scion of a rich, entrepreneurial Welsh–Chilean dynasty.

Williamson, moreover, did not rely wholly upon argument, for he was careful to collect depositions from witnesses. Of the surviving letters, two in English were written by Percy Edmunds (1916), the company's island manager from 1908 into the 1920s, and Frank Green (1916), photographer for the Routledge expedition. A letter in French was collected from J. Dillinger

(1918), captain of the *Jean*, which was sunk off Easter Island by a German cruiser in 1914.

Dillinger lived on Easter Island for 6 months before a ship arrived to take him to Chile. His letter indicates his considerable powers as an amateur ethnologist, based on experiences in the tropical regions of three continents. Comparing the Easter Islanders with other Polynesians, he noted that: their way of life was in no way abnormal; any food received by company workers would be shared out through the kinship network; regular sustained work was not part of their cultural heritage; and their state of dress was not wholly unsuitable for the climate. Dillinger observed no brutality on the part of employer towards employee, but reported that one of his French crew members had been killed by the Rapanui.

Green, less sympathetic, had spent 9 months on the island. He believed that all the islanders were well provided with cows, pigs, horses and fish, and that any case of food deprivation was related to fecklessness or lack of planning. As yams and sweet potatoes were a staple, flour was not an important dietary item. The case of the 100 peso sack of flour he attributed to the islanders' propensity to exaggerate and to agree with the burden of any leading question put to them. In contrast with Bishop Edwards, Green regarded clothing as detrimental to native health, as islanders were prone to exchange garments and often failed to remove damp clothing before retiring. In a sure thrust at the Chilean authorities, he suggested that they first direct their charity towards the hungry and ill clad urchins of the Chilean cities and the nude Indians subsisting in the raw climate of Tierra del Fuego. Finally, the Easter Islanders had plenty of clothing, but on the approach of a boat would hide it and beg for more, though rather for 'pleasure than for gain'.

As company manager, the testimony of Edmunds is more suspect. He noted that the *kanakas* had 500–1000 acres (200–400 hectares) at their disposal in Hangaroa, but cultivated only 10 per cent of this. At least five ploughs were in use, and abundant Polynesian foodstuffs were produced, as well as a variety of European vegetables and non-native fruits. Milk and fish were available. The company had lent plough oxen, but these were so abused that two had had to be slaughtered.

Flour was not generally used, the only sale in 1915 being 20 lb at 20 centavos per lb (0.45 kg), a price far from the alleged 100 peso sack. Although there was abundant food and at least a dozen sewing machines on the island, natives went aboard ships half-naked and hungry, 'as naturally as if they had said they had clothes they would get none given to them; the same with food'. Meat was fairly plentiful and was freely distributable by the shearers to their families. No lock-out ever existed, and all CEDIP workers were paid in cash as well as food and merchandise. No punishments were meted out except the occasional fines; these were either returned later or given to the *subdelegado marítimo*. As for the lepers, they were so well provided with free rations, including daily meat, that the healthy islanders shared their supplies. Four buildings were originally provided for the lepers. The two which had disappeared by the arrival of Bishop Edwards were either burnt down or dismembered by other natives for house construction. In concluding, Edmunds struck a paternalistic note:

> 'The Kanakas are what you would call "muy simpaticas" to strangers who have never seen Kanakas before. They are first class liars, will cry for nothing and are really a lot of grown up children.'

Although the company treated the islanders paternalistically, and in leaving them largely to themselves was guilty of some inhumanity, it is unlikely that the tales of slavery, outright oppression, starvation and brutality broadcast throughout the Chilean press can be taken wholly at face value. The three pro-company accounts outlined above were no doubt solicited by CEDIP. Nevertheless, one derives from them a strong suspicion that the indigenes were quite capable of manipulating the opinions of temporary visitors. Bishop Edwards and his followers, ignorant of Polynesian folkways and sensitive to suffering and distress by virtue of their calling, may have been thoroughly humbugged.

One cannot ignore the possibility of self-seeking and a desire for publicity on the part of the anti-company campaigners. Unlike the mundane social problems of Chilean cities, those of exotic Easter Island stirred the public imagination. Yet, in

> '. . . Valparaiso alone, where there are thousands of poor girls who have no alternative but the streets to make a living . . . there are people . . . who are trying to make themselves famous by lecturing on the "Poor Kanakas" of Isla de Pascua, when they have so much under their noses to remedy first' (Edmunds 1916).

For many Chileans during World War I the Easter Island question provided a convenient external focus of attention, effectively diminishing the perceived importance of the growing social crises of the mainland.

Conflict resolution

Objections to company rule on Easter Island had roots in the late 19th century. Bishop Edwards provided a focus for the anti-company campaigners, including a motley group of anonymous press correspondents. Opposing them was Merlet, now merely the CEDIP manager, and Henry Williamson, scion of the family that had expanded its interests into five continents.

The campaign came to a climax in November 1916. During the whole of November a lengthy anti-company article appeared almost every day in the influential Valparaiso newspaper *La Unión*. Bishop Edwards gave lectures and addresses to general audiences, to ecclesiastical groups and to select social gatherings. A variety of subjects was covered, but again the bishop lost few opportunities to castigate CEDIP as the source of all evil on Easter Island. These lectures were extensively reported in the Santiago and Valparaiso press, and Edwards wrote a series of supplementary letters and reports which were printed with equal avidity.

The campaign was monumentalised in two hurriedly produced volumes. In *La Isla de Pascua* (1918), Rafael Edwards repeated his allegations of misery, want and brutality, and spoke of 'the slaves whose chains have been broken'. He asserted that the chief requirement of the indigenes was for reasonably compensated work, possibly only through the planned development of resources, but added 'this will be useless unless there is maintained in Easter Island an authority independent of the economic interest which alone exists at this time' (Edwards 1918, 25). The company's rebuttal of all allegations was contained in a volume of the same title (Rocuant 1916), which brought together in printed form a large number of the documents that Merlet had been collecting for some time. The aim of this book was to 'dissipate in the minds of the Government, the Magistracy, and Public Opinion, the anti-company feelings which, although no doubt well-intentioned, are rooted in lack of knowledge' (Rocuant 1916, 2). CEDIP proposed that the government should take back its lands and work them itself, leaving the company free to develop its own territory.

Newspaper vituperation, however, was chiefly instrumental in sensitising Chileans to the dispute. Anti-company writers asserted that CEDIP, with complete control of Easter Island, had acted 'as one might expect, exploiting its island as absolute lord and exercising, over the unfortunate [islanders], a medieval despotism' (*La Unión* 8 November 1916). In contrast, Bishop Edwards was referred to as a 'worthy apostle' engaged in a 'modern crusade' which was 'as much patriotic as Christian'. The bishop himself attested that the campaign united the worthy causes of patriotism, religion and charity.

La Unión eagerly published an exchange of letters between the bishop and Williamson. Edwards accused CEDIP of being in illegal control of Easter Island in that the land claims of the company were not legitimate in Chile. Williamson replied that the titles were drawn up legally when Easter Island was under French jurisdiction. The rather unusual situation under which French courts in 1893 made rulings on land titles in an island already Chilean now became a burning issue. Williamson was accused of imperialist designs; a Briton merely resident in Chile, his reference to French jurisdiction was designed to intimidate Chile. His suggestion to turn to France as arbitrator generated howls of protest; a well-spring of anti-imperialist sentiment broke out. The bishop declared him an 'insolent . . . vulgar . . . exploiter'. Other writers echoed these accusations of 'intolerable insolence'.

Williamson was now forced into the position of having to defend both the motives of his company and his own impugned loyalty to Chile. Declaring himself a traditional friend of Chile, he reminded Chileans that his distinguished father's support of Chilean interests in the British parliament had earned him the title of 'Member for Santiago'. Referring to the 60 years of Williamson–Balfour operations in Chile, Williamson declared that he would not be guilty of dishonouring his chosen country of residence by making the Easter Island question an international affair. By keeping the issue an internal one he would safeguard Chile's integrity at a time of global war.

Besides this attempt to reconcile public opinion to CEDIP's continued operation, Williamson was careful to reassure the Chilean president, the Minister for External Affairs and other high functionaries of his loyalty to Chile. Simultaneously, he challenged the veracity of Bishop Edwards by rejecting trial by press campaign and demanding that an impartial investigatory committee be set up to review the evidence against CEDIP.

Meanwhile, government officials had conducted hearings on the Easter Island question, taking special note of the report of the captain of the corvette *General Baquedano*. In November 1916 the Ministry of External Affairs, Colonisation Section, decided that Merlet and CEDIP had not complied with the obligations set forth in their lease of 1895, and that the 'prevailing regime on Easter Island has resulted in the misery of its inhabitants, is a hindrance to its progress, and will cause further evils if it is not immediately terminated' (Vergara 1939). Accordingly, the recently signed lease of 1916 was revoked. The Inspector General of Colonisation and Immigration was instructed to take immediate control of the government lands and to provisionally set aside further portions of land for the use of the Rapanui.

A commission was set up to investigate the judicial and administrative problems of the island with a view to safeguarding government interests and improving the living conditions of the inhabitants. Among the appointed commissioners were Bishop Edwards, the captain of the *General Baquedano*, government officials from several departments and a rehabilitated Policarpo Toro. The commission met several times during November 1916. It considered a project for a model agrarian colony, and began to plan a second colonisation strategy. A little of the optimism of the group must have evaporated when an anonymous correspondent of *La Unión* asserted that such schemes were mere soap bubbles, and that the best use of Easter Island would be as a penal colony where exiles could be accompanied by their families. Only a single *colono* was induced to settle on the island.

As is usual in the modern history of Easter Island, mainland events intruded and a temporary solution, rapidly found, became the basis for future operations. A court case between CEDIP and the government ground to an inconclusive halt, allegedly because of 'instructions from above' (Bulnes 1927). International incidents called Bishop Edwards from Santiago. Without his driving presence the commission also collapsed. Because of the continuing mainland 'social crisis', Easter Island was once more relegated to the status of a very minor issue.

During this period of tension CEDIP, with its exceptionally good contacts in influential circles, was able to convince the Ministry of External Affairs to grant a new lease of the government-owned lands. Known as the *Temperamento provisorio*, the new lease treated the island as a single unit for the first time. In this way the government asserted its claim to ownership of the entire land surface in a manner least offensive to the company, which remained in effective control.

The document enjoined CEDIP to regulate land use, conserve the stock, prevent any further loss of statues or other artefacts to occasional visitors, provide land for a leprosarium, give help to the native fishery, provide the *subdelegado* with meat for native use, provide provisions for naval vessels and support a Chilean administrator and his family. Three thousand hectares in the Hangaroa area were to be given to the Rapanui. The lot of the islanders was somewhat improved by these measures. Unlike the original lease, however, these duties were balanced by the omission of any obligations with regard to rent, maintenance of Chilean settlers, construction and maintenance of piers and coaling stations, provisions of medical assistance to ships' crews or maintenance of annual links with mainland Chile. A more realistic stance was clearly being taken by government circles, themselves unable or unwilling to devote the energies of the state to the development of their Pacific island.

Although some of the omitted clauses had become unnecessary, their omission seemed significant to certain Chileans. To these it appeared that the company now had even greater control over the destiny of Easter Island than before their hard-fought campaign.

Later problems

It was not until 1929 that the Chilean government, led by Ibañez, attempted once more to gain effective control of the island. Mainland political instability prevented this, and in 1935 CEDIP was able to win a further 20 year lease, although recognising 'the absolute dominion of the government over all the lands and shores which comprise Easter Island' (Vergara 1939). A *Reglamento de régimen interno de vida y trabajo en la Isla de Pascua*, whose motive was to enforce mainland labour codes on the island, effectively regulated CEDIP into a position of even greater paternalistic control. Both the Rapanui and the few Chilean officials seconded to the island in the 1930s remained wholly dependent upon CEDIP for shelter, food and communication with the mainland.

Only in the 1950s, with a new perception of Easter Island's value as a trans-Pacific stopover for scheduled air flights, did the national government eventually take effective action to gain *de facto* control of the island. Government in Chile at this time was radical in tone, and in 1953 revoked CEDIP's lease 3 years before its termination. There was apparently no objection from the Rapanui, who were reported to be *impregnados de Chilenidad* (*El Mercurio* 29 January 1952).

President Ibañez's decree states why the Chilean government was eager to assume total control: 'the island's position in the Pacific Ocean renders it of overwhelming geostrategic importance for national defence, and especially for the defence of the continent' (*El Diario Oficial* 5 October 1953). Accordingly, company rule was replaced by a Chilean navy administrator. This proved to be yet another of the temporary expedients by which Chile had succeeded in keeping Easter Island under autocratic rule since 1888. Many Rapanui compared the naval authorities unfavourably with CEDIP, and a mild 'revolution' occurred in the mid-1960s. This secured the Rapanui voting rights in Chile for the first time, and led to the establishment of a municipality. But after less than a decade of civilian government, the island reverted to the military authorities following the Chilean coup of 1973.

Conclusions

The melange of multinational corporation, host government and native population is at best a volatile one. Of the actors in the Easter Island drama, the company proved by far the most powerful during the long period of *de jure* Chilean sovereignty from 1888 to 1953. Successive attempts by government officials to implement their legal authority were repelled by corporate strategies from reasoned argument to covert influence of persons in high positions. Indeed, it appears that between 1888 and 1953, Chile, beset by recurrent mainland problems, not only lacked the will to organise its Polynesian colony, but also was unable even to sustain a high degree of interest. Despite the efforts of the Chilean government, the company was seen by outsiders as able to 'impress its will on the land and exercise a godlike power over life and death' (Casey 1942). Casey's, however, was a somewhat exaggerated view of company power.

On the island itself the contention was ultimately between the company manager and the Rapanui. According to a manager of the 1930s: 'There's no law out here. This place is like the American frontier in "forty-nine"' (see Casey 1942, 248). Agitation, unrest and labour troubles continued into the 1940s, but these feeble Rapanui protests could often be quelled by withholding cash, sugar, flour and other items in great demand.

Moreover, the sheep masters demonstrated an acute perception of Rapanui psychology in their selective support of Polynesian life-styles. The manager's ranch-house was built upon the sacred site of the island-wide Orongo cult ceremony. This sacred rite was then secularised in the annual sheep shearing festivities (Porteous 1978b). The non-regular demands for work typical of a sheep ranch, the occasional largesse in the form of mutton, and frequent Rapanui sheep rustling, usually condoned, all contributed to the creation of a *modus vivendi* which proved acceptable to company and Rapanui alike. Both missionaries and government officials remained largely on the periphery of this mutual-support system.

The Rapanui, indeed, were able to adjust to their changed circumstances after 1888 by, in effect, 'being all things to all men'. The naked, starving wretches seen by the missionaries became daring sheep rustlers by night, some of them having the effrontery to sell the rustled sheepskins back to the company. Occasionally aroused by some grave injustice to murder or brief rebellion, they were unwilling or unable to generate a sustained anti-company effort. For, as in most company estates, the benefits of company rule, in this case in the form of free meat and occasional work, greatly outweighed the paternalistic disadvantages. Even today it is not uncommon for elderly Rapanui to lament the passing of the CEDIP era. Although it is unlikely that the Rapanui, under the present regime, will ever control their own destiny (Porteous, 1980), they at least have the satisfaction of telling visitors that 'it now takes 500 Chileans to do what one company manager did thirty years ago'.

References

Bienvenido de Estella, R. P. 1919. Ocho meses entre los canacas pascuences. *Revista Católica* **19**, 182–91.

Bienvenido de Estella, R. P. 1920. *Los misterios de la Isla de Pascua*. Santiago: Cervantes.

Bulnes, A. 1927. *Informe sobre concesion de la Isla de Pascua*. Report to the Controller General, Chile.

Casey, R. J. 1942. *Easter Island: home of the scornful gods*. London: Elkin, Mathew & Marrott.

Dillinger, J. 1916. Letter to M. Williamson. La Escocesa archive, Santiago.

Edmunds, P. H. 1916. Letter to Compañía Esplotadora de la Isla de Pascua. La Escocesa archive, Santiago.

Edwards, R. 1918. *La Isla de Pascua*. Santiago: San José.

El Mercurio newspaper, Santiago.

Green, F. T. 1916. Letters to Messrs The Easter Island Co. La Escocesa archive, Santiago.

La Escocesa archive, Santiago. Uncatalogued CEDIP documents, located at Compania de Inversiones 'La Escocesa' Limitada, Calle MacIver 142, Santiago.

La Unión newspaper, Valparaiso.

Mamak, A. and G. McCall 1978. *Paradise postponed: essays on research and development in the South Pacific*. Oxford: Pergamon.

Porteous, J. D. 1972. Urban transplantation in Chile. *Geogr. Rev.* **62**, 455–78.

Porteous, J. D. 1973. The company state: a Chilean case-study. *Can. Geogr.* **17**, 113–26.

Porteous, J. D. 1974. Social class in Atacama company towns. *Ann. Assoc. Am. Geogs* **64**, 409–17.

Porteous, J. D. 1978a. Urban symbiosis: a study of company town camp followers in the Atacama desert. *Can. J. Latin Am. Stud.* **3**, 210–21.

Porteous, J. D. 1978b. Easter Island: the Scottish connection. *Geogr. Rev.* **68**, 145–56.

Porteous, J. D. 1980. The development of tourism on Easter Island. *Geography* **65**, 137–8.

Porteous, J. D. 1981. *The modernization of Easter Island*. Victoria, BC: Western Geographical Series Vol. 19.

Rocuant, D. E. 1916. *La Isla de Pascua*. Valparaiso: Universo.

Routledge, S. 1919. *The mystery of Easter Island*. London: Sifton, Praed.

Vergara de la P., V. 1939. *La Isla de Pascua: dominacíon y dominio*. Santiago: Instituto de Geografía Militar.
Vives Solar, J. I. 1920. Review of Bienvenido de Estella, *Los misterios de la Isla de Pascua*. In *El Mercurio*, 14 November 1920.

7 Gender versus ethnic pluralism in Caribbean agriculture

JANET D. HENSHALL

The commercialisation of agricultural production, consequent on the world wide expansion of capitalism from the 16th century onwards, led to a variety of labour practices in the colonial periphery. In the West Indies, the introduction of plantation agriculture, which required a large, easily controlled but relatively unskilled labour force, led to an influx of different ethnic groups into the region. Thus the demands of colonial agriculture created the basis of the plural society of the contemporary Caribbean (M. G. Smith 1965). From the beginning, women of all ethnic groups have been part of this capitalist expansion, contributing both directly with their labour and, also, by providing support for the family through their subsistence farming activities, releasing the men to work on the production of commercial crops.

Only in the last decade has research on the role of women in the Third World been seen as vital in understanding the processes of change in rural areas. This interest was stimulated by the publication of Boserup's *Women and development* in 1970. Boserup's most important contribution was to draw attention to cross-cultural diversity in the division of labour by sex in agriculture. Her analysis suggests that this division is not based on particular cultural perceptions of what is correct or proper nor on physiology or biological determinants. Moreover, the agricultural role of women is not immutable but can vary over time in accordance with changes in socio-economic variables. Primarily, she sees changes in the division of labour between men and women as the result of changes in population density and farming techniques (Boserup 1970, 18). Boserup also argues that social stratification, as reflected in the composition of the labour force and land tenure systems, is of great importance in the areal differentiation of gender roles (Boserup 1970, 30–1). Thus, where there are few agricultural proletarians, as in Africa, women make up a high proportion of the family labour force, but in areas such as Latin America, where wage labour is important, women form a much smaller part of the workforce. Furthermore, she feels that the national percentage of women as 'own-account farmers' is directly related to their ownership of land, particularly as this is affected by inheritance laws.

The Caribbean is an especially suitable area in which to test some of Boserup's ideas on cross cultural differences in gender roles in farming, because of its ethnic pluralism. The distinctiveness of the region is noted by Boserup herself. She sees the West Indies as an anomalous area in her continental-scale regional classification. She suggests that Jamaica, as distinct from Cuba, the Dominican Republic and Puerto Rico, has a relatively high proportion of women farmers and is thus more similar to West Africa than to Latin America. She explains this Jamaican pattern in ethnic terms, relating it to the preservation of African farming traditions among a population mainly descended from African slaves (Boserup 1970, 63). This explanation appears to contradict her earlier generalisations about the minor importance of ethnic differences in determining gender role differentiation.

Plantation agriculture and ethnic diversity

The development of West Indian sugar plantations in the 17th century created a demand for labour. After the post-Columbian decimation of the Amerindians, African slaves were introduced to work in the fields and mills of the plantations. The abolition of slavery in 1834 in the British territories was followed by another period of labour shortage for the planters, but this time it was accompanied by the growth of an independent peasantry. The former slaves shunned work on plantations and whenever possible moved to the towns or sought to cultivate their own small plots of land. In order to secure a steady supply of labour and keep wages down, the planters once again looked overseas for workers. Many ethnic groups were introduced at this time, including Chinese, Javanese and Portuguese, but the most successful immigrants, from the point of view of the sugar industry, were those from India, who became known in the Caribbean as East Indians. Between 1837 and 1917 about 550 000 East Indians entered the West Indies on contracts binding them to service as indentured labourers on the plantations for a period of 5 years (Roberts & Byrne 1966). About one-quarter of the East Indians went to Jamaica, Martinique and Guadeloupe and a few to the Windward Islands, but they were not numerous enough in these territories to have much impact on the economic or social structure (Lowenthal 1967, 606). Only in the larger, less densely populated territories of Surinam, Guyana and Trinidad, where land was easily available to the ex-slaves, did East Indians come to play a major role.

The East Indian indentured labourers who came to Trinidad were free to leave the island after their period of indenture but many chose to accept free lots of Crown Land after 1869, in lieu of a return passage to India. Possession of land became an obsession and, between 1885 and 1912, 89 222 acres (35 680 ha) of land were sold or granted to East Indians in Trinidad. After 1900 the indentured workers, on arrival, were able to join societies whose members then bought land in the name of one of the group, while others worked the land. In this way, immigrants could become land owners in their first year of indenture and consequently the tendency to desert the estates to work their own land increased (Weller 1968, 51). East Indians came to dominate small farming in Trinidad, growing sugar cane, vegetables and cocoa, and introducing the cultivation of paddy rice.

Both African and East Indian immigrants to the West Indies were forced to mix with people of different tribal, language, caste or religious backgrounds within their own ethnic groups, making the preservation of traditional cultures very difficult. Both groups suffered under forced labour, during which period gender role differentiation was determined by an elite of a different ethnic background. During slavery women toiled as strenuously as men on the plantations. Barbadian slave women, in particular, were expected to carry baskets of manure weighing as much as 70 lb (31.5 kg) and when they returned to their huts at night faced additional household duties (Levy 1980, 10). However, the cost of feeding a large slave labour force persuaded many planters to allow peasant-like activities to develop. Mintz has shown that as early as 1672 in Jamaica, slaves were cultivating subsistence plots at weekends and slave women were involved in buying and selling goods on Sunday mornings in public markets (Mintz 1964, 25–51). This growth of marginal production and internal trade within the plantation slave economy with its concomitant sexual division of labour occurred to varying degrees in Nevis, Montserrat, Tobago, St Vincent, Dominica, Grenada, Barbados and St Kitts, as well as in Jamaica (Edwards 1980, 5).

The mid-19th century in the West Indies saw the introduction by the colonial authorities of Victorian ideas about the role of women. With the ending of apprenticeship in 1838 the women were the first to retire from agricultural work (Morsen 1841) but, as many of the male ex-slaves left the small islands in search of higher wages elsewhere and food prices rose, women began to return to agricultural work in order to support their families. The problems of this inflationary period produced the curious situation described by Levy, in that 'while the planters criticized mothers for neglecting their offspring, they preferred to hire females, whom they considered more regular than males in their work habits' (Levy 1980, 113). In Trinidad, at this time, labour demand was being met by indentured labourers from India and for economic reasons the planters wanted to bring in only able-bodied men rather than women and children (Tikasingh 1973), but the British government insisted on a small proportion of female workers to prevent immoral behaviour and prostitution. These indentured labourers of both sexes were treated as severely as slaves had been, since many estate managers wished to extract the maximum returns from their investment during the period of contract (Lowenthal 1972, 62). Harry (1980, 35) quotes a newspaper report

based on interviews with three women who had been indentured in the late
19th century. According to their story, 'In the cultivation you will find that the
women dominated the group. They were out early in the fields performing
hazardous duties, like dropping lime and phosphate of ammonia, planting
foods on the estates, that is vegetable crops and ground provisions, manuring,
cutlassing, weeding, cutting canes, loading them on carts and most of the time
carrying the canes on their heads.' (*Battlefront* 19 May 1978.) In addition to this
work on the plantations, women were responsible for childcare, housework
and general family maintenance. Thus, during the periods of forced labour
there was very little differentiation of agricultural activities based on either
gender or ethnicity.

Gender roles under a free labour system

Boserup suggests that much of the areal differentiation in gender roles is
related to the structure of the labour force. In those world regions where there
are few agricultural proletarians, as in Africa and parts of South-East Asia,
women make up a high proportion of the family labour force, but in areas
where wage labour is important, as in Arab countries and Latin America,
women form a low percentage of the farm workforce. In the Caribbean today
overall female activity rates appear to reflect ethnic differences within the
region, with those countries such as Jamaica and Barbados where the
population is predominantly Afro-Caribbean having rates similar to those of
European countries but lower than those found in Africa. Trinidad and
Guyana, with large East Indian population components, have female activity
rates about half that of Jamaica but still considerably higher than those of the
Muslim nations of the world. Gordon directly links this difference within the
Caribbean to the influence of Hindu and Muslim cultural attitudes to women's
work outside the home (Gordon 1981, 18). Yet work in agriculture is often
thought of as part of a woman's household responsibilities and areal differentiation in agricultural activity rates for women appears to be more closely
linked to economic rather than cultural or ethnic differences.

The decade following slave emancipation was marked by a rapid decline in
the agricultural labour force as the women and children amongst the ex-slaves
moved into domestic occupations and education, respectively, and, where
land was available, the men became peasant farmers. The economic difficulties
of the mid-19th century brought a slight increase in the rural proletariat, but
this was followed by a century of relative stability in the absolute numbers of
agricultural workers in most of the islands of the Eastern Caribbean. The food
shortages of the Second World War brought the agricultural workforce to its
highest level since slavery, but this peak was followed by a rapid decline as
alternative occupations became available to the proletariat (Momsen 1969,
515–617). In Jamaica the decline in the labour force came earlier, and from

Table 7.1 Percentage of women in the agricultural labour force of selected Caribbean territories in 1946, 1961 and 1970.

Territory	Percentage of women in agricultural labour force			Agriculture's share of total employment, 1970 (%)		
	1946	1961	1970	Male	Female	Total
Antigua	47.6	59.2	25.3	12.0	8.4	10.6
Barbados	48.8	52.5	38.3	16.5	15.3	16.0
Dominica	40.4	55.0	32.8	46.6	27.2	39.5
Grenada	48.9	48.9	40.4	34.2	31.9	33.3
St Kitts–Nevis	44.0	44.4	33.8	36.7	30.1	34.2
St Lucia	39.3	47.0	29.9	46.1	27.8	39.7
St Vincent	46.9	49.9	31.8	32.2	23.1	29.0

Sources: Census Statistics, Jamaica 1950, 1976; British Development Division in the Caribbean 1968.

1890 onwards the rural proletariat began to migrate to the towns (Eisner 1961, 350–1). Women led this urbanward trend and their participation rate in the Jamaican agricultural labour force fell from 49.2 per cent in 1891 to 19.9 per cent in 1943 (Roberts 1957, 87). In the smaller, less urbanised islands the postwar decline in the agricultural workforce was accompanied by a relative increase in female agricultural workers, especially in the unpaid family worker category. Garrett noted a similar change in Chile over the same period and suggested that this represented a serious deterioration in the ability of women to obtain those sorts of jobs which would allow them to support them-selves and their children (Garrett 1976, 30). These postwar changes support Boserup's theory that agriculture comes to depend increasingly on unpaid female family labour as the number of paid agricultural workers declines.

Over the past two decades the decline in the number of farm workers has accelerated and the number of women workers in the agricultural sector has decreased both relatively and absolutely (Table 7.1). At the beginning of the 1960s women provided over half the agricultural labour in many islands and were especially important in the unpaid family worker category. By 1970 only a third of the agricultural workforce was female in most of the Windward and Leeward Islands, and in Trinidad women constituted a mere 22 per cent of the farm workers in 1977 (Trinidad Central Statistical Office 1978). Yet despite this decline, the most striking development in the West Indian labour force since 1970 has been the rapid increase in the growth rate of the female labour force, which has exceeded that of male workers in virtually all territories except Jamaica (International Labour Office 1977). The service sector has now superseded agriculture as the major employer throughout the region. Women have been quick to take advantage of this development and there are now twice as many women as men in white-collar jobs (Hope 1980, 274). Industrial growth has also brought new opportunities for women. Women provide a third of the industrial labour force in Trinidad (Trinidad Central Statistical Office 1978) and Monk (1978) has shown how, in the coffee-growing region of Puerto Rico, government programmes encouraging the dispersal of industries into rural areas have provided jobs for women rather than for men. However, the present economic recession appears to be hurting female non-agricultural employment more than that of men, and in the region as a whole the unemployment rate for women is 10.7 per cent whereas for men it is 6.8 per cent (Women and Development Unit 1981, 15).

The decline in the female agricultural labour force is most marked in those territories where alternative employment opportunities are open to women. There is anecdotal evidence that high inflation is forcing many poor women back into subsistence agriculture in order to feed their families, but this is generally an occupation of last resort. Female participation in the familial labour force is least on those farms which are successful enough to be able to employ wage labour. MacMillan noted this trend some 15 years ago in his study of East Indian market gardening in Trinidad.

'As long as market-gardening in Aranguez remains relatively profitable, there will be a continued decline in the importance of the labour contribution of the women and younger children, and most family labour will be supplied by the head of the family and any adult male dependents. For it is becoming generally accepted that manual work should not be done by women, and that children should only help in the garden if they want to, and if it does not interfere with their studies.' (MacMillan 1967, 195)

Deere (1982, 797) has described a similar relationship in Peru between the larger, more prosperous peasant holdings and minimal female agricultural labour participation.

In the socialist economies of the region it has become public policy to attempt to reverse the decline in female participation in farming. Prior to 1959 only 2 per cent of the Cuban agricultural labour force were female, but because of a post-revolutionary shortage of labour in rural areas women have been encouraged to become rural workers. However, as a result of the seasonal pattern of demand associated with the major Cuban crops, women have tended to form a reserve labour force in both collective and private sectors, as they do in many parts of Latin America (Henshall 1982, 1). In Cuba women were organised into a seasonal labour force for the state farms and co-operatives (Croll 1979, 28–9) and were also given agricultural training. In the first post-revolutionary decade 55 000 Cuban peasant women were taught agricultural skills and in 1973 some 107 000 were shown how to raise livestock and vegetables on their smallholdings for sale to state agencies. Although the Family Code of 1975 formally enforced the principle of the sharing of domestic tasks when both marital partners are employed, there is no evidence that this co-operation has actually occurred in many households. In general, Cuban peasant women have resolved the conflict between their domestic duties and the demands of the farm by co-operating with other women in matters of child care and resisting inducements to take on paid employment outside the home whenever possible. In Jamaica, under Michael Manley's Premiership, women were included in many of the new farm settlements, and in Grenada, after the People's Revolutionary Government came into power in 1979, agricultural development programmes increasingly involved women. In both these islands the decision to increase the role of women in agriculture was necessitated by balance of payments problems which made it essential to improve self-sufficiency in food.

Thus, the historical evidence from many parts of the Caribbean indicates that, as Boserup suggests, gender roles in agriculture are decided by economic necessity rather than cultural attitudes. Whether we look at the matriarchal black societies of Barbados, Grenada and Jamaica, at the patriarchal East Indian families of Trinidad or at the equally patriarchal Hispanic society of Cuba, Caribbean women rarely enter agriculture from choice. At the national level the decision to increase female participation in agriculture may be contrary to the prevailing political ideology, as in 19th century Barbados, or may conform to it as in post-revolutionary Cuba, but it is primarily based on the perceived labour needs of agriculture. Whenever possible Caribbean women of all ethnic groups have sought to move out of agriculture, yet their contribution to work in the fields, care of small stock and decision-making remains significant.

The extent of female agricultural participation

Official statistics led Boserup to suggest that women had an unexpectedly high rate of participation in agriculture in the West Indies, but these statistics may well actually underestimate the true level of involvement of women in the region's farming activities. Rural women are usually multiple job holders, acting as housewives and mothers as well as taking part in remunerated and unremunerated work in income-generating activities. In a patriarchal system, such as that of the East Indians in Trinidad, a woman's first duty is to her home and family and so she will describe herself as a housewife despite her many agricultural activities. Even in matriarchal Afro-Caribbean families women gain most status as mothers, and at the same time agricultural work is held in very low esteem because of its low wages and association with slavery. Consequently, social pressures on both ethnic groups will tend to encourage under-recording of women's role in agriculture.

Female members of Caribbean farm households may play three economic roles related to agriculture. They may be the decision-maker for all or some of the aspects of the family farm, they may be responsible for marketing and even processing the output of their own and other farm enterprises, and they may work as paid or unpaid agricultural labourers on the land. These roles are not mutually exclusive and any one individual may fill all three tasks either at the same time or at various stages in her life. In particular communities, one of these occupations may predominate, but the role is not culturally determined and the activity pattern may change at any time as a result of exogenous factors.

Boserup drew particular attention to the relatively high proportion of women as 'own-account farmers' in the West Indies, but this is the one female agricultural role that is most likely to be under-reported. On most female-operated farms the woman is also the head of the household. In 1970 there were 238 781 such female-headed families in the Commonwealth Caribbean, constituting 35 per cent of all households in the region (Buvinic & Youssef 1978, 59). This regional total blurs many intra-regional variations that reflect, to some extent, ethnic differences in family structure. In those territories which have predominantly Afro-Caribbean populations, the role of women is closely linked to the importance of the matrifocal family so often described in studies of the region. Both R. T. Smith (1960) and Clarke (1957) feel that matrifocality is related to the economic marginality of men in many Caribbean societies. Solien (1959) suggests that migrant wage labour of the recurrent type that is found in so many societies of the region produces an excess of adult females and thus forces households into matrifocality. Male marginality is most common among lower-class families, a large number of whom are dependent on small-scale agriculture. In East Indian societies, on the other hand, the institution of marriage is stronger and women are rarely left as the sole support of their children. These differences in family structure can clearly be seen in the figures on female-headed households, which range from 50 per cent in the highly migratory Afro-Caribbean population of St Kitts–Nevis to 25 per cent in Trinidad and Tobago, where there is a major concentration of East Indians (Buvinic & Youssef 1978, 99).

In questionnaire surveys of 1544 small-scale farmers in nine Caribbean territories taken over the period 1963–1979, women constituted 35 per cent of the farmers (Table 7.2). The proportion of female own-account farmers ranged from 55 per cent in Montserrat, which has had a very high rate of emigration, to 16 per cent in St Vincent. This intra-territorial variation does in part reflect real differences but is also indicative of the various classifications used in the surveys, the attitudes of the investigator and the type of farming being studied. Boserup found it remarkable that official statistics in Jamaica reported that women made up 13 per cent of the farm operators. Yet other studies by the United States Agency for International Development and the Jamaican Ministry of Agriculture found that in the central mountains of Jamaica 22 per cent of the smallholdings are managed by women and, even when they are not the principal farm operators, 47 per cent of female members

Table 7.2 Sex of decision-makers on farms of less than 10 acres (4 ha) in selected Eastern Caribbean territories.

Island	Year of survey	Sample size	Percentage farms with female decision-makers
Barbados	1963	207	53.1
Barbuda	1971–73	234	28.2
Grenada	1969	256	20.7
Martinique	1964	203	35.5
Montserrat	1972	112	54.5
Montserrat★	1973	60	36.6
Nevis	1979	91	30.8
St Lucia	1964	187	42.8
St Lucia★	1971	47	17.0
St Vincent	1972	67	16.4
Trinidad	1979	80	28.8
Total		1544	34.6

★ Sample drawn from vegetable specialists only.

Sources: Field surveys for Barbados, Martinique, Nevis, Montserrat (1973) and St Lucia. Data for St Vincent and Montserrat (1972) based on 10 per cent sample of the 1972 Agricultural Census questionnaires. Data for Grenada from Brierley (1974), for Barbuda from Berleant-Schiller (1977) and for Trinidad from Harry (1980).

of the household regularly help in farm production activities and a further 21 per cent help at least in planting and harvesting (Chaney & Lewis 1980, 23). In a survey in Barbados I found women to be farm operators on 30 per cent of the farms but on a further 22 per cent detailed questioning revealed that women were the major decision-makers, in most cases because the nominal male farm operator had a full time, off-farm job and little interest in agriculture.

In Grenada the relationship between census data and that based on sample surveys is reversed, with census statistics indicating that 24 per cent of farmers are women (Zuvekas 1978, 2), whereas Brierley's enquiry found only 19 per cent of the sample farmers were women (Brierley 1974). Interestingly, Brierley did show that women were more important on the non-commercial farm enterprises, making up 31 per cent of the farm operators in this subgroup. This tendency for women to concentrate in the subsistence sector is supported by evidence from St Lucia and Montserrat. In both islands, the surveys of specialist vegetable producers, taken in 1971 and 1973, respectively, found a smaller proportion of women farm operators than did the earlier surveys of the general small farming population of these same islands. This difference could indicate change over time, although in Montserrat there was a gap of only 8 months between the two studies. It seems more probable that these differences reflect a generally low level of female participation in innovative commercial agriculture.

However, it is not only the actual numbers of individuals participating which enables us to measure gender roles in agriculture, but also the type of agricultural labour performed by different members of the farm family over the annual agricultural cycle. In 1970 Boserup (15–35) suggested an initial division between extensive hoe agriculture, associated with shifting cultivation and principally involving food crops grown by women, and intensive plough agriculture, carried out primarily by men. With modernisation a further dichotomy appears, with men generally in charge of commercial crops whereas women concentrate on food crops for home consumption. Rogers (1980, 166) goes further and suggests that the primary impact of Western influence on gender roles in a society is to transfer much or all of the non-farm subsistence work to women, followed later by a transfer of subsistence farming. Case studies indicate that in many cultures men take care of the larger animals which are grazed away from the homestead whereas women are responsible for the smaller animals which are kept penned in the farmyard. Men clear the land and do the initial ploughing, whereas women plant, weed and help with the harvest. An interesting version of this division of labour is seen in Jamaica, where, on steep hillsides, men do the preparation of the soil with a fork for both subsistence and commercial crops, and such work is often called 'ploughing', perhaps in recognition that a man would do it with a plough if he could (Chaney & Lewis 1980, 27). The tasks that women do also vary by farm size (Deere 1982, 805), especially when implements are involved. On larger farms, using many modern inputs, female participation is limited, but on the smaller farms there is a higher level of sharing of tasks and decisions between the sexes.

Gender roles in Trinidad and Nevis

If the cross-cultural diversity in the division of labour by sex in agriculture, which Boserup drew to our attention, is a stable factor in the pattern of gender roles, then it should be seen most clearly in the plural society of the Caribbean. Two ethnic groups dominate farming in the Commonwealth Caribbean: people of Indian origin in Trinidad and Guyana, and elsewhere descendants of African slaves. Boserup noted that in Africa women play a major part in agricultural production, generally working longer hours than men, whereas in India caste and religion restrict many women to work within the home. She herself felt that there was some transfer of these cultural attitudes in agriculture to the Caribbean.

In 1979 the writer was involved with two field surveys of women farmers in the Caribbean. In the island of Nevis all 99 of the farmers interviewed were of Afro-Caribbean ethnic origin. In Trinidad and Tobago only 40 per cent of the population is East Indian but in Indra Harry's (1980) random sample survey of 130 farmers, 62 per cent were Hindu East Indians, 11 per cent Muslim East Indians, 8.5 per cent Christian East Indians or racially mixed, and only 18.5

Table 7.3 Sexual division of labour on the farm by time of day worked.

Time of day		Percentage of workers			
		Nevis		Trinidad	
		Male (*n* = 71)	Female (*n* = 28)	Male (*n* = 116)	Female (*n* = 114)
very early	(04.00 to 06.00)	12	7	0	0
early morning	(06.00 to 08.00)	63	48	55	77
mid-morning	(08.00 to 10.00)	68	68	72	72
late morning	(10.00 to 12.00)	44	30	60	61
mid-day	(12.00 to 14.00)	16	20	30	57
mid-afternoon	(14.00 to 16.00)	37	21	52	47
late afternoon	(16.00 to 18.00)	35	25	22	18
early evening	(18.00 to 20.00)	1	0	0	0

Sources: for Nevis, fieldwork (1979); for Trinidad, adapted from Harry (1980).

per cent were Afro-West Indians. This distribution illustrates the dominance of East Indians in Trinidad's agriculture. If cultural differences are of any importance in determining gender roles in agriculture, one might expect to see the Asian and African patterns noted by Boserup repeated in Trinidad and Nevis. Boserup presents statistics showing that African women work an annual average of 15–20 hours a week in agriculture whereas men average about 15 hours. In India women tend to put in about as many hours as their sisters in Africa but the men work twice as long (Boserup 1970, 21 & 25). Harry's work in Trinidad revealed no significant differences in the hours worked per day by men and women farmers, either in the busy crop period or in the quieter time of the agricultural cycle (Harry 1980, 76). On average men worked 4.9 days per week and women 4.8, although there were sectoral differences. In the sugar cane sector men worked an average of 5.1 days whereas women worked only 3.0 days. On dairy and rice farms women worked more days per week than men. There was little difference in the number of hours worked per day by each sex on any type of farm, but there were differences in the actual part of the day worked. Women were less likely than men to work in the late afternoon (Table 7.3), because they were usually involved with household chores and meal preparation at that time. Men who had off-farm employment were forced to concentrate their farm work in the early morning and late afternoon.

In Nevis, on the other hand, there were distinct differences in the time spent on agriculture by men and women. On average, women worked 4.8 days per week compared with 5.5 days for men. Seasonal differences were also more apparent among women than men: women averaged 25 hours and men 35 hours per week in the busy time of the agricultural year and 18 versus 27 hours in the quiet time of the year. Thus the weekly hours worked by women fell from 72 per cent of male hours in the busy season to 66 per cent in the quiet season. Nevisian farm women are also much more likely to do all their agricultural work in the morning than are Trinidadian women (Table 7.3). Although men are more likely than women to have off-farm jobs, they still contribute the greater proportion of the farm labour. These results from Trinidad and Nevis appear to contradict the ethnic pattern of the sexual distribution of time spent in agricultural labour in India and Africa.

The particular tasks performed by men and women on the farm vary according to the main product of the holding but are consistent within each sector. In general, in both Nevis and Trinidad, women perform the less strenuous tasks such as planting, weeding, fertilising, mounding up of soil around young plants and harvesting. Men undertake the preparation of the land and the transporting of the produce from the fields. In Nevis there is little differentiation among holdings by type of farming, and cotton is the only major commercial export crop. Subsistence food production is important on most farms and the sexual division of labour shows little spatial variation. Women will do most tasks except soil preparation, especially the digging of yam mounds, and they are usually responsible for weeding, harvesting and the picking of cotton. In Trinidad gender roles are related to farming type. If we ignore the dairy and cacao farms, which in Harry's survey were 25 per cent Afro-Caribbean operated, and look only at those segments of the farm economy totally dominated by East Indians, that is tobacco, cane, rice and vegetable farms, then differences become apparent. The average tobacco farm employed 3.6 male and 4.8 female workers. Preparation of land, nursery care of young plants, spraying, irrigation, transporting of leaves from the field and the stringing and hanging of leaves are male tasks. Hired women workers mound up soil around the young plants in the fields and work with the farm wife in fertilising, picking and packing the leaves. Children help with deflowering the plants, and husband and wife work together in planting, grading and preparing the tobacco for sale. On the sugar cane farms women play a very minor role, with each farm hiring an average of 3.7 men and 1.3 women. The male spouse works on chemical spraying of weed killers, and on burning, cutting and transporting the cane. Hired female workers are involved in planting, fertilising, cutting and loading the cane onto animal-drawn carts or tractor trailers. Female spouses help only in fertilising the cane fields. On cane farms owned by women most of the work is done by hired male workers. On rice farms during the peak labour periods of planting and harvesting, an average of 3.0 male and 4.6 female workers are hired. The male head of the household maintains the banks of the paddy fields and the nursery plots, cuts the ripened stalks, transports the harvest from the fields and beats the stalks to separate the grains of rice. Women's tasks centre on planting, cutting, bundling, winnowing and preparing the rice for sale. Vegetable farms are most intensively cultivated. As is common on the other farms, men are in charge of nursery beds and spraying, whereas women take care of weeding, fertilising and tying plants to stakes. Children, as in the tobacco sector, are involved in many tasks on vegetable farms. Women dominate the post-harvest processing and preparation of crops for sale or home consumption.

These gender role patterns found in Trinidad among East Indians may be compared to those found by Bagchi (1981) in India. Paddy rice cultivation traditionally involved male broadcasting of the seed, and female transplanting, weeding and harvesting, but the introduction of high yielding varieties of rice has changed the sexual allocation of these tasks. Today, sowing, weeding and harvesting have become tasks shared by both men and women (Bagchi 1981, 111). The processing of the crops and preparation for sale, as in Trinidad, is predominantly a female occupation, but mechanisation is rapidly changing these sex roles in India. Bagchi (1981, 113) feels that mechanisation of crop processing is not only eroding female employment and income opportunities but is also interfering with the status of village women by dispossessing them of services they traditionally provided for family and community.

In Trinidad, mechanisation is also changing the pattern of gender roles, although the use of mechanical equipment, fertilisers, weed killers and pesticides, and irrigation on male- and female-operated farms is not statistically different (Harry 1980, 88). Application of both chemical and inorganic fertilisers is generally carried out jointly, but other tasks involving modern inputs are predominantly male. Of the 96 farmers in the Trinidad survey who used insecticides, weed killers and fungicides, men performed the task on 77 farms whereas it was jointly carried out on 10 farms. Only five females, all of whom owned their own farms, sprayed their own crops. On other female-operated farms pest control was delegated to hired or family labour. Most Trinidadian rural women feel that chemical sprays are dangerous and so avoid them whenever possible.

Gender roles in animal husbandry tend to show patterns specific to the type of animal. In most parts of the Caribbean it has been found that women are generally responsible for small animals, whereas men take care of the cattle and equines. In Nevis, where the livestock population doubled between 1946 and 1971, and sheep and goats are of major importance, men are normally in charge of all the animals except poultry and do all the marketing of animal products. In many cases the male farmer does little more than care for his animals morning and evening, and during the day he works off the farm. In Trinidad, men take most responsibility for the care of equines and beef cattle, although work with dairy cattle is shared. All other animals are looked after by women (Harry 1980, 112). Overall, it would appear that in both Trinidad and Nevis it is the level of commercialisation of stock raising that determines the gender roles rather than the type of animal.

Women in both islands take care of the dooryard garden with its fruit, vegetables and spices for home consumption and occasional sale. As in Africa, marketing in much of the Caribbean is a typically female task, and has been seen as such since the days of slavery. In Nevis, most of the marketing of crops is carried out by women, although the sale of animal products is a male prerogative. In Trinidad women are only important in the marketing of minor crops at the farm gate or in the local market. Men organise the sale of major crops to middlemen and marketing boards. With regard to animals, the men generally sell the larger animals and milk, if it has to be transported. Women sell the small animals such as pigs, goats and poultry, which they raise, and when milk is sold at the farm gate, this is a female task. Only six women in the survey sold beef cattle and they all managed their own farms. Thus the survey data do give some indication that East Indian women are less likely to be involved in marketing of farm produce than other Caribbean women.

Surprisingly, despite the differences in family structure, there was little difference in the proportion of small farms run by women in the two islands, but joint management was more common in Trinidad than in Nevis. In Nevis 27 per cent of the holdings were operated by women and 5 per cent jointly by men and women; either husband and wife or mother and son. Of the farms visited in Trinidad 20 per cent were managed by women and 16 per cent were under joint management, but there were some variations between farm types. Women were responsible for farm decision-making on one-quarter of the rice farms and on almost one-third of the dairy farms, whereas over half the cocoa, vegetable and tobacco farms were jointly managed. Only amongst cane farmers was male crop responsibility overwhelmingly pre-eminent (Harry 1980, 69). The traditional export crops of cotton and sugar have almost disappeared in Nevis and the main cash crops grown by small farmers are now peanuts, yams and vegetables for which there seems to be no clear sexual division of responsibility.

In both Nevis and Trinidad women are independent farmers, generally because no male is available to take on the role. In Trinidad, where the tradition of early marriage and many children is only just beginning to break down among East Indians, the women farmers are either widows or separated from their husbands and can call on male members of their extended family for agricultural assistance. Furthermore, the strength of the institution of marriage in Trinidad in the East Indian community encourages joint management of farms to a much greater degree than in Nevis. Among Creole small farmers a variety of non-legalised unions is common, probably because of historical antecedents and as an adjustment to contemporary male marginality. Yet, in Nevis, half the households of women farmers contained adult men, usually sons, who, whether employed or not, had little interest in the farm. Even where marriage or a stable union did exist among Nevisian farm families interviewed, there were several instances of husbands who lived overseas and paid only occasional visits to the wives left behind on the family farm. In some cases where both spouses were able to obtain land in Nevis they each worked their own plots quite separately.

Throughout the Caribbean, land ownership by women is one of the main determinants of female own-account farming (Slater 1977). Inheritance of farmland not only enables a woman to achieve some sort of economic independence but reinforces a social system of matrilocality amongst Afro-Caribbean peoples and patrilocality in East Indian families. However, in neither Trinidad nor Nevis was the variation in tenure types between male- and female-managed farms significant. Thus, in both islands the expected tendency for farms operated by women to be characterised by a predominance of freehold land does not hold true. This unexpected finding is perhaps the result of recent government schemes in both islands, which have made land available to small farmers on leasehold. In Nevis, several estates that have come into government hands have been parcelled out to smallholders of both sexes, and in Trinidad specific projects such as dairy farms have been set up on leased Crown Land. These schemes have attracted the younger women farmers and may well illustrate a growing convergence of independent non-traditional attitudes among West Indian women of all ethnic groups. In both islands land is more easily available for lease, both through government schemes and privately, than elsewhere in the region, so inheritance of land is not such a vital prerequisite for women farmers. In addition, in Trinidad, some of the most prosperous small farms, the market gardens of Aranguez, are all on privately rented land near Port of Spain.

Work elsewhere in the Caribbean has indicated that women farm smaller acreages than men and have holdings with fewer parcels (Henshall 1981). This model tends to hold up in Nevis where the average acreage of the female-managed farm surveyed was only 2.85 acres (1.15 ha) as compared with 6.22 (2.48 ha) for the men, and women's holdings contained an average of 2.1 parcels as against 2.8 for the male-operated farms. In Trinidad, on the other hand, female-operated farms were found to be larger than those of men, with half of them being over 10 acres (4 ha) whereas only 36 per cent of the male- or joint-operated farms were so large. This contrast may be influenced by sectoral differences, as cocoa farms, as a group, had both the largest proportion of women managers and the most freehold land.

It is often suggested that women household heads in the Caribbean are older and less educated than their male counterparts (Buvinic & Youssef 1978, 57–61). This generalisation does not appear to hold true for those household heads who are farmers. In Nevis, the average age of women farmers surveyed was 52.6 years whereas the men were a decade older, with a mean age of 62.4 years. Similar, although somewhat smaller, age differences exist in Trinidad where the average age of the male farmers interviewed was 50.4 years and of females 44.2 years (Harry 1980, 55). These similarities are somewhat surprising given the different life cycle patterns of the two populations. In Nevis, women farm mostly during their 30s and 40s when they have children to feed, or when they are older and have grandchildren dependent on them for subsistence. Nevisian mothers hope that their children will get good jobs and support them in their old age, perhaps even helping them to migrate and join their offspring overseas. Often, however, these migrant children expect their mothers to raise the next generation on the family farm, although they will usually provide some financial support for the children and grandmother. For men the life cycle pattern is very different. They migrate in search of employment at an early age, leaving the mother of their children to maintain the family plot, to which they plan to return on their retirement. Thus Nevisian small farms become increasingly subsistence oriented as the farmer gets older. In Trinidad, both men and women farmers tend to be younger than in many of the smaller islands because of lower rates of overseas emigration and possibly higher levels of economic return from agriculture. Young women often have joint responsibility for the farm with their husbands. East Indian women who are farming because they have lost their husbands will tend to hand over responsibility for the farm to their sons as they become older and much of the woman's work on the holding will be taken over by daughters-in-law.

Elsewhere in the Eastern Caribbean no significant difference in educational levels between men and women farmers has been found (Henshall 1981), despite the contention of Buvinic and Youssef (1978) that female heads of household are less educated than male. The field surveys in Nevis and Trinidad suggest some reasons for these conflicting findings. In Nevis it was found that women were significantly better educated than men, with an average of 8.7 years of schooling as against 7.7 years for the men. There are two major reasons for this difference. It is in part due to the age difference between male and female farmers, with women, because they are generally younger than male farmers, more likely to have benefited from the gradual improvement in educational facilities over the years on the island. In addition, the more educated the man, the more likely he is to be able to emigrate or find work other than in agriculture, whereas a woman may be trapped in subsistence farming because of dependent children and the lack of alternative employment opportunities on Nevis, despite her education. In Trinidad, the situation is somewhat different. Traditionally, East Indian families educated their sons but not their daughters, a discriminatory attitude not generally found among Afro-Caribbean families. Today this attitude is rapidly changing and many young East Indian women are now being educated for urban white-collar jobs. However, the traditional discriminatory view probably explains Harry's findings which revealed that, for her sample, the average male respondent had received 5.3 years of schooling as compared with 3.9 years for the women farmers. The only exception was in dairying, where the mean years of schooling were 4.7 for men and 5.6 for women (Harry 1980, 59). This reversal of the position found in other sectors may be explained by two characteristics of dairying: this sector had both the highest proportion of Afro-Caribbean farmers and the youngest farmers of any sector and both these factors are associated with higher educational levels for women.

Although there was surprisingly little difference between the two surveys in levels of off-farm employment, the constraints are not the same. In both Trinidad and Nevis half the male farmers and one-sixth of the women had off-farm jobs. In Trinidad, cultural constraints among East Indians have inhibited women from working outside the home and family farm, but these barriers are breaking down in the face of Trinidad's booming economy, whereas in stagnant Nevis there is little expansion of work opportunities. Inevitably, in both islands, women farmers are much less likely to rely on income from off-farm employment than are men farmers. In Nevis, 49 per cent of the farmers surveyed received the major part of their income from the sale of farm produce, and in Trinidad this proportion was as high as 65 per cent. Some 59 per cent of the respondents reported using more than half of their farm income for domestic needs (Harry 1980, 110). In Nevis, there is also considerable dependence on the farm for subsistence production. Farmers in both countries receive more income from farming than from outside sources, with the exception of rice farmers in Trinidad, who obtain most of their income from off-farm work, and women farmers in Nevis, half of whom depend on remittances from relatives overseas for the major part of their income. These figures reflect the part time but vital subsistence role of small-scale farming in the Caribbean and the importance of money sent back by migrants in the economic life of the smaller islands. That this remittance income is so clearly linked to female-headed households in Nevis reinforces the evidence for the importance of matrifocality in Afro-Caribbean social behaviour patterns.

Conclusion

Cultivation practices and gender roles for plantation crops were imposed by the colonial elite on both African slaves and Indian indentured labourers and so few differences should be expected. Vegetable cultivation was generally carried on outside the jurisdiction of the plantocracy and, consequently, some traditional practices have survived in this farm sector, particularly in relation to women's role in processing and marketing. East Indians introduced paddy rice cultivation into Trinidad and traditional gender roles have been less affected by modernisation in this sector than they have in India (Bagchi 1981).

Harry notes that the traditional values of East Indians, that is, a desire for large families, protection of daughters, early arranged marriages and land ownership are still important characteristics of many Trinidadian farm households (Harry 1980, 116). The largest families are found on cane, vegetable and rice farms, which are virtually all operated by East Indians. Many children provide extra labour for the farm, and female children, in particular, do a great deal of work in the fields with their mothers and assume many domestic chores. According to Indra Harry, most Indian parents believe that 'education is wasted on girl children' and with the majority of schools controlled for a long time by Christian missionaries, most Hindu farmers have feared that their children would be converted and their daughters exposed to Westernised men (Harry 1980, 116). Families work together and kinship ties are important when extra labour is needed. Differences in time of day worked by male and female are few and spouses usually 'garden' together. Land ownership is most common in the cocoa, cane and rice sectors, but in the more recently developed types of farming, such as tobacco and dairying, land is leased, and the modern commercial vegetable producer looking for a market garden near urban areas is usually forced to rent land privately as it is not otherwise available. Harry feels that the distinctive cultural traits of Indian farmers in Trinidad are slowly being eroded and modified. Today, most Indian families educate all their children and, like their Creole neighbours, wish their children to inherit the family farm but do not wish them to become dependent on agriculture for a livelihood (Harry 1980, 119). Thus the traditional differences between the two ethnic groups of small farmers are rapidly disappearing.

The workload of Caribbean women smallholders of all ethnic and cultural groups is very heavy. They often work a 16 hour day, beginning as early as 3 or 4 o'clock in the morning, preparing the family breakfast. Until very recently in Trinidad, girls born to East Indian families were expected to help with the housework, take care of younger siblings and work in the fields by the age of 10. Marriages were arranged for them in their early teens and as child brides their lives were controlled by their mothers-in-law and by their husbands, for whom they were expected to work both in the house and in the fields. Today, many young East Indian women are not willing to accept what Harry has called the 'female coolie status' of their mothers, and the traditional patrilocal family labour system of small farming is beginning to break down. Women in Nevis also carry a heavy burden of household and farm work but with the Afro-Caribbean matrifocal family system they are more likely to be able to turn to their own mothers for assistance rather than being expected to work for their mothers-in-law. However, even today, the strength of marriage and the family in Trinidad among East Indians does lead to more joint management of farms than elsewhere in the Caribbean. Similarly, inheritance of a farm from one's husband, as usually occurs in Trinidad, results in farms operated by women in Trinidad being larger and generally less marginal than such farms elsewhere in the region. Yet, despite these differences, it is sexual, rather than ethnic, pluralism which has been consistently overlooked as a distinctive ingredient of small-scale farming in the Caribbean.

References

Bagchi, D. 1981. Women in agrarian transition in India: impact of development. *Geograf. Ann.* **63B**, 109–17.

Battlefront 1978. Indentured labour. 19 May, 7, col. 2. Trinidad.

Berleant-Schiller, R. 1977. Production and division of labor in a West Indian peasant community. *Am. Ethnol.* **4**, 253–72.

Brierley, J. S. 1974. *Small farming in Grenada, West Indies*. Manitoba Geographical Studies no. 4. Winnipeg: University of Manitoba.

Boserup, E. 1970. *Women's role in economic development*. New York: St Martin's Press.

British Development Division in the Caribbean 1968. *Census of agriculture, 1961 The Eastern Caribbean*. Bridgetown, Barbados: BDDC.

Buvinic, M. and N. H. Youssef 1978. *Women-headed households: the ignored factor in development planning*. Washington, DC: International Center for Research on Women.

Clarke, E. 1957. *My mother who fathered me*. London: George Allen & Unwin.

Chaney, E. M. and M. W. Lewis 1980. *Women, migration and the decline of smallholder agriculture*. Washington, DC: Office of Women in Development, US Agency for International Development.

Croll, E. J. 1979. *Socialist development experience: women in rural production and reproduction in the Soviet Union, China, Cuba and Tanzania*. Discussion paper 143. Brighton: Institute of Development Studies, University of Sussex.

Deere, C. D. 1982. The division of labor by sex in agriculture: a Peruvian case study. *Econ. Dev. Cult. Change* **30**, 795–812.

Edwards, M. R. 1980. *Jamaican higglers: their significance and potential*. Monograph VII. Swansea: Centre for Development Studies, University College of Wales.

Eisner, G. 1961. *Jamaica 1830–1930: a study in economic growth*. Manchester: University Press.

Garrett, P. M. 1976. *Some structural constraints on the agricultural activities of women: the Chilean hacienda*. Madison: University of Wisconsin, Land Tenure Centre.

Gordon, M. 1981. Caribbean migration: a perspective on women. In *Female immigrants to the United States: Caribbean, Latin American and African experiences*, D. M. Mortimer and R. S. Bryce-Laporte (eds). Washington, DC: Smithsonian Institute.

Government Statistics, Jamaica 1950. *West Indian Census, 1946 Part B. Census of agriculture*. Kingston: Government Printing Office.

Government Statistics, Jamaica 1976. *1970 population census of the Commonwealth Caribbean*, vol. 4, part 16. Kingston: Government Printing Office.

Harry, I. S. 1980 (unpublished). *Women in agriculture in Trinidad*. MSc thesis. University of Calgary.

Henshall, J. D. 1981. Women and small scale farming in the Caribbean. In *Papers in Latin American geography in honor of Lucia C. Harrison*, O. Horst (ed.), 28–43. Muncie, Indiana: Conference of Latin American Geographers.

Henshall (Momsen), J. D. 1982. *Women and rural development in Latin America*. Meeting of the International Geographical Union's Rural Commission, Sergipe, Brazil, unpublished.

Hope, K. R. 1980. Population, labor and employment in Caribbean socioeconomic development: a study of selected Caribbean countries. In *The Caribbean issues of emergence: socioeconomic and political perspectives*, V. R McDonald (ed.). Washington, DC: University Press of America.

International Labour Office 1977. *Labour force estimates and projections, 1950–2000*. Geneva: International Labour Office.

Levy, C. 1980. *Emancipation, sugar and federalism: Barbados and the West Indies 1833–1876*. Gainesville: University of Florida Press.

Lowenthal, D. 1967. Race and color in the West Indies. *Daedalus* **96**, 580–626.

Lowenthal, D. 1972. *West Indian societies*. London: Oxford University Press.

MacMillan, A. A. 1967. *The development of market gardening in Aranguez, Trinidad*. PhD thesis. University of the West Indies, Trinidad.

Mintz, S. W. 1964. Currency problems in eighteenth century Jamaica and Gresham's Law. In *Process and pattern in culture: essays in honor of Julian N. Steward*, P. A. Manners (ed.). Chicago: Aldine.

Monk, J. 1978. *Sexual differences in migration from rural areas in Western Puerto Rico*.

Annual Meeting of the Association of American Geographers, New Orleans, April, unpublished.

Momsen, J. Henshall 1969 (unpublished). *The geography of land use and population in the Caribbean with special reference to Barbados and the Windward Islands*. PhD thesis. University of London.

Morsen, H. 1841. *The present condition of the British West Indies: their wants and the remedy for these*. London: privately published.

Roberts, G. W. 1957. *The population of Jamaica*. Cambridge: Cambridge University Press.

Roberts, G. W. and Byrne, J. A. 1966–7. Summary statistics on indenture and associated migration affecting the West Indies, 1834–1918. *Pop. Studs* **20**, 125–34.

Rogers, B. 1980. *The domestication of women*. London: Kogan Page.

Slater, M. K. 1977. *The Caribbean family*. New York: St Martin's Press.

Smith, M. G. 1965. *The plural society in the British West Indies*. Berkeley: University of California Press.

Smith, R. T. 1960. The family in the Caribbean. In *Caribbean studies: a symposium*, V. Rubin (ed.), 67–75. Seattle: University of Washington Press.

Solien, N. L. 1959 (unpublished). *The consanguineal household among the black Caribs of Central America*. PhD thesis. University of Michigan.

Tikasingh, G. 1973. *The establishment of the Indians in Trinidad, 1870–1900*. PhD thesis. University of the West Indies, Trinidad.

Trinidad Central Statistical Office 1978. *Statistical pocket digest*. Port of Spain: Trinidad Central Statistical Office.

Weller, J. A. 1968. *The East Indian indenture in Trinidad*. Rio Piedras, Puerto Rico: Institute of Caribbean Studies, University of Puerto Rico.

Women and Development Unit (WAND). 1981. *Annual report*. Barbados: University of the West Indies, Trinidad.

Zuvekas, C., Jr 1978. *A profile of small farmers in the Caribbean region*. Working Document Series, Caribbean Region, General Working Document no. 2. Washington, DC: US Agency for International Development.

Part C

*THIRD WORLD COLONISTS IN
THE FIRST WORLD*

8 Migration and social change in Puerto Rico

PETER JACKSON

Introduction

Puerto Rican migration to the continental United States cannot be understood simply as a result of intolerable population pressure on limited resources; more fundamental to an understanding of the migration are the social changes that have resulted from the deliberate integration of the economies of the United States and Puerto Rico in a continuing neocolonial relationship.

Geographical studies of migration rarely go beyond empirical analyses of 'push' and 'pull' factors to offer structural explanations in terms of political economy. The former approach derives from the work of Brinley Thomas (1954) and has been illustrated in the case of West Indian migration to Britain by Ceri Peach (1968); the latter has its roots in the work of Marx and has been illustrated in several recent accounts of the Puerto Rican migration (Nieves Falcón 1975, Campos & Bonilla 1976, History Task Force, Centro de Estudios Puertorriqueños 1979, Maldonado-Denis 1980, Bonilla & Campos 1981). The present paper attempts to combine both approaches to the study of social change in Puerto Rico. Migration is itself seen as an agent of social change (Thomas-Hope 1978). Ultimately, however, it can only be understood in terms of changes in the wider political economy.

The combination of these approaches is guided by Paget's (1960) formulation concerning the disharmonious nature of social and economic change, which reveals the inadequacy of theories linking population and resources in a static conception of 'overpopulation'. The history of Spanish and, later, American colonisation in Puerto Rico is dominated by their exploitation of the island's agricultural and industrial resources. The resulting condition of deep seated economic dependency grew out of a process that involved the marginalisation of the traditional agricultural sector through a narrow specialisation on sugar and a subsequent period of capital intensive industrial development. A labour surplus was created at the periphery which was exported to serve the corporate interests of the metropolitan core. The migration is therefore to be interpreted in the wider context of social change and economic dependency, rather than by focusing on 'overpopulation' which is but a symptom of the real disease.

Population and resources

Paget's (1960) observation on the natural disharmonies between rates of social and economic change was made in the context of rural settlement. He was critical of the concept of an 'optimum population' and of the general assumption that there is a hypothetical balance or harmony between the social and economic requirements of a population. The Puerto Rican migration offers an excellent test-case for evaluating these remarks on the relationship between population and resources, for the island's postwar history has been characterised by extremely high population densities and massive outmigration. To what extent was migration simply a result of 'overpopulation' and how did that condition arise?

Several authors have argued that the Puerto Rican migration is to be understood simply as a matter of excess population in relation to a narrow and finite resource base. Stanley Friedlander (1965), for example, considers that the migration provided an excellent 'safety valve' mechanism for the solution of very serious population problems. He shows that migration reduced the island's rate of population growth from over 3 per cent to only 0.6 per cent, withdrawing large segments of the reproductive age group. Senior and Watkins (1966) apparently share this view, arguing optimistically that the migration has benefited the migrant and his family, the area in which he came to live, and the area from which he migrated. A group of Puerto Rican scholars has recently argued quite a different case. Basing their analysis on Marx and Engels' interpretation of the Irish question, they argue that:

'To propose that it is the population that exerts unbearable pressure on the productive apparatus has entirely different implications than to propose that it is the system of production that has an adverse impact on the population.' (History Task Force, Centro de Estudios Puertorriqueños 1979, 21)

Puerto Rico's resource base is not fixed or static, and the exploitation of those resources has occurred under particular political and economic circumstances. It is this context of political economy which holds the key to understanding the course of social change in Puerto Rico and the role of migration in that process.

Migration and political economy

The massive postwar migration from Puerto Rico to the mainland United States has resulted in a 'colony' of about 1 million Puerto Ricans in New York City and approximately the same number scattered throughout the continental United States outside the main port of entry (US Commission on Civil Rights

1976, Jackson 1980a). Understanding this migration depends on an adequate historical knowledge of the political and economic relationship between Puerto Rico and the United States. One aspect of this relationship is illustrated by the fact that the Puerto Rican migration proceeded in the absence of immigration restrictions, which were being applied to other groups with increasing rigour after 1920 and to West Indian migrants in particular as a result of the McCarran–Walter Act in 1952 (Jones 1960). The Puerto Ricans, though, were granted US citizenship in 1917 and thereafter were entitled to migrate freely to the mainland just as other Americans migrate between states. The course of that migration is fundamentally related to the developing economic ties between Puerto Rico and the United States and citizenship is just one political aspect of that wider relationship which will be considered in detail.

United States' interest in Puerto Rico was dominated in the first place by the island's military and strategic significance, in the heart of the Caribbean and at the gateway to the Pacific via the Panama Canal. Following the invasion of Puerto Rico at the end of the Spanish–American War in 1898, the United States claimed the island as compensation for war damages and continued direct military rule until 1900. Ironically, the Puerto Ricans welcomed US intervention which they hoped would put an end to the quixotic government to which they had been subject under Spanish rule. As a measure of their already declining power, the Spanish had finally granted Puerto Rico autonomy in 1897, but self-government was to be very short lived. A process of Americanisation began immediately, with far reaching consequences economically, technologically, culturally, politically and educationally. It was not just the constitutional change which affected the island, for Gordon Lewis (1963) has characterised the first three decades of American rule as 'the imperialism of neglect'. What was neglected was the Puerto Ricans' voice in deciding their own future. American rule provided not so much a new form of government as a stage for massive foreign penetration of the island's economy; 'a decadent and inefficient capitalism was replaced by a dynamic and efficient capitalism' (Lewis 1963). The richest sugar, tobacco and coffee lands were rapidly bought up by American syndicates and by 1930 the 'big four' US corporations operated 46 per cent of the island's sugar lands. The sugar corporations largely ignored the so-called 500-Acre Law which was enshrined in the Foraker Act of 1900. Despite this law, which was ratified in the island's Second Organic Act in 1917, the *latifundia* remained intact to become a major campaign issue in the rise of Muñoz Marín's Popular Democratic Party in 1940.

A measure of US economic penetration and concentration is given by the figures on absentee ownership which already by 1930 had reached 60 per cent in the case of the sugar industry and 80 per cent in the case of tobacco. Coffee, which had been protected by Spanish tariffs until 1898, was cut off from its European markets and neglected in favour of sugar. As Lewis (1963) argues in his telling account of this period, 'a traditional industry that had long been the natural cash crop of the independent Puerto Rican highland farmer was allowed to languish'. Both coffee and tobacco were rapidly replaced by the tariff-protected sugar empire which accounted for 65 per cent of exports in 1930, with more than five times the capital invested in coffee and tobacco combined. The consequences were disastrous for Puerto Rico when the bottom dropped out of the sugar market with the onset of the mainland Depression.

A growing anti-Americanism developed among the alienated landless workers, especially among those employed in the physically arduous work of cutting cane for processing in the huge sugar *centrales* – an occupation whose rigours are evocatively conveyed in Sidney Mintz's *Worker in the cane* (1960). Politically, the Puerto Ricans were almost equally alienated, as they were not able to restore even the notional autonomy achieved under Spain. Nor were they even consulted about the evolution of that form of government. The Puerto Ricans' almost pathological preoccupation with their constitutional status is said to date from these years of humiliation, bitterness and degradation. Internal self-government was, however, ultimately and grudgingly granted, although the island continued to have American governors until 1947. Finally, in the late 1940s, Puerto Rico moved towards a new political status, that of a commonwealth whose 'free association' with the United States was recognized in the island's official designation (*Estado Libre Asociado*). The granting of commonwealth status also coincided with the beginning of a new phase in the island's economic development.

Puerto Rico's programme of industrial development through economic incentives to US corporate businesses is well known. Operation Bootstrap, as the programme was called, began in 1945 and Puerto Rico's commonwealth status was conferred by Constitutional Amendment in 1952. Operation Bootstrap is also closely associated with the coming to power of the Partido Popular Democrática (PPD), under its energetic and talented leader, Luis Muñoz Marín, in 1940. However, the relationship between the island's new political status, the attitude of Muñoz, and the island's subsequent industrialisation is not totally clear. Although Muñoz was an ardent supporter of commonwealth as a 'temporary solution' to the island's chronic status question, he studiously ignored these issues in the 1940 election, concentrating instead on what he regarded as the more immediate problems, summarised in the PPD's slogan: *Pan, Tierra y Libertad*. Muñoz thus avowedly put economic reform before the question of status, a priority that he defended until his death (Johnson 1979). Moreover, Muñoz did not himself invent the commonwealth idea. The concept of a Free Associated State as an autonomous form of government on the Irish model was first mooted by Antonio Barceló, President of the Puerto Rican Senate, in dealings with Washington in 1922 (Wagenheim 1973). It is thus something of an oversimplification to argue that 'the necessary economic and social operations envisioned by Bootstrap were to be carried out through the agency of a newly designed political structure, the commonwealth', although it is perhaps less of an exaggeration to argue that commonwealth status was responsible for providing 'a low-cost approach to channel the movement of redundant Puerto Rican workers abroad while drawing energetic entrepreneurs to the island from the United States' (Bonilla & Campos 1981).

Operation Bootstrap, administered by the island's Economic Development Administration (Fomento), aimed to attract foreign investment in Puerto Rican industries and to generate local employment by offering a package of incentives, including long periods of tax exemption. Already by 1953, Fomento had brought over 300 manufacturing plants to Puerto Rico, creating more than 25 000 new jobs. In the mid-1950s, industry supplanted agriculture as the major sector of the economy and by 1960 the total number of factories established had risen to over 660, providing nearly 46 000 new jobs (Lewis 1963). There were almost 2000 factories on the island in 1970, although many plants closed down once the period of tax exemption (originally 12–17 years, later extended to as much as 25 years in certain cases) came to an end, sometimes only to reopen under a new name in order to receive renewed government incentives (Steiner 1974). The prime stimulus to US investment in recent years has been the Industrial Incentives Act (1978), giving up to 25 years exemption from corporate income and property tax, with the possibility of further 10 year extensions after the initial investment period under certain circumstances.

Despite the 1967 plebiscite which gave commonwealth status a total of 60.5 per cent of the vote (with only 38.9 per cent favouring a move towards greater integration with the mainland by supporting statehood), many would agree that Puerto Rico remains self-governing only in name (Lewis 1963, Maldonado-Denis 1972). Eighty-five per cent of the basic means of government that constitute national sovereignty remain under the jurisdiction of the US Congress, over which the Puerto Ricans have no control in terms of a shared Presidential vote or elected congressional representation (Lewis 1974). The independence parties have repeatedly boycotted elections where the status question was at issue and no reliable estimate of their electoral support is readily available. The United States, however, continues its rather cavalier attitude towards the island's political destiny, and former President Gerald Ford's vain proposal that 'the moment has arrived for Puerto Rico to be fully assimilated as the 51st state', in January 1977, is just one recent example of that attitude (Rodriguez Beruf 1977).

The commonwealth's per capita income rose from $279 in 1950 to $582 in 1960, reaching $1417 in 1970 (US Commission on Civil Rights 1976). It is currently (1978) estimated to be around $2000. But while the labour force increased from 686 000 to 827 000 over the 20 year period up to 1970, the official unemployment rate, which excludes those who are no longer 'actively seeking employment', has remained high. Unemployment levels have been constantly above 11 per cent since 1940, involving 89 000 persons in 1970. In

1981, unemployment rates rose to around 17 per cent and may rise even higher, above 20 per cent, as a result of planned federal cuts in programmes such as those administered by the Comprehensive Employment and Training Act. Unofficial estimates already quote levels above 34 per cent (Bonilla & Campos 1981). These figures suggest that Puerto Rico's 'economic miracle' (Hanson 1955) was not achieved without cost and that the Fomento programme has failed in one of its main objectives – to eliminate mass unemployment.

What Operation Bootstrap did achieve, however, was an unprecedented degree of overseas capitalist penetration by large US corporations in Puerto Rican industries, with few of the benefits 'trickling down' to locally controlled enterprises and with only limited generation of local employment. Over 60 per cent of total Puerto Rican investment currently comes from the US mainland, mainly in manufacturing, but also in construction, real estate and commerce. Puerto Rico's 'total dependency' is now spreading further through multinational (US-based) domination of the petrochemical, pharmaceutical, machinery and metals industries. Puerto Rico's dependence on the continental economy continues to grow, with the island acting as little more than a distributive entity, undertaking the sale and consumption of goods produced in the US economy (Lewis 1963). In 1979, over 80 per cent of the island's $6 billion exports went to the United States; more than two-thirds of her imports (over $7 billion) came from the mainland. Puerto Rico has become an economic 'theatre of the absurd', producing what she does not consume, and consuming what she does not produce (Lewis 1980). Labour migration has naturally followed this pattern; as a result, 'Puerto Rican workers move within what is essentially a unitary labour market, the defining parameters of which are determined by US corporate and governmental decisions or programs' (Bonilla & Campos 1981).

Economic dependency has been further increased by frustrating the emergence of indigenous manufacturing industry. US corporations have repeatedly been accused of 'dumping' goods at artificially low prices to prevent the emergence of local competition. Minimum wage legislation has until recently operated in a similar way, with local unions unable to enforce federal standards for fear of driving overseas industries elsewhere. US investment in Puerto Rico is still openly canvassed. The island's Economic Development Administration recently placed an advertisement in the *International Herald-Tribune* which included the phrase, 'Puerto Rico, USA: the ideal second home for American Business'. The paper itself gave encouraging advice to potential investors:

'Puerto Rico's appeal is based on a highly skilled labor force, an attractive tax incentive program, duty-free entry into the U.S. market, well-developed industry services, a prime location and a sophisticated banking and financial sector with no exchange risk.' (*International Herald-Tribune* Special Supplement on Puerto Rico, July 1981)

Operation Bootstrap has had a profound impact on other West Indian economic aspirations, the latest example being Seaga's plans for US-backed economic development in Jamaica. The exportability of the Bootstrap model can, however, be questioned because of the unique dependence of the Puerto Rican economy on the United States. The desirability of such an export is also open to debate, the whole exercise having been accurately caricatured as 'Operation Boobytrap' because of its unequal rewards for Puerto Rican labour and US capital.

As the Puerto Rican government co-operated so closely with the United States in implementing the island's industrial development programme, its role in encouraging outmigration becomes a highly contentious issue. Officially, the commonwealth government neither encourages nor discourages migration (Commonwealth of Puerto Rico, Migration Division, Department of Labor 1975). But the establishment of a Migration Division of the Commonwealth Department of Labor in New York in 1948 can be taken as *prima facie* evidence of encouragement to further migration as well as simply offering assistance to those who had already migrated. Others have argued that the commonwealth government played a much more active role. Maldonado-Denis (1973), for example, argues that there was a declared policy to foster mass migration to ease 'insupportable population pressure' in the island.

We have already suggested the limitations of this kind of argument and offered an alternative theory which sees migration as an aspect of social change in the context of changes in the wider political economy. Before considering the implications of the economically dependent relationship between Puerto Rico and the United States for Puerto Rican social and cultural identity, therefore, it is worth reviewing the empirical evidence that links the migration to economic change in Puerto Rico and the United States.

The migration

There is, of course, not just one Puerto Rican migration but several. Besides the net transfer of population from Puerto Rico to the mainland on a more or less permanent basis, there is a significant component of seasonal labour migration and an increasing component of return migration back to the island. There is a constant flow of migrants in either direction rather than a permanent movement either way. If internal migration within Puerto Rico, largely rural to urban in character, and tourist travel between the United States and the island are added to this movement, the total migration flows that result are of truly massive proportions.

Data for net migration (Fig. 8.1) thus comprise the balance of several separate streams, moving in opposite directions. In the peak years, 1952–7, net migration exceeded 50 000 per year on several occasions. During the same period, there was a vast upheaval in the island's population, with internal

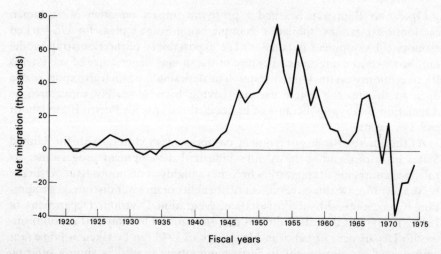

Figure 8.1 Net migration between Puerto Rico and the US mainland, 1920–1975. The 'positive' part of the graph indicates net migration to the US mainland; the 'negative' part indicates net return to Puerto Rico (source: US Commission on Civil Rights 1976).

migration reflecting rapid urbanisation (Macisco 1966, Boswell 1973). In the 1970s, annual net migration began to favour a return to the island and return migration has become an increasingly important component of local population shifts, a fact recognised in the growing body of academic literature stimulated by Hernández Alvarez's (1967) classic study (see, for example, Cintrón & Vales 1975, Torruellas & Vázquez 1976, Jackson 1980b). To what extent can these broad trends in the migration be related to economic trends in Puerto Rico and on the mainland?

The question seems particularly pertinent as the main period of outmigration coincided with the advent of industrial development in Puerto Rico under the Bootstrap programme. Despite the island's rapid postwar population growth (from 2.3 million in 1960 to an estimated 3.2 million in 1980), one might have expected Puerto Rico's rapid economic growth over these years to have absorbed at least some of the potential migrants. The dominance of the United States' economy has been such, however, that the Puerto Rican migration has generally fluctuated in response to booms and slumps in the demand for labour in the United States, rather than to conditions on the island. After the Second World War, a labour vacuum existed on the mainland with vacancies in unskilled and semi-skilled jobs in marginal sectors of the economy, not yet fully mechanised. There may be a parallel here, though on a different scale, with seasonal labour migration. Seasonal demand for labour in the Puerto Rican sugar harvest and the accompanying slack period from July to December (*tiempo muerto*) effectively complement the seasonality of demand for agricultural labour on the mainland, giving rise each year to seasonal migration by some 20 000 farm workers whose contracts are supervised by the commonwealth's Migration Division, with an additional 30 000–40 000 who migrate each year without formal contracts (Wagenheim 1975a). Annual fluctuations in migration show a similar correspondence with periods of relative prosperity and recession in the United States. The Columbia study (Mills *et al.* 1950) reported a correlation of 0.73 between the physical volume of business activity on the mainland and net migration from the island in the early years, between 1908 and 1948. The recession periods of 1907 and 1921–2 gave rise to small reverse flows, and the Depression of the early 1930s caused a more significant net return. There have been repeated attempts to demonstrate this relationship for the postwar period.

The high correlation between economic conditions in the United States and Puerto Rican outmigration has been clearly established in several investigations (see the references in the article by Myers 1967). Paradoxically, the relationship is often easier to demonstrate for periods of recession on the mainland when the scarcity of unskilled and semi-skilled labour is at its lowest. Thus Carleton (1960) argues that the return migration of 60 000 Puerto Ricans in 1957–8 was related to conditions of recession and unemployment prevailing on the mainland at that time.

A satisfactory economic explanation of the migration must involve more than these extreme conditions of occasional labour surplus, however. Fleisher (1963) provided the first regression analysis of annual migration from Puerto Rico to the United States for the period 1947–58, indicating that changes in unemployment and transportation costs were important in explaining yearly fluctuations in net migration. Using national data, Fleisher found migration to be more closely related to labour market conditions in receiving areas than in source areas. Relative hourly wage rates in either area were a poor predictor of population flows in comparison with employment rates or job availability. Unemployment rates in Puerto Rico had practically no independent influence on migration to the United States. Relative wage levels correlated poorly with net departures from Puerto Rico (regression coefficient $R^2 = 0.09$), compared with the unemployment ratio, which produced an R^2 value of 0.61. Substantial residuals were associated with cheaper air transportation, increasing incomes in Puerto Rico, the size of the Puerto Rican population in the United States, industrialisation in Puerto Rico and non-economic aspects of family migration.

A second regression analysis (Gallaway & Vedder 1971), which concentrated on the distribution of Puerto Ricans within the United States at the state level in 1960, apparently contradicted Fleisher's (1963) conclusions. In the second study, the location of Puerto Ricans on the mainland was shown to be extremely sensitive to income differentials by state (and to relative accessibility to the port of entry), but relatively unaffected by the distribution of job opportunities, as measured by unemployment rates. The contradiction may be, at least in part, artefactual, with Fleisher's analysis showing that *yearly migration* was related to unemployment rates, and Gallaway and Vedder's synchronic analysis of the *distribution* of Puerto Ricans in the United States at a particular time indicating a closer relationship with wage rates. Clearly, the decision to migrate in a particular year might be postponed because of poor employment prospects on the mainland. Once the decision to migrate has been made, however, location within the United States might then be expected to vary according to income differentials between states.

A third regression analysis (Maldonado 1976) considered the period 1947–73 and related net migration to measures of economic opportunity in the states of New York, New Jersey, Connecticut and Illinois. The study concluded that income and unemployment differentials between Puerto Rico and the United States were the main variables in the explanation of migration ($R^2 = 0.57$), especially for the earlier period, 1947–67 ($R^2 = 0.81$). Thereafter, non-economic factors gained in weight, appropriate to an increasingly 'family migration' (Chenault 1938, Fitzpatrick 1971). Contrary to the view that sees the Puerto Rican migration as a response to the opportunity of registering for social security on the mainland, differential welfare rates were not significant in either period. Variables that were significant (at the 0.01 level) in this study included the ratio of annual unemployment in Puerto Rico and in the four designated mainland states, and average hourly earnings in manufacturing, with income being the slightly more powerful factor overall. For the earlier period, 1947–67, unemployment was a better predictor than income differentials. Maldonado suggests that the smaller significance of unemployment in the more recent period, 1968–73, may indicate the changing composition of migrants, away from unskilled and semi-skilled, poorly educated (often unemployed) workers, towards a more skilled, educated and professional group which therefore responded more readily to income differentials than to employment levels.

In general, then, a relationship can be shown to exist between the demands of the continental economy and the migration of Puerto Rican workers to meet those demands. But this kind of structural explanation leaves many of the more interesting qualitative elements of the migration out of account. Understanding the social changes that accompany migration therefore also involves a consideration of the changes in Puerto Rican social and cultural identity which are part of the experience of migration.

Social change and Puerto Rican identity

United States' involvement in Puerto Rico has been dominated by economic interests but has also had a widespread and devastating effect on Puerto Rican social and cultural life, aside from the uprooting of those who have migrated to the mainland. In the words of one observer, Puerto Rico has become 'the garbage can of the Americas' (Lewis 1974).

Our conception of social change needs to be broader than that implied in much of the writing on economic dependency. A necessary complement to the account by the Centro de Estudios Puertorriqueños of 'labour migration under capitalism' (History Task Force 1979), therefore, is the historical research of the Centro de Estudios de la Realidad Puertorriqueña (CEREP), admirably represented by Quintero Rivera's (1976) recent documentary history of the Puerto Rican working class movement. It is qualitative material of this kind which can help to answer the questions that the History Task Force asks about the meaning of dependency for Puerto Rican migrants in New York:

'. . . what do revolution and socialism have to do with the concrete day-to-day struggles of this community, which seem to center on modest goals of recognition, inclusion, equity, and the winning of small spaces of relative autonomy in U.S. institutions? These goals do, after all, reflect only the secondary contradictions in the United States today, residual inequities in education, housing, health, and the sharing of all other values. The system holds out the hope of eventual equality in two forms: (1) the dispersal and assimilation of Puerto Ricans, and (2) under the new label of pluralism, a simulation within the United States of the common-wealth idea. In this vaguely formulated corporatism, national and cultural minorities would be free to cultivate their languages, life-styles, and institutional preferences within a common economic and political framework. To the extent that Puerto Ricans, in resisting assimilation and affirming their democratic rights, reject both these solutions, their movement inevitably takes on a revolutionary cast. The combination of national and class goals can find no resolution within the existing U.S. structure. Daily experience drives home this reality to Puerto Ricans in every sphere of activity, making it harder and harder to imagine a satisfactory state of the world without a socialist transformation.' (History Task Force, Centro de Estudios Puertorriqueños 1979, 160–1)

Although one might remain sceptical about the ability of socialism to transform marginality and dependence in practice as well as in theory, it is useful to explore the implications of recent social change for the nature of Puerto Rican identity – an identity that is itself moulded by the experience of migration. Here, the evidence leads one to reject the notion of unilinear 'assimilation' or 'acculturation' in favour of a more complex notion of social change which interprets ethnicity as a shifting identity that is negotiable according to particular circumstances (Jackson 1981a).

The Puerto Ricans' US citizenship affords them little protection from the impact of racial discrimination on the mainland, where they are treated as black. Their own attitudes to race and colour are typical of the more tolerant, multidimensional qualities of West Indian attitudes (Lowenthal 1972). Only a minority of Puerto Ricans, probably less than 10 per cent, have fully Negroid features, although census-type definitions, even when based on self-enumeration, are notoriously unreliable in assessing racial differences. Most Puerto Ricans, though, have some combination of 'black' and 'European' features, and the range includes the whole spectrum from black to white. Multiple criteria of skin colour, facial appearance, hair type and so on, as well as economic status, are aspects of racial identity in Puerto Rico, recognised in a diverse terminology which runs quite counter to the typically unhesitating dichotomy of the mainland, where everyone who is not demonstrably 'white' is automatically classed as 'black'. American social scientists have not therefore been conspicuously successful in conveying an understanding of Puerto Rican attitudes. According to one observer (Fitzpatrick 1971), the following terms are commonly used in Puerto Rico to distinguish 'racial' differences: *trigueño* (wheat-coloured), *Indio* (having Amerindian features), *grifo* (kinky haired). The term 'Negro' is never used, except in the form *Negro/Negrita* which is reserved as a term of affection or endearment. The phrase *pelo malo* (lit. 'bad hair') refers to coarse or kinky hair, supposedly less desirable than fine, straight hair. These are literal translations, of course, and do not convey the full nuances of their meaning in actual use. Their importance in the present context is the contrast with North American norms and the effect that consequent misunderstandings have had on Puerto Rican identity.

A dark skinned Puerto Rican, Piri Thomas, has described the difficulty of coming to terms with his racial identity in the neighbourhoods where he grew up in New York, in his autobiographical novel, *Down these mean streets* (1967). His own self-conscious Puerto Rican identity was widely rejected and he was faced with accepting a new 'racial' identity whether at work or with friends. A more telling incident is taken from Fitzpatrick's work:

'I had met a young Puerto Rican man in New York who would be taken as white even in Mississippi. I met him later in Puerto Rico after he had been back on the Island for some time. He mentioned one point of great distress. He had started going with one or two young ladies, but after a while they had both dropped him. This had happened, he mentioned, after they had run their fingers through his hair. The young man was in a state of anxiety because he was afraid they had the opinion he was partly colored.' (Fitzpatrick 1971, 106)

The position of the return migrant, especially youngsters brought up in New York or Chicago, can be particularly tragic. In places such as Levittown in Puerto Rico, as many as two-thirds of the 25 000 residents are 'New Yoricans' or 'Neoricans'. Their cultural deracination is emphasised by classes in schools specifically designed to teach them Spanish, their 'mother tongue' which was despised on the mainland (see *New York Times* 10 May 1978). At another time, in New York, Spanish was at a premium among migrants who saw an advantage in distinguishing themselves from other dark-skinned

stumbling block, temporarily delaying progress towards Puerto Rican independence. He argues that:

'Once Puerto Ricans pierce the veil of imperialist propaganda and realize the extent to which "association" with the United States is resulting in the massive immiserization of the Puerto Rican working class rather than its enrichment, support for independence will rapidly develop.' (Dietz 1976, 7)

The principal reason for scepticism over Dietz's optimism is, of course, the nature of Puerto Rico's deeply structured economic dependency. More than half the population currently rely for their existence on the federally funded Food Stamps programme (Choudhury 1980, Bonilla & Campos 1981). Independence is thus often viewed as economic suicide and successive Puerto Rican governments are judged by how much 'assistance' they can inveigle from federal funds. The Puerto Rican Resident Commissioner in Washington is similarly put in an unenviable 'broker' role, ill placed to further radical alternatives to continuing commonwealth status or ever-deepening welfare dependency. It is hardly surprising, therefore, that support for independence derives largely from academic intellectuals such as the University Federation for Independence (FUPI) or that dissatisfaction with a continuing neocolonial relationship is measured in terms of student riots (see Maldonado–Denis 1972).

For the immediate future, statehood now seems as unlikely as independence, as virtually half the Puerto Rican electorate recently expressed themselves at least tacitly against it (Lidin 1981). The United States Congress has similarly not been interested in Puerto Rican statehood both for political reasons, as the island's voting strength would outnumber more than 20 states in the House of Representatives (Wagenheim 1975b), and because of a latent racism against a population which is, in North American terms, 'black' as well as Spanish-speaking.

Public opinion in the United States remains woefully ignorant of conditions in Puerto Rico. No spokesman has emerged in recent years to follow the example of Vito Marcantonio who, in the 1940s, drew the nation's attention through Congress to the Puerto Ricans' plight as 'the most exploited victims of a most devastating imperialism' (Lopez 1979). Most Americans' only knowledge of Puerto Ricans is through those who have migrated to the mainland where they are vilified as shiftless welfare-recipients whose youth are organised into violent gangs, roaming the streets and engaging in the most threatening types of criminal behaviour (Jackson 1979). The most popular sources of information on the Puerto Ricans to date have been *West side story* and Oscar Lewis' (1965) *La vida* – a story of family life and prostitution in the 'culture of poverty'. Neither is likely to lead to any radical reassessment of the United States' relationship with Puerto Rico.

Economic dependency also affects Puerto Rico's future wellbeing in that the island is poorly placed to defend herself from mainland recession. During the 1970s, job losses through recession were concentrated in the very sectors in which Puerto Ricans were most heavily concentrated. Return migration rapidly increased as a result (see *New York Times* 7 September 1971, 8 February 1972). New York City alone lost over 180 000 manufacturing jobs between 1960 and 1970, including 137 000 in clothes manufacturing, the largest single employer of New York's Puerto Ricans (US Department of Labor 1975). The secular decline of light manufacturing in the northeastern region of the United States, especially in clothing and textiles, and the consequent loss of jobs in that region, has also been mentioned as a factor in the decision of many Puerto Ricans to return to the island (Torruellas & Vázquez 1976). The New York fiscal crisis also took its toll of city-funded and administered welfare and anti-poverty programmes, again particularly affecting the Puerto Rican population who in 1975 comprised 42 per cent of the city's welfare case load on the major Aid to Families with Dependent Children and Home Relief programmes (New York State Department of Social Services 1977).

Conclusion

In the light of the foregoing argument, one cannot view the Puerto Ricans' future either on the island or on the mainland with much optimism. The exact configuration of their future is indeed uncertain (US Commission on Civil Rights 1975). What does seem clear, however, is that the future wellbeing of those Puerto Ricans who remain on the island will continue to be closely associated with Puerto Rico's chronic economic dependency on the United States. Similarly, the wellbeing of the migrants in New York and other American cities cannot but be affected by the future political status of the island. In both respects, the Puerto Ricans' destiny rests in hands other than their own.

This chapter has sought to analyse social change in Puerto Rico in terms of economic dependency and the continuing neocolonial relationship between the island and the mainland. It has attempted to extend our understanding of the migration beyond the empirical analysis of 'push' and 'pull' factors by looking at the structural determinants of capital investment and labour demand. The theory of social change which it suggests is rooted in the historical context of American colonisation and industrialisation in Puerto Rico, but remains sufficiently broad to incorporate a qualitative understanding of the meaning of migration as it affects Puerto Rican identity both on the island and on the mainland. It is an approach that links population and resources not in a static framework but dynamically, through the operation of specific economic processes.

Acknowledgements

The author is grateful to the US–UK Educational Commission for a Ful-bright–Hays Award which enabled him to conduct a year's fieldwork in the Puerto Rican *barrio* of East Harlem in New York (1978–9) and to visit Puerto Rico. The chapter is a development of the author's doctoral thesis which was sponsored by an SSRC Studentship and supervised by Ceri Peach. David Lowenthal, Clyde Mitchell and Susan J. Smith read the manuscript at various stages and, together with the editors, made many valuable comments.

References

Bonilla, F. and R. Campos 1981. A wealth of poor: Puerto Ricans in the new economic order. *Daedalus* **110**, 133–76.

Boswell, T. D. 1973 (unpublished). *Municipio characteristics as factors affecting internal migration in Puerto Rico: 1939–40 and 1955–60*. PhD thesis. Columbia University.

Campos, R. and F. Bonilla 1976. Industrialization and migration: some effects on the Puerto Rican working class. *Latin Am. Persp.* **3**, 66–108.

Carleton, R. O. 1960. New aspects of Puerto Rican migration. *Mthly Labor Rev.* **83**, 133–5.

Chenault, L. 1938. *The Puerto Rican migrant in New York City*. New York: Columbia University Press.

Choudhury, P. 1980. The dynamics of the Food Stamps program in Puerto Rico. *Puerto Rican Bus. Rev.* **5**, 10–14.

Cintrón, C. F. and P. A. Vales 1975. *Social dynamics of return migration to Puerto Rico*. Río Piedras, Puerto Rico: Social Science Research Centre.

Commonwealth of Puerto Rico, Migration Division, Department of Labor. 1975. *Puerto Ricans in the United States*. New York: Commonwealth of Puerto Rico, Migration Division, Department of Labor.

Dietz, J. 1976. The Puerto Rican political economy. *Latin Am. Persp.* **3**, 3–16.

Fitzpatrick, J. P. 1971. *Puerto Rican Americans: the meaning of migration to the mainland*. Englewood Cliffs, NJ: Prentice-Hall.

Fleisher, B. 1963. Some economic aspects of Puerto Rican migration to the United States. *Rev. Econ. Stats* **45**, 245–53.

Friedlander, S. L. 1965. *Labor migration and economic growth: a case study of Puerto Rico*. Cambridge, Mass.: MIT Press.

Gallaway, L. E. and R. K. Vedder. 1971. Locational decisions of Puerto Rican immigrants to the United States. *Soc. Econ. Stud.* **20**, 188–97.

Hanson, E. P. 1955. *Transformation: the story of modern Puerto Rico*. New York: Simon & Schuster.

Hernández Alvarez, J. 1967. *Return migration to Puerto Rico*. Berkeley: University of California Press.

History Task Force, Centro de Estudios Puertorriqueños. 1979. *Labor migration under capitalism: the Puerto Rican experience*. New York: Monthly Review Press.

Jackson, P. 1979. Puerto Rican culture and community in New York. *Anthropology* **3**, 131–7.

Jackson, P. 1980a (unpublished). *A social geography of Puerto Ricans in New York*. D.Phil thesis. University of Oxford.

Jackson, P. 1980b. Social and spatial aspects of Puerto Rican migration. *Singapore J. Trop. Geog.* **1**, 37–45.

Jackson, P. 1981a. A transactional approach to Puerto Rican culture. *Revista/Rev. Interam.* **11**, 53–68.

Jackson, P. 1981b. Paradoxes of Puerto Rican segregation in New York. In *Ethnic segregation in cities*, C. Peach, V. Robinson and S. Smith (eds), 109–26. London: Croom Helm.

Johnson, R. A. 1979. An interview with Luis Muños Marín. *Revista/Rev. Interam.* **9**, 189–98.

Johnson, R. A 1980. *Puerto Rico: commonwealth or colony?* New York: Praeger.

Jones, M. A. 1960. *American immigration*. Chicago and London: University of Chicago Press.

Kantrowitz, N. 1969. *Negro and Puerto Rican populations of New York City in the twentieth century*. New York: American Geographical Society.

Lewis, G. K. 1963. *Puerto Rico: freedom and power in the Caribbean*. New York and London: Monthly Review Press.

Lewis, G. K. 1974. *Notes on the Puerto Rican revolution: an essay on American dominance and Caribbean resistance*. New York and London: Monthly Review Press.

Lewis, G. K. 1980. Foreword to Johnson, R. A. *Puerto Rico: commonwealth or colony?* New York: Praeger.

Lewis, O. 1965. *La vida: a Puerto Rican family in the culture of poverty – San Juan and New York*. New York: Random House.

Lidin, H. 1981. Puerto Rico's 1980 elections. *Caribbean Rev.* **10**, 28–31.

Lopez, A. 1979. Vito Marcantonio: an Italian-American's defense of Puerto Rico and Puerto Ricans. *Caribbean Rev.* **8**, 16–21.

Lowenthal, D. 1972. *West Indian societies*. London: Oxford University Press for the Institute of Race Relations.

Macisco, J. J. 1966 (unpublished). *Internal migration in Puerto Rico, 1955–1960*. PhD thesis. Brown University.

Maldonado, R. M. 1976. Why Puerto Ricans migrated to the United States in 1947–1973. *Mthly Labor Rev.* **99**, 7–18.

Maldonado-Denis, M. 1972 *Puerto Rico: a socio-historic interpretation*. New York: Random House.

Maldonado-Denis, M. 1973. Puerto Ricans: protest or submission. In *The Puerto Rican experience: a sociological sourcebook*, F. Cordasco and E. Bucchioni (eds), 222–30. Totowa, NJ: Littlefield, Adams.

Maldonado-Denis, M. 1980. *The emigration dialectic: Puerto Rico and the U.S.A*. New York: International Publishers.

Marqués, R. 1962. El puertorriqueño dócil. Cuadernos Americanos: reprinted in *Ensayos, 1953–1966*. R. Marqués (ed.), San Juan, Puerto Rico: Ediciones Antillana.

Mills, C. W., C. Senior and R. K. Goldsen 1950. *Puerto Rican journey: New York's newest migrants*. New York: Harper & Row.

Mintz, S. W. 1960 (republished 1974). *Worker in the cane: a Puerto Rican life history*. New York: Norton.

Myers, G. C. 1967. Migration and modernization: the case of Puerto Rico, 1950–1960. *Soc. Econ. Stud.* **16**, 425–31.

New York State Department of Social Services. 1977. *Characteristics of public assistance cases in January 1975*. Program Brief no. 3. New York: State Department of Social Services, Bureau of Research.

New York Times 1971. Puerto Rican migration dwindles in a recession. 7 September.

New York Times 1972. Many from Puerto Rico flee city for homeland. 8 February.

New York Times 1978. Puerto Ricans accelerating return to crowded homeland. 10 May.

New York Times 1980. Puerto Rican Governor's race still a dead heat; recount pending. 10 November.

Nieves Falcón, L. 1975. *El emigrante puertorriqueño*. Río Piedras, Puerto Rico: Ediciones EDIL.

Paget, E. 1960. Comments on the adjustment of settlements in marginal areas. *Geograf. Ann.* **42**, 324–6.

Peach, C. 1968. *West Indian migration to Britain: a social geography*. London: Oxford University Press for the Institute of Race Relations.

Quintero Rivera, A. 1976. *Workers' struggle in Puerto Rico: a documentary history*. New York and London: Monthly Review Press.

Ribes Tovar, F. 1971. *Albizu Campos: Puerto Rican revolutionary*. New York: Plus Ultra.

Rodriguez Beruf, J. 1977. *Puerto Rico, 51st State?* London: Committee for Puerto Rican Independence.

Senior, C. and D. O. Watkins 1966 (reprinted 1975). Toward a balance sheet of Puerto Rican migration. In *Status of Puerto Rico: selected background studies prepared for the United States–Puerto Rico Commission on the Status of Puerto Rico*, 689–795, New York: Arno Press.

Silén, J. A. 1971. *We, the Puerto Rican people: a story of oppression and resistance*. New York and London: Monthly Review Press.

Steiner, S. 1974. *The islands: the worlds of the Puerto Ricans*. New York: Harper & Row.

Thomas, B. 1954. *Migration and economic growth*. London: Cambridge University Press.

Thomas, P. 1967. *Down these mean streets*. New York: Knopf.

Thomas-Hope, E. M. 1978. The establishment of a migration tradition: British West Indian movements to the Hispanic Caribbean in the century after emancipation. In *Caribbean social relations*, C. G. Clarke (ed.), 66–81. Monograph no. 8. Centre for Latin American Studies, University of Liverpool.

Torruellas, L. M. and J. L. Vázquez 1976. *Labor force characteristics and migration experience of the Puerto Ricans*. New York: Fordham University, Institute for Social Research.

US Commission on Civil Rights 1976. *Puerto Ricans in the continental United States: an uncertain future*. Washington, DC: US Commission on Civil Rights.

US Department of Labor. 1975. *A socio-economic profile of Puerto Rican New Yorkers*. Regional Report no. 46. New York: Bureau of Labor Statistics.

Village Voice 1975. What do the Puerto Rican bombers want? 10 November.

Wagenheim, K. (ed.) 1973. *The Puerto Ricans: a documentary history*. New York: Anchor Books.

Wagenheim, K. 1975a. *A survey of Puerto Ricans on the U.S. mainland in the 1970s*. New York: Praeger.

Wagenheim, K. 1975b. *Puerto Rico: a profile*, 2nd edn. New York: Praeger.

9 The force of West Indian island identity in Britain

CERI PEACH

Introduction

There are in social geography two basic approaches to pluralism. The first, championed by the followers of M. G. Smith, insists on the element of compulsion and of domination of one group by another. The second group, championed by the followers of Milton Gordon, sees pluralism as simply a state that can exist without the necessary presence of compulsion. Pluralism, for this school, is seen as the coexistence of distinct social groups in the same territory without their large-scale social interpenetration. This is to say that there is not a random selection by one group of the other for its close friendship patterns. My argument is that compulsion and domination will certainly produce plural societies, as shown in Chapter 4 by Western; and that domination may continue to exist even when the original dominant colonial powers are removed, as shown by Demaine in Chapter 1. However, pluralism exists independently of compulsion, as demonstrated by Walter with regard to the Irish (see Chapter 11) and by Robinson in Chaptrer 10 on Asians in Britain. Dominance is a sufficient reason for pluralism but it is not a necessary condition.

In this chapter, I wish to show that plurality can exist even within groups that are perceived as highly homogeneous. I wish to argue also that the characteristics that define ethnicity are not inherent or fixed but transactional and negotiable. Ethnic or other characteristics of social plurality can expand or collapse like a sectional telescope, to fit the situation. I am Welsh in England, British in Germany, European in Bangkok. I wish to show how this argument applies to West Indian islanders in Britain.

Imposed perceptions of homogeneity

In Paget's terminology, the West Indies are a formal region rather than a functional unity. Their economies are integrated not with each other but with the metropolitan power. The insularity of West Indian island societies and the parallelism of their economies has made it difficult to foster either political or economic integration in the former British West Indies. The fear of the small islands, on the one hand, that development would concentrate on the bigger and stronger economies, and of first Jamaica and then Trinidad, on the other, that they would have to support the smaller, weaker island economies led to the collapse of the West Indies federation in the early 1960s.

As Lowenthal and Clarke (1980) have shown, on the smaller islands people know each other on an individual basis and the alienating possibilities of political labelling are not present as they are in larger societies. Everyone knows everyone else's business. However, things that you would not be prepared to do in your own back yard, so to speak, you might be prepared to do in another island. From this situation has developed an acute sense of island identity which involves a corresponding distrust of and also stereotyping of people from other islands. The most acute development of such attitudes can be found in some of the smallest and closest groupings. Anguilla demanded separation from its connection with St Kitts, and Nevis also wanted separation. Barbuda strove for separation from Antigua (Lowenthal & Clarke 1980); Tobago feels itself overshadowed by Trinidad. Barbados, perhaps the most chauvinist of all of the societies, thinks itself superior to its more distant arch-rival, Trinidad. The examples could be multiplied. On the other hand, there are also links. Grenadians may invoke relationship with Trinidad (although Trinidadians may not reciprocate). Dominicans and St Lucians have close linguistic affinities through their common French heritage (Midgett 1975, 64).

Thus, it is not totally surprising that a British perception that conceived of the West Indies as a set of homogeneous societies, a job lot to be disposed of in a simple action at the end of Empire, also saw the West Indians who migrated to Britain in the postwar years as a single, homogeneous group. Political activists at opposite ends of the spectrum compounded this view. Marxists, because of their desire to foster functional class unity and, indeed, because of many of the problems which the groups had to face in common, linked the Afro-Caribbeans and Asian immigrants as blacks. Racialists, making little allowance for ethnic differences and looking for a formal object of hate, labelled all South Asians as 'Pakis', all West Indians as Jamaicans and, like the Marxists, but for very different reasons, lumped West Indians, Pakistanis, Bangladeshis and others together as blacks.

Functionally, it is true, West Indians, Indians, Pakistanis and Bangladeshis played very similar roles: they formed a reserve army to man the postwar expansion of the British economy. The rises and falls of net West Indian movement to Britain paralleled, but slightly lagged behind, the cycles of the British economy (Peach 1965, 1968, 1978–9). Robinson (1980) shows similar but rather weaker correlations for the somewhat later arrival of the Asian immigrants.

Occupationally, both the West Indian and the Asian immigrant groups formed replacement populations. They were drawn into jobs that were

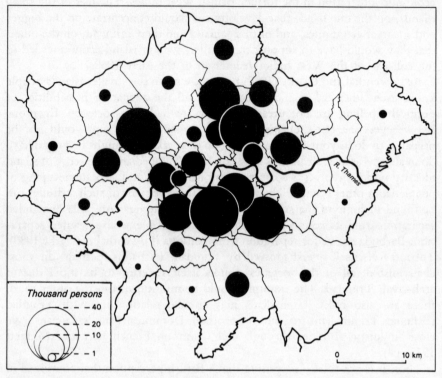

Figure 9.1 Number of West Indians in Greater London by borough, 1977.

proving unable to attract white workers (Peach 1968). These jobs were overwhelmingly urban, and were found mostly in the large city centres that were declining in population (Peach 1982). Thus, occupationally and geographically, black immigrants were perceived as fulfilling similar functions in similar kinds of areas. This perception of homogeneity was increased by virtue of the fact that black immigrants were concentrated in places and in jobs that whites were leaving. Again, as Paget has argued (though not in this context), although black workers were economically integrated, they met social rejection.

Social distinctiveness within imposed homogeneity

Despite this macro-scale formal similarity of black immigrant groups, they remained socially distinct and their settlement patterns show spatial sorting. West Indians and Asians may have experienced a similar functional relationship to the British economy, they may have lived in the same *kind* of areas but they

Figure 9.2 Location of local government boundaries in London.

tended to avoid living in the same areas. West Indians avoided Asians; Sikhs avoided Muslims; Bengalis avoided Punjabis.

West Indians arrived in London in large numbers before the Asian immigrants and they settled predominantly in the inner boroughs (see Fig. 9.1). In 1977 the National Housing and Dwelling Survey showed that over 57 per cent of the Afro-Caribbean populations lived in inner boroughs compared with over two-thirds in 1971. However, the correlation between West Indian concentration and overall decrease in population remained strong. Correlating absolute change in the 33 boroughs between 1971 and 1981 with the absolute West Indian population in these boroughs in 1977 gives an inverse relationship of −0.71.

West Indian concentrations are particularly marked near the railway termini north of the river and around Brixton in the south. Paddington, Euston and King's Cross stand out north of the river, split apart by a white wedge from Hampstead through to Camden and Islington. The Paddington concentration spreads northwestwards into Brent along the Harrow Road. The northeastern nucleus extends in two prongs northwards from Hackney and Haringey and Waltham Forest and eastwards from Hackney and Tower Hamlets into

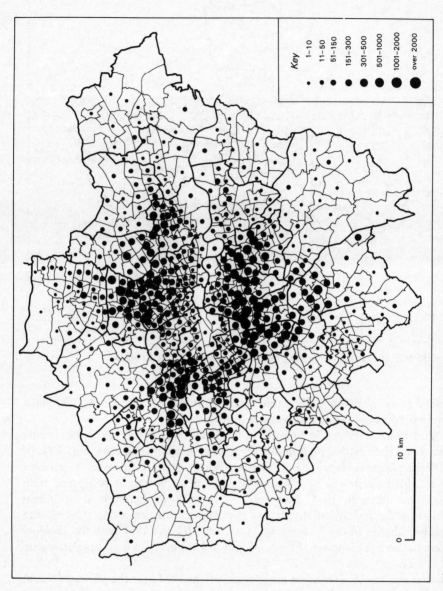

Figure 9.3 Number of Jamaicans in Greater London by ward, 1971.

Key

1–10
11–50
51–150
151–300
301–500
501–1000
1001–2000
over 2000

10 km

0

Newham. South of the river the belt from Wandsworth through central Lambeth and central Southwark and Lewisham extends southwards into Croydon.

The overall distribution of West Indians in London (reflected by the ward level distribution of Jamaicans) may be visualised as falling into three sectors: two north of the river (like an open-winged butterfly) and one to the south (see Fig. 9.3). The northwest sector forms a wedge with its apex in the inner borough of Kensington and Chelsea (around Paddington), and broadening out to Brent and Ealing. This sector is separated from the other by the boroughs of Barnet and Camden, which have few West Indians. The second sector has a broadly northeasterly trend from Tower Hamlets and Hackney north to Haringey and east into Newham. The settlement to the south of the river is also wedge-shaped with its broad base in the north towards the centre of the city in Wandsworth, Lambeth, Southwark and Lewisham and tapering southwards into Croydon.

Asians arrived later than West Indians and were associated with the airport and the docks rather than the railway termini. The distribution of Asian immigrants is in outer rather than inner boroughs (see Fig. 9.4). Half of the

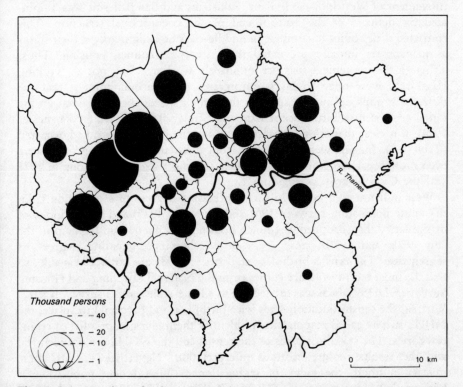

Figure 9.4 Number of Indians, Bangladeshis and Pakistanis in Greater London by borough, 1977.

Pakistanis and two-thirds of the Indians live in outer boroughs. Hounslow, Ealing and Brent stand out. Exceptions to outer borough distribution are the Bengalis (still classified as Pakistanis in the 1971 census) of the East End in Tower Hamlets and Newham. Ethnic sorting has operated among the Asians in the western boroughs, so that Harrow has a concentration of Ugandan Asians, whereas Hounslow and Ealing, Southall and Gravesend are more Punjabi dominated (Simmons 1981, 93). Although Heathrow is important both as a port of entry and as a workplace, it is perhaps worth noting that other factors were important in locating Sikhs in this part of London. The Wolf rubber factory recruited labour directly in the Punjab, and Walls pie factory, also in Southall, is a big employer. Indirectly, the proximity of London Airport had a major impact by lowering the price of middle-class, interwar housing directly under its flight path. Ian Simmons (1981) has shown how the concentration of Asian settlement in Hounslow lies directly beneath the flight path in the area where the government offers 100 per cent grants for sound insulation. Again, the replacement population aspect of immigrant settlement is in evidence.

From this analysis, two important conclusions emerge. The first is that the movement of West Indians, Indians, Pakistanis and Bangladeshis was dominated by demand at the bottom end of the occupational structure. This restricted their ability to compete in middle-class housing markets; their status as newcomers initially prevented their access to council housing. Thus, although the movement was predominantly working class, not all working class areas were open to black immigrants. The second point is that the different groups did not all settle in the same parts of the city. Even on the rather crude census birthplace statistics that are available (Peach & Winchester 1974), it is clear that ethnic separation among the major groups had occurred (Table 9.1). Indians were segregated from Pakistanis and both groups were even more separated from West Indians. The most segregated group in 1971 was the Cypriot-born population.

West Indians, who began to show increasing degrees of segregation from the white population between 1961 and 1966 (Lee 1977) and whose index of dissimilarity then dropped as council housing was opened up to them in the late 1960s and 1970s, now seem to be showing increasing degrees of segregation. The census birthplace statistics for 1981 are not yet available, so that the most recent evidence comes from the National Dwelling and Housing Survey (NDHS) which was carried out as a large-scale sample survey in 1977. Whereas the census question deals with birthplace and parental birthplace, the NDHS survey asked respondents to identify themselves from a list of ethnic categories. The statistical bases of the census and the NDHS are not identical and the results require cautious interpretation. Nevertheless, with these caveats in mind, the index of segregation of West Indian population at borough level increased from 37.7 in 1971 (Woods 1976, 171) to 41.5 in 1977.

Discrimination in the housing market, discrimination in the allocation of

Table 9.1 London: indices of residential dissimilarity for selected birthplaces, by ward, 1971.*

	(1)	(2)	(3)	(4)	(5)	(6)	(7)
(1) England and Wales	–						
(2) Irish Republic	29.92	–					
(3) Old Commonwealth	41.34	39.03	–				
(4) Caribbean	50.92	39.70	63.64	–			
(5) India	38.18	34.46	46.64	50.30	–		
(6) Pakistan	48.96	42.83	54.82	51.85	35.20	–	
(7) Malta	34.42	35.74	48.54	46.47	43.54	45.34	–
(8) Cyprus	53.57	47.42	63.55	47.22	59.88	61.26	54.13

* To find the index of dissimilarity between, for example, the Irish (2) and the Pakistanis (6), read row (6) against column (2). This indicates an ID of 42.83.
Source: special tabulations supplied by Office of Censuses and Surveys of 1971 Census.

council housing (Burney 1967, Political and Economic Planning 1967, Smith & Whalley 1976, Parker & Dugmore 1977–8) and the continued outward movement of the white population have combined to bring about this increasing polarisation. Significantly, the two areas that Ruth Glass (1960) mapped to show the centres of West Indian settlement in London have become the foci of two of the traumatic events of racial confrontation in Britain – the Notting Hill riots of 1958 and the Brixton riots of 1981.

Differentiation among West Indians

Although the movement from the West Indies has been treated as if it were homogeneous, the island identity, particularly among those from the small islands, has remained strong. Regrettably, the British census does not distinguish all island or territorial groups. Separate enumerations are given for those born in Jamaica, Trinidad and Tobago, Barbados and Guyana, but all other islanders are lumped together as 'other Caribbeans'. However, it is very evident to anyone working in the field that the process of chain migration produced a clustering of particular island or even village groups in their British destinations. From the very first piece of fieldwork which Paul Paget encouraged me to do in High Wycombe in 1962 (reputed at that time to have the highest concentration of West Indians in any urban area in the country), it was apparent that this was substantially a St Vincent colony. Leicester, taking another example, is a Leeward Island concentration. Of the West Indians there, 25 per cent are from Antigua, 10 per cent from Nevis, 7 per cent from St Kitts, 7 per cent from Montserrat and 6 per cent from Barbuda (Pearson 1981, 44). Leicester contains almost all of the 500 immigrants into Britain from the tiny island of Barbuda, according to one of the leaders (Rev. M. Roberts, personal communication, 26 March 1982), with only a few in Slough, London and Manchester. Similarly, the 1000 Barbudans who are thought to live in the United States are concentrated in New York and, within New York, in the Bronx. The Jamaicans living in Wolverhampton, to take another example, are very largely from the western extremity of the island – from the parishes of Hanover and Westmoreland, and so on.

Pearson, giving an account of small island West Indians in Leicester, writes:

'Island affiliation is extremely influential in maintaining communal ties among West Indians. Thus "close friends", those who are seen more frequently, whom one trusts with confidential information or relies upon for financial assistance are invariably fellow islanders. When situations become less intimate, kin and island affiliation become less important. A Barbadian may not bother about the island affiliations of his West Indian companions if he is involved in a casual conversation in a pub, but in other situations their origins in the Caribbean will be important'. (Pearson 1981, 64)

A neat, though fictional example comes from the Jamaican organiser of a pardner (savings club), discussing the advisability of bringing in hands from other islands:

'"We are all Jamaicans here", said Mrs. Mackfarley. ". . . I talk plain. I not fighting Bajans. Out there in the street, on the bus, we are one. I ready to stand by them in anything. But – and this is a big but – when it come amongst us I touch them with a long stick."' (Hinds 1970, 117; quoted by Midgett 1975, 66)

Brown quotes a Nevisian saying in the late 1960s:

'When I first came here in 1958, the feeling was terrible. At parties in particular there was always fear of trouble. You never knew when arguments and fights would spark off . . . It's quietened down now, and there's far more mixing. Even mixed marriages between Jamaicans and Barbadians, those most at loggerheads. Ten years ago that would have been impossible. Everyone kept to his own kind.' (Brown 1970, 105; cited by Sutton & Makiesky 1975, 128)

A further example of the specificity of chain migration comes from Midgett (1975, 57–81) in which he shows the migration from the pseudonymously named village of Two Friends in St Lucia to the Harrow Road ward of Paddington: '. . . there was only one primary settlement area for migrants from Two Friends, a locale popularly known as Paddington, to which nearly all villagers first gravitated' (Midgett 1975, 68). 'Within the West Indian population it is notable that Jamaicans, who comprise a majority in many areas of West Indian concentration, account for less than one quarter of the black population of Paddington. On the other hand, St. Lucians and Dominicans probably outnumber all the other West Indians in the area.' (Midgett 1975, 68.)

Midgett also gives evidence of the close island ties among his St Lucian group, even down to the village level. He claims that among villagers who had established conjugal relationships in London, a majority had selected spouses from the same village (Midgett 1975, 72–3). Of the 59 men who had married in England, 30 had married women from the same village, a further 12 had married women from elsewhere in St Lucia, 5 had chosen wives from Dominica and only 6 had chosen brides from elsewhere in the Caribbean. Similarly, out of 54 marriages made by St Lucian women in England, 30 bridegrooms were from the same village, 8 were from elsewhere in St Lucia, 3 were from Dominica and 2 were from other parts of the West Indies. Younger people, however, displayed a greater tendency to select spouses from outside the village. Thus, for younger groups, the wider range of opportunities for interaction with others seems likely to loosen the village, and ultimately the island, bonds.

Perhaps the most interesting of all the documentations on West Indian communities in Britain is Stuart Philpott's (1977) account of the Montserratians. Philpott calculated that in the early 1970s there were 4000–4500 Montserratians in Britain, of whom over 3000 had settled in London. Of these, he calculated that about 2500 were found in North and East London, particularly Stoke Newington, Hackney and Finsbury Park (Philpott 1977, 108). He argued that chain migration and island ties meant that islanders helped find jobs for fellow islanders. In the economic sphere relations cannot be based solely on island ties; outside it, however, island ties were even stronger.

'I have already suggested that kin and friendship ties with other Montserratians are continued through residential proximity. These tendencies are further reinforced by a strong tendency towards island endogamy among migrants marrying abroad . . . Eighty per cent (44 out of 55) of the marriages I recorded in Britain in which at least one partner was Montserratian were contracted with other Montserratians.' (Philpott 1979, 109)

One curiosity of these accounts is that those dealing with West Indians from the small islands are peppered with references to relations with other islanders, whereas accounts of Jamaicans rarely comment on Jamaican attitudes to those from the small islands (see, for example, Foner 1978).

The Caribbean map in London

The island identities have manifested themselves on the map of London. The island groups can still be picked out in the clusters of settlements in different parts of the city. There is an archipelago of Windward and Leeward islanders north of the Thames; Dominicans and St Lucians have their core areas in Paddington and Notting Hill; Grenadians are found in the west in Hammersmith and Ealing; Montserratians are concentrated around Stoke Newington, Hackney and Finsbury Park; Antiguans spill over to the east in Hackney, Waltham Forest and Newham; south of the river is Jamaica.

That is not to say that Jamaicans are found only south of the river or that the only West Indians in Paddington are from St Lucia. The mixture is much greater than that. The populations overlap and interdigitate: there are no sharp edges. Barbadians are the most scattered and mixed of all. Nevertheless, it is possible to demonstrate that when the settlement patterns are stripped down to their essences, fairly marked differences of emphasis appear. If one takes the distribution of Jamaicans by borough for Greater London in 1971 (Fig. 9.3), the map looks like a general reflection of West Indian settlement in Greater

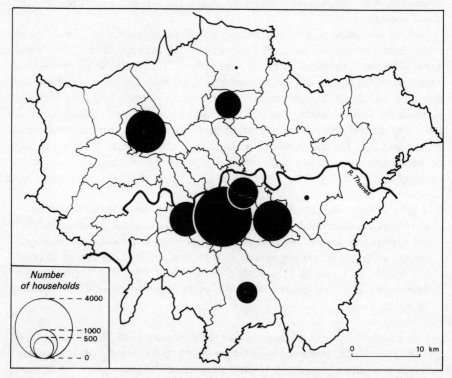

Figure 9.5 Positive deviations from 'expected' Jamaican population in Greater London by borough, 1971 (based on 51.47 per cent of total West Indian population).

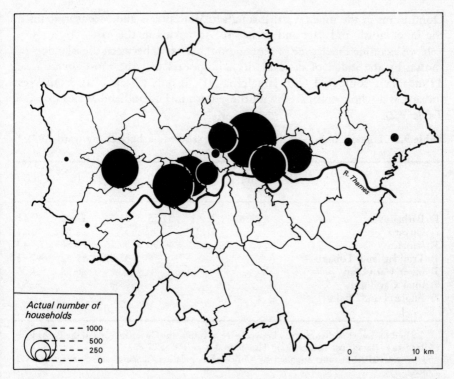

Figure 9.6 Positive residuals of 'other Caribbeans' in Greater London by borough, 1971.

London as a whole (cf. Fig. 9.1: the map for West Indians in Greater London in 1977). This is not surprising, since Jamaicans formed over half (51.4 per cent) of the total population of West Indians in London. However, we can use this overall percentage to highlight the areas where there are more Jamaicans than would be expected on statistical grounds alone (see Fig. 9.5). The map shows the number of Jamaican-born in each borough over and above the number expected from applying the 51.4 per cent to the total number of West Indians. The four southern boroughs of Wandsworth, Lambeth, Southwark and Lewisham stand out, with a smaller group in Croydon even further to the south where dispersal from the inner boroughs has taken place. North of the river only two concentrations stand out, in Brent and Haringey.

If one applies a similar standardisation exercise to 'other Caribbeans' (Fig. 9.6), the term given by the 1971 census to Windward and Leeward islanders, an even more striking geographical pattern emerges. An east to west belt of boroughs north of the river appears, extending from Ealing, through Hammersmith, Kensington and Chelsea, Westminster, Camden, Islington, Hackney and Tower Hamlets to Newham. Within this pattern, there is a west–east change with clusters of Grenadians in the west giving way to St Lucians and

Dominicans in the inner west, through to Vincentians and Montserratians in the inner north and east and thence to Antiguans in the east.

If we examine the degree of segregation that exists between the islanders (as shown by the index of dissimilarity), it appears that the most severe case, Trinidadians compared with Jamaicans (41), is only a step away from West Indians as a whole compared with those born in England and Wales (51) (see Table 9.2).

Table 9.2   London: indices of dissimilarity for selected birthplaces, by ward, 1971.*

	(1)	(2)	(3)	(4)	(5)	(6)	(7)
(1) Barbados	–	27.83	26.41	31.73	31.31	17.45	49.11
(2) Guyana		–	31.91	29.99	37.76	24.82	46.21
(3) Jamaica			–	40.90	39.16	14.86	57.13
(4) Trinidad and Tobago				–	37.59	31.62	44.45
(5) other Caribbean					–	26.34	54.36
(6) total Caribbean						–	50.92
(7) England and Wales							–

* To find the index of dissimilarity between, for example, the Guyanans (2) and the Barbadians (1), read row (1) against column (2). This indicates an ID of 27.83.
   Source: Special tabulations supplied by Office of Population Censuses and Surveys of 1971 Census.

Language and ethnic identity

Despite the island identities which have been brought over from the Caribbean and despite the mistrust of Jamaicans by those from the small islands, there is some evidence for the convergence of the patois spoken by young blacks in Britain. Midgett argued from his fieldwork among St Lucians in London that 'there has developed a youth dialect, a kind of generalized West Indian English, which is not attributable to any single island but which has numerous Jamaican and Cockney elements' (Midgett 1975, 75). Jamaican Creole seems to be the dominant element in this linguistic convergence but this does not mean that other Creole is not used nor that the convergence is universal. There are insufficient investigations to allow this degree of generalisation. It is clear also that the linguistic evolution varies from place to place, according to the degree of dominance of a single island group. Jamaicans constitute over half the West Indian-born population and thus there is a tendency for theirs to be the dominant speech style. However, in towns like Reading, Barbadians constitute the majority of the West Indian-born, and there are differences between Barbadian and other Creoles. In Jamaican Creole, 'im' is used as the pronoun for female, neuter and male cases, whereas in Bajan 'shi' is used for all cases. In

Jamaican Creole 'she is my friend' is rendered 'im a mi fren' and in Bajan 'shi is mi fren' (Sutcliffe 1982, 140).

Language, like ethnicity itself, is often transactional rather than being absolute or fixed in character. That is to say that its use depends on the situation – who is interacting with whom; who is saying what to whom. There is often a whole series of asymmetrics involved in the use of Creole. Parents use it more to children than *vice versa* (Sutcliffe 1982, 150 & 152–3). Young people use it as a refuge from outside authority and often in conflict situations with whites (Sutcliffe 1982, 148). It is also used in directly symmetrical ways by young blacks talking to their peers.

Sutcliffe uses the following piece of dialogue to illustrate asymmetrical change. The mother has caught her daughter fighting in the street when she thought that she was in bed and asleep. The exchanges start with Creole from the mother, English from the daughter. When deferential use of English does not pacify her mother, the daughter shifts toward Jamaican Creole to express her peer group concerns which are of no consequence to her mother:

'Mother: Whey you a dhu out yah? Is whey you deh?
Lorna: I was at the party, mommy, oh please don't beat me.
Mother: Noh beat you noh. Is what you was fighting ovah gal?
Lorna: Dem trying to teck whey my boyfriend.
Mother: You what? Man? You have man? Gal, you can't even wash you
   draws good an' a fight over man when you suppose fi deh a you bed.
You have man. Well I going show you 'bout man you see, love.'
                                                    (Sutcliffe 1982, 153)

Sutcliffe states that it is a commonplace that black British speakers do not sound like those brought up in Jamaica. They tend to use much more of the English part of the continuum from Creole to Standard English. Nor does their patois sound quite the same as the Caribbean variety. 'This phenomenon has given rise to the term London Jamaican. So it is suggested that what we have . . . are West Indian populations where the rising generation, although speaking the local variety of English to varying degrees, are also able in the majority of cases to broaden Jamaican features of their speech to a point where it becomes patois, a variety squarely in the Creole half of the range. At the same time, this patois differs from the original Caribbean variety in ways that have still to be pinpointed.' (Sutcliffe 1982, 152.)

Class, life-style, and stage of life have an appreciable impact on the extent to which Creole is used. The more conformist or accommodating, the less the use of Creole. At the most extreme end of the continuum, where rejection of white racist society is most complete, is Ras Tafari. Here, it is not simply the use of Creole but the evolution of new forms of speech to express the concepts of the belief system: 'I and I' instead of 'we', and so on (see Cashmore 1979, 12).

The more isolated the life-style from white society, the higher the content of patois. Thus one of Ken Pryce's informants explains:

'. . . a lot of white women can't understand patois – well I know I don't talk all that much patois and I always try to speak proper English to them. And because I don't speak patois like all dem other res' o' guys, they [the women] always think I am American. Nothing hurt a woman more than when she is in a group of West Indians and they are talking and she can't understand a word. Then you hear her ask: "What is that bloke saying?" But, you see, that's the thing with a lot of coloured guys, they don't change at all, they will live in this country for years and they continue in the same old Jamaican way. You don't have to be educated but if you are a man who can pick up things fast, you should be able to pick up little phrases and speak so that English people can understand you. The reason why these guys are like that is because they don't know any white folks, so they don't know how to talk to them.' (Pryce 1979, 43)

The emergence of a converging black English vernacular reflects that for many of the second and later generations there is a converging black British identity. Interest in and identity with the sending island societies has diminished for many of the second generation. Rastafarianism and reggae have taken over as the new symbols.

Conclusion

Paradoxically, the early British attitudes that viewed all West Indians as Jamaicans may be becoming true. The Jamaicanisation stems more at this moment from an identity forged by white racism than from a Marxist class consciousness. What has happened so far has been the convergence of second generation West Indians to form a modified ethnic group rather than convergence of those groups within the working class structure. Racism in British society is pervasive but British blacks confront it most commonly in the working class. The Rasta and the skinhead are the product of this confrontation. The most alienated sections of the Afro-Caribbean youth possess what Vidal de la Blache would have described as a *genre de vie* – a life-style complete with distinctive dress, language, music and religion. The street life-style together with its different attitudes to marijuana has prompted police antagonism and this antagonism has spread from the immediate perpetrators of police-defined crime to the wider black community.

But if police hostility to blacks constitutes the fire that is forging a new black identity, it is able to do so also because of the nature of economic change in British society. West Indians were drawn into Britain because of the postwar surge in demand for labour. Since that time two major changes have occurred.

On the one hand, the economy has gone into long-term decline, especially since the 1973 world oil crisis. On the other hand, the technicological labour-saving changes in the British economy have meant that even if the economy had remained on an even keel, jobs would have been shed. The combination of the cyclical and structural impacts have compounded each other. They have also been spatially uneven in their impact, being felt most strongly in inner city areas. The job losses have been socially selective in affecting the young, unskilled school-leaver particularly strongly, and they have affected blacks more than whites. The cumulative effects on young, unskilled blacks in inner cities have been explosive. The police have frequently lit the match.

The Scarman report (1981) showed how the Brixton riots erupted from insensitive policing of blacks in an area of social and economic malaise. Bristol and Toxteth had similar ignition patterns in 1980 and 1981, respectively. In areas of similar racial and social ecologies, however, where policing was more attuned to the community – in Handsworth in Birmingham, for example – the troubles were contained.

This chapter opened by arguing that British opinion had been insensitive to significant inter- and intra-island differences of West Indian ethnicity. It went on to demonstrate how the island differences manifested themselves in the settlement patterns of West Indians across London. It concludes that the very British insensitivity that failed to notice the heterogeneity of West Indians has finished by producing the homogeneity that it perceived.

References

Brown, J. 1970. *The un-melting pot – an English town and its immigrants*. London: Macmillan.

Burney, E. 1967. *Housing on trial*. London: Oxford University Press.

Cashmore, E. 1979. *Rastaman: the Rastafarian movement in England*. London: George Allen & Unwin.

Foner, N. 1978. The meaning of education to Jamaicans at home and in London. In *Adaptation of migrants from the Caribbean in the European and American metropolis*, H. E. Lamur and J. D. Speckman (eds). Department of Anthropology and Non-Western Sociology, University of Amsterdam and the Department of Caribbean Studies of the Royal Institute of Linguistics and Anthropology at Leiden, Netherlands.

Glass, R. 1960. *Newcomers*. London: Centre for Urban Studies and George Allen & Unwin.

Hinds, D. 1970. Small islan' complex. In *Island voices*, A. Salkey (ed.). New York: Liveright.

Lee, T. R. 1977. *Race and residence: The concentration and dispersal of immigrants in London*. Oxford Research Studies in Geography. Oxford: Clarendon Press.

Lowenthal, D. and C. G. Clarke 1980. Island orphans: Barbuda and the rest. *J. Commonwlth Comp. Polit.* **18**, 293–307.

Midgett, D. K. 1975. West Indian ethnicity in Great Britain. In *Migration and development*, H. Safa and B. M. du Toit (eds). The Hague: Mouton.

Parker, J. and K. Dugmore 1977–8. Race and the allocation of public housing – a G.L.C. survey. *New Commun.* **6**, 27–40.

Peach, C. 1965. West Indian migration to Britain: the economic factors. *Race* **7**, 1.

Peach, C. 1968. *West Indian migration to Britain: a social geography.* London: Oxford University Press for Institute of Race Relations.

Peach, C. 1978–9. British unemployment cycles and West Indian immigration. *New Commun.* **7**, 40–3.

Peach, C. 1982. The growth and distribution of the black population in Britain 1945–1980. In *The demography of immigrant and minority groups in the United Kingdom*, D. Coleman (ed.). London: Academic Press.

Peach, G. C. K. and S. W. C. Winchester 1974. Birthplace, ethnicity and the enumeration of West Indians, Indians and Pakistanis. *New Commun.* **3**, 386–93.

Pearson, D. G. 1981. *Race, class and political activism: a study of West Indians in Britain.* London: Gower.

Philpott, S. 1977. The Montserratians: migration, dependency and the maintenance of island ties in England. In *Between two cultures: migrants and minorities in Britain*, J. Watson (ed.). Oxford: Blackwell.

Political and Economic Planning 1967. *Racial discrimination.* London: PEP.

Pryce, K. 1979. *Endless pressure: a study of West Indian life-styles in Bristol.* London: Penguin.

Robinson, V. 1980. Correlates of Asian immigration: 1959–74. *New Commun.* **8** (1 & 2), 115–22.

Scarman, Lord 1981. *The Brixton disorders 10–12 April 1981: report of an inquiry by the Rt. Hon. the Lord Scarman, O.B.E.* Cmnd 8427. London: HMSO.

Simmons, I. 1981. Contrasts in Asian residential segregation. In *Social interaction and ethnic segregation*, P. Jackson and S. J. Smith (eds). Special Publication no. 12. London: Academic Press for the Institute of British Geographers.

Smith, D. and A. Whalley 1976. *Racial minorities in public housing.* London: Political and Economic Planning.

Sutcliffe, D. 1982. *British black English.* Oxford: Blackwell.

Sutton, C. R. and S. R. Makiesky 1975. Migration and West Indian racial and ethnic consciousness. In *Migration and development*, H. Safa and B. M. du Toit (eds). The Hague: Mouton.

Woods, R. I. 1976. Aspects of the scale problem in the calculation of segregation indices: London and Birmingham, 1961 and 1971. *Tijdschr. Econ. Soc. Geograf.* **57**, 169–74.

10 *Asians in Britain: a study in encapsulation and marginality*

VAUGHAN ROBINSON

Peach (1975a) has suggested that the residential and activity segregation of a minority after migration can be conceptualised as the product of two major sets of forces: first, the negative forces, or structural constraints, which act upon a group and are generated by external pressures emanating from members of the core culture; and secondly, the positive forces of association which are internal to the group, and stem from a sense of community and identity built upon shared origins, cultures, value systems and futures. Peach went on to state that in most situations, one of these sets of forces may be regarded as dominant, whereas the other is recessive.

This chapter presents evidence to demonstrate the way in which these two sets of forces coincide for Muslim and Hindu South Asians in Britain to produce an unusually highly encapsulated minority. The situation of South Asians will be contrasted with that of East African Asians for whom the positive forces of association appear weaker. It will be suggested that the dominant forces most directly affecting the life of the average South Asian are positive in nature, whereas those bearing most directly upon the East African Asian are negative. Finally, it will be indicated that the East African Asians are, as a result of conflicting aspirations and opportunities, likely to become 'marginal' within British Society. In this context, the concept of 'marginality' can be narrowed to a definition revolving around the purely sociological view of the marginal situation; this has been defined by Dickie-Clarke (1966, 21) as

> 'the fairly long-lasting, large-scale, hierarchical situation in which two or more whole groups or even nations exist together. The groups vary in degree of privilege and power and there is inequality of status and opportunity. The barriers between the groups are sufficient to prevent the enjoyment by the subordinate group . . . of the privileges of the dominant, non-marginal group, but do not prevent the absorption by the former of the latter's culture.'

In other words, marginality results where an individual's reference group is not his membership group because of barriers to entry (Kerckhoff & McCormick 1955). Such an approach seeks explanation for group relations in terms of stratification theory and status inconsistencies while also being devoid of the psychological overtones that were heavily criticised (Goldberg 1941, Green 1947, Golovensky 1952, Antonovsky 1956) when they appeared in the early works on marginality by Park (1928) and Stonequist (1935, 1937). Such a definition does not, however, preclude the formation of a 'marginal man' (Park 1928) with characteristic personality traits, but it does suggest that further preconditions, other than group marginality, must exist prior to this happening. Membership of a marginal culture may produce personality disorders similar to those outlined by Stonequist (1937), but in other circumstances it produces a life-style and orientation that are as satisfying as those found in the dominant group. This has been demonstrated empirically by Child (1943), Kerckhoff and McCormick (1955), Antonovsky (1956) and Mann (1957). Whether East African Asians are members of a marginal culture and whether this does predispose them towards 'increased sensitiveness, self-consciousness, and race-consciousness' (Stonequist 1935, 6) can only be judged from empirical evidence.

The data, and therefore the conclusions of this study, relate to Gujarati, Punjabi and East African Asians in the northern mill-town of Blackburn in Lancashire. The total Asian population there numbers approximately 12 000 and therefore forms nearly 11 per cent of the town's overall population. The information is derived from three major sources: first, a social survey undertaken in 1977 of nearly 1700 Asian households. These households contained nearly 9000 individuals who represented over 80 per cent of the Asian population of the town. The survey elicited basic census-type information from the head of household in an effort to provide an up-to-date and accurate data bank comparable with the national censuses; secondly, a more detailed profile of 364 households was gained by a further survey, undertaken in 1978, which aimed to interview around 20 per cent of the original sample. The response rate was, again, encouragingly high, and well over 300 separate variables were collected for each household from a 90 minute interview with the head of household and his spouse. Thirdly, educational data were collected during the early summer of 1980 by sociometric testing and non-participant observation within selected schools.

Positive and negative association

Before considering the empirical evidence, it is apposite to expand the notions of positive and negative association outlined by Peach, and to discuss these in relation to the Asian minority in the UK.

Modern sociology has consistently decried the importance of ethnicity as a major force in contemporary group organisation. Ethnicity, and the desire to restrict primary group relations to those with fellow ethnics, has been linked increasingly with primordial instincts and tribalism. Nineteenth century liberalism thus viewed the basic indivisible unit of society as the nation, and any smaller-scale divisions were seen purely as vestiges to be tolerated only in the short term. Later, the 'rationalist–liberal school' extended this reasoning to the point where nations themselves were outmoded sociopolitical entities and ethnicity came to be seen merely as a synonym for the 'brotherhood of all men'. The standardising nature of the process of industrialisation and the greater size of geopolitical alliances has helped strengthen the view that ethnicity is at best a spent force and at worst, a false consciousness. In short, the consensus of opinion is that *Gemeinschaft* has been replaced by *Gesellschaft*, and that ethnicity has become only a transient, or manufactured, starting point in the chronology of assimilation and uniformity. In social–geographic thought such a view was epitomised by the work of the Chicago school who described how the huddled masses arrived from Europe, took up residence in centrally situated colony areas, gradually shed their ethnicity, and became spatially and socially indistinguishable from members of the core culture.

Since divisions based upon ethnic identity were viewed as too transient and superficial, it was natural that the emphasis should shift towards horizontal or class divisions. The prime focus of interest, then, for the study of any group, be it ethnically organised or otherwise, became that group's class affiliation and the relations between its own class and those which were superordinate, and subordinate, to it. For the study of the decline of ethnic groups, the key feature thus became the attitude of the host population towards immigration in general and, in the case of the UK, towards coloured immigration in particular. Rex and Tomlinson (1979) argued that this attitude was shaped long before coloured immigrants reached Britain and that it can, in fact, be traced back to colonial experience when white settlers maintained social distance by stereotyping. According to Rex, Asians were stigmatised as vanquished peasants. Asians thus migrated to Britain against a backdrop of potential, but latent, hostility. This hostility could not, however, become respectable or active without the leadership and initiative of the country's decision-makers. Rex suggests that the legislation of the 1960s, Enoch Powell, and the rise of the National Front all legitimised racial prejudice and escalated racial discrimination. Moreover, government use of ethnic minorities as scapegoats encouraged the public to see them as competitors for, and unlawful usurpers of, scarce jobs, houses and school places. The net result of such a view is that ethnic minorities are seen as the lowest stratum, or under-class, within a social structure where ascriptive status can only be combated by perpetual usurpationary closure against the overlying white working class which is bent upon exclusionary closure (Parkin 1979).

Moreover, in addition to those ceilings proscribed by the broader white society, migrants must also contend with limits created by their movement from a relatively underdeveloped country. Key features that may act as barriers to social mobility are factors such as industrial experience, skill, educational experience and linguistic ability.

However, not all commentators have been so happy to relegate ethnic subdivisions to the role of outdated primordial bonds. Of late, a growing body of work has proclaimed ethnicity and ethnic associations to be a more fundamental and permanent part of societal organisation (see Burgess 1978 for discussion). The essential thesis of Milton Gordon's influential book on assimilation (Gordon 1964) was that even in contemporary urban America, ethnic bonds and ties remained unweakened. As Gordon notes:

> 'As though with a wily cunning of its own, as though there were some essential element in man's nature that demanded it – something that compelled him to merge his lonely individual identity in some ancestral group of fellows smaller by far than the whole human race, smaller often than the nation – the sense of ethnic belonging has survived. It has survived in various forms and with various names, but it has not perished and twentieth-century urban man is closer to his stone-age ancestors than he knows.' (Gordon 1964, 24)

Gordon's theme has more recently been taken up by Glazer and Moynihan (1975) and Ward (1981), and empirical evidence for the persistence of ethnic association has been forthcoming from Kantrowitz (1969) in New York and Hechter (1975) in the Celtic fringe of Western Europe.

However, for the purpose of this chapter, by far the most important piece of work on the maintenance of ethnic communality is that of Philip Mayer (1961), who studied the differential urbanisation of Red and School Xhosa Indians in the Locations of East London in Cape Province. Mayer ultimately concluded that the continued existence of an encapsulated Red community in the Locations could only be attributed to a matter of aspirations and choice. The limited aspirations of the group and strong moral sanctions against deviants ensured that the Reds retained relatively undiversified institutions. Interaction was consequently group-orientated and there developed shared social networks of a close knit and multiplex nature. Mayer thus concluded his research as follows: 'The suggestion is, then, that the general relegation of Red migrants to the bottom of the class ladder in town does not *only* reflect their inability to rise by reason of lack of skill, but is also due to their persistence in acting out parts according to the expectations of the home peasant society instead of the expectations of local society.' (Mayer 1961, 286.)

Asians in the UK

When considering the balance of positive and negative factors for the South Asian and East African Asian populations, four key areas can be isolated for further analysis. The first of these is concerned with the motivation behind migration to the UK and, in parallel, group expectations upon arrival. The second area is that of residential location, a factor which not only reflects social distance (Park 1926) and acts as a symbol of status (Firey 1947), but which also determines, to a large extent, access to services, and therefore to life chances. The third area is that of the workplace and its concomitant primary and secondary group relations. The rationale behind such a focus is provided by Hechter (1978), who notes the way in which a concentration of ethnics in certain industrial categories acts to stimulate and support a strong ethnic identity. Peach (1975b) has also underlined the importance of patterns of day-time activity, as has Hagerstrand through his use of time–space budgeting. The final area of analysis is the school within the educational system. This is of interest for two reasons: first, the educational system forms a method of social selection for adult life, and secondly, geographical concern about the interaction and decision-making of adults is rarely supported by similar concern for those of children.

Motivations and aspirations

As Mayer (1961) pointed out, it is important to consider the willingness of a group to change as well as the opportunities presented to it. In the particular case of South Asians in Britain, the desire for positive association is considerably strengthened not only by religious fervour but also by the existence of a 'myth of return', which emphasises the temporary nature of residence overseas and the importance of retaining strong links with the village of origin. Migration to Britain was originally undertaken as an economic expedient made necessary by population pressures and stagnating opportunities for social mobility within the sending society (Brooks & Singh 1979a). South Asians thus came to Britain as target migrants intent upon accumulating wealth to improve or stabilise the *izzet*, or social position, of their families in the sending society (Dahya 1974). Once sufficient capital had been remitted to the village, the migrant would retire there himself to enjoy his new found status as someone who has 'made good'. While in Britain, though, the life-style of Asians is characterised by frugality and saving, and the overriding need to maintain both cultural purity and boundaries in an effort to ensure ready readoption by fellow villagers. Evidence from Blackburn bears out the South Asian 'myth of return': over 58 per cent of respondents had migrated to Britain to find work or to improve the standard of living of their family. Mr A, a Gujarati, typifies this desire – when asked why he had come to Britain, he replied by saying that in India he had no land, no money and was from a very low class. Since migrating, he has regularly sent remittances to relatives at home and professed himself keen to return to India in the future. In fact, of the total sample, over 35 per cent were sure that they would return home, and 62 per cent still sent remittances to kin despite the fact that several of them had been in the UK for more than 20 years. Finally, when asked to what use they would put an extra £10 per week income, more than 28 per cent said that they would save the money for their return or send it home immediately. In short, South Asians lead a frugal existence orientated to saving and an eventual return home. However, it is important that such motives are not attributed to East African Asians, many of whom were from a predominantly literate and educated middle class prior to migration. These professional or clerical workers did not leave their homes voluntarily in an effort to improve their social standing or their economic prospects. They were forcibly ejected at short notice as a result of the Africanisation programmes of leaders such as President Amin. This difference in motivation is clearly seen in their responses to a question seeking to ascertain why they had migrated to Britain; one man simply replied that he had been 'kicked out' and others commented on the unfavourable attitude of African governments or the feeling that they no longer 'had a future' in East Africa. It is hardly surprising, then, that over three-quarters of Asian respondents from East Africa reported that they would not contemplate moving back there, although several also went on to say that they intended to leave Britain soon since economic opportunities were greater in the United States or Canada. A final pointer to the fundamental difference in aspirations is the fact that less than 32 per cent of interviewees still sent any money to overseas kin. It is clear then that East African Asians were not voluntary migrants and that it might be more appropriate to regard them as refugees intent upon starting a new life, and keen to compete and succeed both economically and socially.

However, in the case of both the South and East African Asians, differences in aspirations must be set within the context of those structural constraints which bear upon the group. Again, evidence from Blackburn suggests that members of both groups are aware of the existence of prejudice and discrimination, although this realisation seems to be more partial in the case of South Asians. Thus when asked whether they felt that whites treated them differently because of their colour, over 58 per cent of East African Asians agreed, and only 24 per cent disagreed. The same question, however, elicited a different response from South Asian interviewees, with 49 per cent agreeing with the statement, 31.7 per cent disagreeing, and 1.2 per cent disagreeing strongly. In short, East African Asians are more aware of white hostility than are South Asians, and the latter group were more predisposed to regard the host society as either ambivalent or kindly disposed. One could argue, though, that such differences result from a discrepancy in the ability of the two groups to communicate in English. Further analysis reveals this assumption to be incorrect since approximately 80 per cent of both South and East African Asians in the sample were able to speak English. It would thus appear that both groups are equally capable of discovering the attitude of the host society towards them, but that South Asians have been less successful in achieving this.

Residential patterns

The early South Asian immigrants arrived in Britain with scarce resources and often with few contacts. In part this was an inevitable outcome of pioneering new overseas destinations, but it was also a direct result of the conditions that stimulated migration. Those families which despatched their sons abroad to provide an additional income were often the least able to afford expenditure on travel costs and other essentials. Consequently, they were unable to provide the emigrant with working capital, and the latter was therefore forced to rely upon a pre-arranged contact at an address in Britain. The contact would then be responsible for finding work and accommodation for his new charge. This is reflected in the fact that nearly 90 per cent of respondents in the 1978 survey admitted that they had no employment arranged in Britain prior to their arrival. Moreover, as we have already seen, many lacked fluency in English or a full education. Only 18 per cent of Asians in Blackburn have experienced education at or above Matriculation level (secondary school). Somewhat inevitably then, the early phases of Asian settlement were characterised by a narrow range of alternative housing options. In practice, 49 per cent of the 1978 South Asian respondents initially stayed with relatives upon arrival in Britain and a further 19 per cent stayed with friends. The typical tenure pattern of the early migrant was thus lodging in, or joint ownership of, a small terraced tunnel-back with similarly placed fellow ethnics. Upward housing mobility was not easy even had it been desired: Asians were not entitled to council housing and remained largely ineligible for private sector mortgages. The need to send regular remittances to the family at home also acted to constrain possible upward mobility via the alternative methods of saving or rotating credit. Even in 1978 the majority of South Asian households sent money overseas, the average monthly amount being in the region of £19 or approximately 9 per cent of household income. The absence of possible avenues for legitimate upward residential mobility, the emphasis upon remittances, and the desire for communal living all ensured that the 1960s were a period of tight residential clustering.

The arrival of dependents in the late 1960s produced a much more demographically balanced South Asian minority with, in Blackburn, 1 female for every 1.1 male. The change in demographic balance and the consequent shift to single family dwellings did not materially affect the pattern of Asian residence. Multi-occupied terraced houses became single family homes and the displaced relatives or lodgers moved to nearby terraces vacated by whites who had moved to the suburbs. Again, a lack of legitimate finance and a desire for positive association locked the South Asian population into the substandard dwellings of the central reception areas. Indices of dissimilarity calculated for the period 1968–73 (Table 10.1) demonstrate the increasing segregation of the Asian population (see Robinson 1981 for a discussion of the mechanics of this

Table 10.1   Residential segregation between
the indigenous and Asian populations,
Borough of Blackburn 1968–73.

Year	Ward level index of dissimilarity
1968	50.37
1969	51.98
1970	54.27
1971	56.20
1972	58.71
1973	58.74

Source: counts of Asian voters on electoral registers.

Table 10.2 Differences in housing quality between the
indigenous and Asian populations, Borough of Blackburn.

Criterion	Percentage of the Asian population*	Percentage of the white population†
no bath	57	21
no inside WC	84	33

Sources: * 1977 survey: data relate to Trinity ward only; † 1971
census.

process), and census and survey data show the inferior quality of much of
the housing involved (Table 10.2).

In contrast, the 1970s have seen a weakening of structural constraints upon
housing choice. The more widespread availability of local authority mortgages
and hardship loans for inner-city residents, and the creation of parallel
institutions allowing Asians to purchase houses from Asian estate agents,
borrow money from Asian banks and finalise the purchase through an Asian
solicitor has significantly increased potential housing choice in the private
sector. Moreover, for those content to stay in their existing homes, the 1969
and 1974 Housing Acts introduced improvement grants to allow upgrading of
inner-area properties. Finally, in the public sector the phasing out of residence
qualifications and the introduction of rent rebates made council occupancy a
more realistic and attractive alternative. At the macro-level, the weakening of
these structural constraints and the increased joint income of the reunited
family should have made widespread residential dispersal a viable proposition.
Analysis of the trend in residential segregation does reveal a decrease but this
has not been as substantial as one might have expected (Table 10.3).

Table 10.3 Residential segregation between the indigenous and Asian populations, Borough of Blackburn, 1973–80.

Year	Ward level index of dissimilarity
1973	58.74
1974	56.96
1975	55.96
1976	56.14
1977	55.39
1978	56.92
1979	54.09
1980	54.76

Source: counts of Asian voters on electoral registers.

Within the ebb and flow of structural constraints, the positive forces of association are also clearly visible. Evidence from the 1978 survey suggests that the high degrees of Asian residential segregation are, at least in part, the product of a positive desire to retain community contact and spatial centrality. When asked why they lived in their present neighbourhood, over 31 per cent of respondents quoted a desire to be near kin as their first-ranked reason, and an additional 12 per cent named the proximity of friends as the dominant factor. A further 21 per cent thought that the proximity of the mosque or temple was the most crucial single feature and 3 per cent listed the closeness of Asian shops and services. Thus 43 per cent of all respondents considered the maintenance of social contacts with their transplanted village/kin network to be the single most important factor determining their residential location, and in total 67 per cent of all residential location decisions were taken on the grounds of community proximity alone. An open ended follow-up question failed to reveal any response that considered compulsion or structural constraints to be the vital factor. Moreover, a further question asking respondents to state in which area of Blackburn they would most prefer to live, in the absence of any constraints, produced a solid desire for residence in Asian core areas.

Similar evidence can be derived from a study of patterns of Asian residence in public housing. In Blackburn there are nearly 40 council estates varying in age, density and location. In general, houses on the more peripheral of these have lower rents. However, as Figure 10.1 shows, Asian applicants overwhelmingly prefer residence in central estates that adjoin existing core areas of owner-occupied housing. Reasons of community centrality dominate the locational decision of applicants, who are willing to remain on waiting lists for almost twice as long as whites in order to gain vacancies on their preferred

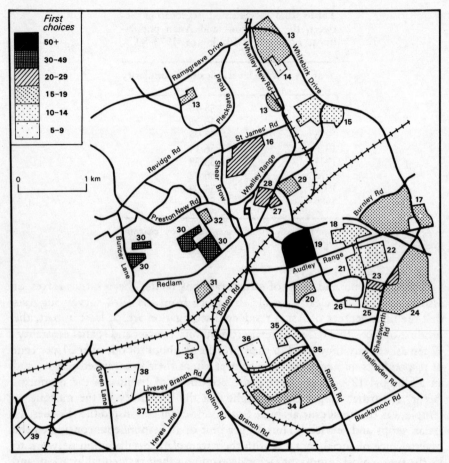

Figure 10.1 Pattern of Asian council estate preference, Borough of Blackburn 1969–78 (*source:* Borough of Blackburn unpublished records).

estates. The pattern of residence consequently mirrors that of preference (Robinson 1980a, 1981b).

Similar conclusions concerning the strength of community association can be gained from a consideration of clustering within the Asian community. The 1977 survey provided data on the birthplace, language and religion of respondents. When combined, these allowed the calculation of indices of dissimilarity between subgroups within the Asian minority. As has been demonstrated elsewhere (Robinson 1981b), clustering within Asian ethnic space reached considerable levels, with a maximum of 70 per cent dissimilarity between Urdu-speaking Muslim Indians and Gujarati-speaking Hindus. In several cases, subgroups were more segregated from each other than they were from the indigenous population, although one must be aware of the impact of

Table 10.4   Residential isolation of the Asian
population, Borough of Blackburn, 1968–80.

Year	Ward level $_aP^\star_a$	Expected $_aP^\star_a$
1968	0.05	0.02
1970	0.11	0.03
1972	0.14	0.04
1974	0.18	0.06
1976	0.21	0.07
1978	0.26	0.09
1980	0.31	0.10

Source: counts of Asian voters on electoral
registers.

group size upon the index of dissimilarity (Woods 1976).

Finally, the data showing residential dispersal of the Asian population
during the 1970s are also amenable to alternative interpretations. Use of a
different measure of residential segregation, the $P^\star$ index (see Robinson
1980b), which takes into account the size of a group as well as its spatial
dissimilarity, reveals that, despite the apparent weakening of structural
constraints, the average Asian became progressively *more* residentially encapsulated throughout the 1970s. In 1968, the average Asian lived in a ward
where approximately 5 per cent of the population was also Asian. By 1980,
this figure had risen to 31 per cent (see Table 10.4). The weakening of
structural constraints has thus had little impact upon the residential encapsulation of South Asians when mediated through the strong forces working
towards community association.

Consideration of the position of East African Asians again shows the
different aspirations of this group when compared with South Asians. Many
of the former arrived as refugees in the early 1970s only to find themselves in a
paradoxical situation. They possessed a preference for middle-class housing
and a middle-class life-style, yet they did not have the necessary capital to
finance these tastes. Moreover, the desire to return to self-employment as
retailers, manufacturers or professionals was strong, and this consequently
imposed contradictory demands upon the limited resources that were available. In view of their mercantile heritage it was not altogether surprising that
the compromise that East Africans made was firmly weighted towards
economic gain at the expense of other considerations. They sought the
primary and secondary statuses which provided monetary gain and not
prestige. This meant that the maintenance of status through higher housing
standards was subjugated to the accumulation of capital for later reinvestment.
In consequence, although 32 per cent of the East African sample in 1978

regarded themselves as 'middle class' in outlook (compared with 20 per cent of
the South Asian sample), housing standards were lower than those of their
South Asian counterparts. East Africans lived in houses with an average of 5.4
rooms, whereas South Asians had an average of 5.9 rooms at their disposal.
The average value of a house owned by an East African was £4307, whereas
the equivalent value for one owned by a South Asian was £4478; in addition,
East Africans were heavily over-represented in the ward that had fewest houses
with baths or inside toilets. Lower housing standards did not, moreover, result
from greater conspicuous consumption – fewer East Africans owned refrigera-
tors, telephones, TVs and cars. However, such a life-style *could* be attributed
to the relative recency of migration and the failure to establish an occupational
niche by the time of the surveys. Further analysis reveals this to be a doubtful
explanation, though, since average annual household income for those East
Africans in full time employment was £3439 compared with the £3092 of
South Asians. Even allowing for the higher rate of unemployment amongst
East Africans (28 per cent as opposed to 25 per cent), the average annual
income for all East African households was £3057, whereas it was £2700 for all
South Asian households.

One is therefore left with a paradoxical situation. Both East African and
South Asians employ the same methods to achieve their different aims. Both
groups depress expenditure on housing to allow the accumulation of capital
for either investment in business or for remittances. But, the paradox is that
the group with the higher income (the East Africans) is the one which, in the
short-term at least, depresses housing standards and quality of life-style
more. One can explain this situation by reference to the targets of the two
groups. The South Asians are saving over a long period to allow the purchase
of more land in the subcontinent. Even at the inflated, and unrepresentative,
prices in the Punjab (Brooks & Singh 1979a), an acre can be purchased for
£1387. The average landless labourer or tenant could thus become a prosperous 'second rank' landowner (Etienne 1973) for approximately £8800. If one
added to this amount the cost of investing in high yielding varieties of crops
(about £430 for such a farm; Ladejinsky 1970) and the price of a new *pakka*
house (£1500; Dahya 1973), the transformation of the economic and social
prospects of a family would be complete. Such a transformation might
therefore cost £11 000. The more modest purchase of 2 acres of land by a
landless labourer might, at the opposite extreme, cost only £2800 saved over
the entire duration of overseas residence. In contrast, the East African Asian
intent upon establishing himself as an entrepreneur in the UK might expect to
have to invest at least £2100 per annum merely to gain entry into the saturated
retail trade via rental of a run-down corner-shop in a neighbourhood suffering
outmigration (Mullins 1980). One must add to this cost the purchase of both
stock and a vehicle with which to visit local wholesalers. If the individual
wishes to purchase such a shop freehold it would cost about £36 000 (Mullins
1980), although sites in less marginal areas could cost up to £110 000,

excluding stock. The cost of entry into manufacturing, even on a small scale, would clearly exceed even this figure. The East African Asian must thus save a proportionately higher percentage of his income than the South Asian in order to stand any chance of achieving his aims.

Despite these indications of relative deprivation, there are signs that this temporary period of austerity might be close to an end, for some East African Asians at least. East Africans have demonstrated that they are more willing, and better able, to compete and participate in the legitimate housing markets controlled by the indigenous population; 43 per cent of East African Asians employ mortgages from conventional sources whereas only 22 per cent of South Asians use this method of financing owner-occupation. In a similar fashion, East Africans were the first to overcome the desire for cultural isolation and preservation which had, amongst other things, prevented the renting of local authority housing. East Africans now occupy 43 per cent of all properties let to Asians in Blackburn, despite the fact that they form only 15 per cent of the town's Asian minority. This shift in tenure patterns has allowed improved housing standards while reducing housing costs (Robinson 1980a). Finally, several East Africans in Blackburn show clear evidence of success. When Mr B arrived in Britain he had no prearranged employment and was forced to live in a hostel. He now owns a house that he considers to be worth £10 000, and his annual earnings exceed £6200 per annum (in 1978). The property, which is a large Victorian terraced house, is situated in a ward where only 3 per cent of the population is of Asian origin. Mr B possesses a car, a hifi, a private telephone, a washing machine, a refrigerator and a colour TV. Mr C is very similar, but he had lodged with relatives on his arrival in the UK in 1968. He now holds a professional post of some standing and, in view of this, he refused to declare his income. He owns a large detached house which he bought for cash in 1974. This, he estimates, is now worth £17 000. The existence of East Africans such as Mr B and Mr C, who live in less central areas, is reflected in the levels of residential segregation between East Africans, South Asians and local whites. Ward level indices of dissimilarity reveal that East Africans are more segregated from Pakistanis and the admittedly small number of Bangladeshis than they are from whites.

Patterns in employment

The second area of analysis is that of the work-place. As Brinley Thomas (1954) demonstrated for the Atlantic economy and as Peach (1968, 1979) showed for the Anglo-Caribbean economy, the exact timing of, if not the original motive for, migration may well be internal to the receiving rather than the sending society. This seems also to be true of net Asian immigration to the UK (Robinson 1979). Robinson showed that there was a significant inverse relationship between unemployment, and therefore job vacancies, in the UK and lagged Indian and Pakistani net immigration to the UK. This relationship was not, however, as strong as that which related to net West Indian immigration. As was the case with West Indians, UK conditions contributed not only to the timing of Asian migration but also to the regional and industrial concentration of the minority upon arrival. Robinson (1979) also demonstrated how at the micro-scale the net movement of Asians was sensitive to employment opportunities, the correlation between the two factors being 0.55 for Blackburn (over what was admitted to be a small data set). According to Peach's notion that Commonwealth immigrants act as a regional and industrial 'replacement population', migrants were attracted to two types of areas: those undergoing economic decline and suffering population loss and those undergoing economic expansion at a rate which exceeded population growth. Jones' (1978) analysis of the 1971 census demonstrates that this holds good for the Asian, as well as the West Indian, population. Census data also show that this concept of a replacement population was valid for industrial sectors as well as for regions. As Anwar (1979) has demonstrated, in 1971 Pakistanis were heavily concentrated in a small range of industries at the national level. These industries included declining sectors offering poor job opportunities, low pay, working conditions that the indigenous population regarded as unacceptable, and a lengthy working week. Examples included the textile industry which employed nearly 20 per cent of the Pakistani working population, and metal manufacture which accounted for nearly 10 per cent. In contrast, several industries attracted Asian labour because at the time they were enjoying a rapid expansion which could not be matched by the growth of the indigenous labour force.

The concentration of much of the Asian labour force in these two types of industries ensured not only a degree of sectoral encapsulation but also an above average vulnerability to economic depression. Table 10.5 illustrates the sectoral encapsulation of the South Asian labour force in Blackburn, with over 56 per cent of economically active South Asians being connected with the precarious fortunes of the textile industry. It is hardly surprising that as early as 1977 over 21 per cent of all economically active Asians were looking for work at a time when the average unemployment rate for Blackburn was around 3 per cent. Again, however, further analysis shows that differences exist between South and East African Asians. Table 10.5 demonstrates the lower reliance of the latter group on employment in the textiles industry and the more balanced employment structure of the minority. In particular, the secondary concentration of East Africans in the growing, and more buoyant, electrical engineering category bodes well for future prospects, since many of these employers are actively engaged in advanced electronics, a sector that the Organisation for Economic Co-operation and Development considers will form the pole 'around which the productive structures of advanced industrial societies will be reorganised' (*Economist* 1981). One should also note that despite their more recent arrival, a higher percentage of East African Asians are

Table 10.5 The employment structure of the South and East African Asian minorities, Borough of Blackburn, 1977.

Industrial category	South Asian		East African Asian	
	Number*	Percentage	Number*	Percentage
agriculture	1	0.07	—	—
food, drink and tobacco	24	1.67	11	2.03
chemicals	25	1.73	8	1.48
metal manufacture	10	0.69	3	0.55
mechanical engineering	84	5.83	57	10.51
electrical engineering	158	10.96	88	16.24
vehicles	1	0.07	3	0.55
textiles	814	56.49	203	37.45
leather and furs	6	0.42	—	—
clothing and footwear	53	3.68	70	12.91
glass	1	0.07	—	—
timber and furniture	5	0.35	—	—
paper and printing	65	4.51	16	2.95
construction	5	0.35	5	0.92
transport	53	3.68	17	3.14
distributive trades	62†	4.30	37†	6.82
insurance, banking and finance	12	0.83	5	0.92
professional and scientific	39	2.71	12	2.21
miscellaneous services	11	0.76	2	0.37
public administration	11	0.76	5	0.92

* Includes males and females.

† South Asians enumerated all family members as shopkeepers, East Africans only head of household.

Source: 1977 household survey.

found in the (predominantly self-employed) distributive sector, even though it is likely that the East African figures underestimate employment in this category because of a widespread failure to record members of the family who also acted as assistants in the shop or café. However, whether retailing will act as a route to economic success for the Asian minority remains hotly contested (Aldrich 1980).

Those Asians who were fortunate enough to have gained employment, even in a declining sector of industry, are in many ways constrained to retain that job rather than seek upward mobility. The need to maximise income and savings ensures that many South Asians would rather retain a dirty, or heavy job, involving shift work than seek a more congenial working atmosphere with lower potential earnings. In short, they seek a higher gross pay rather than a high rate per hour. This is borne out by work on the Gujaratis in the Midlands (Desai 1963) and on the Patidars in London (Tambs-Lyche 1980). In fact, Tambs-Lyche goes so far as to suggest that 'the calling for money-making is bound up with a morality for hard work, and overtime thus acquires a social value as well' (Tambs-Lyche 1980, 134). In Blackburn, there is clear evidence concerning the extent of overtime: the average shift worker in the textile industry works $37\frac{1}{2}$ hours per week, whereas, in 1978, the average for Asians was $41\frac{1}{2}$ hours. Overtime appeared almost universal amongst manual workers. Despite this need to work harder and for longer periods in order to maximise income, 93.2 per cent of South Asian respondents were either very satisfied or satisfied with their current job. Most mentioned their high potential earnings as the reason behind this. Those dissatisfied with their job did not mention the disruptive nature of shift work or the poor working conditions; instead, they bemoaned the lack of overtime and their low gross wage. In contrast, over 13 per cent of East African Asians were dissatisfied, or very dissatisfied, with their current job.

In addition to self-imposed constraints concerning the need to maximise earnings, Asians also face constraints resulting from their pre-migration background. Foremost amongst these is linguistic competence but, in the industrial sphere, it is also important to consider job qualifications and previous work experience. Only 4.7 per cent of the Asian population interviewed in 1977 had either completed vocational training or gained professional qualifications. Furthermore, of the 1978 respondents nearly 40 per cent had been employed in the agricultural sector prior to migration and only 10 per cent could be said to have had relevant industrial experience. In view of these factors, it is clear that even though employment in declining and undesirable industries may be viewed as satisfactory by the Asian population, it is unlikely that they could achieve rapid upward mobility should they desire it. This conclusion would be strengthened by the acknowledged presence of discrimination in hiring and promotional procedures (Smith 1974). However, as with residential distributions, different patterns of positive association are apparent in industry, within the shell of structural constraint. Respondents in the 1978 survey were asked to give the name and location of their current employer. This allowed a consideration of whether Asians were concentrated into a small number of plants, or whether they were more widely dispersed. The analysis suggested a high degree of concentration in a relatively small number of plants. Only 74 different places of work were recorded for those respondents who were not self-employed. But within these 74 plants, eight accounted for nearly 60 per cent of the workforce in full time employment, and the largest alone (an electronics firm) employed over 10 per cent. If the 1978 sample is representative of the town's entire Asian population, nearly 76 per cent of South Asians are employed in plants where there are at least another 10 Asian workers. The converse is that only 19 per cent work in plants where there are less than 10 Asian employees (the remaining 5 per cent being self-employed). This suggests that encapsulation is present not only on the criterion of industrial sectors but also on a plant-by-plant basis within these sectors.

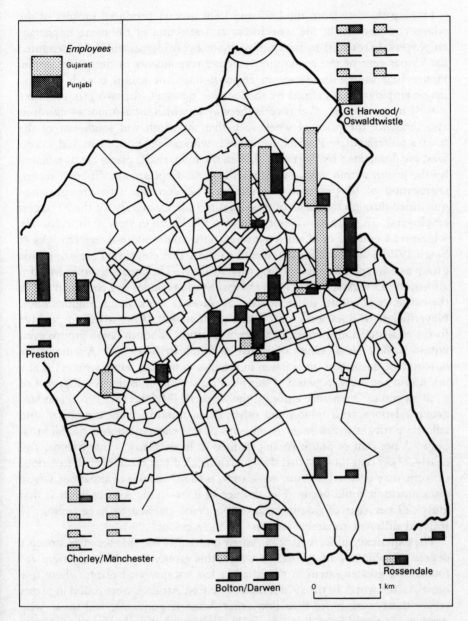

Figure 10.2 The distribution of Asian employees in the 1978 sample by regional origin.

Linking the data from the 1977 and 1978 surveys produced profiles of the ethnic composition of the workforces at a selection of the more important employers. In total, 31 major employers were considered, and these accounted for 75 per cent of the economically active respondents in the 1978 sample. Figure 10.2 shows the dominant regional–linguistic group at each of these major employers, as defined by the location quotient (for two groups where $n = 81$ in both cases). This reveals the way in which intra-minority divisions also influence the place of work such that the south and south-east of the town's hinterland are Punjabi dominated, whereas the north, east and south-west are dominated by Gujaratis. Within the town itself, plants are dominated by the group within whose territory they fall. Expressed in different terms, segregation of 61 per cent was recorded between the two groups when quantified through the index of dissimilarity (calculated only for the 30 largest employers). This situation is not unique to Blackburn in view of the relatively widespread practice of chain recruitment into ethnic work gangs (Brooks & Singh 1979b), and occasional evidence to show that employers use one ethnic group as a weapon against another (Marsh 1967). The predominantly Muslim affiliation of the Asian population in Blackburn precludes any comment about the existence of similar differentiation of places of work along religious lines. Nevertheless, it does seem clear that a combination of negative and positive forces of association encourages the encapsulation of South Asian groups even within a very small range of plants and industrial sectors. An inevitable outcome of this is that 'interaction in this situation with white workers is at a minimum and a consequence of this physical separation is the development of a "them and us" mentality amongst the workers' (Marsh 1967, 19). Secondary group relations with whites and other Asian minorities are minimised and cultural purity is maintained. A measure of this encapsulation is the fact that only 7.5 per cent of South Asians claimed to have 'many' white friends, and nearly 29 per cent thought that they had none. A direct result of such isolation, or some may even say a major cause of it, is the avoidance of situations where discrimination could occur. The absence of inter-ethnic contact ensured that 'only' 29 per cent of South Asian respondents claimed to have personally suffered different treatment because of their colour.

The experience of East African Asians underlines the absence of as strong a degree of voluntary encapsulation within this group. East African Asians are found to a greater extent in the smaller, less encapsulated plants where few other Asians work. In the 1978 sample, few East Africans were found in plants where there were more than two other Asian respondents, and those who were, were found in skilled jobs such as electrical engineering or aerospace engineering where work-gangs are less common. The greater willingness of East Africans to come into contact with the core culture at their place of employment (and the greater necessity for this in the absence of a vacant occupational niche) is shown by the higher percentage of men claiming friendships with whites. Nearly 17 per cent of interviewees claimed to have many such friends, whereas less than 17 per cent thought that they had none. Inevitably though, a greater willingness to discard ethnic encapsulation results in a higher potential for discrimination by the core group. Thirty-six per cent of East Africans thought that they had experienced such treatment, and 13 per cent of interviewees described the attitude of the indigenous population as unfriendly, hostile or indifferent.

Patterns in education

Many local authorities organise school attendance on the basis of *de jure* or *de facto* spatially contiguous catchment areas (Williamson & Byrne 1979). This ensures that Asian children resident in the encapsulated inner-city areas will attend schools where many, if not actually a majority, of their class-mates are also Asian. Encapsulation is thus perpetuated to the detriment of spoken English, which has therefore to be learned rather than adopted casually. The predominant mode of communication in schools where Asians are concentrated is somewhat naturally Punjabi, Gujarati or Urdu. Use of English becomes the formal exception to the general rule since its use is largely restricted to the class-room. In the playground, in the street of residence, in the home and in the cinema, the child must speak in his mother tongue. In view of this, deficiencies in reading age can amount to an average of 11 months when a comparison is drawn between Asian and white 9 year olds (Robinson 1980c; see Tomlinson 1980 for a broader discussion of ethnic underachievement), although analysis of test scores on subjects other than English language revealed a greater degree of parity. Driver and Ballard (1979) have shown how the greater tenacity and motivation of Asian children (particularly girls) help to remedy any disparities by school-leaving age and they suggest that minority ethnic affiliation may therefore be seen as a positive resource once the problem of language is overcome. The findings of Taylor (1976), and of Brooks and Singh (1978) confirm these conclusions although various methodological problems are evident in their work. Nevertheless, it is clear that later achievement is inhibited by the need to devote an undue proportion of energies to overcoming the language barrier at an earlier age. However, the younger child not only has to accommodate the use of the mother tongue as a passive, inherited phenomenon, but he or she has also to sustain the active steps taken by parents to encourage attendance at mosque schools. Within these schools formal classes are organised on religious education and, more importantly, instruction is given in both spoken and written Asian languages. Several headteachers and community workers told me that they considered that compulsory attendance at such classes during the evenings and at weekends produced Asian children who were very tired during the day, and therefore less receptive to learning. The average Asian child thus spends a high percentage of his work and leisure time in the company of other Asian children and adults, and he or she consequently gets little opportunity for interaction with English children.

Additional to the question of encapsulation is the fact that Asian children are often forced (along with other deprived inner-city residents) to attend the older inner-city schools where facilities are outdated and teacher:pupil ratios are high. The poorer standard of education in such an environment ensures that inequality or disadvantage is passed from one generation to the next. In Blackburn, these spatial inequalities have been compounded by demographic trends. The suburbanisation of the white working class in the town to peripheral council estates and the planned clearance of large areas of inner-city terraces all pointed to a declining need for educational places in the inner city. Schools were not refurbished and facilities were channelled elsewhere to cope with the problem of the 'rising 5s' in the outer areas. However, the rapid movement of Asians into the inner areas of the town, and their high birth rate (one of the highest in the country according to the Office of Population Censuses and Surveys) created an unexpected need for school places in the inner part of the town at a time when shrinking resources were committed elsewhere. Although the Borough responded to this, the provision of mobile classrooms was insufficient to prevent 54 Asian children being kept at home in 1977 because of the lack of school places for them. This figure represented nearly 2 per cent of enumerated Asian children. Structural forces thus ensure that, in general, those Asian children who are able to attend school have restricted opportunities for interaction with English children and, in addition, many Asian children are not even presented with such restricted opportunities since they are forced to remain at home within ethnic space.

Fortunately, within Blackburn, the Borough pursues a more enlightened policy than is the norm, since it allows parental choice of primary schools rather than operating through the strictures of a catchment area system. In Blackburn, then, Asian parents choose which school their children attend, thereby allowing a clearer view of the positive forces of association. Despite this greater measure of choice (a policy that has generated a great deal of animosity amongst suburban whites), the calculated index of dissimilarity between Asian and white children in July 1980 was 62 per cent at the primary school level. Furthermore, although Asians form only 11.8 per cent of the primary and infant school population of the town, they form more than 64 per cent of one school roll. Asians remain clustered in a small number of schools. However, as well as choosing not to send their children to schools with a high percentage of indigenous white children, Asian parents are careful to select schools for their children that are dominated by their own ethnolinguistic group within the Asian minority. The index of dissimilarity between Gujaratis and Punjabis at 29 primary and infant schools shows segregation of approximately 40 per cent between these two groups.

However, several parents to whom I talked revealed a desire for their children to attend schools where they would be able to mix freely with English children, and hence broaden their cultural experience. A small minority of parents consequently go to great personal expense to ensure that their children attend a school where they can be less encapsulated. It is important within this context, and also with regard to the broader issue of bussing, to ascertain whether *opportunities* for interaction with whites are actually productive. With this end in mind sociometric testing was recently undertaken in a large primary school in Blackburn (see Northway 1952 for a discussion of methodology). The three-choice, three-criteria test was used, whereby children were asked to name the individuals with whom they most liked to play at school, with whom they preferred to sit in the classroom, and with whom they most liked to work. In each case respondents were asked to list three individuals in rank order. Tests were given to three classes of 9–10 year olds. These yielded 69 completed responses, and 621 bits of information concerning patterns of preference within and between white and Asian peer-groups. The percentage that Asians formed of the register in these three classes varied between 50 and 77 per cent.

The results of this testing revealed the extent of South Asian encapsulation. As Figures 10.3 and 10.4 demonstrate, even where schools or classes are

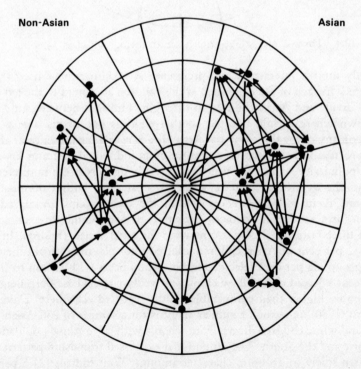

Figure 10.3 Three-choice, three-criteria target sociogram: class 14, boys.

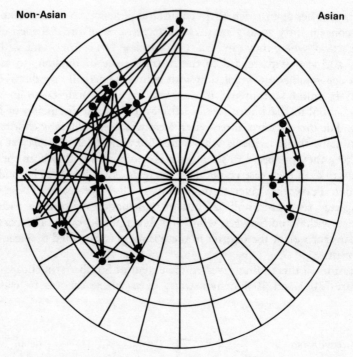

Figure 10.4 Three-choice, three-criteria target sociogram: class 14, girls.

ethnically mixed, interaction and preference are compartmentalised and encapsulated. In each of the diagrams, white children are found to the left of the
vertical divide and Asian children to the right. Linkages between individuals
are shown where a child selected another child as one of his nine possible
choices on any of the three criteria. Arrowheads reveal the presence or absence
of reciprocity, and the relative centrality of an individual indicates his or her
overall popularity within the peer-group. Although cross-ethnic preferences
do exist, the overriding pattern is one of separation, with a dominance of
close-knit, reciprocal preferences within the two groups. Analysed in a
different form, of the nine choices given to each Asian child (three choices for
each of three criteria), 87.4 per cent were for other Asian children. In more
detail, 82 per cent of Asian children selected only playmates from their own
ethnic group, 68 per cent selected only in-group peers with whom to sit, and
58 per cent selected only fellow ethnics as workmates. These percentages are
considerably higher than comparable results reported elsewhere. Davey and
Norburn (1980) undertook a similar analysis for a sample of 238 Asian, West
Indian and white children drawn from schools with large ethnic populations in
Yorkshire and the South. They found that expressed friendship patterns were
least often solely in-group in character amongst West Indians (21.5 per cent)
and most often in-group amongst Asians (44.6 per cent). Davey and Nor-

burn's findings on patterns of friendship amongst white children are also divergent from those discovered in Blackburn. They state that almost 64 per cent of white children had friendships exclusively restricted to their own ethnic group. The comparable figure for Blackburn was 90.3 per cent.

Unfortunately, the Blackburn sample contained only one child of East African Asian origin, and one child of a mixed white–Asian marriage (see Robinson 1980d for a discussion of the characteristics of this group). Despite this, these two children, YL and SN, displayed considerable variety in their choice of partners, selecting members of both ethnic groups without favour. This feature is clearly apparent in the three-choice, three-criteria graphs. However, Figures 10.3 and 10.4 are sociometric portrayals of those links of preference which exist only *within* school classes. Scrutiny of the network of *all* friendship preferences (including those directed to individuals in other school classes) reveals that ethnicity and group consciousness appear to unite South Asians from different school classes to form a larger community. In contrast, white children select primary group contacts largely from within their own school classes; this consequently produces several mutually exclusive social networks rather than a larger unified body (see Figs. 10.5 and 10.6). In the case of Asians, over 18 per cent of first choice primary contacts were amongst Asians in other school classes. South Asian children thus become

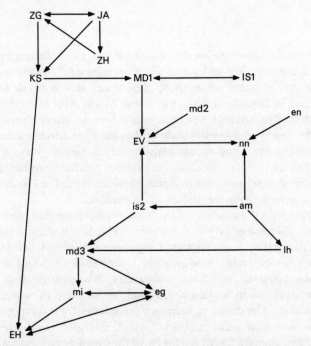

Figure 10.5 Topological representation of patterns of in-school play: Asian boys, classes 12 (lower case initials) and 14 (initials in capitals).

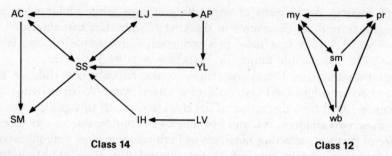

Figure 10.6 Topological representation of patterns of in-school play: white boys, classes 12 and 14.

encapsulated not only within the classroom but also within the school as a whole. One could argue that this results from a poorer level of spoken English, which prevents contact with indigenous children. This, however, would be contradicted by the ability of certain children to create primary group contacts across ethnic lines where they wished to do so. Moreover, an ability to converse in English may not be accurately measured by formal testing of grammar.

Conclusion

Within the Asian minority in Britain there are clear differences in backgrounds, aspirations, life-styles and attitudes towards British society. This chapter has concentrated upon those differences which mark off the East African Asians in Blackburn from the South Asians who arrived in Britain at an earlier date. No attempt has been made here to study those differences which can be found on a smaller scale within the East African minority, most notably between the Hindus and Muslims. In a similar way, the data for Blackburn (which is 92 per cent Muslim) are not conducive to consideration of the differences that separate South Asian Muslims from the Hindus and Sikhs who also migrated from the Indian subcontinent.

However, within the confines of the data, several important conclusions are relevant to a discussion of plural societies. The South Asians to which the Blackburn data relate have restricted aspirations while in the UK, centred upon the myth – or reality – of an early return to the sending society. This factor, when allied to structural constraints, has ensured that the group remains encapsulated in its neighbourhood, in its place of work, and in its place of learning. The desire to maintain boundaries by introspection and the retention of close-knit social networks, which minimise cross-ethnic primary group relations, shelters South Asians from the hostility and inequality present in the wider society. South Asians consequently hold a rather idealistic view about the attitudes of British society towards them (although this may well change under the pressure of economic recession and physical attacks), and they, moreover, remain unaware of many of the constraints that would bear upon them if they decided to venture more widely into the 'host' society. In Mayer's words, 'the processes are two way or circular ones. It is by refusing to branch out into new habits that . . . migrants retain a basis for close-knit networks; while it is by keeping the networks close-knit that they inhibit cultural branching-out' (Mayer 1961, 292).

In contrast, those East African Asians studied here have no such restricted aspirations, possess a more limited desire to retain community association, and wish fervently to compete, and succeed, within the white-dominated society. The removal of their cultural defence inevitably exposes them to the full extent of the constraints that bear upon them, and consequently alerts them to the hostility of the core culture. Unprotected by an encapsulated society and unable to gain full acceptance to the core culture because of their racial origin and ethnic background, East African Asians seem set on a route that may well end in increased inter-ethnic conflict and ultimately group marginality.

References

Aldrich, H. 1980. Asian shopkeepers as a middleman minority. In *The inner city: employment and industry*, A. Evans and D. Eversley (eds), 389–407. London: Heinemann.

Antonovsky, A. 1956. Toward a refinement of the 'marginal man' concept. *Social Forces* **35**, 57–62.

Anwar, M. 1979. *The myth of return: Pakistanis in Britain*. London: Heinemann.

Brooks, D. and K. Singh 1978. *Aspirations versus opportunities. Asian and white school leavers in the Midlands*. London: Walsall CRC, Leicester CRC and the Commission for Racial Equality.

Brooks, D. and K. Singh 1979a. Ethnic commitment versus structural reality. *New Commun.* **7**, 19–31.

Brooks, D. and K. Singh 1979b. Pivots and presents; Asian brokers in British foundries. In *Ethnicity at work*, S. Wallman (ed.), 93–115. London: Macmillan.

Burgess, M. E. 1978. The resurgence of ethnicity. *Ethnic Racial Stud.* **1**, 265–86.

Child, I. 1943. *Italian or American?* New Haven: Yale University Press.

Dahya, B. 1973. Pakistanis in Britain: transients or settlers? *Race* **14**, 241–77.

Dahya, B. 1974. The nature of Pakistani ethnicity in industrial cities in Britain. In *Urban ethnicity*, A. Cohen (ed.), 77–118. London: Tavistock.

Davey, A. G. and M. V. Norburn 1980. Ethnic awareness and ethnic differentiation amongst primary school children. *New Commun.* **8**, 51–61.

Desai, R. 1963. *Indian immigrants in Britain*. London: Oxford University Press.

Dickie-Clarke, H. F. 1966. *The marginal situation: a sociological study of a coloured group*. London: Routledge & Kegan Paul.

Driver, G. and R. Ballard 1979. Comparing performance in multi-racial schools. *New Commun.* **7**, 143–54.

Economist 1981. Where will the jobs come from? 3 January, 45–62.

Etienne, G. 1973. India's new agriculture; a survey of evidence. *S. Asian Rev.* **6**, 197–213.

Firey, W. 1947. *Land use in central Boston*. Cambridge, Mass.: Harvard University Press.

Glazer, N. and D. P. Moynihan 1975. *Ethnicity: theory and experience*. Cambridge, Mass.: Harvard University Press.

Goldberg, M. M. 1941. A qualification of the marginal man theory. *Am. Sociol. Rev.* **6**, 52–8.

Golovensky, D. I. 1952. The marginal man concept: an analysis and critique. *Social Forces* **30**, 333–9.

Gordon, M. M. 1964. *Assimilation in American life: the role of race, religion and national origins*. New York: Oxford University Press.

Green, A. W. 1947. A re-examination of the marginal man concept. *Social Forces* **26**, 167–71.

Hechter, M. 1975. *Internal colonialism. The Celtic fringe in British national development*. London: Routledge & Kegan Paul.

Hechter, M. 1978. Group formation and the cultural division of labour. *Am. J. Sociol.* **84**, 293–318.

Jones, P. N. 1978. The distribution and diffusion of the coloured population of England and Wales. *Trans Inst. Br. Geogs* **3**, 515–32.

Kantrowitz, N. 1969. Ethnic and racial segregation in the New York metropolis, 1960. *Am. J. Sociol.* **74**, 685–95.

Kerckhoff, A. C. and T. C. McCormick 1955. Marginal status and marginal personality. *Social Forces* **34**, 48–55.

Ladejinsky, W. 1970. Ironies of India's Green Revolution. *Foreign Affairs* **48**, 758–68.

Mann, J. W. 1957 (unpublished). *The problem of the marginal personality*. PhD thesis. University of Natal.

Marsh, P. 1967. *The anatomy of a strike*. London: Institute of Race Relations.

Mayer, P. 1961. *Townsmen or tribesmen*. Cape Town: Oxford University Press.

Mullins, D. 1980 (unpublished). Race and retailing. Annual Conference of the Institute of British Geographers, Lancaster.

Northway, M. L. 1952. *A primer of sociometry*. Toronto: University of Toronto Press.

Park, R. E. 1926 (reprinted 1975). The urban community as a spatial pattern and a moral order. In *Urban social segregation*, C. Peach (ed.), 21–35. London: Longman.

Park, R. E. 1928. Human migration and the marginal man. *Am. J. Sociol.* **33**, 881–93.

Parkin, F. 1979. *Marxism and class theory; a bourgeois critique*. London: Tavistock.

Peach, C. 1968. *West Indian migration to Britain*. London: Oxford University Press.

Peach, C. 1975a. Immigrants in the inner-city. *Geogr. J.* **4**, 372–9.

Peach, C. 1975b. The spatial analysis of ethnicity and class. In *Urban social segregation*, C. Peach (ed.), 1–17. London: Longman.

Peach, C. 1979. British unemployment cycles and West Indian immigration 1955–74. *New Commun.* **7**, 40–4.

Rex, J. A. and S. Tomlinson 1979. *Colonial immigrants in a British city*. London: Routledge & Kegan Paul.

Robinson, V. 1979. Correlates of Asian immigration to British, 1959–74. *New Commun.* **8**, 115–23.

Robinson, V. 1980a. Asians and council housing. *Urban Stud.* **17**, 323–31.

Robinson, V. 1980b. Lieberson's P^* index; a case-study evaluation. *Area* **12**, 307–12.

Robinson, V. 1980c. The achievement of Asian children. *Educ. Res.* **22**, 148–50.

Robinson, V. 1980d. Patterns of South Asian ethnic exogamy and endogamy in Britain. *Ethnic Racial Stud.* **3**, 427–43.

Robinson, V. 1981a. *The dynamics of ethnic succession: a British case study*. Working paper no. 2. Oxford: University of Oxford School of Geography.

Robinson, V. 1981b. The development of Asian settlement in Britain and the Myth of Return. In *Ethnic Segregation in cities*, C. Peach (ed.), London: Croom Helm.

Smith, D. J. 1974. *Racial disadvantage in employment*. London: Political and Economic Planning.

Stonequist, E. V. 1935. The problems of the marginal man. *Am. J. Sociol.* **41**, 1–12.

Stonequist, E. V. 1937. *The marginal man*. New York: Charles Scribner's Sons.

Tambs-Lyche, H. 1980. *The London Patidars*. London: Routledge & Kegan Paul.

Taylor, J. H. 1976. *The half-way generation*. Windsor: National Foundation for Educational Research.

Thomas, B. 1954. *Migration and economic growth*. Cambridge: Cambridge University Press.

Tomlinson, S. 1980. The educational performance of ethnic minority children. *New Commun.* **8**, 213–35.

Ward, D. 1981 (unpublished). *Ghettos; past and present*. Social Science Research Council lecture, Annual Conference of the Institute of British Geographers, Leicester.

Williamson, W. and D. S. Byrne 1979. Educational disadvantage in an urban setting. In *Social problems and the city*, D. T. Herbert and D. M. Smith (eds), 186–201. London: Oxford University Press.

Woods, R. I. 1976. Aspects of the scale problem in the calculation of segregation indices: London and Birmingham, 1961 and 1971. *Tijdschr. Econ. Soc. Geograf.* **67**, 169–74.

11 Tradition and ethnic interaction: second wave Irish settlement in Luton and Bolton

BRONWEN WALTER

'My wife's parents are here and our friends are Irish, so it's like home.'

(Luton, married man, arrived in Britain 1964, came to Luton from London 1964)

'I've settled in. I feel like a Boltonian.'

(Bolton, married man, arrived direct from Ireland 1966)

Time is an essential ingredient of the assimilation process. Many studies present snapshot views of ethnic interaction, dictated by census or sometimes survey data. Evidence that assimilation is culture specific (Bagley 1973), however, suggests that the process should be viewed cumulatively. At any given moment, the relationship between different ethnic groups living side by side reflects attitudes and shared experiences developed over time, as well as immediate circumstances. Both contemporary processes and the contribution of the past must therefore be examined if recent developments are to be understood.

An approach that recognises the dynamic aspects of ethnic relations and allows the mechanism of change to be examined is that based on primary group composition. Primary groups comprise those with whom an intimate face-to-face relationship is maintained, involving the whole personality rather than segmented roles (Cooley 1909). Eisenstadt (1954) related the changes in role-expectations necessary for immigrant 'resocialisation' to the 'formation of new channels of communication with the wider society' and ultimately 'the establishment of new primary groups in common with them'. Similarly, Gordon (1964) made structural assimilation or 'large-scale entrance into the primary groups of the majority society' the key process in his typology, which also included cultural, marital, identificational, behaviour receptional, attitude receptional and civic assimilation. If structural assimilation occurred, progress towards loss of a separate group identity would follow; if not, cultural pluralism, in which intrinsic ethnic traits are retained, would persist. Thus in order to examine processes of change, attention must focus on the formation of primary groups. In turn, this may provide a crucial link between social interaction and residential clustering.

Many studies, notably those of the Chicago School of Ecology, have found parallels between the distribution pattern of an immigrant group and the strength of external ties. Park's (1926) dictum concerning the inevitable association between spatial and social relationships has been amply illustrated (Peach 1975). However, the precise nature of the process linking the two aspects of segregation remains obscure. In particular, the social change that precedes or follows residential movement is little understood. Even Lieberson (1963), whose study of the relationship between degree of segregation and a number of significant indices of assimilation remains one of the most thorough objective attempts to relate the outcomes of the two processes, could only assume the existence of such a link: 'This study, applying the perspective of human ecology to the assimilation of immigrant groups and their children in our society, finds fairly orderly and consistent patterns which can best be interpreted *on the assumption* that the process of assimilation *is bound up with* the process of residential segregation in American cities' (my italics).

A key to the clarification of the link between spatial and social processes may lie in the concept of the primary group. By definition, primary groups rely on propinquity, at least in the formative stages. The extent to which the neighbourhood itself fosters close friendships outside the family is a measure of the active contribution of spatial factors to inter-group relationships. Initial immigrant settlement is often clustered for mutually reinforcing reasons such as information flow, practical assistance, housing availability and access to ethnic institutions (MacDonald & MacDonald 1962, Hyland 1970). Thus initial members of reformed primary groups are likely to be confined to the ethnic group for both social and spatial reasons. Subsequent voluntary movement away from immediate contact with the initial group members is an indication either of a willingness to expand the range of potential primary group members through exposure to neighbours of a different background, or of indifference to distance travelled to maintain the original contacts (Etzioni 1959, Jakle & Wheeler 1969). Involuntary moves, though they may eventually result in the ethnic intermixture of primary groups, are likely to be accompanied by further shrinkage of the field of contacts unless these can be maintained over a distance (Young & Willmott 1962).

Rex and Moore (1967) have suggested a five stage model which links size and content of primary groups to spatial change. The first stage is characterised by 'anomie' experienced by some migrants cut off from their home culture and lacking ties with the new society. At the second, immigrants join a primary community of people from their country of origin, thus re-establishing a wider social network within the 'colony' as a stable base from which to acquire new norms. The third and fourth stages result in the establishment of formal and informal social ties respectively with the new society, and the fifth involves a spatial move away from the colony 'except for reasons of retrospective sentiment'. According to this predicted sequence, the neighbourhood plays two roles in the assimilation process. It provides a stable background within which new ties may be established on first arrival and subsequently gives opportunities to confirm and strengthen the process of assimilation that follows such re-socialisation. This assumes that neighbours are significant members of prim-ary groups. Unless this is true then the links between social and spatial processes are ecological correlations reflecting simply the social structure of the two groups.

A number of studies have shown that physical distance is positively related to friendship formation (Beshers 1962, Timms 1971). Clearly, two major effects are involved. One is social homogeneity of neighbourhood, given the tendency to select friends of similar background (Gans 1968, Boal 1971). Secondly, opportunities and preference for contact, both initial and repeated, increase with propinquity (Moore & Brown 1970, Johnston 1974, Ley 1974). Mobility, both in daily activity patterns and longer-term residential relocation, is a crucial factor. Thus the importance of the neighbourhood, or familiar area surrounding the home, varies for different subgroups of the population (Western 1973, Stutz 1976). Many examples of tightly knit locality-based social networks among less mobile working-class groups are available (Young & Willmott 1962, Bott 1971), whereas more widely dispersed structures and even 'non-place realms' have been shown to typify middle-class behaviour (Webber 1964). Age is also a major variable. Children, housewives and the elderly spend a large part of their leisure time in or close to the home even in very mobile societies (Everitt 1976). Married men with young children also increase the number of local contacts at this time (Fischer 1977). Since a large proportion of the British population falls into one or more of these subgroups, it may be assumed that the neighbourhood is a major area for the formation of social contacts. Moreover, the Irish-born population in Britain is dispropor-tionately concentrated in the lower socio-economic categories and in family groupings at the child-rearing stage. In 1971 43.8 per cent of males born in the Irish Republic were classified as belonging to the Registrar General's Socio-Economic Groups IV and V compared with 28.6 per cent of the total population, and 51.5 per cent lived in one-family households comprising a married couple with children compared with 43.0 per cent of the total population.

An analysis of the content and residential distribution of primary group membership over time is thus an index of the changing degree of structural assimilation of an immigrant group. It is a significant index because it concerns the process by which the change is accomplished, though clearly the mechan-ism of residential allocation is also crucial in providing the opportunity surface from which neighbours may be chosen.

Theories and empirical studies of assimilation have largely been developed in the context of colonisation, particularly in North America and Australasia

(Gordon 1964, Taft 1966). But the postwar expansion of immigration to Britain has underlined the need to examine ethnic relationships in more stable and homogeneous receiving societies (Banton 1967). Most migration streams into Britain are either completed or of very recent origin. The only flow that may be studied longitudinally over at least five or six generations and which continues to be reinforced by new arrivals is that from Ireland (Fig. 11.1). This provides a valuable case study of the effects on present-day immigrants of inter-ethnic social relationships in the past. Not only have shared experiences and attitudes been inherited, but inter-marriage has blurred the distinction between immigrant and receiving societies. The impact of past immigration has not been uniform throughout Britain, however. Whereas the 'first wave', in the 19th century, was concentrated in Scotland and the North-West, the 'second wave', dating approximately from the 1930s, focused on the South-East and the Midlands, with more recent extensions into the South-West and East Anglia (Fig. 11.2) (Walter 1980). By comparing Irish communities in the newer and long established areas of settlement, the consequences of length of contact may be clarified.

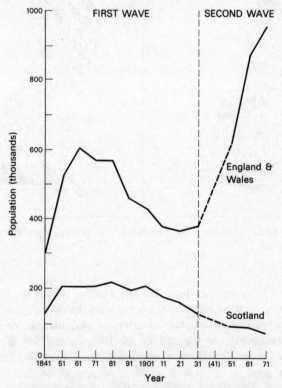

Figure 11.1 Total Irish-born population resident in Great Britain, 1841–1971 (*sources*: Census of Great Britain 1841, 1851; Census of England and Wales 1921, 1951, 1961, 1971; Census of Scotland 1951, 1961).

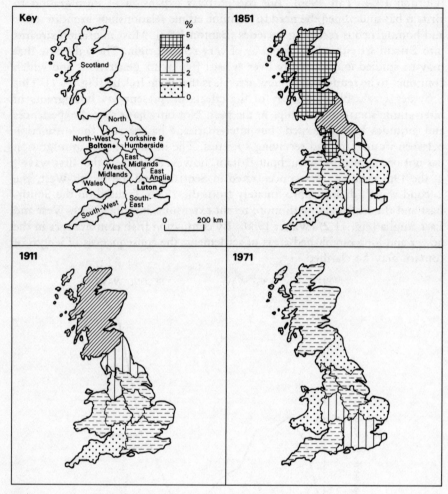

Figure 11.2 Total Irish-born as percentage of regional population, 1851–1971 (*sources*: see Fig. 11.1).

The study of Irish immigration also has a wider relevance. It is frequently used comparatively in studies of contemporary black migration to Britain. Thus the apparent loss of separate identity, or assimilation, of earlier immigrants has encouraged the forecast of an 'Irish future' for West Indians in contrast to the 'Jewish future' of continued cultural pluralism for Asians. The Irish are also used as a 'colour control' group in studies of immigrant settlement (Jones 1967, Peach 1968, Lee 1977). As yet, however, little research has focused on the Irish themselves in order to provide a firm basis for such comparisons.

Methods

The empirical data for this investigation are drawn from detailed interviews carried out between 1973 and 1975 with Irish immigrants and people of Irish descent. Respondents were selected randomly from a comprehensive list of residents with Irish names, or of known Irish origin, compiled at two levels of areal stratification. At the regional scale, two medium-sized towns, Luton (total population, 1971: 161 405) and Bolton (total population, 1971: 154 702), were selected to represent areas of substantial recent and long-established Irish settlement, respectively. Luton had 5.8 per cent (total: 9340) Irish-born inhabitants in 1971, a proportion exceeded only by Stretford (7.0 per cent) and Coventry (6.1 per cent). Although Bolton had 7.9 per cent Irish-born inhabitants in 1861 at the height of the 'first wave' of immigration, by 1971 only 1.7 per cent (total: 2593) had been born in Ireland. From data available in the census,[1] it is known that the population characteristics of the Irish-born in the two towns correlated closely with those of the total Irish-born in their respective regions.

At the intra-urban scale, four enumeration districts in each town were identified by Social Area Analysis (1966 census data) (Fig. 11.3). These corresponded to the distribution of social and demographic characteristics of the total Irish-born population in the town, and in each group the enumeration district with the highest percentage of Irish-born was selected. In both towns this resulted in the choice of two areas in the denser 'core' of Irish settlement, located at the centre and periphery, respectively, and two suburban areas, one inner and one outer. However, the contrasting histories of the development of the towns and their Irish communities produced considerable differences in the character of these areas. Most conspicuous was the density of the Irish-born population. In Luton, the core areas contained 15.7 and 10.5 per cent Irish-born respectively, compared with 6.0 and 4.2 per cent in Bolton. A time-lag in the spread of Catholic church and school provision in the suburbs had resulted in secondary clustering in Luton, so that 16.3 per cent of the population of the inner suburban area were Irish-born and 4.1 per cent of the outer. Religious institutions had diffused more evenly through the urban fabric of Bolton and the proportions were 5.2 and 2.3 per cent, respectively.

Those finally contacted included both Irish-born and people of Irish descent who retained an Irish surname. Only 3 of the 89 respondents in Luton had been born in Britain, all being in the second generation. In Bolton, however, 59 of the 115 had been born in Britain, including 29 second-, 23 third-, 6 fourth- and 1 fifth-generation immigrants. Those of Irish descent were asked about a number of factual aspects of their genealogy in the direct line, including migration history, occupations, marriage partners and religious affiliation. The last two were used as surrogate indices of structural assimilation in the absence of any primary group information. The Irish-born[2] total (142) gave a longitudinal profile of the migration process from the decision to

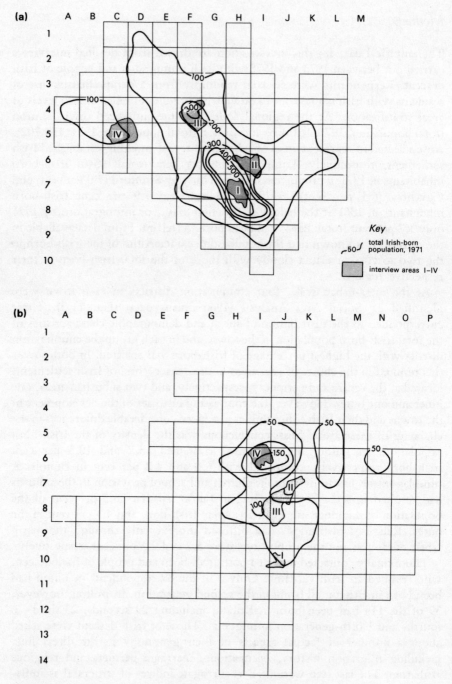

Figure 11.3 Map of (a) Luton and (b) Bolton showing distribution of total Irish-born population and interview areas. Grid squares 0.77 km.

leave, through stages of movement to residential settlement within towns. In this chapter, however, interest is restricted to a series of indicators showing the character of primary groups, based on the responses to questions concerning both attitudes and behaviour. Although the results are presented quantitatively, comments and qualifications were encouraged in the interviews and quotations are used to illuminate and extend the figures.

Representatives of primary groups were identified by the technique widely used in sociological research of asking about the 'three people seen socially most often in the last month' (Goldthorpe *et al.* 1969, Richmond 1973). This overcomes the insoluble problem of defining the intensity of friendships, although contact rates alone cannot indicate the subjective meaning attached to different relationships (Allan 1979). It also provides a selected form of 'personal star' (Barnes 1972) in which best friends are over-represented, and from which several attributes of primary group networks may be measured. These include size, up to a maximum of three, and some aspects of content, namely ethnic composition (nationality), spatial pattern (home address) and nature (kin, friend, workmate).

Structural assimilation

The extent to which individuals of Irish descent and Irish birth living in Britain could be regarded as structurally assimilated was assessed, using Gordon's criterion of 'large-scale entrance into the primary groups of the majority society'. Although inter-marriage was specified by Gordon as a separate subprocess, which could proceed independently from structural assimilation though it would inevitably follow from it, it was used as the principal surrogate for primary group content in the case of the descendants.

English-born respondents at least two generations removed from their Irish origins ($n = 30$), all living in Bolton, were asked about the ethnic group of marriage partners (Irish-born, Irish descent, English, other) as far as such information could accurately be recalled. The results showed that whereas one-third of the immigrant generation were known to have an Irish-born spouse, none of the succeeding generations had married Irish-born people. Approximately two-thirds were known to have married Boltonians with no Irish connections and a maximum of three in any generation had married a spouse also of Irish descent. Outmarriage was accompanied in many cases by lapsing from the Catholic faith. Of the immigrant ancestors, 22 were known to have been Catholic and 2 Protestant, but only 13 of the respondents themselves claimed to be Catholics and 12 were Protestants. Finally, none of the respondents identified themselves as Irish. These findings support the view that first-wave Irish immigrants were rapidly assimilated and made a significant contribution to the social mix of the receiving society. They suggest that the present Catholic proportion of the Bolton population (15 per cent) understates by at least half the numbers of people of Irish descent, and many more may have distant kinship ties. For recent arrivals, therefore, the line between immigrant and majority society is by no means clear cut (Lieberson 1963).

All migrants experience a shrinkage of social network after migration (Bott 1971). For resocialisation to take place, an adequate network must be re-established in order for norms to be transferred (Eisenstadt 1954). Stability cannot be achieved while a state of 'anomie' is being experienced (Rex & Moore 1967). Size of network is thus a crucial index of receptivity to change. It must be remembered, however, that class differences account for some of the variation in network size. Members of the working class in Britain typically have fewer friends than are found in the middle classes. Since respondents in both towns were concentrated in the manual working groups (social classes IIIM–V: Luton 89 per cent, Bolton 82 per cent), conformity to social class norms in Britain would result in relatively attenuated networks. The number of close friends, defined as those 'seen socially most often in the last month', was recorded for each subsample. Table 11.1 shows that the majority of the total sample (56 per cent) could name at least three close friends, and that a further 20 per cent could name two. However, there was a significant difference between the two subsamples. In Luton only half (49 per cent) had well developed networks compared with 67 per cent in Bolton. This may in part reflect the 'privatised' life-style of affluent workers in Luton, resulting from an instrumental attitude to work noted by Goldthorpe et al. (1968). A large number of Irish immigrants in Luton were also isolated from contacts of any kind, 16 per cent being unable to name any friend and 15 per cent giving only one, compared with an overall total of only 10 per cent in Bolton. These respondents were found particularly in the inner core areas of settlement in Luton and their responses reflected a lack of integration into either community.

Table 11.1 Number of close friends (max. = 3).

Number	Luton n	Luton %	Bolton n	Bolton %	Total n	Total %
0	13	16	2	4	15	12
1	12	15	3	6	15	12
2	15	19	10	20	25	20
3	39	49	33	67	72	56
NI	–	–	1	2	1	1
total	79	99	49	99	128	101
average	2.0		2.5		2.2	

NI = no information.
Observed chi-square 9.25; critical value 5% level 7.82.

Table 11.2 Question: Would you say your friends are mostly Irish or English?

	Luton		Bolton		Total	
Score	n	%	n	%	n	%
1 all Irish	4	5	–	–	4	3
2 mostly Irish	23	30	10	18	33	25
3 about the same	29	38	15	27	44	33
4 mostly English	13	17	18	32	31	23
5 all English	7	9	13	23	20	15
6 no friends	1	1	–	–	1	1
total	77	100	56	100	133	100
average score		2.9		3.6		3.2

Observed chi-square 20.83; critical value 5% level 9.49.

'I don't have any friends. I keep to myself.'

(Luton, single male lodger, shiftworker, 8 years in Luton)

'I don't know where they live. They're casual friends except Francis and Pat [both Irish] who live here.'

(Luton, single male lodger, unemployed, 3 years in Luton)

'I don't go out much. I have one friend in Saxon Street, an Irishman from my home area who married an English woman. I knew him before.'

(Luton, married man, 15 years in Luton)

Although single people were significantly over-represented among those who had no close friends (observed chi-square 4.08, critical value 5 per cent level, 3.84), when those with only one are included the distribution by marital status (72 per cent married) conforms closely to the proportion married in the total Luton subsample (71 per cent). The overall proportion married was similar for Bolton (77 per cent), so that this was unlikely to account for the difference observed between the two towns.

Limited social interaction with the majority society is clearly illustrated for those with small networks. In order to examine the extent to which all respondents remained ethnically enclosed in their friendships, the ethnic origin of the contacts was recorded. The information was collected in two forms, the first being an attitudinal measure indicating a general impression of the ethnic background of friends. Answers were pre-scaled into five classes and given scores (Table 11.2).

The results show that the average for the sample was 3.2, suggesting no ethnic bias, but the two subsamples differed significantly. Whereas the Luton average was slightly towards the Irish end of the scale, the Bolton score was

Table 11.3 Numbers of non-Irish close friends (max. = 3).

Number	Luton		Bolton		Total	
	n	%	*n*	%	*n*	%
0	44	56	11	21	55	42
1	20	25	14	27	34	26
2	11	14	12	23	23	18
3	3	4	14	27	17	13
NI	1	1	1	2	2	1
total	79	100	52	100	131	100
average		0.64		1.54		1.00

NI = no information.
Observed chi-square 19.34; critical value 5% level 7.49.

closest to a 'mostly English' response. More than half of the respondents (55 per cent) in Bolton said that their friends were more English than Irish, compared with only 31 per cent in Luton. Only 18 per cent had mostly Irish friends compared with 30 per cent in Luton, where a further 5 per cent had no English friends. A number of factors must be taken into account, however. The Irish-born comprised only 5.9 per cent and 1.8 per cent, respectively, of the total populations of Luton and Bolton, so that a random selection of friends would be 'mostly English'. Responses may also reflect a desire to conform to a non-discriminatory norm. One respondent replied, 'It's all the same to me', but later revealed that his three closest friends were Irish. Finally, no definition of friend was given so that acquaintances as well as primary group members may have been included. For all these reasons, the responses probably under-stated the ethnic bias in friendship groups, though they are a useful guide to general attitudes to the majority society.

A second index of ethnic content of social relationships was drawn from accounts of actual behaviour and focused on a limited range of contacts defined by frequency of meeting. Proportions of non-Irish close friends were calculated (Table 11.3). The overall result suggests a much higher degree of enclosure than the attitudes expressed earlier revealed. Two-thirds of the sample (68 per cent) had less than half (0–1) the potential maximum friends outside their group, but whereas over half the Luton subsample (56 per cent) had no English close friends, this was true of only 21 per cent of the Bolton subsample. On the other hand, 50 per cent of the Bolton subsample had well developed networks, including only, or mainly (2–3), English people compared with only 18 per cent in Luton. The high proportion of Irish friends is not explained by the widespread inclusion of kin. In Luton only 11 per cent of contacts mentioned in this context were related, although 59 per cent of the sample had kin living in the town and reported frequent meetings. Presumably, such interactions were taken for granted.

A further behavioural measure concerned the practice and frequency of home visiting. This was designed to test the intensity of friendships mentioned and to determine one aspect of their spatial context. Again, however, cultural and class norms must be taken into account before conclusions are drawn. The majority of respondents (85 per cent) were from rural backgrounds in Ireland. In the past, home visiting had been customary, at least for men. 'Night walking' to rotating venues among peer groups was common (Arensberg & Kimball 1968). But subsequent studies have reported a reduction in this kind of informal contact as a result of increasing contact with urbanisation during the postwar period, so that neighbours rarely saw inside each other's houses (Limerick Rural Survey 1962, Brody 1973). In Britain class norms again differ substantially. Whereas the middle classes frequently entertain at home and, indeed, deliberately remove friendships from the constraints of their original setting in this way, working class sociability does not 'flower out' from specific contexts of meeting and home visiting is restricted to 'popping in' for a chat or the provision of day-to-day aid (Allan 1979). Young and Willmott (1962), for example, found that only one-third of their sample in the East End of London had friends with whom they were on visiting terms. Conformity to British norms would therefore suggest restricted activity in both towns.

The responses again indicated the gap between generalised feelings and revealed behaviour (Table 11.4). Although 51 per cent had said that their friends were mostly or all English, only 30 per cent frequently visited English homes. Nearly half the Luton sample never visited, though the proportion declined sharply from 67 per cent in the central core to none in the outer surburban area. In Bolton, however, only 20 per cent never visited and the highest subarea proportion was 33 per cent. As suggested above, conformity to neighbourhood norms may explain these findings. This was indeed expressed by some respondents.

> 'We never visit. The English don't do that.'
> (Bolton, married couple, arrived 1956–57)
> 'I never visit – only in Ireland. I've never done that here.'
> (Luton, single man, lodger, arrived direct 1955)

Nevertheless it is likely that meetings in the home provide the greatest opportunity for informal exchange of information leading to adaptation of norms.

Friendship formation is the key to changes in primary group composition which will lead to structural assimilation. Inclusion of people from another ethnic group among close friends not only implies shared norms, but is the context within which transference of information by example may take place most thoroughly and with least stress. Evidence presented so far suggests that

Table 11.4 Question: Do you visit English people in their homes?

Score	Luton		Bolton		Total	
	n	%	n	%	n	%
0 never	36	47	11	20	47	35
1 sometimes	23	30	21	38	44	33
2 frequently	18	23	22	39	40	30
no reply	–	–	2	4	2	2
total	77	100	56	101	133	100
average	0.76		1.21		0.93	

Observed chi-square 10.25; critical value 5% level 5.99.

the two subsamples had reached different stages in the process. The Luton Irish community as a whole had not reached the stage of 'large-scale entrance into the primary groups of the majority society'. The pattern of extensive external contacts typical of fully socialised residents had not yet been re-established. Moreover, even among those naming three close friends, 69 per cent included two or more Irish people. Both attitudinal and behavioural measures suggest a considerable degree of ethnic enclosure typical of Rex and Moore's (1967) stage two, so that the group as a whole must be regarded as integrated on plural lines. Thus the presence of friends and relatives ranked high among reasons for satisfaction with Luton as a place to live.

'My mates are here.'
(Luton, married man, arrived Britain 1957, came to Luton 1968)
'There are many Irish here. It feels homely. I know people.'
(Luton, single woman, arrived Britain 1972, came to Luton 1973)

In Bolton, on the other hand, it may be argued that structural assimilation had been achieved for the group as a whole. Social networks were well developed and included a majority of non-Irish members. This corresponds more closely to stages four and five of Rex and Moore's model. More references to the friendliness of the population as a whole were included in reasons for satisfaction with the town.

'You couldn't find more friendly people.'
(Bolton, married woman, arrived direct 1957)
'They're the nicest people in England.'
(Bolton, married couple, arrived in Britain 1951, 56, came to Bolton 1957, 58)

The findings suggest that degree of assimilation is place specific, so that no general conclusions can be drawn concerning the Irish in Britain. The sample totals could only be interpreted as an aggregate of two contrasting case studies. Since the towns were selected to represent distinctive types of Irish settlement in Britain, however, it may be possible to interpret the differences observed in the light of length of settlement. Moreover, piecemeal evidence from other sources lends support to these regional contrasts. Marked similarities with Luton were reported from Birmingham by a journalist who found 'only the beginning of social or geographical integration' (Harrison 1973). In an oral history account of St Helens (Forman 1979), on the other hand, a miner recalling young Irishmen arriving in the 1920s commented: 'Many of these men are now assimilated in the area. They're married and they're all Lancashire people in effect.'

Reasons for these differences must now be considered. One possible explanation is that different social attitudes have developed among the majority society. Where exposure to an ethnic group has occurred over several generations, especially in the absence of social tension and widespread acceptance of inter-marriage, subsequent immigrants may experience a greater degree of acceptance on the part of the receiving groups. It is difficult to measure such attitudes objectively, but various indirect indicators may be used. Content analysis of local weekly newspapers was carried out for the census years 1961 and 1971. All references to the Irish and other ethnic groups were noted. The most striking result was an absence of direct references to the Irish community and its activities in the *Luton News*. Although Catholic church attendances were higher than Protestant ones, no Catholic parish news was reported and even major events in the calendar were passed by. For 3 months in 1961, however, an active and sometimes bitter correspondence continued over the educational 'apartheid' principle of separate Catholic schooling as well as doctrinal matters. In the *Bolton Journal and Guardian*, by contrast, Catholic parishes had sections of equal status with Protestant ones, and Irish activities, such as St Patrick's Night celebrations, received full and sympathetic coverage. Although editorial policy must be considered, the findings suggest that the Luton Irish community was excluded from local press coverage and must have found alternative outlets for advertising and circulation of news. The role of newspapers in influencing as well as reflecting the views of their readers must also be remembered.

Irish respondents were asked for their perceptions of town and neighbourhood friendliness as a general indication of their feelings of acceptance (Table 11.5). Clearly, there was a marked difference in the opinions expressed in the two towns. At both urban and neighbourhood level, Bolton was perceived to be much more friendly, 92 and 86 per cent of respondents, respectively, expressing positive reactions. In Luton, by contrast, although the majority believed that people were at least 'quite friendly', a considerable proportion at the urban level had definitely negative feelings (31 per cent). For some at least this had the effect of reinforcing internal community ties.

Table 11.5 Question: Do you think that on the whole this is (a) a friendly town and (b) a friendly neighbourhood?

| | Luton | | Bolton | |
	n	%	n	%
(a)				
very friendly	23	30	40	77
quite friendly	23	30	8	15
neither	7	9	1	2
quite unfriendly	18	23	1	2
very unfriendly	6	8	–	–
don't know	–	–	2	4
total	77	100	52	100
(b)				
very friendly	19	24	35	67
quite friendly	37	47	10	19
neither	6	8	1	2
quite unfriendly	9	12	1	2
very unfriendly	3	4	1	2
don't know	4	5	3	6
NI	–	–	1	2
total	78	100	52	100

(a) Observed chi-square 34.45; critical value 5% level, 4 degrees of freedom 9.49.
(b) Observed chi-square 14.43; critical value 5% level, 3 degrees of freedom 7.82.
NI = no information.

'They're rather unfriendly in this town, so I stay with the Irish.'
(Luton, married woman, arrived 1960 from Cheshire)

But although such opinions were expressed more strongly in areas with lower proportions of Irish-born residents, it is not possible to attribute them to a lack of acceptance of Irish people in the town. Again, it may be a reflection of the 'privatisation' resulting from the rapid influx of migrants from all parts of Britain in the postwar period. This was supported by one respondent who said:

'It's rather an unfriendly town. Even the Irish are not very friendly. Everyone keeps themselves to themselves.'
(Luton, married man, arrived 1972 from London)

Nevertheless, impressions of neighbourhood friendliness were somewhat higher, only 16 per cent feeling that they lived in an unfriendly neighbourhood. The contrast was brought out by a respondent from the heart of the 'secondary' area, who was probably referring to her Irish neighbours.

'It's rather unfriendly. Both English and Irish that is. Both parents work and have no time to be friendly. But this street is very friendly.'
(Luton, married woman, arrived 1963 from Nottingham)

The differing histories of settlement in the two towns may also affect present-day relationships in other ways. The rapid expansion of 'second wave' immigrants in Luton has provided potentially greater support for ethnic institutions, which in turn help to increase intra-ethnic contact. In the early 1970s, in addition to a large Irish club, the Luton community supported two hurling teams, two flourishing branches of Comhaltas na Eireann, the cultural association fostering Irish music and dancing, and *de facto* Irish clubs attached to each of the seven Catholic parishes. Bolton had no specifically Irish activities of this kind. Greater numbers also provided a large pool of neighbours, friends and marriage partners. Together these factors may help to explain the different degree of endogamous marriage in the two towns. Table 11.6 confirms that endogamy was significantly greater in Luton, though similar proportions of each subsample were married (Luton 71 per cent, Bolton 77 per cent) and had arrived as single people (Luton 69 per cent, Bolton 64 per cent). When partners who met after migration are considered, the difference was even more pronounced, 71 per cent of the Luton married sample having Irish-born spouses compared with only 38 per cent in Bolton. Moreover, 33 per cent in Bolton had married a person with no Irish connection, compared with only 8 per cent in Luton.

Table 11.6 Ethnic background of spouse.

	Luton n	Luton %	Bolton n	Bolton %
both Irish-born	55	89	23	53
met in Ireland	21		11	
met in Britain	33		12	
met elsewhere	1		0	
one Irish-born spouse	7	11	20	47
self migrated as child	0		3	
spouse of Irish descent	2		7	
non-Irish spouse	5		10	
total	62	100	43	100

Observed chi-square 13.41; critical value, 5% level 3.84.

Table 11.7   Question: Are your friends mostly Irish or English?

	Average score by period of arrival*			
	Luton		Bolton	
	Arrival in		Arrival in	
	Britain	town	Britain	town
pre-1950	3.1	2.6	3.8	3.8
1951–5	3.1	3.3	4.0	4.2
1956–60	3.0	2.8	3.5	3.4
1961–5	2.7	2.8	3.0	3.4
1966–70	2.9	2.5	3.5	3.6
1971–5	2.0	3.1	3.0	3.3

* See Table 11.1.

Another factor could be the greater average length of residence of Irish respondents in Bolton (22 years) compared with Luton (12 years), though the distribution by period of arrival in the two towns was not significantly different at the 5 per cent level. Scores for responses to the attitudinal question on the ethnic mix of friends indicate a general, though not regular, increase with length of residence in Britain (Table 11.7). For each period, however, the Bolton scores were higher, often substantially so, than those of the Luton Irish-born, suggesting that variation in individual assimilation was not sufficient to account for the differences between the two towns.

Finally, the longer-established Bolton Irish-born residents had fewer kin living in the town. At least one related household was reported by 46 per cent of households, though a further 11 per cent had lost local kin through death or further migration. In the Luton subsample, 59 per cent had kin living in the town. Other researchers have concluded that the presence of kin retards assimilation by reinforcing the norms of the society of origin and reducing contact with the receiving society (Rose & Warshay 1957). This might be particularly applicable to Irish immigrants since kin dominate primary groups in rural Ireland (Arensberg & Kimball 1968). But when the association between presence of kin and degree of structural assimilation, indicated by opinion of ethnic mix of friends and the practice of home visiting in Luton was measured, the reverse was found to be true. Those without kin were less likely to visit English homes (observed chi-square 6.93, critical value 5.99) or to have English friends (observed chi-square 5.83, critical value 5.99). Kin may thus have passed on some measure of their own achieved assimilation and provided a 'springboard' from which to enter the wider society.

It would seem, therefore, that apart from variations in size of community, whose effects are difficult to isolate in a study based on two cases, attributes of the immigrants themselves do not explain the difference in degree of assimilation confirmed by each of the indices. Longer exposure to Irish immigration appears to have blurred the religious and inherited cultural divide in Bolton, reducing the sharp distinction from the remainder of the population experienced by Irish immigrants in Luton. Whereas Irish accents heard on the streets, the colonisation of particular pubs and the appearance of new Catholic churches and schools are recent intrusions into an albeit increasingly heterogeneous population in Luton, in Bolton they have been commonplace for several generations and, indeed, more widespread in the past.

Spatial pattern of primary groups

The residential distribution of primary group members is an indication of the relative importance of the neighbourhood as the milieu for establishing close social contacts, or at least for their maintenance. If the majority of close friends named by the respondents are also neighbours, then support is given to the widely held belief that ethnic clustering leads to and perpetuates social segregation. Those living in dense ethnic residential clusters will have a higher proportion of neighbours and therefore friends of the same background, though where densities are low a considerable latitude of choice may still be exercised. If members of primary groups are widely spread, however, there are fewer constraints on selection. Where those from the same ethnic group are selected, it must be concluded that an urban rather than neighbourhood community exists. Residential proximity does not therefore play a major role in the assimilation process and any spatial clustering is likely to have resulted from factors other than the preference of the ethnic group. Similarly, scattered networks of friends from outside the group reduce the importance of residential distribution as an active influence on ethnic interaction.

When the pattern of friends' home addresses is mapped for the two towns, some similarities may be seen in the overall numerical distribution (Fig. 11.4). In both cases, about one-third were located in the interview area and a further quarter within the radius of approximately 1 km (Table 11.8). The remaining 40 per cent were widely scattered and a small number (Luton 7, Bolton 8) lived in neighbouring towns. Thus, though dispersed friends may reflect residential movement (Beshers 1962), present proximity was not essential for the maintenance of significant sociable ties.

In each town the proportion of Irish-born among close friends was considerably higher than would be expected from a random distribution, taking account of proportions of each group present. Whereas in Bolton the highest proportion of Irish-born (56 per cent) was in the extended neighbourhood of the surrounding grid squares, in Luton it was in the remainder of the town (72 per cent). At the level of the interview area, however, there was no positive correlation between density of Irish-born population and proportion

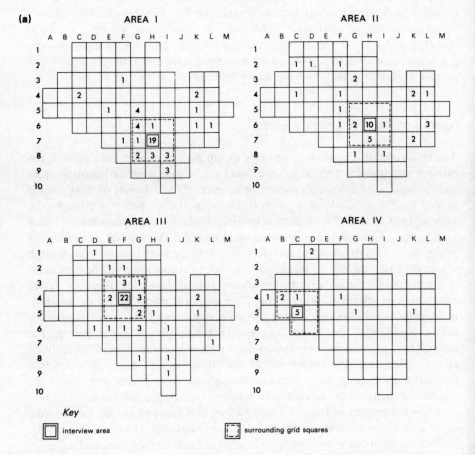

Figure 11.4 Map of (a) Luton and (b) Bolton showing distribution of three closest friends by interview area. The numbers in the grid squares refer to total numbers of close friends present in separate households. Thus in (a), four close friends of respondents in area 1 lived in G6.

(b)

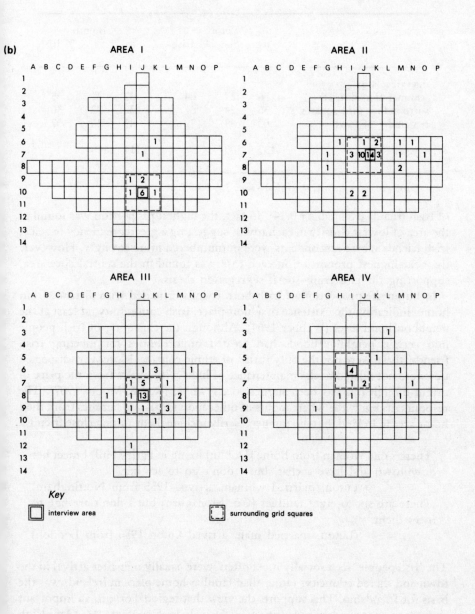

Table 11.8 Spatial distribution of people's close friends within the towns (max. = 3).

	Luton			Bolton		
	n	%	% Irish	n	%	% Irish
interview area						
(enumeration district)	56	37	64	37	32	35
surrounding grid squares	36	24	67	36	32	56
remainder of town	60	39	72	41	36	37
total	152	100		114	100	

Observed chi-square 1.97; critical value, 5% level 3.84.

of Irish friends (Kendall's τ 0.14). In fact, the highest proportion was found in the area of lowest density in each town, suggesting a greater tendency to select Irish friends where respondents were outnumbered more strongly. However, the next highest proportion in each case was found in the central core area, supporting the clustering–social segregation thesis.

In Luton the proportion of Irish-born friends increased with distance from home, indicating the existence of a 'non-place' Irish community, at least at the neighbourhood level (Webber 1964). Although the clustering of Irish people into certain neighbourhoods had created opportunities for meeting Irish friends, these were not the only forms of ethnic contact. Moreover, dispersed ties were not related to the maintenance of links with others from the place of origin though this has been suggested elsewhere (Rex & Moore 1967). The respondents knew the whereabouts of other individuals and families from their home area in Ireland, but did not necessarily include them among close friends.

'There's one woman from home [Dublin] living in Farley Hill. I meet her downtown and have a chat, but I don't go to see her.'

(Luton, married woman, arrived 1955 from Nottingham)

'There are six to eight families [Co. Monaghan] but I don't arrange to meet them.'

(Luton, married man, arrived Luton 1956 from London)

The Irish people 'seen socially most often' were usually met after arrival in the town and shared ethnicity, rather than familiar home place in Ireland, was the basis for friendship. This supports the view that regional origin, an important element in an individual's identity in exclusively Irish contexts (MacAmhlaigh 1964), loses its significance in face of greater ethnic difference encountered in Britain (Fox 1975), in contrast to its retention by West Indian immigrants (Philpott 1977).

The network of kinship ties was even more widely dispersed than that of friends (Fig. 11.5). In Luton 19 per cent lived in the interview area, and 60 per cent were located outside the surrounding grid squares. Only two children remained in the same area after marriage, the remainder being located on the newer estates on the outskirts. However, distance seemed to have little effect on the frequency of visiting (cf. Stutz 1973), though only those who lived very close met daily. The majority met at least once a week.

The Irish community in Luton, therefore, seemed to be maintained at an urban rather than a neighbourhood scale, significant numbers of primary group members living at some distance from the respondents' homes. But the inclusion of more non-Irish elements in the neighbourhood suggests that resocialisation through intensive external social contact might be taking place in this area. The findings for Bolton, on the other hand, offered no support for the existence of an extended Irish community. There was a slight decline in the ethnic proportion with distance, though this could reflect the overall distribution of the Irish-born in the town. Non-Irish friendships were maintained in all areas of the town, indicating structural assimilation at both neighbourhood and urban levels, and according with the widespread perception of friendliness recorded earlier.

Conclusions

Primary group analysis is a valuable measure of social relationships between immigrants and other members of society, because it concerns the process by which change takes place. Resocialisation to the norms of the receiving country is brought about by intense, informal contact outside the ethnic group. These findings suggest, however, that the process does not take place simply at the individual level, but is significantly affected by the characteristics of particular locations. Although it is not possible to weigh up the various factors involved, tradition of immigration in a settlement appears to influence present attitudes to new arrivals. Both structural and social links, strengthened over time, have eased the path of subsequent migrants. However, the connections between primary group membership and neighbourhood are complex and need further investigation. Propinquity appeared to play an important part, but by no means all close friends lived in the neighbourhood. Moreover, respondents living in least 'Irish' areas were not always the most structurally assimilated, although those with least developed and predominantly Irish social networks were generally found in areas of higher concentration.

The degree of structural assimilation displayed by Irish respondents in Bolton confirms the widely held belief (Patterson 1965, Rose et al. 1969, Johnston 1971) that the Irish in Britain have lost their separate identity over time. This does not conform, however, to Richmond's (1969) typology,

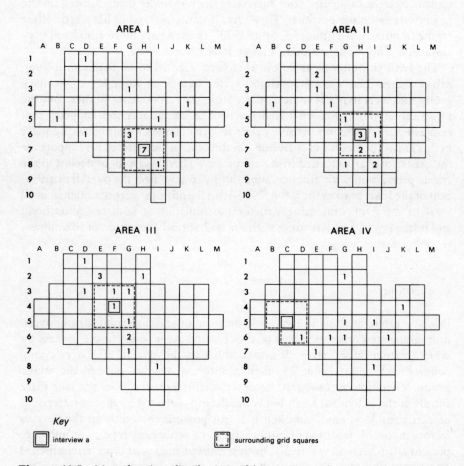

Figure 11.5 Map showing distribution of kin in Luton by interview area. The numbers in the grid squares refer to total number of separate households containing kin, other than children. Thus three households in G6 were related to households in area 1.

which suggests that pluralistic integration is the expected 'mode of coaptation of migrants' in industrial societies. During two centuries of industrialisation, the Irish in Bolton have become identifiable only fragmentedly by name and religion.

Yet time has context as well as duration. The experience may not necessarily be projected on to the Luton Irish nor yet the West Indian populations. Changes in the rate of structural assimilation or even regression could occur. In 1975, for example, reports in the national press (see, for example, *The Times* 17 January 1975) described a 'backlash' of antipathy towards Irish communities in Britain following IRA bombing campaigns, though respondents claimed not to have experienced this personally. Increasing levels of unemployment could also generate resentment against all immigrant workers. Thus although the epithet 'toasted Irish' for the West Indian community carries with it the implication of rapid assimilation, this may be neither universal nor inevitable.

Notes

1 Rate of community growth (birth place totals), sex ratios and proportions born in Northern Ireland.
2 Those born in the Irish Republic (119) and Northern Ireland (23) are treated as a single sample because of the small totals. Despite Boal's (1976) comments on the lack of ethnic homogeneity of the Irish in London, many similarities were found in the structure and motivation of those interviewed (Walter 1979). However, the difference in class structure of the total populations must be borne in mind. In 1971, 44.9 per cent of those born in the Republic of Ireland were classified in Socio-Economic Groups IV and V compared with only 36.7 per cent of those from Northern Ireland.

References

Allan, G. A. 1979. *A sociology of friendship and kinship*. London: George Allen & Unwin.
Arensberg, C. and S. Kimball 1968. *Family and community in Ireland*, 2nd edn. Cambridge, Mass.: Harvard University Press.
Bagley, C. 1973. *The Dutch plural society*. London: Oxford University Press.
Banton, M. 1967. *Race relations*. London: Tavistock.
Barnes, J. A. 1972. *Social networks*. Reading, Mass.: Addison-Wesley, Module in Anthropology.
Beshers, J. M. 1962. *Urban social structure*. New York: Free Press.
Boal, F. W. 1971. Territoriality and class: a study of two residential areas in Belfast. *Irish Geog.* **4**, 229–48.
Boal, F. W. 1976. Ethnic residential segregation. In *Social areas in cities*, D. T. Herbert and R. J. Johnston (eds), vol. I, 41–79. London: Wiley.
Bott, E. J. 1971. *Family and social network*. London: Tavistock.
Brody, H. 1973. *Inishkillane*. London: Allen Lane.
Census of England and Wales 1921. *General tables*, Table 52.
Census of England and Wales 1951. *General tables*, Table 39.
Census of England and Wales 1961. *Birthplace and nationality tables*, Table 1.

Census of England and Wales 1971. *Great Britain country of birth tables*, Table 3.

Census of Great Britain 1841. Vol. II, Preface, 14–16.

Census of Great Britain 1851. *Population tables II*, Vol. 1, Tables XXXIX, XL.

Census of Scotland 1951. Vol. III, Table 31.

Census of Scotland 1961. Vol. V, Table 1.

Cooley, C. H. 1909. *Social organization*. New York: Charles Scribner's Sons.

Eisenstadt, S. N. 1954. *The absorption of immigrants*. London: Routledge & Kegan Paul.

Etzioni, A. 1959. The ghetto – a re-evaluation. *Social Forces* **37**, 255–62.

Everitt, J. C. 1976. Community and propinquity in a city. *Ann. Assoc. Am. Geogs.* **66**, 104–16.

Fischer, C. S. 1977. *Networks and places*. New York: Free Press.

Forman, C. 1979. *Industrial town*. London: Granada.

Fox, R. 1975. The vanishing Gael. In *Encounter with anthropology*, R. Fox (ed.), 116–22. London: Penguin.

Gans, H. 1968. *People and plans*. New York: Basic Books.

Goldthorpe, J. H., D. Lockwood, F. Bechhofer and J. Platt 1968. 1. *The affluent worker: industrial attitudes and behaviour*. Cambridge: Cambridge University Press.

Goldthorpe, J. H., D. Lockwood, F. Bechhofer and J. Platt 1969. 3. *The affluent worker in the class structure*. Cambridge: Cambridge University Press.

Gordon, M. M. 1964. *Assimilation in American life*. New York: Oxford University Press.

Harrison, P. 1973. Culture and migration: the Irish English. *New Soc.* 20 September, 699–702.

Hyland, G. A. 1970. Social interaction and urban opportunity: the Appalachian in-migrant in the Cincinnati Central City. *Antipode* **2**(2), 68–83.

Jakle, J. A. and J. O. Wheeler 1969. The changing residential structure of the Dutch population in Kalamazoo, Michigan. *Ann. Am. Assoc. Am. Geogr.* **59**, 441–60.

Johnston, R. J. 1971. *Urban residential patterns*. London: Bell.

Johnston, R. J. 1974. Social distance, proximity and social contact. *Geog. Annal.* **56B**, 2.

Jones, P. N. 1967. *The segregation of immigrant communities in the city of Birmingham, 1961*. Occasional Papers no. 7. Department of Geography, University of Hull.

Lee, T. R. 1977. *Race and residence*. London: Oxford University Press.

Ley, D. 1974. *The black inner city as frontier outpost*. Monograph no. 7. Washington, DC: Association of American Geographers.

Lieberson, S. 1963. *Ethnic patterns in American cities*. New York: Free Press.

Limerick Rural Survey 1962. Third interim report. *Social structure*. Tipperary: Muintir na Tire.

MacAmhlaigh, D. 1964. *An Irish navvy*. London: Routledge & Kegan Paul.

MacDonald, J. S. and L. D. MacDonald 1962. Urbanization, ethnic groups, and social segmentation. *Social Res.* **29**, 433–48.

Moore, E. G. and L. A. Brown 1970. Urban acquaintance fields: an evaluation of a spatial model. *Environ. Plan.* **2**, 455–68.

Park, R. 1926. The urban community as a spatial pattern and moral order. In *The urban community*, E. W. Burgess (ed.). Chicago: University of Chicago Press.

Patterson, S. 1965. *Dark strangers*. London: Tavistock.

Peach, C. 1968. *West Indian migration to Britain*. London: Oxford University Press.

Peach, C. (ed.) 1975. *Urban social segregation*. London: Longman.

Philpott, S. B. 1977. The Montserratians: migration dependency and the maintenance of island ties in England. In *Between two cultures*, J. L. Watson (ed.), 90–119. Oxford: Basil Blackwell.

Rex, J. and R. Moore 1967. *Race, community and conflict*. London: Oxford University Press.

Richmond, A. H. 1969. Sociology of migration in industrial and post-industrial societies. In *Migration*, J. A. Jackson (ed.), 238–81. Cambridge: Cambridge University Press.

Richmond, A. H. 1973. *Migration and race relations in an English city*. London: Oxford University Press.

Rose, A. M. and L. Warshay 1957. The adjustment of migrants to cities. *Social Forces* **36**, 72–6.

Rose, E. J. B. *et al.* 1969. *Colour and citizenship*. London: Oxford University Press.

Stutz, F. 1973. Distance and network effects on urban social travel fields. *Econ. Geog.* **49**, 134–45.

Stutz, F. 1976. *Social aspects of interaction and transportation*. College series. Washington, DC: Association of American Geographers.

Taft, R. 1966. *From stranger to citizen*. London: Tavistock.

Timms, D. W. G. 1971. *The urban mosaic*. Cambridge: Cambridge University Press.

Walter, B. M. 1979 (unpublished). *The geography of Irish migration to Britain since 1939, with special reference to Luton and Bolton*. PhD thesis, University of Oxford.

Walter, B. M. 1980. Time–space patterns of second-wave Irish immigration into British towns. *Trans Inst. Br. Geogs New Ser.* **5**, 297–317.

Webber, M. M. 1964. Culture, territoriality and the elastic mile. *Paps Reg. Sci. Assoc.* **13**, 59–70.

Western, J. 1973. Social groups and activity patterns in Houma, Louisiana. *Geogr. Rev.* **63**(3), 301–21.

Young, M. and P. Willmott 1962. *Family and kinship in East London*. London: Penguin.

Contributors

Colin Clarke. Colin Clarke is a University Lecturer in Geography at Oxford University and an Official Fellow of Jesus College. He studied geography while an undergraduate at Jesus College and completed his doctorate for Oxford in 1967. He has taught at the universities of Toronto and Liverpool, where he was Reader in Geography and Latin-American Studies, and has carried out numerous field investigations in Mexico and the Caribbean. His publications deal with race relations and pluralism, urbanisation, demography, politics and social history. He is the author of *Jamaica in maps* (London: University of London Press 1974) and *Kingston, Jamaica: urban development and social change 1692–1962* (Berkeley: University of California Press 1975), and the editor of *Caribbean Social Relations* (Liverpool: Centre for Latin-American Studies, Monograph Series number 8 1978) and *Modernization in Mexico*, a special issue of the *Bulletin of the Society for Latin-American Studies* number 32, 1980.

Harvey Demaine. Harvey Demaine was an undergraduate at Jesus College, Oxford, and is now a Lecturer in Geography with reference to South-East Asia at the School of Oriental and African Studies, University of London. His main research interests are in the field of development studies, particularly agricultural and rural development which was the focus of his PhD thesis completed in 1977. He has written several papers on aspects of agricultural development and planning in Thailand and Burma and has been involved in several research and planning projects for the Mekong Committee, the Royal Thai Government and the World Bank. He is currently completing an edited text entitled *The geography of South-East Asian development*.

Geoffrey Hawthorn. Geoffrey Hawthorn read geography at Jesus College, Oxford, and is now a University Lecturer in Sociology at Cambridge and a Fellow of Clare Hall. He has also taught at Essex and Harvard and been a Visiting Member at the Institute for Advanced Study at Princeton. He has written *The sociology of fertility* (London: Collier-Macmillan 1970) and a history of social theory, *Enlightenment and despair* (Cambridge: Cambridge University Press 1976), edited a collection of papers on population and development, and published articles and reviews on a variety of other subjects.

Janet Henshall. Janet Henshall Momsen was an undergraduate at Lady Margaret Hall, Oxford, and did postgraduate work at Oxford, McGill and London universities. She is currently a Lecturer in Geography at the University of Newcastle upon Tyne. She has taught at King's College, University of London, the University of Calgary, Canada, the Federal University of Rio de Janeiro, Brazil and the InterAmerican Institute of Agricultural Sciences, Turrialba, Costa Rica and has been a consultant on agricultural development in Brazil and the Caribbean. Her current research concerns the role of rural women in development and the use of biomass energy sources in Latin America. Dr Momsen is co-author with R. P. Momsen Jr of *The geography of Brazilian development* (London: Bell 1974) and has written many papers on Latin American topics.

Peter Jackson. Peter Jackson was an undergraduate at Keble College and has a first degree, a Diploma in Anthropology and a doctorate from Oxford. He is now a Lecturer in Geography at University College London. He was a Fulbright scholar at Columbia University in New York (1978–9) and a visiting Scholar at New York University (1982), undertaking research on migration, residential segregation, and ethnic competition. His current research concerns a comparative analysis of ethnicity in

American cities which he is studying as a Fellow of the American Council of Learned Societies, based at the University of Chicago (1983). He is co-editor, with Susan J. Smith, of *Social interaction and ethnic segregation* (London: Academic Press 1981).

David Ley. David Ley is Professor of Geography at the University of British Columbia, Vancouver. He studied at Jesus College, Oxford, and he obtained the BA in 1968: he took his PhD at Pennsylvania State University in 1972. His doctoral dissertation was published in the Monograph Series of the Association of American Geographers as *The black inner city as frontier outpost: images and behavior of a Philadelphia neighborhood* (1974). Other publications include *A social geography of the city* (New York: Harper and Row 1983) and a jointly edited volume, *Humanistic geography* (London: Croom Helm 1978). His research and published papers are concerned with the social geography of the inner city, urban politics, and issues of philosophy and social theory in human geography.

Ceri Peach. Ceri Peach is a Lecturer in Geography at Oxford University and a Fellow of St Catherine's College. He was both an undergraduate and research student at Merton College where he completed his doctorate in 1965. He has taught at Oxford since 1964. His field work on urban ethnic segregation has taken him to India, South Africa, Australia and the United States. He was a Visiting Fellow at the Department of Demography at ANU and Visiting Fellow at the Department of Sociology, Yale University. He is the author of *West Indian migration to Britain* (Oxford University Press 1968); editor of *Urban social segregation* (Longman 1975) and co-editor of *Ethnic segregation in cities* (Croom Helm 1981).

J. Douglas Porteous. Douglas Porteous is Professor of Geography at the University of Victoria, British Columbia. He studied at Jesus College, Oxford, Hull University, Harvard and MIT. Previous publications include numerous papers on such diverse topics as: the planning of remote resource communities; territoriality in teenage gangs and Third World beggars; the urban history of the Canal Age; environmental aesthetics; urban planning problems; and the geography of fantasy. Books include *Canal ports: the urban achievement of the canal age* (1977), *Environment and behaviour: planning and everyday life* (1977), and *The modernization of Easter Island* (1981). He has conducted fieldwork in Britain, North America, Latin America, Europe, the Middle East, and Polynesia. Current research interests are surname geography, environmental aesthetics, trends in geographical thought, and autobiogeography.

Vaughan Robinson. Vaughan Robinson is Lecturer in Human Geography at University College, Swansea. Formerly, he was an undergraduate at St Catherine's College, Oxford, a Heyworth Prize Research Fellow at Nuffield College, Oxford, and between 1980 and 1981 Oxford University's Frere Exhibitioner in Indian Studies. During 1982 he was a Visiting Scholar at Gujarat State University in India. His main areas of interest are urban social geography, South Asian studies and demography. His previous publications are mainly within these areas, though they also take in geographical methodology and quantitative methods. He co-edited *Ethnic segregation in cities* (London: Croom Helm 1981) with Ceri Peach and Susan Smith, and is the author of a forthcoming book on Asians in Britain.

Bronwen Walter. Bronwen Walter was an undergraduate at St Hugh's College, Oxford, and has been a Lecturer in Human and Social Geography at Cambridgeshire College of Arts and Technology since 1974. After obtaining a BA degree in geography at Oxford in 1969, she spent a year as a Thouron Scholar at the University of Pennsylvania and was awarded an MA in international relations. She completed a

D.Phil. thesis in 1979 and her current research interests include Irish migration, rural social integration and comparative minority group relations in Europe.

John Western.   John Western is Associate Professor of Geography at Syracuse University. After studying at Jesus College, Oxford, he gained a BA in geography in 1968. In 1972 the University of Western Ontario conferred his MA, after fieldwork on racial–ethnic patterns in the Louisiana bayou country. In 1978 he gained his PhD from the University of California, Los Angeles, following a two-year research scholarship at the University of Cape Town; *Outcast Cape Town* (Minneapolis: University of Minnesota Press and London: George Allen & Unwin and Cape Town: Human & Rousseau 1981) resulted. He has also taught at the Ohio State University in Columbus and Temple University in Philadelphia. Research interests revolve around ethnic and racial cleavages in both Third World and revitalising North American cities.

List of subscribers

Dr D. J. Acheson		Jesus College, Oxford OX1 3DW
Polly Amos	(Jesus 1979)	75 Cavendish Road, Clapham, London SW12 0BM
Stuart A. Atkin	(Jesus 1968)	c/o Miyamoto, 12–5 Ichibancho, Chiyoda-ku, Tokyo 102, Japan
A. Sarah Bendall	(Jesus 1979)	25 Millington Road, Cambridge CB3 9HW
T. J. Betts } Mrs T. Betts }	(Jesus 1961) (St Hugh's 1961)	1 Fordwich Hill, Hertford, Herts SG14 2BG
Dr David Browning		St Cross College, Oxford
Elspeth Buxton	(Lady Margaret Hall 1944)	School of Geography, Mansfield Road, Oxford OX1 3TB
V. Bywater	(Campion Hall 1938)	Campion Hall, Oxford OX1 1QS
J. A. Campbell	(Jesus 1969)	Department of Geography, Queen's University, Belfast BT7 1NN
J. Roger Chapman	(Pembroke 1971)	Flat 6, 19 Bolton Gardens, London SW5 0AJ
David N. Cockcroft	(Jesus 1980)	Department of Geography, The University of Keele, Staffs ST5 5BG
Jean B. Collier	(Pembroke 1979)	Mount Pleasant, Foss Cross, Chedworth, Cheltenham, Glos GL54 4NN
D. J. Collins-Taylor	(Pembroke 1946)	Auchencalzie, Kirkbean, by Dumfries DG2 8DW
Dr Paul Coones	(Christ Church 1973)	Hertford College, Oxford OX1 3BW
Stephen M. Criddle	(Jesus 1979)	45 Devonshire Road, Oxton, Birkenhead, Merseyside L43 4UP
Dr Robert Crittenden	(Jesus 1971)	The Southern Highlands Rural Development Project, PO Box 98, Office of Project Coordination, Mendi, Southern Highlands Province, Papua, New Guinea
Dr R. Timothy Coupe	(Jesus 1967)	198 Woodside Avenue South, Coventry, West Midlands CV3 6BG
Professor Derek R. Diamond	(Pembroke 1952)	Department of Geography, London School of Economics & Political Science, Houghton Street, London WC2A 2AE
Dr A. J. Downs		Jesus College, Oxford OX1 3DW
P. A. Doye	(Merton 1958)	Byways, Beesfield Lane, Farningham, Kent DA4 0BZ

P. C. Ebbutt	(Jesus 1959)	2 Oddfellows Cottages, Wolds Lane, Wolvey, Nr Hinckley LE10 3LL
Richard Emmens	(Pembroke 1973)	47 Essex Street, Oxford OX4 3AW
John T. Enticott	(Merton 1956)	57 Bostock Road, Abingdon, Oxon OX14 1DW
Dr B. H. Farmer		St John's College, Cambridge CB2 1TP
Brian Finlayson		Department of Geography, University of Melbourne, Parkville 3052, Victoria, Australia
John Fisher	(Pembroke 1966)	146 Freer Road, Birchfield, Birmingham 6
Dr S. J. Gale	(St Catherine's 1973)	Jesus College, Oxford
Dr Alan George	(Pembroke 1970)	36 Clonmore Street, London SW18
M. J. Goddard	(Jesus 1978)	2 Abraham Close, Botley, Southampton, Hants SO3 2RQ
Professor Jean Gottmann	(Hertford)	19 Belsyre Court, Oxford OX2 6HU
Dr A. S. Goudie		Hertford College, Oxford
John Gyford	(Jesus 1958)	Department of Town Planning, University College London, 22 Gordon Street, London WC1H 0QB
Sir John Habakkuk		The Lodgings, Jesus College, Oxford OX1 3DW
Graham Hadley	(Jesus 1978)	45 St James' Road, Dudley, West Midlands DY1 3JD
John F. Hamilton	(Pembroke 1965)	9 Dene Avenue, Westmore, Newcastle upon Tyne 12, NE12 0EX
Martin J. Harris	(Jesus 1962)	Orchard House, 9 Butts Road, Horspath, Oxford OX9 1RH
Myszka Hogan-Guzkowska	(Jesus 1979)	School of Geography, Mansfield Road, Oxford OX1 3TB
Dr Colin Humphreys		Jesus College, Oxford
Hugh Ibbotson	(Pembroke 1958)	Little Priors, 34 Station Road, Bishops Cleeve, Cheltenham, Glos GL52 4HH
Antony E. Ives	(Jesus 1960)	25 Russell Court, Woodstock Road, Oxford OX2 6JH
Richard T. Jackson	(St Edmund Hall 1960)	University of Papua, New Guinea, PO Box 320, University, Papua, New Guinea
Nicolas Jacobs		Jesus College, Oxford OX1 3DW
Mark N. James	(Jesus 1974)	14a Rochford Road, Southend-on-Sea SS2 6SP
Dr Mark R. D. Johnson	(Pembroke 1967)	Research Unit for Ethnic & Racial Studies, St Peter's College, Aston University, Birmingham B8 3TE

John Jones	(Jesus 1966)	Rossmere, 31 High Street, Gravesend, Swansea
Dr Anthony Lemon	(St Edmund Hall 1964)	Mansfield College, Oxford OX1 3TF
Library		School of Geography, Mansfield Road, Oxford OX1 3TB
David Long	(Jesus 1973)	67 Plantation Road, Oxford OX2 6JE
Keith L. Maclean	(Pembroke 1971)	c/o 26 Ashdale Road, Kesgrave, Ipswich IP5 7PA
G. W. Marshall	(Jesus 1957)	Salle Place, Salle, Reepham, Norfolk NR10 5SF
M. A. N. Martin	(Jesus 1952)	Chestnut Cottage, Cowers Lane, Derby DE5 2LF
Gordon Moss	(Jesus 1968)	32 Tournay Road, London SW6
Peter Page	(Jesus 1966)	50a Wigstone Lane, Leicester LE2 8TL
W. A. Parker	(Jesus 1966)	Stowe Grange, St Briavels, Lydney, Glos GL15 6QH
Professor John T. Parry	(Jesus 1953)	Department of Geography, McGill University, 805 Sherbrooke Street West. Montreal, Quebec, Canada H3A 2K6
Professor Allan Patmore	(Pembroke 1949)	Department of Geography, The University, Hull HU6 7RX
Stewart N. Pearson	(Jesus 1966)	18 McGrath Court, West Hill, Scarborough, Ontario, MIC 3B5, Canada
Professor R. Mansell Prothero		Department of Geography, University, Liverpool L69 3BX
Peter Radmall	(Jesus 1973)	20 Paterick Place, Holt, ACT 2615, Australia
Adrian Read	(Pembroke 1963)	c/o Department of Geography, Mansfield Road, Oxford OX1 3TB
C. J. Read	(Jesus 1969)	Low Sipton Shield, Spartylea, Hexham, Northumberland NE47 9UZ
Dr D. A. Rees		Jesus College, Oxford OX1 3DW
Dr Neil Roberts	(Jesus 1975)	Department of Geography, Loughborough University of Technology, Leics LE11 3TU
Peter John Robertson	(Jesus 1971)	Calima, High Street, Ardingly, Haywards Heath, W. Sussex RH17 6TG
Miss H. J. Ross	(Jesus 1978)	c/o 8 Northleigh Avenue, Weston-Super-Mare, Avon BS22 8HA
P. T. Sandry	(Jesus 1954)	Headmaster's House, High Street, Chipping Campden, Glos
Dr D. I. Scargill	(St Edmund Hall 1954)	School of Geography, Mansfield Road, Oxford OX1 3TB
Geoffrey Schofield	(Jesus 1955)	Hillrise, 3 Springfield Lane, Kirkbymoorside, York YO6 6LU

Ian Simmons	(Jesus 1975)	1A Victoria Road, Twickenham, Middlesex TW1 3HW
C. G. Smith	(Keble 1946)	235 Woodstock Road, Oxford OX2 7AD
N. P. T. Staunton	(Jesus 1962)	c/o 23 Albert Road, Caversham, Reading, Berks
Professor Robert W. Steel	(Jesus 1934)	12 Cambridge Road, Langland, Swansea SA3 4DE
Theo Steel	(Pembroke 1967)	383 Woodgrange Drive, Southend-on-Sea, Essex
A. J. J. Street	(Jesus 1958)	30 The Moor, Carlton, Bedford MK43 7JR
Dr David E. Sugden	(Jesus 1959)	Department of Geography, University of Aberdeen, Aberdeen, AB9 2UF
Dr M. A. Summerfield	(St Catherine's 1971)	Department of Geography, University of Edinburgh, Drummond Street, Edinburgh EH10 6TU
Dr C. Swithinbank	(Pembroke 1946)	7 Home End, Fulbourn, Cambridge CB1 5BS
Dr Fred Taylor		Jesus College, Oxford OX1 3DW
F. C. E. Telfer	(Pembroke 1951)	West End House, Frensham, Surrey
Ian Tempest	(Jesus 1977)	74 Windmill Rise, Acomb, York YO2 4TX
Paul Thomas ⎫ Gillian Thomas ⎬	(Jesus 1964) (Lady Margaret Hall 1964)	2 Bloomfield Cotts., Timsbury, Bath BA3 1LH
John Langton Tyman	(Pembroke 1956)	Brisbane College of Advanced Education, Box 82, Mount Gravatt, Australia 4122
Karl Vanters	(Jesus 1974)	9 Cuckoo Street, Pantygog, Pontycymmer, Mid Glamorgan CF32 8DR
Dr Iain Wallace	(Jesus 1964)	Department of Geography, Carleton University, Ottawa, Canada K1S 5B6
Dr Colin Webb		Jesus College, Oxford OX1 3DW
Professor Martyn Webb	(Balliol 1943)	Department of Geography, University of Western Australia, Nedlands, Western Australia 6009
Robert C. Williams	(Jesus 1958)	Via Maffei 45, Cortona (AR), Italia
Bradley A. J. Wilson	(Jesus 1967)	779 Worthington Road, Wayne, Pennsylvania 19087, USA
Richard Workman	(Pembroke 1966)	
Rodney D. Wright	(Jesus 1962)	B3, 11th Floor, Lockhart House, 440 Jaffe Road, Hong Kong
Dr G. T. Young		23 Northmoor Road, Oxford OX2 6UR

Index